THE FEDERALIST SOCIETY

THE FEDERALIST SOCIETY

How Conservatives Took the
Law Back from Liberals

◆

Michael Avery and Danielle McLaughlin

Vanderbilt University Press

NASHVILLE

This book is printed on acid-free paper.
Manufactured in the United States of America

Library of Congress Cataloging-in-Publication Data on file

LC control number 2012031471
LC classification number KF294.F43A94 2012
Dewey class number 349.7306--dc23

ISBN 978-0-8265-1877-4 (cloth)
ISBN 978-0-8265-1879-8 (e-book)

For my children, Katherine, David, and Samantha.

My love for them knows no bounds.

—Michael Avery

For my parents, Adam and Patti McLaughlin,

who taught me that anything is possible.

—Danielle McLaughlin

Contents

—✦ PREFACE ✦—

This is a book about the power of ideas. The Federalist Society has been extremely effective over the past thirty years in translating the intellectual capital of its members into law and policy. We have traced the development of the ideas of society members from articles, books, panels, and debates into legislative proposals, citizen referenda, legislation, legal briefs, court opinions, and White House policy. We have followed key Federalist Society members from law schools into private practice, public interest law firms, the Department of Justice, and the White House, as well as onto the bench. Our narrative is primarily based on what the subjects of our study have said and written, the ideas they have propagated and embraced, and the ideas that they have rejected.

We wrote this book to shine a light on the forces at play in the making of law and policy in the United States. There is much that citizens from all points on the ideological spectrum can learn from the story of the Federalist Society. We also hope, as the story unfolds, that our readers will stop to think about what they believe the Constitution stands for, how it should be interpreted, and its influence on their lives.

To do justice to the ideas and the considerable scholarship of our subjects, it is necessary to discuss in some detail political philosophy, Supreme Court jurisprudence, and legal doctrine. We have tried to explain the law and the history of legal doctrine in the Supreme Court in a common-sense way, and have tried to steer a middle course between the lengthy footnotes that legal writing demands and the dearth of footnotes often found in popular publications. To assist the reader further, we provide an explanation of how legal citations work in Appendix A.

Many of the members of the Federalist Society who have had great influence over law and politics are relatively unknown to members of the general public. We supply an alphabetical list and basic information about important Federalist Society members and allies in Appendix B.

We conducted the research by reviewing the voluminous written work of Federalist Society members and allies, transcripts and recordings of panels and symposia, legal briefs and court opinions, government reports, contemporary published accounts of the activities of the Federalist Society, and existing scholarship regarding the conservative legal movement. We also attended Federalist Society conferences and meetings. The society posts a great deal of the output of its members on its website (*fed-soc.org*), including videos of speeches and panels. We have based our analysis on the public record rather than on private interviews, with the exception of some statements that Federalist Society members have made to other researchers.

This book consists of chapters on substantive areas of law where Federalist Society members have been active, including property law, international law, privacy, race and gender discrimination, and access to legal remedies. We also discuss the success the Federalist Society has enjoyed in getting its members and other conservative lawyers appointed to influential positions in government. There are many more areas of law for which a similar analysis would yield interesting results, such as administrative law, intellectual property law, and criminal law, but we leave those for others to investigate.

We are grateful to the many people who supported and assisted us in the preparation of this book. Margaret Hagen, Brett Haywood, Katie Powell, Rebekah Provost, Dave Samuels, and Charu Verma were students at Suffolk Law School who conducted invaluable research. David Avery assisted with cite checking. Suffolk Law School legal reference librarians Diane D'Angelo, Steve Keren, and Susan Sweetgall were very helpful in providing research advice and obtaining necessary materials and resources. We appreciate the critical insights provided by the lawyers and professors who read drafts of some of the chapters, including Nan Aron, Marie Ashe, Mark Brodin, Barry Brown, Lee Cokorinos, Sara Dillon, Steven Ferrey, Robert Friedman, Sheldon Goldman, Page Kelley, David Murphy, Natsu Saito, Elizabeth Trujillo, and Hazel Weiser. Helene Atwan, director of Beacon Press, and attorney Ike Williams read early drafts of the manuscript and generously gave us advice about how to proceed with our project.

Suffolk Law School provided Michael Avery with a sabbatical semester and summer writing stipends to do much of his work on the project. The staff at the Harvard Law School Library provided Danielle McLaughlin with invaluable research resources. Chip Berlet and his colleagues at Political Research Associates made their superb library available to us. We are extremely grateful for the support, assistance, and advice from our families, friends, and colleagues, who are too many to name, but to some we are especially indebted. Michael Avery would like to thank the many students in his constitutional law classes over the years whose interest in the subject was a principal motivation for doing this book. Danielle McLaughlin would like to thank Brendan Hall for his unfailing encouragement and support. Any mistakes that remain in this work are entirely our responsibility.

⟶ ◆ INTRODUCTION ◆ ⟵

Law schools and the legal profession are currently strongly dominated by a form of orthodox liberal ideology which advocates a centralized and uniform society. While some members of the legal community have dissented from these views, no comprehensive conservative critique or agenda has been formulated in this field. This conference will furnish an occasion for such a response to begin to be articulated. —*Steven Calabresi, Lee Liberman, and David McIntosh, statement of purpose for "A Symposium on the Legal Ramifications of the New Federalism"*[1]

You are more likely to convince people of your viewpoint if they feel the other side has been given a fair hearing. —*Liberman and McIntosh, in an early Federalist Society guide on how to establish campus chapters*[2]

In 1980, Steven Calabresi, Lee Liberman [Otis], and David McIntosh were young, conservative law students—Calabresi at Yale, and Liberman and McIntosh at the University of Chicago—alienated from the prevailing political orientation of their classmates and their schools. Their professors' ideologies, for the most part, reflected the dominance of liberal politics in the sixties and seventies. The New Deal, the civil rights movement, and the Great Society antipoverty programs had led to widespread faith that government could and should supply the solutions to the country's social, political, and economic problems. Calabresi, Liberman, and McIntosh disagreed, believing that big government posed a fatal threat to individual rights and the sanctity of private property. In their view, the liberals had distorted important constitutional principles. The three law students started to raise questions.

Over the next thirty years, the questions they and their conservative colleagues would raise identified many of the crucial issues of twentieth-century America. What is the appropriate balance between an individual's right of self-determination and the powers and responsibilities of government? Should Americans pursue collective or individual solutions to social problems like poverty, care of the elderly, and education? How much regulation of private property and economic behavior is appropriate in a capitalist, free-market country? Is racial and gender diversity in education and employment an appropriate goal for government to pursue and what means are acceptable for achieving it? In the face of increasing economic and social globalization, what is more important—protecting national sovereignty or establishing international norms? Should judges interpret the U.S. Constitution to keep pace with the moral, economic, and social tenor of the times, or should they read the text in the light of its eighteenth-century meaning unless it has been formally amended?

The law students not only began to ask these questions, they began to answer them. And they began to organize. Chief Justice John Roberts's law clerk, George Hicks, described the conservative students at Harvard Law School in the early eighties as "ideological outliers who struggled to gain credibility in class and acceptance on campus."[3] Soon enough, however, they got help from conservative professors who were themselves struggling with the prevailing liberal ideology of their colleagues. Professors Ralph K. Winter and Robert Bork helped Calabresi start the Federalist Society at Yale, and Professors Antonin Scalia, Richard Epstein, Richard Posner, and Frank Easterbrook were advisors to Liberman and McIntosh at Chicago. A couple of years earlier, Spencer Abraham and Steven Eberhard, students at Harvard Law School, had started the *Harvard Journal of Law and Public Policy* as a vehicle for conservative ideas. Eventually this would become the official law journal of the Federalist Society.

The Federalist Society's first major event was a symposium on federalism in April 1982. It was cosponsored by the Yale and Chicago law school groups, the *Harvard Journal of Law and Public Policy*, and a similar group at Stanford Law School, the Stanford Foundation for Law and Economic Policy. The Institute for Educational Affairs, the Olin Foundation, and the Intercollegiate Studies Institute funded the conference.[4] The seminar was a huge success, and the Yale and Chicago law students soon began assisting conservatives on other campuses with the organization of their own Federalist Society chapters. At the time of the society's inception, conservative law students felt isolated in an academic world dominated by a liberal mindset; the fledgling Federalist Society provided "a social club for students to come comfortably out of the political closet."[5]

Within one year of the first symposium, there were seventeen Federalist Society chapters, all on law school campuses.[6] The society grew continuously over the next several years. By 2000, former federal appellate judge Abner Mikva, a liberal, would say, "Where so many of the nation's leaders are groomed, the Federalists manipulate the landscape. It was once held that liberals ran the law schools. The liberals had the name but the Federalists own the game. For students on the go, there is nowhere else to go."[7] At that point, the society had 25,000 members, lawyers chapters in 60 cities, and law school chapters on 140 campuses.[8]

Today the Federalist Society for Law and Public Policy Studies claims that over 45,000 conservative lawyers and law students are involved in its various activities. There are only approximately 13,000 dues-paying members, however.[9] Four Supreme Court justices—Antonin Scalia, Clarence Thomas, John Roberts, and Samuel Alito—are current or former members of the Federalist Society.[10] Every single federal judge appointed by President George H. W. Bush or President George W. Bush was either a member or approved by members of the society. During the Bush years, young Federalist Society lawyers dominated the legal staffs of the Justice Department and other important government agencies. The dockets of the federal courts are brimming with test cases brought or defended by Federalist Society members in the government and in conservative public interest firms to challenge government regulation of the economy; roll back affirmative action; invalidate laws providing access to the courts by aggrieved workers, consumers, and environmentalists; expand state support for religious institutions and programs; oppose marriage equality; increase statutory impediments to women's ability to obtain an abortion; defend state's rights; increase presidential power; and otherwise advance a broad conservative agenda.

There are Federalist Society lawyers chapters in every major city in the United States, and in London, Paris, Brussels, and Toronto. It has established student chapters at every accredited law school in the country (as well as at a handful of unaccredited law schools, and at the business schools at Harvard and Northwestern). It has also recently launched law school alumni chapters, to enable alumni to better reconnect. With revenues of $9,595,919 in 2010, the 75 lawyers chapters sponsored nearly 300 events for more than 25,000 lawyers, and the society sponsored 1,145 events at law schools for more than 70,000 students, professors, and community members.[11] The Federalist Society's membership includes economic conservatives, social conservatives, Christian conservatives, and libertarians, many of whom disagree with each other on significant issues, but who cooperate in advancing a broad conservative agenda. As professors on the faculties of law schools, its members have succeeded in gaining respect and traction for conservative legal ideas, which stem in large part from an originalist interpretation of the Constitution. Academics associated with the Federalist Society have not only educated a new generation of conservative law students but played a role in the rise of openly conservative law schools such as Pepperdine and George Mason. The high point for Federalist Society influence in government was the second term of George W. Bush. By the time President Bush left office, what had begun as a counterestablishment movement had become the establishment.

The Federalist Society has been described as "quite simply the best-organized, best-funded, and most effective legal network operating in this country."[12] Although its leaders have described the group as an intellectual forum, operating above the fray of government, the academy, and the private sector, there can be no doubt that many of its members have wielded extraordinary influence in all these arenas.[13] Professor Jerry Landay's account of the 1999 Federalist Society National Lawyers Convention at the Mayflower Hotel in Washington, D.C., gives us some flavor of the organization at that time:

> Tonight at the Mayflower you get a sense of just how powerful and far-reaching the Society is. There are stars from every corner of the Republican establishment in the room. From snippets of conversation, one concludes that they are joined not only at the ideological hip but by a collective hatred for President Clinton—perhaps more for standing in the way of their Revolution than for any moral or legal lapses. Members of Starr's old team like constitutional law advisor Ronald Rotunda (who counseled Starr that he could indict a sitting president) rub shoulders with old-timers from the Reagan administration—former Attorney General Edwin Meese, Solicitor General Charles Fried, and Civil Rights commissioner Linda Chavez—and with former Bush White House Counsel C. Boyden Gray. The room bulges with partners from among the most powerful law firms in the land. . . . And then there

are the judges. No fewer than eight federal judges, most of whom are still active on the bench, will sit on panels or speak from the podium during this three day affair.[14]

This book describes how the Federalist Society grew from a small student organization into a dominant force in law and politics. Primarily, this book is about the power of ideas. Analyzing five substantive areas of the law, it identifies ideas about the Constitution, government, and individual rights that were created, adopted, and proliferated by the Federalist Society and its members. It demonstrates how those ideas have taken hold in the mainstream of legal thought and contributed to the creation of law and policy. The society's success is due to the extraordinary network it has created, the support it receives from wealthy conservative patrons (whose agendas it advances), and the intellectual work that its members have done. The Federalist Society has created an interdependent network of conservative think tanks, public interest law firms, prominent lawyers, elected representatives, judges, and law professors. To fuel this network, the leading Federalist Society members publish prolifically. The sheer output of speeches and the number of conferences and debates at which they promote their views is staggering.

Their success demonstrates the truth of Sidney Blumenthal's argument that "ideas themselves have become a salient aspect of contemporary politics."[15] The adoption of the ideas of Federalist Society members in briefs, court opinions, foreign policy, and municipal, state, and federal legislation has been unprecedented in speed and scope. Former vice president Dick Cheney has said that the Federalist Society "changed the debate."[16] Abner Mikva has characterized the society as a once-small "band of legal conservatives" whose ideas, at the time they began organizing, were "scorned by academics, ignored by judges and unknown to the public" but who ultimately succeeded, persevering to "build a powerful movement and reshape our world according to their notions."[17]

Yet the critical role that the Federalist Society has played in the resurgence of conservatism is largely unknown to the general public and has only recently become the object of academic study. Even in law schools, for the most part students study Supreme Court cases and legal doctrine without considering who filed the cases, who paid to litigate them, and whether the ideology of the judges who presided over them had an effect on the outcome. The fact is that much of what may have appeared as a haphazard or spontaneous legal development to a casual observer over the past two decades has been the result of deliberate tactics and a finely honed strategy to move the law in a conservative direction.

This book does not take the position that the law is the product of secret conspiracies. Nonetheless, the influence of the Federalist Society is often difficult for the general public to discern. The society itself does not take public positions on policy issues, legislation, the outcome of Supreme Court cases, or judicial appointments. Articles are written, briefs are filed, and cases are brought by individual members or by sister organizations, such as conservative public interest law firms. This allows the society to maintain a "big tent" that promotes cooperation among conservatives with different views by avoiding internal battles over official policies. It also avoids visibility for much of what the Federalist Society accomplishes. For example, Lee Liberman Otis, one of the founders, vetted judicial nominees during the administration of George H. W. Bush. Although the Federalist Society does not formally endorse judicial nominees, it would be highly artificial to consider her influence on judicial selection as the business of a single member.

The society, however, is keenly aware of the power of branding and rhetoric. Named for the Federalists and "the principles of the American Founding," its magazine is named the *Federalist Paper*.[18] The bust of its founders' hero, James Madison, serves as the society's logo. Madison was in fact given a nose job by Robert Bork's son, Charles, who remarked that the original silhouette was "too ugly" to adorn a brochure.[19] From 2001 to 2010, the amount that the society spent on its public relations firm, Creative Response Concepts, grew as reflected in Table 1.

TABLE 1. Annual Expenditures for Creative Response Concepts

Year	Amount (in dollars)
2001	$ 0
2002	0
2003	0
2004	214,500
2005	324,878
2006	536,134
2007	728,622
2008	557,922
2009	710,916
2010	917,705

Source: Federalist Society for Law and Public Policy Studies, Form 990, 2001–2010.

The society's publications and projects currently include the following: *ABA Watch, Bar Watch Bulletin, State Court Docket Watch, Class Action Watch*, and *State AG Tracker. NGO Watch*, a Federalist Society project in collaboration with the American Enterprise Institute, also features *UN Treaty Watch*. These titles place the society firmly in the role of defender of the ideals on which it asserts the republic was founded—ideals supposedly eroded by the individuals and organizations the society keeps watch over. For example, consider the explanation for founding the *State AG Tracker*; "There has been increasingly pronounced discussion concerning the appropriate role of state Attorneys General. Some argue that state AGs have overstepped their role by prosecuting cases and negotiating settlements that have had extraterritorial effects, and sometimes even national effects. Others argue that state AGs are simply serving the interests of their own citizens and, at times, appropriately filling a vacuum left by the failure of others (for example, federal agencies) to attend to these issues."[20] Although the situation is characterized as a debate, it is clear that the views of the society align with the first proposition.

The society is aware of its tremendous potential to move law and policy in a conservative direction after training, within its first thirty years, "two generations of lawyers" who actively participate at various levels of government and in the community outside of government, promoting originalism, limited government, and the rule of law.[21] David McIntosh has stated that "[p]utting them in place means we'll have fifty years of seeing what that actually means for impact."[22]

Among other tactics, leading Federalist Society members are prolific authors of amicus (friend of the court) briefs. The initiative for filing such briefs may come from individual Federalist Society members or conservative groups with which they have ties. On other occasions, parties before a court may solicit amicus briefs from organizations they believe will support their position, in order to put arguments before the court that the parties either do not want to make themselves or simply do not have space to address in their briefs. This is a common practice, used by all parties, irrespective of ideology. The chapters that follow will demonstrate how effective Federalist Society members have been in using amicus briefs to move the law in a conservative direction.

The fifteen practice groups and nine special projects of the Federalist Society both support and publicize the work of its members. The conservative network that the society has fostered provides a platform for the projects of its members, even though the Federalist Society name is not formally associated with them.

Another element of the Federalist Society network is an online pro bono center that pairs lawyers with opportunities for conservative public interest pro bono work.[23] Its mission is to "match lawyers nationwide with opportunities for pro bono service in the cause of individual liberty, traditional values, limited government and the rule of law." The executive director is Margaret ("Peggy") A. Little, a Stamford, Connecticut, lawyer engaged in commercial litigation, a Yale Law graduate, and a former clerk to federal judge Ralph K. Winter. Federalist Society member Ilya Somin lauds the center as a means of addressing the need for lawyers to conduct follow-up litigation to enforce favorable precedents obtained by conservative public interest law firms, a problem that he described as a key weakness of conservative public interest law.[24]

THE LIBERAL ESTABLISHMENT

As noted above, when the founders of the Federalist Society began law school in the early nineteen eighties, they found themselves in institutions dominated by liberal ideas. Professor Steven Teles, who has studied the conservative legal movement, has analyzed the dominance of the liberal legal network at that time.[25] The foundation of liberal dominance was the New Deal. The work of the NAACP Legal and Defense Fund, the American Civil Liberties Union, the National Lawyers Guild, and other advocacy organizations contributed to the preeminence of liberal legal thought and action. During the sixties and seventies, there were several significant developments, including the Supreme Court's decision in *Gideon v. Wainwright*, which mandated court-appointed counsel for criminal defendants; a subsequent explosion in the numbers of legal services lawyers and programs; an expanded interest on the part of the American Bar Association in legal aid programs; the growth of clinical education in law schools; the development of liberal public interest law; and crucial support from the Ford Foundation for many of these initiatives.[26] Furthermore, in the late sixties and early seventies, there was enormous growth in the size of law faculties in the United States, just as "the law students who would fill those positions were moving decisively to the left."[27] The new generation of liberal law professors "sought to legitimize the expanded role of the judiciary ushered in by the Warren Court," as compared with the previous generation, who had "cut their teeth on legal realism and judicial restraint."[28]

Fundamentally, in the post–civil rights movement era, individual rights were identified as crucial to achieving equality and social justice. Sanctioned by federal government programs and the decisions of the Supreme Court, the claims and arguments of legal liberals who sought to achieve those ends seemed "identical to morality, progress and common decency" and "a part of elite common sense."[29] From a progressive point of view, however, the liberal legal network achieved only qualified success. In fact, according to many progressives, liberal legal goals were never more than partially realized. Social and racial justice remained elusive in significant and enduring respects, and prevailing corporate interests were never seriously compromised. Structural and political forces, and the limitations of the liberal ideology itself, curbed the success of legal liberalism.

THE CONSERVATIVE RENAISSANCE

Although the predominant values when Calabresi, McIntosh, Liberman, and Abraham arrived in law school were liberal, a wave of conservative political resurgence was reaching its crest as the students began to organize. The election of Ronald Reagan as president in 1980 has been described as a triumph of the new conservative "Counter-Establishment" movement that had slowly been gathering strength over the preceding thirty years.[30] The role of ideas and ideology in the development of this movement was critical. Friedrich von Hayek's *The Road to Serfdom* (1944) and the ex-communist Whittaker Chambers's *Witness* (1952) were seminal publications that influenced the conservative resurgence. It was William F. Buckley's journal *National Review*, which appeared in 1955, and Buckley's subsequent personal celebrity, however, that "cover[ed] the conservative movement with the mantle of respectability."[31] Buckley introduced the concept of the conservative "Remnant"—what Blumenthal calls "the last defenders of the old values against modern liberal decadence."[32] Barry Goldwater's run for the presidency in 1964 and Ronald Reagan's California gubernatorial campaign in 1966 moved the conservatives actively into the world of electoral politics. By 1980, conservatism was in full bloom. Buckley's "Remnant" had become an ideological movement, consisting of institutes, think tanks, and publications that nurtured and promoted the ideas of conservative intellectuals, lawyers, and policymakers. And the Reagan presidency created a powerful platform—in all three branches of government—for the members of that movement.[33]

So when the young Federalist Society lawyers burst onto the scene, there was a political apparatus waiting to put them to work. After law school, Calabresi clerked for Judges Bork and Scalia on the Court of Appeals for the D.C. Circuit. He then worked in the White House and the Justice Department from 1985 to 1990. McIntosh became a special assistant to President Reagan and to Attorney General Meese. Liberman clerked for Scalia on the Court of Appeals, then served as an assistant attorney general under Attorneys General William French Smith and Edwin Meese. When Scalia was appointed to the Supreme Court, she clerked for him there. Later she worked in the White House with C. Boyden Gray when George H. W. Bush was president and was in charge of vetting judicial nominees.

A large number of young conservative lawyers joined the Federalist Society founders in government. Charlie Savage describes the Justice Department under Meese as "a giant think tank where these passionate young conservative legal activists developed new legal theories to advance the Reagan agenda."[34] Professor Ann Southworth, who has written extensively about conservative lawyers, reports that many of the people she interviewed found jobs in the Reagan administration. One of them observed that "[t]he credentialing of lawyers during the Reagan [years] is probably the single biggest factor, along with the selection of conservative judges, in . . . really launching the [conservative law] movement into a more prominent and successful role."[35] During the Reagan administration, membership in the Federalist Society was a passport to career opportunities. The same has remained true with Republican presidents since then.

The young lawyers from the Federalist Society were far more extreme than the older conservatives in the Justice Department. Charles Fried, the solicitor general under Reagan from 1985 to 1989, described the speeches they wrote for Meese as containing "extreme positions such as questioning the constitutionality of independent agencies or suggesting that the president need not obey Supreme Court decisions with which he disagrees."[36] Many of these older lawyers retired by the time George W. Bush was elected president, and the Federalist Society lawyers in his administration were able to put into practice some of the theories they had developed during the Reagan years.

The society's promotion of originalism as the only legitimate method of constitutional interpretation was given a solid beginning in the Reagan Justice Department under the stewardship of Meese. Meese has described originalism as the notion that "judges should issue rulings based on the original understanding of the authors and ratifiers of the Constitution and the Bill of Rights, rather than on outcomes that reflect the judges' own biases or policy preferences."[37] Meese became interested in the subject while serving in Reagan's California administration and made it a national priority while serving as attorney general.

Meese launched his originalism campaign in a speech to the American Bar Association in July 1985.[38] It evoked harsh criticism from the liberal establishment. Supreme Court Justice William J. Brennan Jr., in an address at Georgetown University just months later, called attempts to divine the intent of the framers as "arrogance cloaked in humility." According to Brennan, it was "arrogant to pretend from our vantage we can gauge accurately the intent of the framers on application of principle to specific, contemporary questions."[39] Meese responded a few months later in a speech before the Federalist Society's lawyers division in Washington, D.C.; the society's current executive vice president, Leonard Leo, attended the meeting and described it as "a heady moment for me as a student."[40] To preserve the momentum of what would come to be known as the "great debate," Meese scheduled breakfast and lunch lectures on originalism at the Justice Department, and he promoted originalism as applied to issues such as civil rights and criminal justice in a series of seminars with conservative groups.[41] These groups included the fledgling Federalist Society.

Twenty years after the debate began so publicly, Harvard professor Lawrence Tribe said that Meese was "successful in making it look like he and his disciples were carrying out the intentions of the great founders, where the liberals were making it up as they went along. It was a convenient dichotomy, very misleading, with a powerful public relations effect."[42] What Meese sought to achieve with originalism—with considerable success to date, not least because of the endeavors of the Federalist Society—is what the Federalist Society itself has achieved with a broader base of conservative legal principles. Charles Cooper, who worked under Meese in the Office of Legal Counsel, described it thus: "Ed really brought it out of the pages of law review articles and the rarified atmosphere of faculty lounges and academic debates and made it a highly important and visible public policy debate."[43]

Calabresi published many of the important speeches and panel discussions on the debate about originalism in a single volume in celebration of the twenty-fifth anniversary of the Federalist Society.[44] Calabresi labels Robert Bork as the "intellectual godfather" of originalism. Yet he criticizes Bork on one point that has become a crucial development in the doctrine. Bork spoke of the need to interpret the Constitution's provisions "according to the intentions of those who drafted, proposed, and ratified them." Calabresi argues that it is the *words* of the Constitution that are the law, not the *intentions* of its authors.[45] The prevailing thought in the Federalist Society today, exemplified by the jurisprudence of Justice Scalia, is that to interpret the Constitution, one must search for the original meaning of its provisions, not the original intent of the framers. The argument is that the original meaning of words may be objectively determined by recourse to historical sources that reveal how the words were used at the time, whereas determining the intent of the framers is subjective and speculative.

The doctrine of originalism continues to develop, and there continue to be disagreements and debates among Federalist Society members and other conservatives about the correct approach. One current issue is the difference between "interpretation" and "construction" in determining what the Constitution requires in individual controversies. Professor Randy Barnett explains that discovering the original semantic meaning of the Constitutional text, i.e., "interpretation," is not always sufficient to resolve a case.[46] One must also engage in "construction," i.e., applying that meaning to particular factual circumstances. Some of the terms in constitutional provisions are vague. For example, the Fourth Amendment requires that searches be "reasonable," but what does "reasonable" mean in the context of a specific case? The text of the Constitution "does not say everything one needs to know to resolve all possible cases and controversies." When the information provided by interpretation "runs out," as Barnett puts it, one must turn to construction. Here is the rub—the rules for construction "are not found in the semantic content of the written Constitution." Thus, originalists will disagree among themselves about how to engage in constitutional construction partly because of "their differing normative reasons for favoring originalist interpretation."[47]

Ted Olson maintains that originalists are not motivated by "the desire to achieve any particular political outcome or result." "What drives originalists is nothing more, and nothing less, than the noble pursuit of a coherent and principled approach to interpreting and implementing the various provisions of our written Constitution."[48] Nonetheless, the doctrine of originalism does lead to some fairly predictable conservative outcomes. Calabresi closes the introduction to his collection of originalist documents by noting "some good consequences that would flow from adopting originalism":

> This country would be better off with more federalism and more decentralization . . . with a president who had more power to manage the bureaucracy . . . if we did not abort a million babies a year as we have done since 1973 . . . if students could pray and read the Bible in public school and if the Ten Commandments could be posted in public places . . . if citizens could engage in core political speech by contributing whatever they wanted to contribute to candidates for public office . . . if we could grow wheat on our own farms without federal intrusion . . . if criminals never got out of jail because of the idiocy of the exclusionary rule . . . if our homes could not be seized by developers acting in cahoots with state and local government . . . [and] if state governments could not pass laws impairing the obligations of contracts.[49]

GROWTH AND INFLUENCE

Federalist Society members have thoroughly infiltrated the executive and judicial branches, but have not been as successful in getting elected to public office. The historic 1994 election resulted in a fifty-four seat swing from Democrats to Republicans and gave Republicans a majority in the House for the first time since 1954. The new Republican majority included Federalist Society founder David McIntosh, elected as a representative from Indiana. Federalist Society members in the House formed a caucus called the New Federalist, "aimed in part at reducing the number of federal agencies in the government and restoring the balance of power between the federal government and the States." Rep. McIntosh reported, "Every day, as I travel to and from my committee meetings and the House floor, I seem to run into someone I originally met at a Federalist Society conference."[50] Nonetheless, the 1994 election sent only fifteen Federalist Society members to the House and Senate. McIntosh served six years in the House, and then ran for governor of Indiana in 2000, losing to Democrat Frank O'Bannon.

The membership and the financial resources of the Federalist Society have grown steadily from its inception. Between 2004 and 2010, for example, the number of members involved in local and national programs grew from 35,000 to over 45,000, and the number of members paying dues to the national organization went from under 8,000 to approximately 13,000. In the same period, the number of programs offered increased from approximately 900 to nearly 1,400. Over those six years, annual revenue more than doubled, from somewhat over four million dollars to more than nine million.[51] There are now more than three hundred student, faculty, lawyer, and alumni chapters in the United States and abroad.

The society has also begun to expand beyond the borders of the United States, with chapters in London, Brussels, Paris, and Toronto. In 2010, the society's International Law Project reached out to leaders of European public policy organizations "friendly to free markets and rule of law principles" and assisted European lawyers in starting groups modeled on the Federalist Society's lawyers and student chapters, all of whom are collectively termed the "European Sovereignty Network."[52] In 2010, the society anticipated participating with groups in Bulgaria, Macedonia, Serbia, Estonia, Latvia, and Lithuania.[53]

Federalist Society members reached the height of their political influence in the George W. Bush administration. Vice President Cheney, addressing the Federalist Society at its national convention in 2001, underlined the close ties between the society and the administration: "There are many members of the Federalist Society in our Administration. We know that because they were quizzed about it under oath. We're especially proud to have two of your founders at the Department of Energy—the general counsel, Lee Liberman Otis, and Secretary Spence Abraham."[54]

In 2001, three cabinet members were either Federalist Society members or active participants: Energy Secretary Spencer Abraham, Interior Secretary Gale A. Norton, and Attorney General John D. Ashcroft. Federalist Society stalwart Ted Olson was the solicitor general. Five of the eleven lawyers in the White House Counsel's Office were members.[55] Sidney Blumenthal took a dim view of the influence of Federalist Society members: "On every issue, from the gutting of the civil rights division of the Justice Department, where 60 percent of the professional staff was driven out and not a single discrimination case was filed, to the implementation of the so-called 'war paradigm,' including abrogation of Article Three of the Geneva Convention against torture, (which then White House counsel Alberto Gonzales termed 'quaint' in a memo to the president), Federalist Society cadres were at the center."[56]

The appointments of Chief Justice Roberts and Justice Alito doubled the Federalist Society influence on the Supreme Court. The *Wall Street Journal* noted: "[T]he Alito-Roberts ascendancy also marks a victory for the generation of legal conservatives who earned their stripes in the Reagan Administration. The two new justices are both stars of that generation—many others are scattered throughout the lower courts—and they are now poised to influence the law and culture for 20 years or more. *All those Federalist Society seminars may have finally paid off. Call it Ed Meese's revenge.*"[57]

A few examples suffice to illustrate the ideological content of the Roberts Court's jurisprudence. Professor Jeffrey Rosen describes the current direction of the court as "exceptionally good for American business."[58] In Chief Justice Roberts's first two terms, the court heard seven antitrust cases, compared to less than one per year during the Rehnquist Court.[59] The court resolved them all in favor of the corporate defendants and in the process overruled an almost one-hundred-year-old precedent holding minimum price restraints to be per se anticompetitive.[60] Consumers lost when the court held that regulatory action by a federal agency preempted a state tort action against an allegedly defective medical product in one case, and in another when the court afforded insurance companies a good faith defense for a mistaken reading of a regulatory statute.[61] The court has continued to protect corporate defendants against large punitive damage awards.[62] Environmental claims have had mixed success, with parties favoring regulation winning some procedural victories, but losing on the merits in other cases.[63] In a sharp departure from a decision just seven years earlier, the court upheld a law criminalizing abortion by means of intact dilation and evacuation, despite the fact that the statute made no exception for the need to protect the health of the mother.[64] Important decisions on the Fourth Amendment have run against criminal defendants.[65] The court struck down as unconstitutional voluntarily adopted school integration efforts in Seattle, Washington, and Louisville, Kentucky, over a passionate dissent by the moderate justices.[66] In a failure to follow what was arguably a controlling precedent, the court held that taxpayers had no standing to bring an establishment clause challenge to a federal agency's use of federal money to fund conferences to promote the president's faith-based initiatives.[67]

In one of the more controversial decisions handed down in recent memory, the court held in *Citizens United v. Federal Election Commission* that First Amendment protections extended to corporate-funded independent political broadcasts.[68] This case had been shepherded through the lower courts by society member James Bopp, and was argued before the court by Ted Olson. Common Cause, a reform group, subsequently argued that Justices Scalia and Thomas should have declined to participate in the case because they had associated with corporate leaders whose political aims were advanced by the ruling. Those corporate leaders included David and Charles Koch, staunch supporters—and funders—of the Federalist Society. Further media fallout highlighted both justices' personal ties to the Federalist Society.

In 2012, the Supreme Court decided one of the most politically charged cases in recent years, ruling on the constitutionality of provisions of the Patient Protection and Affordable Care Act of 2010, popularly known as "Obamacare."[69] In *National Federation of Independent Business v. Sebelius*, twenty-six states, together with private individuals and business organizations, filed suit seeking to have the statute declared unconstitutional. Questions concerning two provisions of the statute were before the court: (1) whether Congress had the power to require individuals to purchase and maintain health insurance (the "individual mandate"), and (2) whether Congress had the power to give the secretary of health and human services the authority to penalize states that chose not to participate in the statute's expansion of the Medicaid program. The court held that the individual mandate could be justified under the power of Congress to lay and collect taxes, treating the penalty for not purchasing health insurance as a tax. In addition, the court in effect upheld a penalty provision in connection with the expansion of Medicaid, although it narrowed the scope of the penalty. In practical terms, the result was a victory for President Obama and liberals who supported the health care reform measure. At the same time, the underlying rationale of the decision was a significant legal victory for conservatives, and advanced constitutional principles important to the Federalist Society.

Federalist Society members, including many the reader will encounter frequently in this book, were heavily involved in the case. Paul Clement represented the states that challenged the law and Michael A. Carvin represented the National Federation of Independent Business and the individual private challengers. Clement and Carvin participated in the oral argument at the Supreme Court. Karen R. Harned and Professor Randy Barnett also represented the private challengers. Some commentators described Barnett as the "key legal thinker" behind the challenge to the individual mandate.[70] Several influential Federalist Society members and allies authored amicus briefs on behalf of organizations supporting the challenge to the law.[71] Leading Federalist Society members fanned out across the country to speak at lawyers and student chapters both before and after the decision. The Federalist Society set up a dedicated webpage on which it hosted video from debates at Federalist Society chapters around the country discussing the act and its constitutional implications, as well as scholarly articles and podcasts by Federalist Society members.[72]

As we discuss in greater detail in the chapters that follow, members of the Federalist Society favor constitutional principles that limit the size of the federal government, protect states' rights, and protect private property from government regulation. Congress's power to enact legislation is limited by its constitutionally enumerated powers. As relevant here, in the late nineteenth and early twentieth centuries, the Supreme Court took a very narrow view of what Congress could do under the power given to it by Article I of the Constitution to regulate interstate commerce—the "commerce clause." During the Depression and in response to New Deal legislation, however, the court changed its philosophy and began to read the commerce clause extremely broadly. This continued through the civil rights era, when federal antidiscrimination statutes were passed under the commerce clause. Between 1937 and 1995, the Supreme Court did not strike down any federal legislation on the ground that Congress had exceeded its power under the commerce clause. This has been of ongoing concern to conservatives because it extended the reach, scope, and size of government. On two occasions, the Rehnquist Court held that legislation enacted by Congress exceeded its power under the commerce clause, striking down as unconstitutional the federal Gun-Free School Zones Act in 1995 and the civil remedy provision of the Violence against Women Act in 2000.[73] The court reasoned that the relationship between guns in school zones or domestic violence and interstate commerce was too attenuated. The decisions suggested that the commerce clause did not justify the regulation of non-economic activity based on its cumulative effect on interstate commerce. The effect of those decisions on the scope of the commerce clause, however, has been more limited than conservatives hoped.[74]

In *Sebelius*, Federalist Society lawyers argued that the health insurance individual mandate was unconstitutional under the commerce clause, in part because it *created* commerce rather than regulating it, and because it regulated *inactivity* (failing to purchase health insurance) rather than activity. Chief Justice Roberts's opinion accepted that argument, concluding, "The Framers gave Congress the power to *regulate* commerce, not to *compel* it."[75] It is too early to tell how many future laws the "inactivity" limitation on the commerce clause may invalidate, but the net result of the decision, although the act was upheld, was the creation of a new principle limiting Congress's power under the commerce clause. Following the decision, Randy Barnett blogged, "Who would have thought that we could win while losing?" Barnett stated the court had "accepted all of our arguments about why the individual insurance mandate exceeded the commerce power," and that the court had reaffirmed the "first principle" from *Lopez v. United States*, that "the federal government is one of limited and enumerated powers."[76]

In addition, the court held that the provision penalizing states that refused to participate in the expansion of Medicaid was unconstitutional under the spending clause. In earlier cases, the Supreme Court had read that clause to give Congress the power to condition federal grants on whether the recipient states met certain requirements. In this case, the court held for the first time that the requirements were too onerous and amounted to coercion, rendering the penalties provided by the statute unconstitutional.[77]

Thus, although the Supreme Court for the most part upheld the health care reform legislation, conservatives succeeded in establishing two important constitutional principles that they will be able to use in future cases. These doctrinal victories may, in the long run, prove to be more important than the fate of a single program.

Justices Scalia, Thomas, and Alito make no secret of their close connection to the society. The justices are highly prized and relatively frequent attendees at the society's major events. Justice Alito, hosted by the society's Paris chapter, traveled to France in December 2010 to participate in a panel discussion regarding judicial review and separation of powers with Judge Jean-Claude Bonichot of the European Court of Justice.[78] Justice Scalia was advertised as a copresenter at a September 2011 Continuing Legal Education (CLE) session sponsored by the society's Federalism and Separation of Powers Practice Group.[79] The CLE was held at the Ritz-Carlton in Lake Tahoe and was open to Federalist Society members only.

Scalia and Thomas attracted negative press just two months later as guests of honor at the fundraising dinner associated with the society's 2011 National Lawyers Convention, held at the Omni Shoreham Hotel in Washington, D.C. (Alito was also present, but was not an honoree).[80] Media outlets and various liberal groups decried the appearance of the justices at the gathering, in view of its temporal proximity to the court's decision as to whether it would hear the challenge brought by twenty-six states to President Obama's health care law (the conference in chambers was held the day of the dinner, and in conference, the justices decided to hear the case). The critics also pointed out that society member Paul Clement, who would likely argue the case before the court (and subsequently did), would not only be in attendance, but that Clement's firm was one of the nearly two dozen firms sponsoring the dinner. Jones Day, a firm that represented one of the trade associations that challenged the law, was another sponsor, as was Pfizer, the pharmaceutical giant, who would be greatly affected by the court's decision to hear the case.

Some federal judges and many lawyers are less public about their ties to the Federalist Society. Michael Mukasey was a judge on the Second Circuit Court of Appeals and was named attorney general by President George W. Bush after Alberto Gonzales resigned. Mukasey spoke about the war on terror and military commissions at the 2009 Federalist Society National Lawyers Convention. Earlier that morning, President Obama had announced that he intended to try several Guantanamo detainees in civilian courts in the United States, and Mukasey was harshly critical of the proposal. He said, "One of the benefits of leaving public service is that I got to be a member of this organization. Given today's announcement I can't think of anywhere else I would rather be. I felt uncomfortable being here when I was on the bench and when I was AG, but I don't criticize those who are on the bench or in public service who are members."[81] Of course, Mukasey had the same views about law and politics when he was a judge and attorney general as he did after he left public service—he simply did not acknowledge his affinity for the Federalist Society. Now he is on the organization's board of directors.

FINANCIAL SUPPORT

The Federalist Society's success is in great part due to the willingness of conservative philanthropists to make very large contributions year after year and to do so, for the most part, in unrestricted funds. In the first decade of the twenty-first century, the financial base of the society grew enormously, as illustrated in Table 2.

TABLE 2. Financial Base of the Federalist Society

Source: Federalist Society for Law and Public Policy Studies, Form 990, 2001–2010.

Table 3 lists the five largest Federalist Society funders as of 2010 and shows their cumulative contributions as of that time and the amounts that constituted unrestricted funds.

The society is the beneficiary of a cohesive and strategic approach to shaping public policy by philanthropy, begun in earnest by conservatives in the 1960s.[82] The John Olin Foundation, for example, which Steven Calabresi described in the early years of the society as "absolutely number one in terms of foundation support," gave financial support to the idea of the society before it came into existence.[83] The 1982 national symposium happened, in part, because of Olin monies that were used for grants to enable out-of-state law students to travel to Yale. That same year, Olin had donated $6,000 to the *Harvard Journal of Law and Public Policy*. Of those early years, Calabresi would say that Olin was "indispensable."[84] Olin's most significant contribution to the society was the creation and support of the John M. Olin Lectures in Law series. This program of debates, sponsored on campuses around the country, has since 1983 been the backbone of the Federalist Society's programming in law schools.[85] The debates, often structured as a conversation between a liberal and a conservative on an issue of law or particular case, allowed the society to air conservative views in a neutral environment. Olin's funding also meant that the Federalist Society exposed law students

TABLE 3. Cumulative Contributions as of 2010

Funder	Total Contributions[a]	Unrestricted Funds[b]
John M. Olin Foundation	$5,657,000	$1,268,000
Lynde and Harry Bradley Foundation	4,965,000	4,592,000
Sarah Scaife Foundation	4,405,000	4,405,000
Claude R. Lambe Charitable Foundation (Koch Family)	1,431,500	971,500
Charles G. Koch Charitable Foundation (Koch Family)	862,499	378,200
Total	$17,320,999	$11,614,700

a. Federalist Society for Law and Public Policy Studies, Form 990, 2005–2010; *Federalist Society: Funders,* Media Matters Action Network, *mediamattersaction.org/transparency/organization/Federalist_Society_for _Law_and_Public_Policy_Studies/funders* (last visited Feb. 25, 2012) (financial data prior to 2005).
b. *Id.* Any grant indicating a dual purpose for general support and another use was treated as a grant for general support unless specific amounts were indicated for each type of use.

to very high-profile conservatives, including Supreme Court justices, in a way no organization before it had.

As Table 3 demonstrates, other than Olin, the principal benefactors of the Federalist Society made unrestricted grants. As compared to grants that are earmarked for a specific project or program, and therefore require grantees to justify the details of specific expenditures and meet specific benchmarks, unrestricted funds give recipients the freedom for long-term goal setting and institution building.

Conservative philanthropists understood much earlier than their liberal counterparts that what they were seeking to win was a war of ideas, and that winning that war requires patience. James Piereson, who led the Olin Foundation for more than twenty years, has discussed the stylistic difference in grant making between conservative and liberal foundations. He noted that liberal foundations tended to stay with things "less for the long haul than we do." The idea that funded programs should become self-sustaining was not an idea that Olin subscribed to.[86] Perhaps because they are conservative by nature, Piereson said, conservative donors have fewer grand expectations about their work than their liberal counterparts—"they know that the world is going to be changed in increments, by and large."[87] The Olin funds were granted to the ambitious law students with little or no expectation—with some skepticism, even—but the society came to be one of Olin's great successes: a "significant voice in the national political debate."

ORGANIZATIONAL PRINCIPLES

The Federalist Society's success is also due in large part to decisions its leaders have made about organizational policies. As noted above, the Federalist Society itself does not take formal policy positions on legal or political questions. Teles analyzes this as the organization's approach to "boundary maintenance."[88] The members of the Federalist Society represent a broad range of conservative and libertarian view-points and may disagree about particular legal issues. The society sponsors frequent debates on legal issues, openly exploring disagreements among its members. By avoiding contests about which positions the organization should adopt, however, it avoids disputes that might drive some members away.[89]

Disagreements among conservative lawyers may reflect significant differences in their basic values. For example, conservative public interest firms eventually moved away from representing business interests toward litigation that reflected libertarian values. Federalist Society member Ilya Somin finds it surprising that "it took so long for right of center public interest lawyers to realize that business interests weren't necessarily their friends." He notes that many conservative economists recognized that whether business supports expansion of government depends on whether it serves their interests.[90]

Professor Ann Southworth's empirical research shines a light on the "striking differences" among the lawyers who represent conservative causes, both with respect to their political views and their social and educational backgrounds.[91] For example, "social conservatives are at odds with business elites, who are generally uncomfortable with the Republican Party's association with Protestant fundamentalism, pro-life advocacy, prayer in the schools, and traditional 'family values.' . . . Social conservatives tend to dislike big business and tax policies that favor the wealthy."[92] With respect to their backgrounds, "[r]eligious conservatives usually come from rural and less economically privileged environments, and many of them openly invoke God as a source of inspiration and guidance. Lawyers for libertarian groups also generally come from modest backgrounds, but they are less religious and more enamored with markets and personal liberty. Most of the business representatives come from economically secure circumstances and describe their advocacy for business-oriented causes as work rather than activism."[93] Southworth characterizes the Federalist Society and the Heritage Foundation as "mediator organizations" that have successfully established common ground among the various conservative constituencies and their lawyers.[94] Ed Meese directs the foundation's efforts to keep conservative legal principles alive in public debate and discourse.

The Federalist Society provides organizational, financial, political, intellectual, and social support that is crucial to the empowerment of conservative lawyers, scholars, and judges. For example, debates organized by the Washington, D.C., chapter have created networks that are "especially valuable in overcoming the intrinsic informational challenges of coordinating action across the executive branch."[95] The debates are also crucially important, of course, because as Teles explains, "ideas do not develop in a vacuum. Ideas need networks through which they can be shared and nurtured, organizations to connect them to problems and to diffuse them to political actors, and patrons to provide resources for these supporting conditions."[96] The debates and symposia offer many lawyers the opportunity to engage in intellectual discussion and analysis, which is rare in post–law school practice.

Teles identifies the problems conservatives faced in mobilizing against liberal control of crucial legal networks and institutions as fundamentally *organizational*.[97] The conservative legal movement challenged the entrenched liberal legal polity through the development of an "alternative governing coalition."[98] Of necessity, such a coalition must comprise "*intellectual, network*, and *political entrepreneurs*, and the *patrons* that support them."[99] All of these pieces came together for the Federalist Society.

The Federalist Society has been so successful that organizations outside the field of law and policy have adopted its model for their own ends. The Benjamin Rush Society, launched in 2008, was formed in reaction to the prevailing liberal bias in medical school curricula. It seeks to educate medical students on free-market solutions to health care, and to question government intervention in the relationship between physicians and patients.[100] The Alexander Hamilton Society, dedicated to foreign, economic, and national security policy, was founded in 2010. The group believes that foreign and domestic policy must be shaped to defend the principles of individual liberty, limited government, economic freedom, the rule of law, human dignity, and democracy.[101] The Adam Smith Society was formed very recently to achieve in business schools what the Federalist Society achieved in law schools, exposing students to the philosophical and moral underpinnings of capitalism.[102] All three groups are building institutions based on student chapters. All three groups subscribe to principles of individual liberty, limited government, and free markets.

The American Constitution Society for Law and Policy (ACS) was founded by Georgetown Law School professor Peter Rubin in 2001 as a counterweight to the Federalist Society. Rubin told the *New York Times* that year that the Federalist Society "has been extraordinarily successful in taking, in some cases, extreme views, views outside of the mainstream, and moving them into the center stage of American law."[103] Rubin's goal was to "emphasize legal values like compassion, equality and respect for human dignity," values he believed "have largely been read out of American law through the ascendancy of various strands of legal thought over the last 20 years."[104] The ACS shares many institutional features with the Federalist Society: a nationwide network of student and lawyers chapters, an official journal (the *Harvard Law and Policy Review*), sponsorship of debates and conferences as a means to proliferate its ideas and ideology, and an annual convention featuring legal luminaries with liberal and progressive leanings. The ACS motivates its members by citing the humble beginnings of its rival: "ACS's goals are ambitious but attainable. Those who would despair of our success need only think of the small band of legal conservatives of twenty-five years ago—their ideas then scorned by academics, ignored by judges and unknown to the public—who persevered to build a powerful movement and reshape our world according to their notions. If you seek their works, look around you. Our work is just beginning. Don't just stand there—join us."[105] Justice Ginsburg addressed the 2012 ACS national convention as a featured speaker.

The Federalist Society's membership includes many brilliant and sincere theorists who raise important and interesting issues. Their intellectual endeavors, their creativity, and their willingness to discuss and debate controversial ideas are admirable. They argue that their answers to fundamental political and legal questions preserve the essence of the American constitutional system. On the other hand, their critics say that the overall impact of Federalist Society thought is reactionary. Critics argue that by glorifying private property, demonizing government intervention (particularly at the federal level), insisting that originalism is the only legitimate method of constitutional interpretation, embracing American Exceptionalism, and advocating related policies, the Federalist Society advocates a form of social Darwinism that has been discredited by the mainstream of American legal thought since the 1930s.

The chapters that follow describe and analyze the thinking and writing of influential Federalist Society members in specific areas of law. We track their views as they are planted as intellectual seeds in law journals, germinate in legal briefs, and eventually blossom in court opinions, legislation, and public policy. A measure of the success of the Federalist Society is that the current Supreme Court can generally be relied on to protect business interests against legislation designed to protect workers, consumers, and the environment; to halt the judicial expansion of personal liberty interests while expanding judicial protection of property interests; to interpret a "colorblind" Constitution by rolling back affirmative action and school desegregation plans; to restrict access to the courts through a variety of procedural and substantive doctrines; and to weaken the boundaries between church and state.

— 1 —

THE NETWORK

The White House, The Department of Justice, and The Bench

One fact is clear and compelling. No President exercises any power more far-reaching, more likely to influence his legacy, than the selection of federal judges.

—Edwin Meese III[1]

Since the early years of the Federalist Society in the 1980s, its members have believed that the easiest way to change the law is to change the judges. They have been phenomenally successful in doing so. The Federalist Society came into being at a catalytic moment for remaking the judiciary. Southern resentment at the integration that followed *Brown v. Board of Education*, disenchantment by "law and order" citizens with the criminal procedure rulings of the Warren Court, and profound disagreement with the right to choose an abortion recognized in *Roe v. Wade* made large sectors of the conservative and Republican base angry at the Supreme Court. Ronald Reagan's election campaign and presidency and the general renaissance of conservative ideas created an opportunity both to galvanize the base to demand change on the bench and to recruit, educate, and groom a new generation of elite lawyers as judges. The nascent Federalist Society benefited from this confluence of events. Throughout the administrations of all three Republican presidents since its founding, Federalist Society members occupied key positions in the White House, the Department of Justice, and as outside advisors with respect to the nomination of federal judges. Working together with other conservatives, they have moved the federal judiciary significantly to the right over the past thirty years. And as they predicted it would, the law has followed.

The most obvious success of the Federalist Society is that it has four justices on the U.S. Supreme Court. Antonin Scalia helped found the society as a faculty advisor at the University of Chicago Law School. His sons Eugene and John are members; Eugene is the chairman of the Employment and Labor Law Practice Group, and John is the chairman of that group's publications subcommittee. Federalist Society members were key supporters of Clarence Thomas's nomination to the Supreme Court. Thomas remains a major figure in the Federalist Society and delivered the keynote speech at the 30th Annual Federalist Society Student Symposium in February 2011, where the theme was "Capitalism, Markets, and the Constitution."[2] Later in the year, as noted in the Introduction, Thomas and

Scalia were honored at the annual black-tie dinner of the society, a major fund-raising event. They participated despite the fact that their activities as guests of honor would have been a clear violation of the Code of Conduct for United States Judges, for any federal judge other than Supreme Court justices.[3] Samuel Alito is a longtime member of the Federalist Society. He addressed the annual dinner of the group in 2009. Chief Justice John Roberts claimed during his confirmation hearings to have no recollection of being a member, although his name appeared in the organization's 1997–1998 leadership directory as a member of the steering committee of the Washington, D.C., chapter.[4] His support of the Federalist Society and its principles is evident from his appearances before the group, including his video tribute to the society, which is featured on its website.[5]

Success in obtaining Supreme Court appointments was the result of a long-term strategy by the Federalist Society and other conservatives in the Reagan administration. The first move was to get young members and friends of the society who were potential Supreme Court justices onto the lower federal courts. As David Kirkpatrick noted in the *New York Times*, the appointment of Alito to the Supreme Court was "the culmination of a disciplined campaign begun by the Reagan administration to seed the lower federal judiciary with like-minded jurists who could reorient the federal courts" toward the philosophy of originalism.[6] Those who made it to the Supreme Court were first appointed to one of the courts of appeals.

The eventual Supreme Court justices were part of a much larger pool of Federalist Society members or close friends named to the federal bench by Republican presidents, advised by lawyers who either were, or would become, Federalist Society members. Among those Reagan appointed to the lower federal courts were the original Federalist Society faculty advisors. He appointed Scalia to the D.C. Circuit; Ralph K. Winter, Yale Law School, to the Second Circuit; and Robert Bork, Yale Law School, to the D.C. Circuit. Other important appointments were Richard Posner (Seventh Circuit), Frank Easterbrook (Seventh Circuit), J. Harvie Wilkinson (Fourth Circuit), Edith Jones (Fifth Circuit), Alex Kozinski (Ninth Circuit), and Kenneth Starr (D.C. Circuit). Reagan later appointed Scalia to the Supreme Court. These judges were young when appointed and are either still on the bench or otherwise active in the law.[7] Among those George H. W. Bush appointed to the lower federal courts were Thomas (D.C. Circuit), Roberts (D.C. Circuit), Alito (Third Circuit), and Michael Luttig (Fourth Circuit). Bush Sr. later appointed Thomas to the Supreme Court, and Roberts and Alito were appointed to the Supreme Court by his son, George W. Bush.

From the moment they graduated from law school, the Federalist Society founders secured important positions in the White House and the Department of Justice (DOJ). The young Federalist Society lawyers, under the tutelage of Ed Meese, had a remarkably significant impact on legal and policy decisions during the Reagan administration, and their successors continued to do so, particularly in the administration of George W. Bush. At the same time, the White House and the DOJ served as incubators for conservative lawyers, predominantly members of the Federalist Society, who would go on to take judicial appointments or be-come powerful lawyers or policymakers. Scalia served as assistant attorney general in the Office of Legal Counsel under President Nixon. Roberts, Alito, and Thomas all worked in the Reagan administration. Roberts was a special assistant to the at-torney general and later associate counsel to the president. Alito was assistant to the solicitor general and later deputy assistant to Attorney General Meese. Thomas was assistant secretary for civil rights at the DOJ and later the chairman of the Equal Employment Opportunity Commission (EEOC). Roberts later became the principal deputy solicitor general under George H. W. Bush. Scalia's service un-der President Nixon predated the founding of the Federalist Society, but once the group was in existence, its networking resources made placing Federalist Society members and other conservatives in the federal legal apparatus much easier.

Once a large number of conservative judges and Supreme Court justices were on the bench, Federalist Society law graduates obtained clerkships with them, an important career stepping-stone. Edward Lazarus, a former Supreme Court clerk, called membership in the society during the eighties "a prerequisite for law students seeking clerkships with many Reagan judicial appointees as well as for employment in the upper ranks of the Justice Department and the White House."[8] Eventually the Federalist Society developed a powerful pipeline from the law schools to judi-cial clerkships, White House and DOJ positions, judgeships, and other positions of power and influence.

As an example, consider two of the staff lawyers involved with judicial selection during the Bush administration, Rachel Brand and Kate Comerford Todd. Rachel Brand graduated from Harvard Law School in 1998, where she was the deputy edi-tor in chief of the *Harvard Journal of Law and Public Policy* (the Federalist Society's law journal). She then clerked for Justice Charles Fried on the Massachusetts Supreme Judicial Court. After a brief stint as general counsel to Elizabeth Dole's Presidential Exploratory Committee, she worked two years for Cooper, Carvin & Rosenthal (where lead partner Charles J. Cooper is a Federalist Society member and former DOJ lawyer). She followed that with two years at the White House, as associate counsel to the president, one year as a clerk for Supreme Court Justice Anthony Kennedy, and four years at the DOJ. She left the DOJ to join the D.C. office of law firm behemoth WilmerHale in its Regulatory and Government Affairs and Litigation/Controversy Departments.[9] Kate Todd graduated from Harvard Law School in 1999. She clerked for two Federalist Society stalwarts, first for Judge Luttig on the Fourth Circuit Court of Appeals, and later for Justice Thomas on the Supreme Court. She became a partner at the Washington firm Wiley Rein & Fielding, at which time she was a vice chair of the Federalist Society's Federalism and Separation of Powers Practice Group. She went to the White House as associate counsel to the president when Fred Fielding became White House counsel. Kate's husband, Gordon Todd, also worked for the Office of Legal Counsel in the Bush administration, where he was special counsel for Supreme Court nominations, in-cluding that of Justice Alito. After Alito joined the court, Gordon Todd was hired as one of his clerks. In June 2011, the Litigation Center of the U.S. Chamber of Commerce announced that it had hired both Rachel Brand and Kate Todd, Brand as chief counsel for regulatory litigation and Todd as chief counsel for appellate litigation. The chief legal officer of the chamber said their hiring "couldn't be more timely, given the aggressive regulatory overreach America's job creators now face."[10] If they want to go on the bench, Rachel Brand and Kate Todd are highly likely to be appointed to federal judgeships during the administration of the next Republican president.

At a Federalist Society conference entitled "The Presidency and the Courts," near the end of the president's second term in office, keynote speaker George W. Bush thanked the members of the "mighty Federalist Society" for their hard work in recruiting more Americans to the selection of good judges. He declared that with their support he had fulfilled his campaign pledge to appoint judges who would "faithfully interpret the Constitution—and not use the courts to invent laws or dictate social policy."[11]

To select judges who will be effective in moving the law in the direction he desires, the president has to be able to predict how a judicial candidate will rule, in general terms, once he or she is on the bench. It is generally agreed, however, that it is inappropriate to ask judicial candidates how they would decide specific issues likely to come before the courts. At various times, both Republicans and Democrats have accused presidents of the opposing party of employing ideological "litmus tests" in selecting judges. Presidents and their top advisors, of course, deny such charges, asserting that they choose judges based on their legal acumen, background and experience, and judicial temperament. Yet few would deny that President Franklin Roosevelt selected judges who would be more supportive of his New Deal policies than their predecessors, or that President Reagan nominated judges who shared his conservative social and economic views.

Federalist Society members and their allies argue that it is appropriate for a president to select judges based on their "judicial philosophy," which they define as the principles that determine the role that the judicial branch plays under our Constitution. They distinguish judicial philosophy from a judicial candidate's views on specific political issues that might arise in cases before the courts, such as abortion, prayer in schools, criminal procedure questions, and the like. In their view, it is inappropriate for presidents to ask judicial candidates about their opinions on such issues, but permissible and desirable to inquire about judicial philosophy.

Gary McDowell is a professor at the Jepson School of Leadership Studies at the University of Richmond, and he worked as a speechwriter for Meese when Meese was the attorney general. McDowell considers the Federalist Society to be "a revolutionary development in legal education" and a "powerful force for good."[12] In the mid-1980s, he viewed the courts as controlled by liberal judges and liberal thought, and he became a key player in early conservative efforts to remake the federal judiciary. According to Meese, during the Reagan administration McDowell was "instrumental" in developing a strategy in a series of articles and speeches about "judicial allegiance to the Constitution and fidelity to it."[13] McDowell believes the country needs to return to the "old race of judges" who engaged in a strict interpretation of the constitution according to fixed rules. He identifies Clarence Thomas as the paradigmatic example of a judge who takes language and original meaning seriously. Robert Bork is another of his heroes. In McDowell's words, the Senate's rejection of Bork's nomination to the Supreme Court in 1987 was an event "we must never forget, must never forgive."[14] He looks for judges who will engage in judicial review but not "judicial activism," and examines a candidate's views concerning principles of federalism and separation of powers to determine his or her philosophy concerning judicial power.[15] The McDowell-Meese school of judicial selection has guided the thinking of Federalist Society members, and the actions of Republican presidents, for three decades.

The Reagan Administration

President Reagan came to Washington in 1981 committed to enacting a conservative social and economic agenda. Selecting judges who would support that agenda was a critical part of his program. The Republican Party platforms in 1980 and 1984 called for judges who would protect "the rights of law-abiding citizens," favor "decentralization of the federal government" and the return of decision-making power to state and local officials, respect "traditional family values" and "the sanctity of innocent human life," and be committed to "judicial restraint."[16] The Republicans contrasted judicial restraint with reading the Constitution to find individual rights not enumerated in the text. On the other hand, Reagan sought aggressive jurists when it came to enforcing the criminal law: "We don't need a bunch of sociology majors on the bench. What we need are strong judges who will aggressively use their authority to protect our families, communities, and our way of life . . . judges who do not hesitate to put criminals where they belong—behind bars."[17]

For the last three years of Reagan's second term, Federalist Society member Stephen Markman was the assistant attorney general in charge of the DOJ's Office of Legal Policy (OLP), the office that screened judicial candidates.[18] Markman has written that Reagan was determined to appoint only judges who were "committed to the rule of law and to the enforcement of the Constitution and statutes as those [that] were adopted by 'we the people' and their elected representatives."[19] Changing the philosophical orientation of the courts from the jurisprudence of the Warren Court era was essential to Reagan's overall program. According to Markman, once candidates had been identified, the OLP reviewed their written work, the comments of local bar leaders, and any recommendations by members of Congress. The OLP then determined which candidates to talk to, and invited them to the DOJ for four to five hours of interviews by several different DOJ lawyers. They discussed federalism, separation of powers, statutory interpretation, constitutional interpretation, criminal justice, and the candidate's reasons for wanting to be a judge. Markman asserts that they were interested in whether a candidate "reasoned from constitutional premises," but that they did not ask about a candidate's views on individual issues or employ any "litmus test."

The OLP followed up the personal interviews by talking with public officials, bar leaders, sitting judges, and others in the candidate's home state. It then prepared a summary of each candidate's qualifications, and the attorney general selected one candidate to recommend to the President's Federal Judicial Selection Committee. The counsel to the president chaired the committee, which also included the attorney general, the deputy attorney general, and the assistant attorney general for the OLP. Officials at the White House also did their own background checks on proposed nominees.

If the committee decided to go forward with a nominee, it would send his or her name to the FBI and to the American Bar Association (ABA) Standing Committee on the Federal Judiciary. If they did not turn up information that revealed unfitness, the attorney general and the counsel to the president recommended the person to the president for formal nomination.

Federalist Society members and allies were critical participants in judicial selection in the Reagan administration. The Federalist Society was only formed in 1982 as a law student organization, so many of the important conservative lawyers in the Reagan administration were not initially members. Ed Meese, however, quickly realized the significance of the group and arranged for the Federalist Society founders to get jobs either in the White House or the DOJ after graduation from law school. Conservative lawyers in the administration began attending meetings organized by the society, and many eventually joined it or became frequent contributors to Federalist Society publications or speakers at its debates and panels.

Meese, originally as counselor to the president and later as attorney general, was a key figure in judicial selection. Peter J. Wallison was a principal advisor on judicial selection during Meese's tenure as White House counsel.[20] He later became an advisor on insurance issues to the Federalist Society's Financial Services and E-Commerce Practice Group and a frequent speaker at Federalist Society events. In 1986, Meese named Grover Rees III as a special assistant to review the judicial philosophy of judicial candidates. Rees is a frequent speaker at Federalist Society events. In fact, the first Federalist Society event held at Yale Law School, in January 1982, was a debate over *Roe v. Wade* between Rees, then a professor at the University of Texas Law School, and Burke Marshall, a former assistant attorney general in the Kennedy administration and then a member of the Yale law faculty.[21]

Professor Henry Abraham concluded that the Reagan administration was arguably "more effective than any of his recent predecessors" in selecting judges to pursue a "coherent and ambitiously systematic legal policy agenda."[22] Critics of judicial selection during the Reagan administration claimed that despite their protestations to the contrary, Reagan's advisors did use an "ideological litmus test" to select nominees.[23] Debra Cassens Moss reported in the *ABA Journal* that the DOJ was "thoroughly screening judicial candidates for ideology to ensure a conservative judiciary."[24] Contrary to the assertion by Markman that specific cases were not discussed, she quotes Grover Rees as saying, "Of course we discussed particular cases, real as well as hypothetical, in the course of trying to figure out how the person approached the Constitution. I don't know any other way to do it. Otherwise, you're settling for somebody's slogans."[25] After Judge Roger J. Miner's death on February 18, 2012, his wife, Jacqueline, told the *New York Times* that his failure to tip his hand on how he would vote on the abortion issue may have cost him a seat on the Supreme Court. In 1987, it was widely thought that Miner was next in line when President Reagan's nomination of Robert Bork to the Supreme Court was failing. A Republican senator on the Judiciary Committee called Judge Miner at home to ask his views about abortion. While the judge was telling the senator that he would decide each case on its merits, his wife was shouting at him from the next room to be more politic. Reagan passed over Miner and appointed Anthony Kennedy to the court.[26]

Federalist Society members were heavily involved in the attempt to secure Senate approval for Bork's nomination to the Supreme Court in 1987. Peter Keisler was in the White House Counsel's Office and "was at Bork's side throughout the fight."[27] David McIntosh worked on the nomination at the White House, Clint Bolick at the Department of Justice, and Lee Liberman, who was then teaching at George Mason, recruited support. Nina Easton reports, "Five months after his defeat, an embittered Bork found solace in the embrace of the Federalist Society's annual conference, where he would be treated to four standing ovations and the sight of audience members sporting 'Reappoint Bork' buttons."[28] Ralph Reed, the first executive director of the Christian Coalition, is quoted by Easton as saying, "I have always felt the vicious treatment of Thomas (and Robert Bork) by the radical Left helped inspire our movement." Easton concluded, "And so, the movement would Bork back."[29]

Whether the interviewers asked candidates about specific cases or not, exploration of the potential nominee's "judicial philosophy" in fact provided sufficient information to predict how he or she might rule on many substantive questions. Professor Sheldon Goldman is a leading academic who has studied judicial selection for the past several decades; as he observed, candidates who believed in "judicial restraint" were likely to share President Reagan's views with respect to substantive issues such as the right to abortion, busing to desegregate public schools, the exclusionary rule in criminal cases (under which evidence gathered in violation of a defendant's Fourth Amendment rights is thrown out), the rights of criminal defendants, prayer in public schools, and affirmative action in employment and education.

The influence of the young Federalists and the older conservative lawyers in the Reagan administration whom they recruited into the society was remarkable.[30] Among the Federalist Society members with crucial policy positions were Charles Cooper, head of the Office of Legal Counsel; Stephen Markman, head of the OLP; John Bolton, in the Office of Legislative Affairs; Douglas Ginsburg, in the Antitrust Division; Terry Eastland, in the Office of Public Affairs; and Steven Calabresi, David McIntosh, and Kenneth Cribb as special assistants.[31] Amanda Hollis-Brusky reports that Thomas A. Smith, one of the first Federalist Society members, described the Meese DOJ as a "Federalist Society shop."[32]

The Office of Legal Policy Reports

The young Federalist Society lawyers in the DOJ provided the intellectual capital for a series of government publications that informed the legal and constitutional agenda for conservatives inside and outside the government for the next three decades. The agenda was based on an original meaning method of constitutional interpretation, a limited role for the federal government, and judicial restraint with respect to the recognition of constitutional rights not explicitly enumerated in the text of the Constitution.

In *Report to the Attorney General: The Constitution in the Year 2000*, published in 1988, the OLP described fifteen areas of potential conflict on the Supreme Court between then and 2000. The emphasis on selecting the right judges to resolve these issues was paramount:

> [I]t is hoped that this report will allow Members of Congress of both parties, pursuant to their constitutional responsibilities, to assess judicial nominees in the most thorough and informed manner possible. There are few factors that are more critical to determining the course of the Nation, and yet more often overlooked, than the values and philosophies of the men and women who populate the third co-equal branch of the national government—the federal judiciary.[33]

The report's areas of concern included the exclusionary rule in criminal cases, abortion, homosexual rights, morality as a basis for legislation, affirmative action and disparate impact cases, policies with a disparate impact based on wealth and social welfare spending, private education and the religion clauses of the First Amendment, the free exercise clause and accommodation of religious practices, freedom of association and protection from government policies as applied to private groups, the takings clause and the contracts clause, the authority of the president in foreign policy, protection of the states by the Tenth Amendment, the equity power of the federal courts to restructure local institutions, the rights of aliens, and separation of powers.

The prevailing philosophy of constitutional interpretation among Federalist Society members has been the original meaning school of thought, notably advanced in the opinions of Justices Scalia and Thomas. In a lengthy and detailed argument in favor of the original meaning approach, the OLP characterized the choice of interpretive methodology as "[t]he most basic issue facing constitutional scholars and jurists today."[34] The OLP report defined original meaning jurisprudence as "the enterprise of attempting to interpret the provisions of the Constitution as those provisions were generally understood at the time of their adoption by the society which framed and ratified them."[35]

William Bradford Reynolds, an assistant attorney general under Meese, and later a member of the Federalist Society's board of visitors, was an early proponent of original meaning jurisprudence. In an article about judicial selection, Reynolds wrote that "the Constitution and laws passed pursuant to it have meanings;

otherwise, the very idea of consent—of ratifying or amending the Constitution or voting for or against laws—would be absurd. Consent must mean knowing consent, and knowing consent is possible only if the constitutional provisions consented to have discernable meanings."[36]

Reynolds was also the author of the metaphor that Chief Justice Roberts famously employed to summarize his judicial philosophy in his testimony at his Senate confirmation hearings. To emphasize his contention that judges do not make law, Roberts quipped, "Judges are like umpires. Umpires don't make the rules; they apply them. . . . And I will remember that it's my job to call balls and strikes and not to pitch or bat."[37] In a 1990 article, Reynolds had criticized the manner in which the Senate exercised its advise and consent function in judicial selection: "[T]he job of a judge is much like that of an umpire or referee: simply to call the balls and strikes; not undertake to rewrite the rule book."[38] President George W. Bush quoted the phrase again in 2008 when speaking to the Federalist Society about how proud he was of his nomination of Roberts to the position of chief justice.

The legal theories that the Rehnquist Court later employed with respect to federalism and limits on the power of Congress mirrored those set out in the reports of the OLP during the Reagan administration.[39] In one of the most important of these reports, *Guidelines on Constitutional Litigation* (1988), the DOJ provided government lawyers with a set of positions that were presumptively to be followed unless a deviation from them was cleared with supervisors. The *Guidelines* analyzed the prevailing judicial doctrine on individual issues and identified points at which the administration's views as to what the law should be varied from the current law. The document analyzed Supreme Court opinions that were "consistent" and "inconsistent" with the administration's views. Professor Dawn Johnsen concluded, "The unmistakable premise of the Guidelines was that executive branch lawyers were to seek to advance the administration's understanding of the Constitution— and not simply what the courts said the Constitution means—even when at odds with 'inconsistent' Supreme Court decisions."[40] This is in line with the view that many Federalist Society members came to espouse: that there is a difference between the Constitution (the text) and constitutional law (the text as interpreted by the Supreme Court), and that a lawyer's ultimate loyalty is to the former.[41] The view is at odds with the Supreme Court's opinions in *Marbury v. Madison* and *Cooper v. Aaron*, which held that it is the Supreme Court that determines what the Constitution means.[42]

Professor Johnsen describes the *Guidelines'* success in the Supreme Court's adoption of the principles that the OLP articulated for limiting the power of Congress to enact legislation under section 5 of the Fourteenth Amendment.[43] Section 5 provides Congress with the authority to pass statutes to enforce the due process and equal protection guarantees of the Fourteenth Amendment. The Rehnquist Court adopted a narrow interpretation of Congress's power under section 5, as recommended in the *Guidelines*.[44] As a result, it declared unconstitutional major portions of a series of civil rights acts, including the Religious Freedom Restoration Act, the Age Discrimination in Employment Act, the Violence against Women Act, and the Americans with Disabilities Act.[45]

The ideology of small government and judicial restraint permeated the OLP reports. In *Religious Liberty under the Free Exercise Clause*, the authors asserted that a significant factor that had complicated free exercise clause jurisprudence was the advance of the welfare state. They wrote:

> The so-called "Affirmative Age" of government has transformed the way in which we approach constitutional rights by emphasizing entitlements over responsibilities, equality over liberty, and positive over natural law. Our rights-based era has cast the government—and particularly the courts—in the role of guardian of our rights, and because the influence of government is so widespread the power to determine what rights it will guard has become the power to determine the rights themselves.[46]

Another OLP publication, *Justice without Law: A Reconsideration of the "Broad Equitable Powers" of the Federal Court*, criticized the broad use of injunctions in school desegregation cases and suits alleging unconstitutional conditions in mental hospitals and prisons.[47] Based on its research into the equitable powers of English courts and the history of U.S. constitutional provisions, the OLP concluded that the Supreme Court's unanimous opinion in the remedy phase of *Brown v. Board of Education* was not supported by a proper analysis of equitable principles. It characterized the court's later unanimous decision approving busing as a desegregation remedy as based on "tautological and circuitous reasoning," and representative of the court's assumption of a "license-without-limit to make policy for social institutions."[48] The document reflects the ongoing Federalist Society critique of "activist judges," arguing that equity had become "a special judicial superpower that gives little recognition to issues of jurisprudence, constitutionalism, separation of powers, or federalism."[49]

THE GEORGE H. W. BUSH ADMINISTRATION

George H. W. Bush became president in 1989. In his administration, the person principally responsible for screening nominees for judicial appointments was the White House counsel, C. Boyden Gray, now a member of the Federalist Society's board of directors. Gray's staff was considered "a bastion of bright conservatism."[50] Gray's most important staff member with respect to judicial nominees was Lee Liberman, one of the Federalist Society founders. Murray G. Dickman, Attorney General Dick Thornburgh's chief advisor on judicial nominations, said, "For information about people who are appeals court nominees, Lee has the best view of anyone in the country."[51]

President Reagan had appointed Dick Thornburgh as attorney general during his last six months in office, and President George H. W. Bush retained him. Under

Bush, Thornburgh changed the name of the Office of Legal Policy in the DOJ to the Office of Policy Development, and the selection of judicial candidates was removed from the newly named office. Originally the intent was to make Robert B. Fiske Jr. a deputy attorney general and to put judicial selection activity in his office. Conservative Republicans, however, objected to Fiske because he had been a member of the ABA Standing Committee on the Federal Judiciary. The Bush administration threatened to stop consulting with the ABA on judicial nominees unless it explicitly stated it would not take into account political or ideological views of nominees in considering their qualifications. After some negotiation, the ABA committee agreed. Fiske, however, withdrew his name when it became clear that the White House would not support his nomination. Thornburgh made Dickman, assistant to the attorney general, responsible for coordinating judicial selection at the DOJ.[52]

The Bush administration retained the systematic screening process that Reagan had initiated and also used the president's Committee on Federal Judicial Selection. Lawyers at the DOJ did the interviewing. They claimed that they did not ask candidates about particular cases. To emphasize the point, Gray said that when Attorney General Thornburgh and he appeared before the Judiciary Committee, they were "read the riot act" by Senators Joe Biden, Ted Kennedy, Orrin Hatch, Strom Thurmond, and Patrick Leahy, and told that they would not even give a hearing to a nominee who had been asked about his or her views on a specific issue.[53]

It is clear, however, that the administration, through its Federalist Society aides, did research and inquire into the judicial philosophy of potential nominees. Liberman, as assistant White House counsel, reviewed candidates' histories, including judicial opinions where available. Gray chaired the judicial selection committee, which met weekly at the White House. Dickman and Liberman were members of the committee, as were the attorney general, the deputy attorney general, the assistant to the president for personnel, and the assistant to the president for legislative affairs. The White House chief of staff was on the committee, but attended rarely because of other business.[54]

Roger J. Miner, of the Second Circuit Court of Appeals, was critical of the influence of the Federalist Society over judicial selection during this period, describing it as "in the hands of those who profess a blind adherence to the doctrine of original intent."[55] Noting that it was "well known" that no federal judicial appointment was made without the "imprimatur" of Liberman, Judge Miner wrote that "the hot flame of ideology" burned brightly in Gray's office, "tended by those who consider themselves the descendants of the original Federalists but who indeed are not."[56]

THE GEORGE W. BUSH ADMINISTRATION

During the administration of President George W. Bush, the Federalist Society brought its full weight to bear on the judicial selection process. Both Supreme Court justices appointed by Bush—Roberts, as chief justice, to replace William Rehnquist, and Alito, as associate justice, to replace Sandra Day O'Connor—were members of the society. Both new justices were more conservative than their pre-decessors. Nearly half of the courts of appeals judges Bush appointed were members. As Professor Goldman and his colleagues put it, Bush successfully nominated and got confirmed to the courts of appeals "a veritable all-star team of conservative judges with strong appeal to the Republican base."[57]

The two most important staff lawyers for judicial selection during the first two years of this administration were Federalist Society members. Brett M. Kavanaugh was the associate White House counsel working under Alberto Gonzales, until the president nominated Kavanaugh himself to the D.C. Circuit Court of Appeals. Assistant Attorney General Viet Dinh was head of the reconstituted Office of Legal Policy in the DOJ. Both emphasized the significance of judicial appointments to the president. Kavanaugh stated that Bush "devoted more attention to the issue of judges than any other president."[58] Dinh said that the president's "legal legacy" would be as important as anything the administration did with respect to legislative policy, and that they sought to ensure "a judiciary that will follow the law, not make the law, a judiciary that will interpret the Constitution, not legislate from the bench."[59]

The president's judicial selection committee was the principal group in the government with responsibility for selection of federal judges, and its most important members were the White House counsel and the attorney general. Key staff people were also on the committee, but the Bush administration never made public the identity of all the members.[60] Initially, the committee was chaired by White House Counsel Alberto Gonzales, and the attorney general was John Ashcroft. In Bush's second term, Gonzales became attorney general and was replaced as White House counsel by Harriet Miers. When Gonzales resigned in mid-2007, Michael Mukasey became attorney general. Mukasey was a closet supporter of the Federalist Society during his years in government, and then formally joined it after he retired.[61] He is now a member of the Federalist Society's board of directors. When Miers left as White House counsel at the end of 2007, Fred Fielding took that position, one he had occupied in the Reagan administration. Fielding brought with him Kate Comerford Todd, a vice chair of the Federalist Society's Federalism and Separation of Powers Practice Group, to work on judicial selection.[62] Federalist Society member Rachel Brand had been an associate White House counsel during a portion of the first term before moving to the DOJ. She was promoted to assistant attorney general in charge of the OLP in the second term, where she was responsible for judicial selection.

The basic procedure for selecting judges remained similar through both terms.[63] The judicial selection committee developed lists of potential candidates that were sent to the president for initial approval before detailed vetting began. After the president gave that approval, the OLP would review the nominees and the FBI would do a field investigation. The interviews of potential nominees took place at the White House, with both White House lawyers and DOJ lawyers involved. Once the judicial selection committee finished vetting a potential nominee and found him or her to be appropriate, it forwarded the name to the president for final approval.[64]

According to his biographer, Gonzales, as a Washington outsider, did not know much about the Federalist Society before he began his job as White House counsel.[65] Whether that is accurate or not, Gonzales assembled a staff based on the recommendations of advisors who were heavily involved with the Federalist Society, such as C. Boyden Gray, and which consisted predominantly of Federalist Society members. Gray was Gonzales's principal advisor during the transition period between the election and when the president assumed office.[66] Gonzales's deputy counsel was Timothy Flanigan. The staff included, among others, Brett Kavanaugh, who had been a senior deputy to Ken Starr; Bradford Berenson, at one point the chair of the Federalist Society's Criminal Law and Procedure Practice Group; Christopher Bartolomucci, who had been president of the student chapter of the Federalist Society at Harvard Law School; Noel Francisco, a former clerk for Justice Scalia; and Rachel Brand.[67] Citing the observations of several legal analysts, Gonzales's biographer notes that "the young, hungry attorneys on his staff saw the opportunity to pick such a large number of judges as a once-in-a-lifetime chance to transfer the strict constitutional aims of the Federalist Society to benches across America."[68] Nan Aron from the Alliance for Justice identified the Federalist Society as the "linchpin in the White House for identifying and grooming candidates for the federal bench."[69]

During the George W. Bush administration, Federalist Society members also served as significant outside advisors to the president with respect to judicial selection. There were frequent conference calls between White House staff and the "Four Horsemen," C. Boyden Gray, Jay Sekulow, Leonard Leo, and Ed Meese. According to Sekulow, these advisors were consulted at the beginning of President Bush's first term and had weekly telephone conferences with the White House. They played a "critical role": "We point out people that, we think, will be incredible nominees. But we always keep in contact regularly. This is not haphazard. It's very structured and organized."[70] In 2005, Leo took a leave of absence from his position as executive vice president of the Federalist Society to devote more time to advising the president on judicial selection.

In addition to providing direct advice to the president, Federalist Society members were active in a highly organized public campaign to support conservative judicial nominees. In February 2005, Leo, Meese, and Gray organized a group of grassroots organizers, public relations specialists, and legal strategists to "prepare a battle plan" for vacancies that might occur on the Supreme Court.[71] Roberts and Alito were among the eighteen potential nominees they researched. They worked through the Judicial Confirmation Network, a group that had been set up specifically to ease the path of Bush nominees, to "coordinate grass-roots pressure on Democratic senators from conservative states," and reached out to other conservative groups to coordinate their message.[72]

For five years, the chief counsel of the Judicial Confirmation Network was Wendy Long, a former law clerk to Justice Thomas and Judge Ralph K. Winter of the Second Circuit, and a frequent contributor to Federalist Society publications and debates. Long attempted to preempt criticism of Roberts based on his Federalist Society membership in a "Bench Memo" in the *National Review Online*, asking which senators might be "goaded" at his nomination hearing into asking, "Judge Roberts, are you now, or have you ever been, a member of the Federalist Society?"[73] She was relying, of course, on the antipathy to the McCarthy-era question, "Are you now, or have you ever been, a member of the Communist Party?" In her piece, Long assures her readers that the principles of the Federalist Society are those that "the vast majority of Americans agree with and admire." The executive director of the Judicial Confirmation Network was Gary Marx, also a featured Federalist Society speaker.

Another group that lobbied publicly for the president's judicial nominees was the Committee for Justice, which Gray headed. In 2003, the committee aired television commercials that suggested that opposition by liberal senators to nominees Miguel Estrada and William Pryor was motivated by anti-Catholic bias. The commercials had a sign, "Catholics Need Not Apply," in front of a locked courthouse door.[74] In 2006, Spencer Abraham, one of the founders of the Federalist Society, became the committee's chairman. Curt Levey was the group's executive director during George W. Bush's second term and remains in that position. He is a member of the Executive Committee of the Federalist Society's Civil Rights Practice Group and the former director of legal and public affairs at the Center for Individual Rights.[75]

Although Supreme Court rulings are the decisions that establish the law for all the lower courts, the Supreme Court hears approximately only eighty cases per year. On the other hand, in the twelve-month period ending March 31, 2011, the circuit courts of appeals concluded over fifty-eight thousand cases.[76] The courts of appeals determine how constitutional provisions and federal statutes are interpreted unless and until the Supreme Court decides to consider an issue. And then it is the courts of appeals that subsequently apply the Supreme Court's decision to the multitude of new and different factual situations that may require further interpretation.

The significance of appointments to the courts of appeals is not often highlighted by the media and not appreciated by the general public. It certainly was appreciated, however, by the members of the Federalist Society who influenced the selection process during the Bush administration. As a result, the selection of judges to the court of appeals during the Bush years was skewed by candidates' political views. Indeed, Elliot Mincberg, former legal director of People for the American Way, stated that he had "never seen courts of appeals nominations [as] politicized" as they were during the Bush administration.[77] The Senate had rejected a number of the president's nominations during his first term, but when George W. Bush was re-elected he promptly threw down the gauntlet by nominating them again. Professor Goldman and his fellow authors quote an unnamed senior aide to a Democratic senator on the Judiciary Committee who opined that it was no coincidence that those nominations were announced during the week that the Federalist Society national convention was held in Washington. In his view, the White House made "a great effort to satisfy the appetites of activists from the right."[78] Some of the most controversial nominees the Senate rejected who were repeatedly renominated by President Bush were members or close friends of the Federalist Society: Janice Rogers Brown, Priscilla Owen, and William Pryor (ultimately confirmed); and Peter Keisler, one of the founding directors of the Federalist Society, and William Haynes (never confirmed).

Democratic senators on the Judiciary Committee frequently complained about the influence of the Federalist Society on the nomination process, particularly Senator Patrick Leahy (Vermont) and Senator Richard J. Durbin (Illinois). For example, during the discussion of Estrada's membership in the Federalist Society, Senator Leahy related a story about another judicial nominee who testified that although he had previously not really heard of the Federalist Society, he was told that if he wanted to be a judge during the current administration he should join. He did, and was subsequently appointed.[79] During the hearing regarding the nomination of John Tinder for the Court of Appeals, Senator Durbin asked, "I have a question, too, about one of your affiliations. I have asked this of many nominees, so you probably have been prepped: Durbin's bound to ask you about the Federalist Society. It seems to be the secret handshake here on the way to the Federal bench for many nominees."[80]

On the other hand, conservatives such as Roger Pilon of the Cato Institute, a member of the Federalist Society, criticized the Democratic senators on the Judiciary Committee of erecting "an ideological litmus test" that the Bush nominees could not pass.[81] With characteristic ideological reasoning of his own, Pilon ascribed the problem of ideological litmus tests for judges to the Progressive Era, where "social engineers" attempted to get government to do what properly belonged to the realm of the private sector, necessitating action by the courts to limit government to its constitutional limits. When the Supreme Court abandoned its commitment to laissez-faire economics in 1937 and began to sustain such legislation, "politics trumped law" and the court ultimately went down the wrong road, not only failing to confine government to its constitutionally limited sphere, but even worse recognizing unenumerated constitutional rights not found in the text of the Constitution. The Constitution became "thoroughly politicized" and is now interpreted through "the subjective understandings of judges about evolving social values." As a result, judicial selection has become correspondingly politicized.[82] Pilon believes the only solution is to go back to first principles, to recognize that "most of what the government is now doing is unconstitutional" and for judges to "come to grips" with "the full richness of the Constitution, including its natural rights foundations."[83]

The Department of Justice

During the administration of George W. Bush, members of the Federalist Society also substantially increased their numbers and their power within the federal legal

bureaucracy. Among Federalist Society members with important legal positions in
the DOJ during this administration were Ted Olson, solicitor general (and a member of the Federalist Society's board of visitors); Paul Clement, solicitor general;
Peter Keisler, who held several important positions in the DOJ, including acting
attorney general; Larry Thompson, deputy attorney general; Viet Dinh, assistant
attorney general for legal policy; Thomas L. Sansonetti, assistant attorney general
for the environment and natural resources; J. Michael Wiggins, deputy assistant
attorney general for civil rights (formerly vice chairman of the Federalist Society's
Intellectual Property Practice Group); William H. Jordan, counsel to the assistant
attorney general in the Civil Division (formerly president of the Atlanta chapter of
the Federalist Society); David E. Nahmias, counsel to the assistant attorney general in the Criminal Division; and John G. Malcolm, deputy assistant attorney general in the Criminal Division (formerly chairman-elect of the Federalist Society's
Criminal Law Practice Group).[84]

The DOJ also hired large numbers of Federalist Society members and other conservatives as staff lawyers and immigration judges during the George W. Bush administration. Many of these hires were politically motivated, in violation of written DOJ
policy and federal statutes. Some of the legal positions at the DOJ, of a confidential
or policy-determining character ("Schedule C positions"), are recognized as political,
and it is appropriate to take politics into account in hiring for those positions. Most
staff lawyers, however, are career appointments, as are immigration judges. Both the
policy of the DOJ and federal statutes make it improper and illegal to consider political affiliations or ideology in making career appointments.[85]

As a result of the discharges of nine U.S. attorneys in 2006, which were widely
perceived to be politically motivated, and complaints to Congress by a group of
anonymous DOJ employees in 2006 regarding hiring in the department, there were
several investigations into allegations of improper political influence in hiring. The
Office of the Inspector General (OIG) of the DOJ and the Office of Professional
Responsibility (OPR) of the DOJ conducted investigations into hiring practices
in the Honors Program and the Summer Law Intern Program (SLIP),[86] hiring by
Monica Goodling and other staff in the Office of the Attorney General (OAG),[87]
hiring and other personnel actions in the Civil Rights Division of the DOJ,[88] and
the firing of the nine U.S. attorneys.[89]

The investigations concluded there had been improper political influence
in hiring and other personnel decisions at the DOJ, including favoritism toward
members of the Federalist Society. One report concluded that Goodling, as White
House liaison in the OAG, "inappropriately considered political and ideological
affiliations in the selection and hiring" of certain assistant U.S. attorneys (AUSA)
and other career attorneys in the department. The report also documented that
Goodling, as well as Kyle Sampson (the chief of staff to the attorney general), and
Jan Williams (Goodling's predecessor as White House liaison), "inappropriately
considered political and ideological affiliations in selecting" immigration judges and
members of the Board of Immigration Appeals.[90] Williams was a paid employee of

the Federalist Society from 1997 to 2001, first as the assistant lawyers division director and then as senior deputy lawyers division director.[91]

The report also concluded that Goodling "often used political or ideological affiliations to select or reject career attorney candidates for temporary details to Department offices," which was particularly damaging because "it resulted in high-quality candidates for important details being rejected in favor of less-qualified candidates."[92] Goodling recommended against hiring one AUSA because he was too "liberal," and was in favor of hiring another because he was a conservative "good American."[93] She recommended hiring another lawyer who had worked for the Federalist Society and was, according to Goodling's notes of the interview, "pro-God in public life" and "pro-marriage, anti-civil union."[94] The OIG and OPR report on the Goodling investigation is rife with similar details.

The most systematic use of political or ideological affiliations was in screening candidates for immigration judges. Sampson created the problem in 2004 when he changed the process so that the OAG selected all candidates for immigration judge positions. The White House was the principal source for these candidates, but Sampson, Goodling, and Williams used other Republican sources as well, including the Federalist Society.[95] The report documents that the White House itself often reached out to the Federalist Society for candidates for legal positions in the administration.[96] Although Williams looked to the White House, other DOJ political appointees, and the Federalist Society for potential candidates for immigration judges, she refused to consider candidates supplied by the Executive Office of Immigration Review (EOIR).[97]

Goodling screened the candidates for political acceptability, including researching their political contributions and voting registration records, searching the Internet with a string of political terms (e.g., "iran contra," "spotted owl," "florida recount," "downsiz!," "enron," "wmd," "gay!," "homosexual!," "firearm!"), discussing political topics (abortion, gay marriage) with candidates, and asking candidates political questions during interviews (e.g., "Why are you a Republican?").[98] The political vetting of the immigration judges caused delays in hiring and a shortage of judges that led to backlogs in the immigration courts.[99]

The report found that Goodling provided inaccurate information to a DOJ Civil Division attorney defending a lawsuit by an unsuccessful immigration judge candidate, by falsely stating to the government lawyer that she had not taken political factors into account in hiring immigration judges. The report also concluded that Williams provided false information to the OIG and OPR regarding the Internet searches. She denied using the search string of political terms more than once, but independent records from LEXIS showed that she had used it repeatedly.[100] The report does not mention it, but it is a federal felony to make false statements or misrepresentations of material facts with respect to any matter within the jurisdiction of the executive, legislative, or judicial branches.[101] Neither Goodling, who received immunity from Congress in connection with her testimony before the Judiciary Committee of the House of Representatives, nor Williams was ever indicted. The Virginia State Bar gave Goodling a public reprimand in 2011 for her misconduct in taking political affiliations into account in hiring at the DOJ.[102]

The Honors Program is a competitive hiring program for entry-level law-yers in the DOJ, and SLIP is a competitive paid summer internship program. Individual divisions and components within the DOJ were responsible for hir-ing their own lawyers and interns. In 2002, however, the leadership of the DOJ greatly expanded the involvement of political appointees in the hiring of career lawyers. During the selection process, individual divisions had to submit materi-als on prospective hires to the screening committee of the Office of the Deputy Attorney General. The screening committee was composed primarily of politi-cal appointees from leadership offices in the DOJ. The screening committee had the authority to deselect candidates previously identified by the divisions, which ended their candidacy unless a division appealed its decision and the screening committee reinstated the person.

The OIG and OPR found evidence of reliance on political and ideological con-siderations by the screening committee. There was no evidence of hiring based on political affiliation by the individual divisions and components within the DOJ, except for the Civil Rights Division, which was the subject of a separate report. In 2002, the screening committee deselected candidates with liberal affiliations at a "significantly higher rate" than candidates with conservative affiliations, and in 2006, it "inappropriately used political and ideological considerations to deselect many candidates."[103]

The OIG and OPR data showed that in 2002 the screening committee de-selected 80 of 100 candidates with liberal affiliations (80 percent), only 4 of 46 candidates with conservative affiliations (9 percent), and 223 of 765 candidates with neutral affiliations (29 percent). With respect to the most qualified applicants (based on which law school they attended, their class rank, whether they had a federal judicial clerkship, and whether they were members of the law review), the committee deselected 15 of 18 candidates with liberal affiliations, 0 of 5 candidates with conservative affiliations, and 11 of 48 candidates with neutral affiliations. The committee deselected all 7 applicants who were members of the liberal American Constitution Society (ACS), but only 2 of 29 who were members of the Federalist Society.[104] The data with respect to affiliations were comparable with respect to SLIP candidates who were deselected, including the fact that 12 of the 13 applicants who were members of the ACS were deselected, while none of the 12 applicants who were members of the Federalist Society was deselected. The head of the screening committee was Andrew Hruska, senior counsel to the deputy attorney general; after the OIG and OPR had analyzed the data, Hruska, through his attorney, declined to be interviewed regarding the results.[105] The OIG and OPR found no evidence of the use of political affiliations in hiring between 2003 and 2005.

The OIG and OPR did find substantial evidence of the use of political affilia-tion in hiring again in 2006. The report provided data that established a pattern of reliance on political affiliation, and specific evidence that two of the three members of the screening committee "inappropriately considered political and ideological affiliations in the deselection process."[106] The two were the chair, Michael Elston, the deputy attorney general's chief of staff, and Esther Slater McDonald, a counsel to the associate attorney general.

In 2006, the screening committee deselected 83 out of 150 (55 percent) of Honors Program candidates with liberal affiliations, only 5 out of 28 (18 percent) of candidates with conservative affiliations, and 98 out of 424 (23 percent) of candidates with neutral affiliations. With respect to highly qualified applicants, the committee deselected 35 out of 87 (40 percent) with liberal affiliations, only 1 out of 17 (6 percent) with conservative affiliations, and 35 out of 275 (13 percent) with neutral affiliations. There was little difference in the percentage deselected between applicants who identified as members of ACS and those who identified as members of the Federalist Society, but a significantly higher percentage (48 percent) of those who had Democratic Party affiliations were deselected than those who had affiliations with the Republican Party (27 percent).[107] With respect to SLIP applicants, the committee deselected 82 percent of those with liberal affiliations, only 13 percent of those with conservative affiliations, and 39 percent of those with neutral affiliations. Among highly qualified applicants, the committee deselected 25 out of 31 (81 percent) with liberal affiliations, 1 out of 6 (17 percent) with conservative affiliations, and 77 out of 231 (33 percent) with neutral affiliations.[108] With respect to candidates whose applications indicated membership in the ACS, the committee deselected 5 out of 6 (83 percent), but deselected only 1 out of 10 (10 percent) who indicated membership in the Federalist Society.

The OIG and OPR found that McDonald conducted Internet searches on some applicants and made notations about political affiliations she discovered, identified political items on applications that caused her concern (such as membership in the ACS or employment with a liberal judge), and voiced concerns that certain applicants might have views contrary to those of the administration. McDonald declined to be interviewed by OIG and OPR, hired a lawyer, and then resigned abruptly during their investigation.[109] Elston, who as head of the committee failed to take action against McDonald, also deselected candidates based on their liberal affiliations, and gave reasons for deselection that did not withstand scrutiny. OIG and OPR concluded that the third member of the committee, Daniel Fridman, a career lawyer in the DOJ, did not use ideological or political criteria in making decisions.[110] Elston resigned from the DOJ in June 2007.[111]

It should be noted that Peter Keisler, the then–assistant attorney general for the Civil Division and a prominent Federalist Society member, called to Elston's attention that people within the department thought the deselections were so irrational that it raised the possibility they were motivated by politics. Elston denied political influence. Keisler also raised these concerns with Acting Associate Attorney General William Mercer and Principal Deputy Associate Attorney General Gregory Katsas. There was little or no other complaint or criticism at the time from leadership personnel in the DOJ about the issue.

After these reports were written, in September 2008, the attorney general wrote to Honors Program candidates who had been deselected in 2006, offering them an opportunity to reapply for the positions and giving them two weeks to do so. Some of the deselected candidates who did not reapply filed suit against officials in the DOJ and the government. Judgment was entered in favor of the officials and the government in December 2011, for technical reasons, although the court recognized that the officials had engaged in misconduct.[112]

The OIG and OPR also found that Bradley Schlozman, a deputy assistant attorney general in the Civil Rights Division of the DOJ, "inappropriately considered political and ideological affiliations in hiring experienced attorneys in the sections he supervised and entry-level attorneys throughout the division for the Attorney General's Honors Program."[113] Schlozman actively recruited members of the Federalist Society for positions in the Civil Rights Division. In 2004, he told coworkers that he went to the Federalist Society events and student symposiums specifically to recruit applicants. In one e-mail, he said, "If we get a speaking role, it might be useful to spread the word and get more applications from these fine young Americans."[114] Schlozman boasted about his politically motivated hiring practices. An attorney that Schlozman hired in the Special Litigation Section e-mailed Schlozman that he was so happy to be where he was, and that his office is "even next to a Federalist Society member." Schlozman replied, "Just between you and me, we hired another member of 'the team' yesterday. And still another ideological comrade will be starting in one month. So we are making progress."[115] A statistical overview of the attorneys hired by Schlozman in the Civil Rights Division from 2003 to 2006 showed that 97 percent of them had conservative or Republican affiliations. Attorneys hired by Schlozman were twice as likely to be conservative or Republican than those not hired by Schlozman.[116]

Schlozman was assisted by front office counsels Jason Torchinsky and Matt Dummermuth in screening applicants and deciding who would be interviewed.[117] Torchinsky is a member of the Federalist Society.[118] Dummermuth is on the advisory board and steering committee of the Federalist Society's Iowa lawyers chapter, and he has been a member of the Religious Liberties Practice Group and the Federalism and Separation of Powers Practice Group since law school.[119] His wife, Rebecca Dummermuth, was the associate director for legal affairs of the George W. Bush White House Office of Faith-Based and Community Initiatives, and is the chair of the Publications Subcommittee of the Federalist Society's Religious Liberties Practice Group.[120] Torchinsky declined to be interviewed by the OIG and OPR.[121] Matt Dummermuth admitted to investigators that the hiring committee looked for "candidates who would focus on enforcing the law as it stood and not necessarily pursuing the most creative interpretations of the law as possible." Membership in the ACS or the Americans United for Separation of Church and State indicated a "more activist approach to law enforcement," and was a negative factor in hiring. Conversely, for Dummermuth, membership in the Federalist Society was a positive factor.[122] Following the investigations, Attorney General

Michael Mukasey announced the DOJ would not pursue criminal charges against any of those involved.[123] After serving briefly as the U.S. attorney for Iowa as a result of a recess appointment by President Bush (he was never confirmed by the Senate), Dummermuth went into private law practice in Cedar Rapids, Iowa. In 2011, he made unsuccessful attempts to get a seat on the Iowa Supreme Court and to get the Republican nomination for a state senate seat.

Schlozman's political biases influenced the assignment of attorneys to cases, as well as hiring decisions. The OIG and OPR found that he inappropriately considered political and ideological affiliations when he forced three career attorneys to transfer out of the Appellate Section. He had frequently talked of his plan, once he had the power, to move certain attorneys out of the Appellate Section to make room for "real Americans."[124] He told section chiefs not to assign important matters to lawyers who were "not on the team," "against us," "not trustworthy," or "a pinko." In one case, he directed a section chief not to allow a certain attorney to argue an appeal, because "[t]he potential stakes are too great to entrust this to either a lib or an idiot."[125]

Finally, the report concluded that Schlozman made false statements to Congress about his use of political considerations in hiring, both in oral sworn testimony and in written responses to questions.[126] The OIG and OPR referred the matter for prosecution to the U.S. Attorney's Office in the District of Columbia, but it declined to prosecute Schlozman.[127] Schlozman resigned from the DOJ on August 17, 2007. He is now of counsel to the Hinkle Law Firm in Wichita, Kansas, which notes on its website that he "held a series of high-level posts in the Department of Justice."[128]

The last report in this series, concerning the removal of nine U.S. attorneys, raised multiple issues that are beyond the scope of this book. Its conclusions, however, were consistent with the picture the other investigations painted of the improper politicization of the DOJ. The report found that the "Chief of Staff to the Attorney General Kyle Sampson, with very little input from other Department officials, designed, selected, and implemented the removal process, with little supervision or oversight."[129] As we discussed above, Sampson also engaged in improper activities with respect to hiring immigration judges. The report found "significant evidence that political partisan considerations were an important factor in the removal of several of the U.S. Attorneys."[130] The OIG and OPR, however, were not able to fully develop the evidence because several witnesses refused to be interviewed and the Bush White House refused to make internal documents available to the investigators.

One may expect the influence of the Federalist Society to continue in the administrations of future Republican presidents, at least judged by their influence with presidential hopefuls. Mitt Romney enlisted several prominent Federalist Society members and friends for his Advisory Committee on the Constitution and the Courts during his 2008 campaign, several with previous experience advising presidents on judicial selection. Among them were Bradford A. Berenson, James Bopp Jr., Timothy Flanigan, Tom Gede, Allyson Ho, James Huffman, Gary L.

McDowell, Jay Sekulow, and Richard Willard. Romney contributed $25,000 to the Federalist Society in 2005, and another $10,000 the following year, through his family charitable foundation.[131]

DEMOCRATIC ADMINISTRATIONS

Federalist Society members are also active with respect to judicial nominations when the president is a Democrat. David Kirkpatrick noted that during the Clinton administration, "Federalist Society members and allies had come to dominate the membership and staff of the Judiciary Committee, which turned back many of the administration's nominees."[132] Spencer Abraham was a senator from Michigan and on the Judiciary Committee during this time.

In 2010, the Judicial Confirmation Network, formed to promote George W. Bush's judicial nominations, changed its name to the Judicial Crisis Network (JCN), once President Obama began nominating judges. Carrie Severino, a former clerk for Justice Thomas and Judge David Sentelle of the D.C. Circuit (a Reagan appointee and a frequent speaker at Federalist Society events), took over as chief counsel. Severino is a Federalist Society member and a member of its Northern Virginia Women's Caucus. Severino blogs on the JCN website on a variety of political and legal topics, from a conservative point of view. She attacks judicial nominees by President Obama whom she perceives to be too liberal. Her critique of five Obama nominees in February 2011 runs the gamut of conservative concerns. She described Professor Goodwin Liu, who later withdrew his nomination to the Ninth Circuit Court of Appeals in the face of unrelenting Republican opposition, as "at the top of the list of likely judicial activists," based on his support for constitutional rights in the fields of welfare and health care, busing to achieve school integration, and same-sex marriage. She faulted Edward Chen, later confirmed as a district judge, for acknowledging that a judge's racial and ethnic background might affect his decisions through "understanding the human impact of legal rules upon which the judge must decide." She criticized John McConnell, later confirmed as a district judge, and Louis Butler, whose nomination as a district judge was rejected twice by the Senate, for advocating an enterprise theory of lead paint liability. She stated that Caitlin Halligan, whose nomination to the D.C. Court of Appeals was filibustered by Republican senators, "toes the liberal line on every major issue," including marriage equality and a standard for cruel and unusual punishment that varies with societal norms.[133]

THE AMERICAN BAR ASSOCIATION

Over the years, as the Federalist Society became more influential in selecting federal judges, conservatives have also lobbied to limit or eliminate the role of the American Bar Association (ABA) in the selection process. Presidents since Dwight Eisenhower had furnished the ABA with the names of prospective federal judicial nominees before publicly announcing them, permitting the ABA to conduct an investigation to determine whether the candidates were "qualified" to be federal judges. Beginning with President Reagan, the role of the ABA in the judicial nomination process was gradually diminished under Republican presidents. By the time of the George W. Bush administration, some observers argued that the Federalist Society had "stepped into the breach" left by the removal of the ABA from the pre-nomination process, and that it was "playing an even more central judgemaking role than had ever been attributed to the ABA."[134]

During the Reagan administration, the White House and the DOJ did not furnish candidates' names to the ABA until after the President's Federal Judicial Selection Committee had settled on a presumptive nominee. In 1990, Meese argued that the ABA review process could be helpful to the president's advisors on judicial selection, but that it was important for the ABA committee to stay within proper bounds and avoid making judgments about the judicial philosophy and political ideology of candidates.[135] By 1997, Meese was arguing that Congress should completely strip the ABA of any special role in judicial selection, because in his view the ABA had become a special-interest group by taking substantive (and liberal) positions on a variety of legal questions.[136]

During George W. Bush's presidency, White House Counsel Gonzales announced that the administration would not furnish names to the ABA before their names were submitted to the Senate or released to the public.[137] The ABA was removed from the selection process and had no opportunity to express an opinion on a candidate for the bench until after President Bush had already made a final decision to nominate the person. The ABA did have an opportunity to present its views to the Senate Judiciary Committee before confirmation, but that was very different from the role it had historically played in the process.

Nan Aron of the Alliance for Justice, a liberal critic of many of President Bush's judicial nominees, said that taking the ABA out of the process until after a nomination was made had a "chilling effect" on the willingness of lawyers to criticize the candidates candidly. Moreover, she argued that the administration's purpose was to "shroud the entire judicial selection process in secrecy."[138]

Brett Kavanaugh defended the decision by stating, "The President felt it was unfair and unwise to give one outside group preferential access to the process, particularly when there are a number of bar associations that we hear from and the ABA had this preferred role, which seemed unwise."[139] At the same time, although the Federalist Society had no role in judicial selection as an organization, during the Bush administration the process was almost completely in the hands of Federalist Society members.

How Conservative Are the Judges?

The available data demonstrates that the Federalist Society strategy of changing the law by changing the judges is working. First, judges appointed by Republican presidents render more conservative decisions than judges appointed by Democratic presidents, as empirical research demonstrates. Professor Cass Sunstein and his fellow authors have analyzed "striking evidence" of the relationship between the political party of the president and the way in which his judicial appointees decided cases.[140] Their analysis of 6,408 published opinions of three judge panels from the Circuit Courts of Appeals strongly showed that in "ideologically contested cases, involving the most controversial issues of the day," "Republican appointees vote very differently from Democratic appointees."[141]

The Federalist Society has moved the judiciary further to the right than the traditional orientation of judges appointed by Republican presidents. Sunstein's data demonstrated that the judicial decisions of appointees of Presidents Reagan, Bush Sr., and George W. Bush were more conservative than the appointees of Presidents Eisenhower, Nixon, and Ford.[142] The recent Republican administrations are the ones, as we have seen, where the Federalist Society has exercised decisive influence over the appointments of judges. Moreover, the data in this study documented "a statistically significant trend over time toward more conservative voting," between 1981 and 2004.[143] The authors observed a number of phenomena that may explain the ever increasing influence of Federalist Society approved judges on the law. One is what they term "ideological amplification," the tendency of both Democrats and Republicans to become respectively more liberal or more conservative the more of their party members there are on the panel. Another is "group polarization," or "the tendency of a group of like-minded people, including judges, to move to relative extremes."[144] Overall, they observed that when the federal courts have a growing number of Republican appointees, "they are likely to become more conservative."[145]

The Sunstein data concerned decisions by judges on the courts of appeals. A different empirical study of opinions by federal district court judges reached similar conclusions. Researchers concluded that the trial court judges appointed by George W. Bush "are not only the most conservative of the eight most recent administrations . . . but indeed they are the most conservative for all presidential cohorts going back to Woodrow Wilson!"[146] The authors analyzed more than 75,000 opinions by more than 1,800 judges, from 1933 to 2005, including 795 decisions by George W. Bush appointees. The cases were chosen for the study based on whether they contained clear liberal-conservative dimensions.

Overall, 33 percent of George W. Bush judges' opinions were decided in a liberal direction. By way of comparison, the liberal decision percentages of judges appointed by other presidents were: Johnson, 52 percent; Carter, 52 percent; Clinton, 49 percent; Nixon, 38 percent; Ford, 43 percent; Reagan, 36 percent; Bush Sr., 37 percent.[147] The greatest conservative gap between the George W. Bush appointees and other judges was in the area of civil rights and civil liberties (abortion, freedom of speech, right to privacy, racial discrimination, and the like). In this category, only 27.2 percent of the decisions of the George W. Bush judges were liberal, compared with: Johnson, 57.9 percent; Carter, 50.9 percent; Clinton, 41.2 percent; Nixon, 37.8 percent; Ford, 39.7 percent; Reagan, 32 percent; Bush Sr., 32.1 percent.[148] In the other large categories of cases studied by these authors, criminal justice and labor and economic regulation, the George W. Bush judges were more similar to those of other recent Republican presidents, but still substantially more conservative than judges appointed by Democratic presidents.[149]

Finally, a study of decisions reached by judges who are members of the Federalist Society demonstrated convincingly that such judges are significantly more conservative than nonmembers appointed by Republican presidents.[150] Professors Nancy Scherer and Banks Miller analyzed all courts of appeals "non-consensual" decisions involving a motion to suppress evidence under the Fourth Amendment between January 1, 1994, and December 31, 2005, and those involving a challenge to the constitutionality of a federal statute on Tenth and Eleventh Amendment grounds between January 1, 1996, and December 31, 2006. By "nonconsensual," they mean cases where there was a split decision on the appellate panel, or where the appellate panel reversed a decision by the district court. The Fourth Amendment motion to suppress cases involved the "exclusionary rule," under which courts prohibit the use of evidence that came from an unconstitutional search or seizure. Ideology tends to influence one's view of whether discarding evidence that could prove a defendant guilty is justified by the need to require the police to observe the constitutional rights of suspects. The Tenth and Eleventh Amendments protect states' rights and the sovereign immunity of state governments. Again, ideology influences how one views questions of "federalism," the constitutional division of power between the federal government and the states.

The authors identified judges as belonging to the Federalist Society if they acknowledged membership on their judicial questionnaires, or if they were identified as members in two separate newspaper articles.[151] They analyzed judges' decisions with respect to a number of independent variables in addition to Federalist Society membership, including ranking them on ideological grounds by traditional judicial ideology measures.

The analysis showed that for judges appointed by Bush Sr., Federalist Society membership raised the probability of a conservative vote on Tenth and Eleventh Amendment cases for judges who were deemed less conservative by traditional measures from .52 to .88; for a judge at the median on the ideology scale from .70 to .94; and for judges deemed most conservative on the scale from .72 to .94. For George W. Bush appointees, Federalist Society membership increased the probability of a conservative vote on these questions for the less conservative judges from .59 to .90; for the median judge from .66 to .93; and for the most conservative judges from .73 to .95.[152]

In the Fourth Amendment cases, for judges appointed by Bush Sr., Federalist Society membership raised the probability of a conservative vote for judges who were deemed less conservative by traditional measures from .38 to .75; for a judge at the median on the ideology scale from .42 to .78; and for judges deemed most conservative on the scale from .44 to .80. For George W. Bush appointees, Federalist Society membership increased the probability of a conservative vote on these questions for the less conservative judges from .40 to .77; for the median judge from .41 to .78; and for the most conservative judges from .43 to .79.[153] The authors concluded, "Without question, our results demonstrate that Federalist Society membership has a statistically significant and substantively large impact on judicial decision-making behavior on the U.S. Courts of Appeals."[154] The authors note that the Federalist Society has achieved this in part by "educating young lawyers to reject the conventional method of constitutional interpretation taught in the nation's law schools, and instead, adopt originalism as the only correct method of interpretation."[155]

The results of these empirical studies are probably not surprising to anyone other than those who would argue that law is nothing more than a set of neutral principles mechanically applied to the facts as they vary from case to case. Resolving legal questions, however, is in fact far more complicated than "calling balls and strikes." Often there is no controlling precedent in the case law, or the relevant constitutional or statutory provisions are not specific enough to decide the case at hand without interpretation. Given that, a judge's views on a myriad of questions inform his or her decisions, including: how power should be distributed in a federal system, the role of the courts vis-à-vis the legislature and the executive, what "liberty" means, how fundamental fairness is defined, and many general issues of politics and economics. As Sunstein et al. wrote, "No reasonable person seriously doubts that ideology, understood as moral and political commitments of various sorts, helps to explain judicial votes."[156]

Federalist Society members shared that assessment, and, as we have seen, have worked hard since the administration of Ronald Reagan to influence judicial nominations. This has been a central element of their strategy to move the law in conservative directions. In the remaining chapters of this book, we analyze complementary activities of Federalist Society members in a variety of areas of the law.

2

REGULATION OF PRIVATE PROPERTY

The Takings Clause

This chapter addresses land use regulation and more comprehensive forms
of economic regulation, including wage and price controls, on the assumption
that these are all . . . takings of private property.

—*Richard Epstein*[1]

We now turn to ideological and constitutional law battles over government regulation of economic rights and private property. By "economic rights," we mean the ability of property owners to use and develop private property as they see fit, or the ability of individuals and businesses to
contract with each other for the exchange of goods and services on their own terms.
Obviously, in the United States today, these rights are not absolute and are subject
to a good deal of government regulation. How much power the government has
to regulate these rights, however, has been a matter of intense debate since the late
eighteenth century.

We discuss these issues in the context of the takings clause of the Fifth
Amendment. Most people are familiar with the takings clause as the constitutional
provision that requires government to pay compensation to private owners for property it takes for public purposes (for example, when the state takes someone's land
to build a highway). But in a modern, heavily regulated economy, one may argue
that government regulations that do not physically seize private property but limit the
owner's ability to develop it also amount to a "taking" of that person's property rights.
On the other hand, if government had to pay private property owners compensation
for every regulation it enacted, much of what government does today would have to
be shut down. The question is how and where to draw the line.

As we discuss in greater detail below, a consequence of the Great Depression
and the New Deal in the 1930s was a dramatic change in the Supreme Court's
analysis of when government regulation of private property is constitutional. This
permitted much greater government regulation of wages and hours, occupational
safety, consumer protection, protection of the environment, and many other areas.
Business interests, economic conservatives, and libertarians have attempted to find
new arguments to restrain such regulation. Expanding the takings clause to require
compensation for regulation has been one of their principal strategies. Members

of the Federalist Society are largely responsible for the intellectual resources behind that movement, and for much of the litigation to remake constitutional law
concerning the takings clause. In 1985, society member Richard Epstein published
Takings: Private Property and the Power of Eminent Domain, in which he argued that
any governmental regulation constituted a compensable taking. Epstein's theory
was received as radical by many, including some in the conservative establishment.
It has become the linchpin, however, for conservatives' deregulation efforts. In fact,
it is difficult to overstate the power of Epstein's theory and how far it has carried the
organized Right in the past three decades.

To do justice to the constitutional issues in this area, we will first have to spend
some time exploring the intellectual history and political philosophy of property
rights. What is property? Where does a citizen's entitlement to own and use property come from? What justifies interference with private property by the government in an organized society? Are modern theorists about these matters true to the
ideas of our constitutional framers?

More contemporaneously, we will be discussing how and when the government
can limit the ability of property owners to control what happens on their property:
What and where they can develop on their property? (For example, what are their
rights when building extra floors onto the terminal at New York's Grand Central
Station or excavating valuable minerals from beneath the surface of their land?)
Where and when can environmental agencies limit the impact of private development? (For example, can the agencies enforce limits on the seashore, or on land
with a wetlands designation?) What concessions can government exact from property owners in return for permits to develop their property? (For example, can the
government require a retailer to grant public easements for foot traffic in exchange
for a building permit to increase the size of her store?) Can government force individuals to sell their homes or land if it will bring broad economic benefits to an
entire community?

A History of the Takings Clause and Constitutional Protections of Private Property Rights

The Fifth Amendment to the U.S. Constitution protects citizens against abuse of
government authority:

> No person shall be held to answer for a capital, or otherwise infamous crime, un-
> less on a presentment or indictment of a Grand Jury, except in cases arising in the
> land or naval forces, or in the Militia, when in actual service in time of War or
> public danger; nor shall any person be subject for the same offence to be twice put
> in jeopardy of life or limb; nor shall be compelled in any criminal case to be a wit-
> ness against himself, nor *be deprived of life, liberty, or property, without due process
> of law; nor shall private property be taken for public use, without just compensation.*
> (Emphasis added.)

The amendment contains two distinct protections for private property. The first, that "[n]o person shall be . . . deprived of life, liberty, or property, without due process of law," is termed the "due process clause" and was originally included to ensure fundamental fairness in the way the law is administered. It provides procedural safeguards such as the right to be adequately notified of charges or proceedings, and the opportunity to be heard at these proceedings before an impartial decisionmaker. The final sentence, termed the "takings clause," was included to limit the power of the government to take private property for the performance of government activities (i.e., eminent domain).

The Fifth Amendment is a distant relative of article 39 of the Magna Carta, which states, "No freeman shall be taken, or imprisoned, or disseized, or outlawed, or exiled, or in any way harmed—nor will we go upon or send upon him—save by the lawful judgment of his peers or by the law of the land." The term "disseized" stems from "seisin," which is akin to freehold ownership of land, which was at common law held by the sovereign and was the basis of wealth in the then-feudal economy.

Before the Fifth Amendment was adopted in 1789, few states awarded compensation when they seized private property.[2] Around the time that the Bill of Rights was enacted, regulations governing not only land use but businesses, individuals, and markets were widespread. Peddlers and tavern owners were required to obtain licenses and pay fees. Prior to sale or export, goods and foodstuffs (including beef, pork, tar, pitch, flour, and turpentine) were inspected against statutory quality standards. Laws limiting speculation in the commodities market were enacted that banned engrossing (buying up a large quantity of a given good for resale), forestalling (purchasing commodities while they were en route to market), and regrating (purchasing commodities in a market for resale within the same market). Boston's zoning regulations restricted where slaughterhouses, bakeries, and other merchants could be located. Virginia's statutes limited the amount of tobacco farmers could plant. These laws were grounded in the inherent right of the sovereign (embodied now as state and federal government) at common law to control freehold title to land; a lingering example of this is the control that government retains over activities in coastal areas, including fishing, fowling, navigation, and commerce. Fundamentally, the concept of a "taking" is based on the inherent right of the sovereign to reassert its right to all property.

Our takings clause jurisprudence has evolved considerably. The earliest takings clause cases were narrow, focusing on physical seizure of land by the government. But since the mid–twentieth century, the clause has been invoked to protect private property (real and otherwise) against not only seizure but regulation, including historic landmark designations and environmental laws. Although takings jurisprudence has evolved in an erratic fashion, the inquiry in any takings case remains unchanged and centered on the four key elements in the clause: (1) the definition of a "taking"; (2) what constitutes "private property"; (3) what satisfies the requirement of "public use"; and, (4) how to determine "just compensation."

Defining a "Taking"

Early cases strictly defined what constituted a "taking." Until the second decade of the twentieth century, takings clause jurisprudence applied only to a "direct appropriation" of property or [its] functional equivalent.[3] In 1922, the Supreme Court broadened the definition of a taking to include regulation of property, but only when that regulation went "too far," making it commercially impracticable to use land for the purposes for which it had been purchased.[4] Since that 1922 decision, the court has examined a host of regulations under a takings clause paradigm.[5] These include zoning laws, environmental laws, development restrictions, and rent control.[6] By and large, the court has rejected the characterization of such laws as takings. And although no clear rule regarding what constitutes a regulatory taking has emerged, so far the court has been fairly deferential to government action, so long as the government can demonstrate a legitimate purpose that the regulation is rationally related to, and the property subject to the taking retains some economically viable use.[7]

Defining "Private Property"

The Supreme Court has been inconsistent in its definition of "private property." Most frequently, the court has looked to state court definitions of property. By doing so, it has adopted a positivist understanding of property law. Legal positivism holds that the law is fundamentally the creation of humans, and is valid without any necessary correlation to morals. In comparison, the concept of natural law holds that certain rights or values are inherent and universal by virtue of human nature. Under the positivist construct, the sovereign has the original and inherent right to all property, and any expectation a citizen may have for the use and enjoyment of his or her property is defined by the contours of state law.[8] Therefore, although a citizen may own property, he or she may not exercise unfettered rights of ownership over it. For example, if a property regulation limiting building heights existed prior to the purchase of the land, a new owner could have no expectation of a property right to build a structure in excess of the height limitation.[9] At other times, the court has enunciated a sweeping definition of property based on the theory of natural law. Under the natural law construct, original and inherent property rights rest not with the sovereign, but with individual citizens. In a 1945 case, the court described property as a group of rights people inherently have—to possess, use, and dispose of land.[10] This is the theory to which Epstein and members of the property rights movement adhere.

The court has been equally inconsistent with emerging concepts of property. It has found that trade secrets and interest on client funds held in a trust account by an attorney are property subject to the takings clause.[11] It decided, however, that U.S. creditors' attachments to Iranian assets were not; the assets were subsequently removed by the federal government in the agreement following the 1979–1981 Iranian Embassy hostage crisis.[12]

Public Use

The legislature initially determines what constitutes "public use" under the "police power"—that is, the power to protect citizens' health, welfare, and safety. And historically, the court has shown considerable deference to legislative determinations of public use. If the government reasonably believes that the taking will benefit the general public, even if it takes from one private party in order to transfer it to another private party, the public use requirement is met.[13] "Public use" can include generalized economic benefits such as jobs or sales tax revenues, the paradigmatic example being the condemnation of private homes to make way for a manufacturing plant or business park where the government contends the development will create employment and rejuvenate an ailing local economy.

Just Compensation

The final inquiry is whether "just compensation" has been paid. The Supreme Court has consistently held that "just compensation" should be measured by the economic loss to the property owner.[14] It has also carved out a "nuisance exception" to the takings clause's compensation requirement. First proclaimed by the Supreme Court in 1887, the nuisance exception allows government to prohibit "noxious" uses of property without having to compensate the property owner.[15]

RICHARD EPSTEIN'S TAKINGS THEORY

Epstein's theory is that *any* regulation of private property constitutes a taking. His analysis rests on a theory of property rights attributed to John Locke, one of the philosophers who influenced the Constitution's framers.[16] Locke, like Thomas Hobbes, ascribed to the theory of natural law. He believed that all property was originally subject to common ownership, and was a "natural right" from God.[17] Unlike Hobbes, who believed that men gave up all their natural property rights to a sovereign in order to create civil society, Locke believed that natural property rights remained with the individual.[18] Locke's theory of private property ownership holds that all property was originally in common ownership, but by adding one's labor to the property, a person acquired private ownership. Locke did not believe in unfettered private property rights, stating that the right of private property ownership could be exercised only "where there is enough, and as good left in common for others." [19]

Locke theorized that property ownership constitutes a bundle of rights, often analogized to a bundle of sticks. A property right in a piece of land would include, for example, the owner's right to occupy the land and to exclude others from it, the right to use the land as the owner sees fit, and both the air rights above the land and the mineral rights below it. Epstein's position is that a governmental encroachment—not only on the entire bundle, but on any of the individual sticks—is a taking. That is why in his view any governmental regulation that restricts an owner's absolute use of their land—be it a zoning law, an environmental ordinance, or a health and safety regulation—requires compensation, because it violates the takings clause. Furthermore, Epstein seeks to limit the "nuisance exception" to the takings clause (thus making the class of takings that is noncompensable smaller) while broadening the definition of a taking to include not only complete expropriations of property, but expropriations of a portion of property, which he calls "partial takings."[20]

Epstein argues the takings clause should be used to strike down rent control, zoning laws, welfare and social security payments, workers' compensation, and progressive taxation, on the basis that these are impermissible takings which require "just compensation."[21] In fact, at its broadest, Epstein's theory is that *any* wealth redistribution by government, be it direct or indirect, constitutes a compensable taking.

Epstein was not the first legal scholar to characterize government entitlements as "property." This idea was, in fact, popularized by liberal scholar Charles Reich, a Yale law professor, in the mid-1960s. Reich argued in a famous article, "The New Property," that government benefits, including professional licenses and welfare benefits, ought not to be considered as privileges. Instead, he argued, once transferred, they vested in their holders certain property rights *against* the government.[22] A key difference between Reich and Epstein, however, is that Reich's constitutional basis for protecting these property rights was procedural due process under the Fourteenth Amendment. In a 1970 case, *Goldberg v. Kelly*, the Supreme Court adopted Reich's theory. It ruled that the state could not terminate welfare payments without first affording the beneficiary an opportunity for some type of hearing to contest the decision. The court's rationale was that the beneficiary has a property interest in her welfare payments, protected by the Fourteenth Amendment's requirement of due process before termination.[23]

THE DEBATE OVER EPSTEIN'S THEORY

In 1922, Supreme Court Justice Oliver Wendell Holmes pointed out in *Pennsylvania Coal v. Mahon* that government simply could not function if it had to compensate every person whose property lost value because of a government action.[24] Epstein's critics argue that James Madison, the author of the takings clause, was motivated by the pressing issues arising out of the founding of a nation. The Bill of Rights protected citizens against abuses of government power, like the practice of quartering soldiers in private homes and the government's expropriation of homes and farms to build roads and bridges. The position of takings experts Douglas Kendall, Charles Lord, and William Treanor is that Madison intended the takings clause to apply to dispossession of private property by the government, but not to regulations that might decrease the property's value.[25] Road building was in fact the most common use for which governments in colonial times exercised their power of eminent domain.[26]

Treanor posits that the plain language of Madison's proposal indicates his primary concern was physical seizures. Madison's original text for the takings clause stated, "No person shall be . . . obliged to *relinquish* his property, where it may be necessary for public use, without just compensation."[27] According to these scholars, the Magna Carta's "disseizure," Madison's term "relinquish," and its eventual replacement, "taking," are, by their plain and ordinary meanings, descriptions of complete physical dispossession—not "partial takings" and almost certainly not diminutions in value.

As Kendall has pointed out in articles and Federalist Society debates, early in the construction of his takings manifesto, Epstein casually "corrects" Locke's theory of natural property rights, saying:

> The *proper position would have been reached* if Locke had dispensed with the idea of divine justification for private property and had adopted the traditional common law view of the original position. That is, each individual owns his own labor; no one owned the external things of the world until the first possessor acquired them.[28] (Emphasis added).

Also, while embracing Locke's theory of private property rights—that by combining one's labor with property, one acquires ownership rights in that property— Epstein simultaneously casts aside Locke's limitation on unmitigated property ownership, which posits that property rights should be exercised only "where there is enough, and as good left in common for others."[29] Epstein also rejects the Hobbesian idea that the government is the source of all rights in property, and those that it retains cannot be "taken." He ignores the idea that the bundle of rights that constitute property may also include simultaneously shared rights—and the possibility that rights are shared between the government and the individual property owner.

Epstein's treatment of Locke's theory has been characterized by commentators as "superficial and manipulative."[30] Professor Joseph Sax reviewed Epstein's book in the *University of Chicago Law Review* the year after it was first published. He wrote, "The book is not a developed work of history, of logic, of philosophy, or of textual analysis. Though it is some of all these things, it is none of them consistently."[31] Kendall argues that Epstein's theory is dangerous and disingenuous and that *Takings* "does not offer a principled means of interpreting the takings clause. Rather it offers an abundance of smoke and mirrors that advocates and judges sympathetic with Epstein's distaste of government regulation can use to provide some semblance of authority to their arguments about what the takings clause means."[32]

Prominent conservatives have also agreed that Epstein's property rights movement seeks an unsuitable home in the takings clause of the Fifth Amendment.[33] Robert Bork stated that his difficulty is "not that Epstein's contribution would repeal much of the New Deal and the modern regulatory-welfare state but rather that these conclusions are not plausibly related to the original understanding of the Takings Clause."[34] Charles Fried, solicitor general during President Reagan's term in office, stated that Epstein's reimagining of Locke's theories revealed that he was more Lockean than Locke, writing that "Professor Epstein is moved to complete not only the text of the Constitution by reference to the Lockean spirit, but Locke's text itself."[35] Indeed, in the early 1980s, while many members of the emerging Federalist Society network were entering government and the judiciary via the Reagan administration, Epstein was considered too radical to appoint.[36]

EPSTEIN'S THEORY AND JUDICIAL ACTIVISM

Although most conservatives decry judicial activism, it is a requisite mechanism for outlier legal theories, like Epstein's understanding of the takings clause, to take hold. In an op-ed in the *Wall Street Journal* in 1985 entitled "Needed: Activist Judges for Economic Rights," Epstein argued that his new theory would require a level of judicial interpretation unlike anything current courts had seen.[37] Epstein has come under fire from fellow conservatives for his advocacy of judicial activism. Bork has remarked that Epstein's approach flies in the face of "deference to democratic choice."[38] Justice Antonin Scalia wrote in 1984 that he feared that the "constitutionalizing" of economic rights would reinforce the "liberal brand of judicial activism" he presumably had witnessed, unhappily, in "right to privacy," contraception, and abortion cases.

To the chagrin of liberals and the joy of most conservatives, Epstein's *Takings* started a movement. Epstein's takings manifesto became the basis of deregulatory policy in the Reagan and Bush administrations.[39] According to Fried, "Attorney General Meese and his young advisors—many drawn from the ranks of the then-fledgling Federalist Society and often devotees of the extreme libertarian views of Chicago law professor Richard Epstein—had a specific, aggressive, and it seemed to me, quite radical project in mind: to use the Takings Clause of the Fifth Amendment as a severe brake upon federal and state Regulation."[40]

ECONOMIC DUE PROCESS AND PROPERTY RIGHTS IN THE SUPREME COURT

Economic Due Process and the New Deal

The modern property rights movement's focus on the takings clause results from the 1937 rejection by the Supreme Court of a substantive due process rationale for upholding economic rights against the power of government to regulate. The substantive due process basis for economic rights, heavily influenced by laissez-faire economic theory, had dominated the court's jurisprudence from the late nineteenth century to Franklin Roosevelt's second term. The leading case was *Lochner v. New York*, where the Supreme Court invalidated a New York labor law that limited the number of hours a week a baker could work.[41] The court ruled that the New York law was an unreasonable and arbitrary interference with a person's right to enter into contracts, and not a valid exercise of the state's police power under which it could constitutionally legislate to protect the health, welfare, and safety of its citizens. The court identified the right to purchase or sell labor in the Fourteenth

Amendment's guarantee of the right to life, liberty, and property. [42] The court gave little or no deference to the New York legislature's position that the labor law bore a direct relation to the welfare of the bakers.[43] As between the state's power to legislate and the bakers' freedom of contract, the court upheld the rights of the bakers.[44]

In the three decades following *Lochner*, the Supreme Court maintained a healthy aversion to regulation. In that period, it struck down nearly two hundred regulations on economic due process grounds.[45] The Great Depression, however, threw the U.S. economy into free fall. By 1933, the year Roosevelt became president, the United States was suffering a devalued currency, record unemployment, and widespread poverty. Congress, enacting Roosevelt's New Deal, created new federal agencies with aggressive programs to assert greater federal government control over the economy and the money supply.[46] The president and Congress believed that governmental regulation of economic matters was not only important, but necessary to bring the country back from financial disaster. *Lochner* represented the idea that freedom of contract was a natural right, but legal realists argued that *Lochner* was a political decision that favored employers over employees. Following his election to a second term, Roosevelt threatened to pack the court with an extra justice for every sitting justice aged over seventy to counteract the court's laissez-faire economic philosophy.[47]

The court began to move away from *Lochner* in its 1934 decision in *Nebbia v. New York*. There, it upheld a retail price-fixing statute for milk, giving deference to the legislature's purpose in enacting the law. The court held that the Fifth and Fourteenth Amendments' requirements of due process demand "only that the law shall not be unreasonable, arbitrary, or capricious, and that the means selected shall have a real and substantial relation to the object sought to be attained."[48] The decision demonstrated that neither property rights nor contract rights are absolute.[49] In effect, it anointed a vast swath of the modern regulatory regime as constitutionally sound.[50]

If *Nebbia* was the death of economic substantive due process and the Supreme Court's strict review of economic legislation, then 1937's *West Coast Hotel v. Parrish* was its burial. In *Parrish*, the court upheld the constitutionality of a minimum wage law for women.[51] In doing so, it overruled its 1923 holding in *Adkins v. Children's Hospital* in which it had held that a minimum wage law aimed at women and children violated the individual right to contract.[52] The *Parrish* Court found that the Constitution did not speak explicitly of the freedom to contract, only of liberty, and that the prohibition against depriving a person of liberty without due process of law did not refer to an "absolute and uncontrollable liberty."[53] The court held that the law was a legitimate use of the state's police power because exploiting a class of workers by not paying a minimum wage was detrimental not only to their own health and wellbeing, but created a burden on the community. The court made explicit reference to the Depression, which had gripped the nation: "We may take judicial notice of the unparalleled demands for relief which arose during the recent period of depression and still continue to an alarming extent despite the degree of economic recovery which has been achieved."[54]

One year later, in *United States v. Carolene Products*, the court cemented its new deference to legislative decision making with respect to economic regulation. The court upheld a federal law prohibiting the sale in interstate commerce of a cheap imitation of condensed milk or cream that included coconut and other nondairy fats, called "filled milk." Congress had concluded that sale of the filled milk committed a fraud on the public, and was injurious to public health.[55] The court held that "legislation affecting ordinary commercial transactions is not to be pronounced unconstitutional unless in the light of the facts . . . it is of such a character as to preclude the assumption that it rests upon some rational basis."[56]

In perhaps the most important footnote in Supreme Court history, the court specifically distinguished between the deference the legislature should be shown with respect to economic regulation, and the higher level of scrutiny the court would apply to laws that interfered with noneconomic individual and civil rights, or that implicated minorities' right to equal protection of the law.[57] This distinction, between weak protection for economic rights and vigorous protection for other individual rights, is at the heart of conservatives' complaints about Supreme Court jurisprudence from 1937 to the present.

Post–New Deal Property Jurisprudence: The Takings Clause Takes Hold

The post–New Deal jurisprudence of the court signaled to property rights advocates that the economic substantive due process argument was no longer viable. Since 1937, not a single state or federal economic regulation has been held unconstitutional on substantive due process grounds. Justices Scalia and Thomas, sure allies of the conservative legal movement on the current court, have resoundingly rejected the idea that the due process clause protects economic rights.[58] Conservatives needed a new constitutional hook to regulation of private property. They have attempted to find it in the takings clause.[59]

In 1922, the Supreme Court first held that a *regulation* that went "too far" constituted a taking. In *Pennsylvania Coal v. Mahon*, the court concluded that a Pennsylvania law limiting coal mining was a taking insofar as it rendered certain land "commercially impractical to mine," which had the same effect for constitutional purposes as confiscating or destroying it.[60] In 1935, the Supreme Court held in *Lynch v. United States* that valid contracts were property rights that could not be taken without just compensation.[61]

The court refined *Pennsylvania Coal's* nebulous "too far" test in its 1978 decision in *Penn Central Transportation v. City of New York*.[62] There, the court ruled that the historic landmark designation of New York City's Grand Central Station, which prevented its owners from building above the terminal building, was not a taking that required just compensation (and in fact to do so would mean that all comparable landmark laws in the country were also takings).[63] The court stated that the owners could not establish a taking had occurred just because they had been denied the ability to exploit a property interest they had believed they had.[64] It was an important decision in terms of demarcating when compensation must occur.

The inherent power of the government to regulate means that an owner is not entitled to (and therefore need not be compensated for if he does not achieve) the highest and best use of his property—only some reasonable use must remain. The court also reiterated a firm stance on the parcel on which a takings analysis must be performed—namely, the entire parcel, not the smaller piece of the parcel affected by the governmental action.[65]

The court's *Penn Central* holding was a rejection of what would come to be one of the fundamental tenets of Epstein's takings theory: that a governmental act, which restricted even one stick in the bundle of rights constituting property ownership, was a compensable taking under the Fifth Amendment. Justice Rehnquist took up Epstein's argument in his dissent. Citing the court's 1945 decision in *United States v. General Motors*, which advanced a natural law theory of property as being the group of rights a citizen has in relation to a physical thing, Rehnquist argued that the landmark designation was in fact a taking because it precluded the owners of Grand Central Station from exercising their air rights above the terminal.[66] He stated that the regulation was "for public use" because the owners of Grand Central Station shouldered the landmark designation—an economic burden with purely public benefits—alone. This view was also advanced in an amicus brief submitted by the Pacific Legal Foundation (PLF), which has been heavily involved in most of the important takings cases in the past thirty years; it would later employ several Federalist Society members. The PLF characterized the regulation as a taking, arguing that the benefits conferred on the people of New York in preserving the historic landmark were compelling reasons to distribute the costs of those benefits to those people.[67]

The Supreme Court has not adopted Epstein's "partial takings" theory. In the 1980s and 1990s, however, the court seemed determined, if not impatient, to issue takings decisions.[68] During that period, the court narrowed the "nuisance" exception to the takings clause—a victory in no uncertain terms for Epstein and the property rights movement. As the definition of what constitutes a nuisance is narrowed, more property regulations have the potential to be classified as compensable takings. The court also demonstrated less deference to the declared intent of legislatures regarding conditions on development, and revealed a desire to decide takings claims, even where plaintiffs faced almost insurmountable procedural obstacles that could have kept them out of court altogether.

In *Nollan v. California Coastal Commission*, the court considered the constitutionality of a regulation under which a building permit, granted by the commission to the Nollans, included a condition requiring the owners to grant back a public easement across a portion of their beachfront property.[69] The Supreme Court, in a 1987 opinion authored by Justice Scalia, held that the regulation mandating the conditional permit was a compensable taking. The court overcame considerable standing obstacles to reach the merits. The Nollans had built their house prior to obtaining permission to do so, and under California law, by doing so, they lost the right to challenge any conditions placed on their development permit.[70] Also, a serious question remained as to whether the Nollans owned the land the state "took."

The land that the public access easement would occupy was frequently below the high-tide mark. At common law, the inherent right of a sovereign to control land below the high-tide mark means it is not subject to private ownership.

The commission is charged by both the state constitution and legislature to preserve public access to the California coastline. It argued that the Nollans' home, both alone and part of a larger development problem along the California coast, threatened public access to the shore. The commission argued the Nollans' home would decrease public sight of the beach and increase private use of the beach, and that the encroaching nature of this private use may give the impression that the beachfront is no longer available for public use. Scalia rejected the commission's rationale and created new law, requiring an "essential nexus" between a permit condition and the public good sought in order for the condition to not constitute a taking.[71] This dramatic break from the deferential approach with which the court had treated zoning and other land use legislation for more than fifty years was a huge success for the property rights movement.

In dissent, Justice Brennan accused Scalia and the majority of subjecting the state to "intolerable supervision."[72] The court's lack of deference to the commission was not only contrary to precedent, it was a manifestation of the kind of judicial activism Epstein and other property rights advocates (including Federalist Society members Chip Mellor and Clint Bolick) had called for since the early 1980s. For Bolick, it was a matter of beating liberals at their own game. Attributing the many privacy right cases to activist liberal judges bent on making social policy, Bolick reasoned that liberals could not be defeated "by putting the activist court genie back in the bottle."[73]

Nollan was a significant victory for the Pacific Legal Foundation.[74] The PLF litigation team, representing James and Marilyn Nollan, argued that the permit condition was the equivalent of a physical expropriation. This was the analysis that the court adopted.[75] Property rights activists initially greeted the *Nollan* decision with enthusiasm, believing that it signaled a real change in Supreme Court takings jurisprudence—in their favor. More careful analysis, however, revealed that the decision did not materially alter the power of zoning boards to determine how citizens may or may not use their property.[76]

Five years later, the court granted review of four cases involving economic liberties and private property. Many conservatives hoped this signaled a reexamination of what Epstein called the "troubled Supreme Court's jurisprudence on the takings issue, as crafted during the Warren and Burger years."[77]

One of these four was *Lucas v. South Carolina Coastal Commission*. In *Lucas*, the court held that a state law that prohibited building on beachfront property, in order to protect the sand dunes, was a compensable taking.[78] In 1988, David Lucas had purchased two beachfront lots in Charleston, South Carolina, for just under $1 million. Two years later, the state passed a law preventing him from erecting any permanent, habitable structures on the land. Justice Scalia wrote the opinion in *Lucas*, and as he did in *Nollan*, refused to defer to South Carolina's purpose for enacting the legislation. Scalia clearly believed that such deference would have the effect of eviscerating all regulatory takings claims, writing that it would "essentially nullify [*Pennsylvania Coal v. Mahon*'s] affirmation of limits to the non-compensable exercise of the police power."[79]

In *Lucas*, Scalia also leaped over procedural obstacles to decide a takings case in favor of the property owner. As the case was making its way to the court, South Carolina amended its Beachfront Management Act and under it, Lucas could have applied for a permit to build on his lots. He did not and as a result, his permanent takings claim, on which he prevailed in the Supreme Court, was actually not ripe for judicial review. Scalia acknowledged this early on in his opinion, then proceeded to a decision based on whether Lucas had suffered a "temporary taking" in the two years between the act and the amendment. This issue had not even been briefed by the parties.[80] The trial court below had not found that Lucas had intended to use his property in that two-year span and as a result, Lucas lacked the "injury in fact" necessary to bring even a temporary takings claim. Scalia brushed past this, although in another case just seventeen days earlier, Scalia had denied standing to an environmental group, Defenders of Wildlife, on the basis that they could not show any of the "actual or imminent injury that our cases require."[81]

Scalia's opinion significantly narrowed the nuisance exception to the takings compensation requirement. The ultimate effect of his decision was to make it more likely that a regulation designed to prevent a harmful use of property would be classified as a taking, and would require the government to compensate the land-owner. Before *Lucas*, the court had rejected the idea that the government's power to act without paying compensation turned on whether the prohibited activity was a common-law nuisance.[82] But in *Lucas*, the court ruled that it would determine whether a property was being used for a "noxious use" only by reference to the lim-ited common law understanding of nuisance, rather than the definition of noxious use that a legislative body had set out.

Scalia began his analysis of the history of takings clause jurisprudence in the early twentieth century, when the Fourteenth Amendment made the Fifth Amendment's Takings Clause applicable to the states. This allowed him to begin his analysis in the substantive due process era, rather than by examining the original intent of the takings clause, which explicitly conditioned compensation on loss of possession, rather than loss of value.[83]

A look at the parties that submitted amicus briefs in *Lucas* reads like a mast-head for a Federalist Society newsletter. Kenneth Starr, Richard Epstein, Chip Mellor, and Clint Bolick participated, along with the preeminent conservative legal organizations—the Institute for Justice, the Pacific Legal Foundation, the Mountain States Legal Foundation, and Defenders of Property Rights. *Lucas* was widely criticized as inconsistent with both precedent and the framers' intent.[84] Scalia was said to have heavily relied on Epstein's brief.[85] And yet, Epstein criticized Scalia for not going far enough. He lamented that the reformation of takings juris-prudence he had hoped for had been eclipsed by the justices' intellectual lethargy.[86] For him, *Lucas* was a case of "disappointed expectations."[87]

Two years later, the court again found that a conditional building permit violated the takings clause. In *Dolan v. City of Tigard*, the owner of a chain of hardware stores who had applied for a city permit to expand her premises brought a takings claim against the city of Tigard, Oregon, because it would grant her the permit only if she granted back a public easement for bicycle traffic in front of the store and allocated a portion of her land behind the store as a public green space.[88]

The court held that the city's conditional permit was a taking. The court found that the permit conditions satisfied *Nollan*'s "essential nexus" test, because they were legitimate means by which the increased foot traffic and storm runoff from the expansion of Dolan's store would generate could be offset. But Chief Justice Rehnquist, writing for the majority, and joined by Justices Scalia, Thomas, O'Connor, and Kennedy, found that the state had not met its burden of proving that the achievement of state ends was "roughly proportionate" to Florence Dolan's loss. Rehnquist stated that the city had not sufficiently quantified the effect that the store expansion would have on traffic to show that its permit conditions were justified. That a pathway "could" perform such an offset was not enough. Rehnquist held that in granting a public green space, Dolan's loss of her right to exclude people from her land was a loss of one of the most important "sticks in her bundle of property rights." He opined that it was difficult to see "why recreational visitors trampling along [Florence Dolan's] floodplain easement" was sufficiently related to the city's objective of reducing flooding in the area, and he chastised the city for not offering any proof that it would.[89]

Justice Brennan wrote in dissent that while the record before the court was not illustrative of the dollar value of the harm done to Florence Dolan, the "mountains of briefs" submitted spoke volumes about the keen interest from property rights advocates in the rule of law that would come from it.[90] He disagreed with Rehnquist's burden shifting and argued for a return to more deferential treatment of governmental land conditions so long as they are rational, impartial, and conducive to achieving valid land use plans. He argued that the burden of demonstrating that land conditions constitute a taking should remain on the shoulders of the party challenging the state action, rather than being shifted to the state.

In 2005, the Supreme Court heard a game-changing takings case, *Kelo v. City of New London*. This case expanded the concept of what constitutes a "public use" as justification for a government taking. Suzette Kelo's modest pink Victorian house, one in a neighborhood of 115 homes, was condemned by the City of New London, Connecticut, to make way for a 90-acre proposed redevelopment, including a $300 million Pfizer research facility, a hotel, a marina, a shopping center, parkland, and parking. The redevelopment was managed by a private, nonprofit entity, the New London Development Corporation (NLDC).[91] The City of New London argued that the redevelopment would create over one thousand jobs and bring growth to its ailing economy. Kelo and a handful of other homeowners challenged whether the condemnation was legitimate, taking their case all the way up to the Supreme Court. They lost. The court, in an opinion by Justice John Paul Stevens, held that a taking is "for public use" so long as the government reasonably believes the taking will benefit the public. Justices Scalia, Rehnquist, and Thomas, joined by Justice O'Connor, dissented.

The outcome in *Kelo* lit a fire under not only property rights activists, but ordinary citizens who thought that demolishing a home to make way for a shopping mall just felt wrong. *Kelo* has been described as a "Trojan Horse," because although it was a defeat, it energized the property rights movement by enabling it to capitalize on fears of Wal-Marts invading poor neighborhoods at the behest of state governments.[92] One court stated that "eminent domain may now represent a growth industry for litigation over the purported public uses which have formed the basis for takings of private property."[93]

In the years since *Kelo*, its controversial "public use" ruling has altered the eminent domain landscape in state constitutions, state regulations, and case law. Arguably, the perceived injustice for which the *Kelo* decision has come to stand has been the biggest boost to the property rights movement since Epstein's *Takings*. Although property owners are still losing takings claims, courts appear to be paying more attention to public use challenges than they did before *Kelo*.[94] The courts themselves have recognized this: the New Jersey Appeals Court stated, "Since *Kelo* was decided, greater judicial and legislative scrutiny of redevelopment-based takings has occurred."[95]

Federalist Society members have played no small role in this campaign. Chip Mellor and Scott Bullock, for the Institute of Justice (IJ), were two of the four lawyers representing Suzette Kelo before the Supreme Court. Mellor has said that in the lead-up to *Kelo*, "[w]e had to figure out ways to mobilize people and public outrage around the issue."[96] After *Kelo*, he concluded that "a defeat with the kind of dissent that we got, is as good as it could possibly be."[97]

Within two months of the *Kelo* decision, twenty-eight states had introduced more than seventy bills to limit the use of the eminent domain power for private development.[98] In 2006, one year after the decision in *Kelo*, measures to bolster individual property rights were placed on the ballot in six states—Arizona, California, Idaho, Missouri, Montana, and Nevada.[99] The ballot questions were backed by conservative philanthropists like Howie Rich, a director of the Cato Institute, a public policy research foundation named for the libertarian pamphlets that "inspired the architects of the American Revolution."[100] The questions were also supported by libertarian think tanks like the Reason Foundation, where David Koch is a trustee.[101] The measures had names like "Save our Homes" and "Property Fairness."[102] All but Arizona's failed, due largely to lobbying by environmental groups, farmers, business groups, religious organizations, realtors, and others.[103] Nonetheless, by 2007, just two years after the *Kelo* decision, forty-two states had passed reforms to limit *Kelo*-like use of eminent domain.[104]

The *Kelo* decision and its deference to government was a detour from the court's pro-property rights direction of the previous decades because it broadened the definition of "public use," thus permitting greater government regulation. At the 2010 meeting of the Association of American Law Schools, Dana Berliner, who participated in *Kelo* on behalf of the IJ, said that "when I started litigating eminent domain cases in 1996, absolutely no one thought there was anything left of the public use doctrine except Richard Epstein." A local activist from New London brought the controversy in *Kelo* to the attention of the IJ and they filed it as part of a series of cases to challenge whether takings made solely for economic development satisfied the public use requirement.

Berliner cataloged the enormous difference their challenge had made in the law and in public opinion, although they lost *Kelo* itself in the Supreme Court. They have won several cases in state supreme courts under state constitutions that generally provide greater protection for private property than the federal constitution does. According to Berliner, only New York has ruled against a "public use" challenge to the use of eminent domain since *Kelo*. Immediately after the Supreme Court's *Kelo* decision, polls showed that over 90 percent of respondents thought the Supreme Court was wrong. According to Berliner, "[A]ll of that can be traced to Richard Epstein saying there was something left of public use."[105]

TAKINGS CASES IN LOWER FEDERAL COURTS

Takings clause jurisprudence has also expanded in the lower federal courts, fueled in no small part by conservative legal interest groups and the proclivity of some judges for Epstein's takings theory. State takings cases are heard in state or federal district courts. Federal takings cases are heard in the U.S. Court of Federal Claims. This court sits without a jury and comprises sixteen judges who are appointed by the president for terms of fifteen years. After a judge has completed his or her term, he or she may continue to sit on cases as senior judge of the court, a privilege that the court describes as a "mechanism to ensure judicial impartiality and independence." This extension of tenure—potentially for life—was successfully lobbied for by former chief judge Loren A. Smith. Clint Bolick called the court of claims "a place where the Reagan and Bush Administrations have been able to place top-notch conservative judges without getting much attention."[106] By the end of President George W. Bush's term, eleven of the sixteen sitting judges had been appointed by the three Republican presidents.[107]

Appeals from the Federal Court of Claims are heard in the Federal Circuit Court of Appeals, which has shown some willingness to adopt an expansive reading of the takings clause. Parts of the majority opinions in *Florida Rock Industries v. United States* and *Loveladies Harbor, Inc. v. United States*, for example, read like a précis of Epstein's *Takings*. These two decisions are considered to have ominous implications for federal wetlands and other environmental regulations, because they mean no matter how much profit a land development produces, virtually any federal restriction on that development could be determined by a court to be a partial, compensable taking.[108]

Both cases were decided in 1994, and both opinions were written by Jay Plager, a Federalist Society member and former DOJ appointee under Meese. Plager served during Reagan's second term as executive director of the Vice-Presidential Task Force on Regulatory Relief. He was also the administrator of the Office of Management and Budget's Office of Information and Regulatory Affairs, which was tasked with considering the impact of the takings clause on forthcoming federal regulations.[109]

In *Florida Rock*, Judge Plager ruled for the first time that a governmental regulation—in this instance, a wetlands regulation—violated the takings clause if it constituted a *partial* taking.[110] The case involved the owner of a parcel of land who had sought a permit to mine limestone on ninety-eight acres of his property; the permit was denied because the land in question was designated as wetlands pursuant to the Clean Water Act.[111] Plager remanded the case to the Federal Court of Claims for a determination of the extent of the owner's economic loss due to the regulation, so that the lower court could rule on whether a partial taking of the land had occurred.[112] The case was sent to Judge Loren Smith of the Federal Court of Claims, a Federalist Society member loyal to Epstein's interpretation of the takings clause. Smith created a judicial construct for partial takings cases that has been called a "watershed" by some commentators.[113] Guided by the plaintiff's economist, Smith applied the economic tests outlined in *Penn Central* to the ninety-eight-acre portion of the plaintiff's land.[114] In doing so, he carefully separated noncompensable "diminutions in value" from compensable "partial takings," basing his decision on the theory of "reciprocity of advantage." Judge Smith ruled that the denial of the limestone-mining permit, pursuant to the regulation, constituted a compensable partial regulatory taking because the landowner bore an undue burden, compared to the rest of the community at large, as a result of that regulation.

In *Loveladies Harbor*, Plager affirmed a trial court ruling that where wetlands regulations restricted the use of real property, the takings analysis was not to be performed on the entire parcel, but on the piece burdened by the restrictions.[115] Innocuous as this holding on "segmentation" of the property may sound, it was in direct conflict with the Supreme Court's holding in *Penn Central*, which examined the loss of air rights over the train terminal in the context of the complete parcel of land—all of Grand Central Station. More importantly, it enables savvy landowners to segment their property into smaller increments to call a regulation that might otherwise have only caused a 5 percent diminution in value to the entire parcel—itself noncompensable—to be a "total taking" of a segment of it.[116]

Since 2000, both the Federal Court of Claims and the Federal Circuit Court of Appeals have considerably honed *Penn Central*'s economic test for regulatory takings.[117] The Federal Court of Claims heard *Zoltek Corp. v. United States* in 2006.[118] The plaintiff argued that the government had infringed on its patent and in doing so, violated the takings clause. The Court of Claims held that it had jurisdiction to hear the takings case. On appeal, the Federal Circuit, despite its conservative disposition, decided the lower court had gone too far, and criticized it for attempting to write out of existence the statute authorizing the court of claims to hear patent and copyright cases in its pursuit of a takings remedy for governmental patent infringements.[119] The Federal Circuit stated that by enacting the Patent Act of 1910 and assigning patent infringement jurisdiction to the court of claims, Congress did not create a separate takings remedy in that court. If the right to sue for patent infringement under the takings clause already existed, the court reasoned, the creation of this statutory remedy would not have been necessary.[120] The court also reiterated that patent protection was a creature of federal law and not a private property right granted by the Constitution. The Federal Circuit was dismissive of the multitude of means by which the Court of Claims analyzed Zoltek's claim as a Fifth Amendment taking and reprimanded it for ignoring controlling Supreme Court precedent.[121]

More recently, in the Ninth Circuit Court of Appeals, Judge Jay Bybee, a Federalist Society member and former lawyer in the George W. Bush DOJ, ruled in *Guggenheim v. City of Goleta* that a city mobile home rent control ordinance (in place before the plaintiffs purchased the mobile home park in question) constituted a regulatory taking of their property, requiring compensation.[122] Bybee reached past the fact that the plaintiffs purchased the park at a discount because of the ordinance to find that a regulatory taking had occurred. His decision was subsequently overturned by the full panel of the Ninth Circuit Court of Appeals.[123]

Historically, many conservatives—including many senior members of the Federalist Society—have railed against the brand of judicial activism demonstrated in *Zoltek* and *Guggenheim*. As Epstein, Bolick, and Mellor have articulated, however, judicial activism is necessary to weave outlier legal theories into the fabric of the law. Judicial activism is in part fueled by education. In the property rights arena, the Foundation for Research on Economics and the Environment has taken a leading role in teaching judges about free-market approaches to property rights law and the takings clause.

THE FOUNDATION FOR RESEARCH ON ECONOMICS AND THE ENVIRONMENT

Within one hundred miles of the majesty of Yellowstone National Park, in the mountainside town of Bozeman, Montana, one of the powerhouses of the property rights movement maintains its headquarters. The Foundation for Research on Economics and the Environment (FREE) is a leading proponent of free-market environmentalism and an organization devoted to social and legal change in the property rights arena. FREE's philosophy is grounded in the use of the takings clause as a means to secure individual property rights against environmental and other land use regulation. FREE posits that the dual goals of economic prosperity and environmental stewardship can be met in two ways: first, by utilizing the takings clause to protect private property against government interference, and second, by implementing economic incentives to protect the environment as an alternative to land use regulation.[124]

FREE provides complimentary, live-in, intensive training programs to five key constituencies: Supreme Court justices, law professors, religious leaders, social entrepreneurs, and lower federal court judges.[125] FREE's reach into the judiciary is staggering. Since 1992, a quarter of the chief judges in federal courts have attended one of their programs. Alongside this, a third of the judges from the U.S. Court of Claims and half of the judges from both the Federal Circuit Court of Appeals and the D.C. Circuit are graduates of a FREE program.[126]

FREE and its judicial seminar program are sponsored in large part by charitable donations from foundations such as the Koch family's Claude R. Lambe Charitable Foundation, the John M. Olin Foundation, and the Sarah Scaife Foundation.[127] The patrons of FREE are therefore the same conservative philanthropic foundations that fund the gamut of conservative public interest law firms. The law firms litigate takings claims before judges who have undergone training in the free-market approach to property rights law, sponsored by those very same conservative philanthropic foundations. For example, between 1988 and 2008, the Claude R. Lambe Charitable Foundation donated more than one million dollars to FREE. During that time period, the foundation also made significant contributions to the Cato Institute ($9.5 million), the Federalist Society ($1 million), the Heritage Foundation ($3.4 million), and the Institute for Justice ($1 million).[128] FREE's board of directors includes influential conservatives such as John Kannon, vice president and senior counselor at the Heritage Foundation, and Judge Edith Brown Clement, nominated by President George H. W. Bush to the federal bench and elevated by President George W. Bush to the Fifth Circuit Court of Appeals. Clement was reported to be on President George W. Bush's Supreme Court short list in 2005, but the president instead nominated Harriet Miers and then Samuel Alito.[129] Professor Jonathan Adler of Case Western Reserve University School of Law is the NGO activity liaison on the Executive Committee of the Federalist Society's Environmental Law and Property Rights Practice Group. Ed Meese was formerly a director.

FREE's training programs include educational seminars on such subjects as "Law and Economics" and "Public Policy, Risk Analysis, and the Law." Lecturers at FREE's judicial seminars have included former Reagan-era solicitor general Charles Fried, Judge Loren Smith, and Yale law and economics professor George Priest. Priest studied antitrust law with Richard Posner at the University of Chicago Law School, and Posner remains a "close friend."[130] Priest took over Robert Bork's antitrust class at Yale Law School after Bork's departure and has said that "intellectually, [he] would like to think that [his] antitrust law class closely resembles the class that [Bork] taught or would be teaching if he had stayed."[131] He appeared on a panel discussing Bork's influential book *The Antitrust Paradox* in a conference honoring Bork that was organized as part of the Federalist Society's twenty-fifth anniversary celebration.[132] He also testified before the Senate Judiciary Committee in favor of Bork's confirmation to the Supreme Court.[133] Priest has written extensively in the areas of antitrust and tort reform, and four of his law review articles appear in the Federalist Society's conservative and libertarian bibliography.[134]

DEREGULATION EFFORTS FROM INSIDE GOVERNMENT

Epstein's takings theory has served the creation of judge-made law well. It has also underpinned deregulation efforts from inside government by Federalist Society members and other conservatives.

Society member David McIntosh has been an instrumental figure in realizing conservative goals of preserving individual rights and limiting government. Called the "wonk behind the Right's campaigns to roll back health, safety and environmental protections" and "one of the Republican party's leading defenders of unfettered capitalism," McIntosh has advanced a libertarian agenda from a number of platforms—as an employee of the executive branch, as a member of Congress, as a leader of the Federalist Society, and as a lawyer in private practice.[135]

McIntosh entered the University of Chicago Law School in 1980. During his three-year legal education, this former member of the Progressive Party would come under the tutelage of Epstein and embrace Epstein's belief in the supremacy of individual rights.[136] McIntosh served as special assistant to Attorney General Meese and as President Reagan's special assistant for domestic affairs.[137] In the George H. W. Bush administration, McIntosh was executive director of the President's Council on Competitiveness and assistant to Vice President Dan Quayle. As a congressman from 1995 until 2001, McIntosh represented Indiana's second district, becoming chairman of the Subcommittee on Regulatory Relief, which had oversight of environmental, labor, and FDA regulations.

Reagan proposed dismantling large swaths of the welfare-bureaucratic state that had been in place since the New Deal.[138] Meese was at the helm of this so-called Reagan Revolution. Even Fried, the solicitor general, thought some of Meese's positions were extreme.[139] Fried also thought Meese was more moderate than some of his positions demonstrated, and that they reflected more the ideas of his "cadre of young assistants." The members of this cadre, including the Federalist Society founders, considered themselves revolutionaries in a way that many of the old guard in the DOJ—including Meese and Fried, who were firmly part of the establishment—could not.[140] President Reagan, who campaigned on platforms of limited government and abhorrence of centralized power, created a labyrinth of rules requiring all federal agency rules to be scrutinized by a team of lawyers and civil servants called the Taskforce on Regulatory Relief, in his Office of Management and Budget (OMB). Presidential oversight of executive agencies was not a new or necessarily partisan phenomenon; it had begun under President Nixon and continued through the Ford and Carter administrations.[141] Reagan's system, however, was more rigorous than its predecessors. Under Executive Order 12,291, *Federal Regulation*, the president directed agencies to perform cost-benefit and least-cost analyses on all the rules they intended to promulgate. They were to be guided by the results of those analyses, as interpreted by the OMB.[142] The OMB was to receive advance notice of all significant upcoming regulatory actions, and it would conduct a final review of every proposed major rule prior to the public notice period.[143]

Reagan was accused of giving the OMB a practical veto power over health, safety, and environmental regulations, and of using the OMB to "implement a myopic vision of the regulatory process which places the elimination of cost to industry above all other considerations."[144] Advocates for the environment, consumers, and workers were particularly concerned, and many argued that OMB was unduly interfering with agency authority, operating in an opaque fashion, and abusing its authority.[145] Jay Plager assumed leadership of the Office of Information and Regulatory Affairs (OIRA), a subsection of OMB, during the last few months of the Reagan administration.[146]

Reagan also implemented Executive Order 12,630, *Governmental Actions and Interference with Constitutionally Protected Property Rights*, in May 1988. This order was principally authored by Roger Marzulla, the assistant attorney general in charge of the Environment and Natural Resources Division.[147] Before entering the administration, Marzulla had been president of the Mountain States Legal Fund, a libertarian public interest law firm focused on protecting individual liberties, particularly the rights of property owners.[148] Two years after he left the Reagan administration, Marzulla and his wife, Nancie, founded Defenders of Property Rights, a public interest law firm representing landowners and small business owners.[149] Marzulla is also currently a senior advisor to the Federalist Society's Environmental Law and Property Rights Practice Group.

Executive Order 12,630 required all federal agencies to analyze all proposed federal property regulations for the risk they posed of subjecting the government to takings litigation. This risk assessment was performed ostensibly to head off potentially expensive compensatory awards. The order stated that Attorney General Meese would circulate guidelines against which all agencies were required to measure their proposed regulations. The order (and Meese's eventual guidelines) specifically stated that a proposed regulation that restricted the use of private property must be proportionate to the problem that the regulation sought to address.[150] The idea of "proportionality" had in fact first surfaced in Justice Scalia's dissent in *Nollan*. After the order had been released, Marzulla lauded Scalia for contributing to the evolution of property law by introducing the concepts of nexus and proportionality to the takings analysis.[151]

George H. W. Bush also used OIRA to create a regulation oversight group.[152] His Council on Competitiveness was chaired by Vice President Quayle. Supporters regarded the council as a sensible approach to unburdening the economy. Detractors called it an "anti-regulatory committee" and a "superregulator." The council's remit—to submit all agency rules, including health, safety, and environmental regulations to a cost-benefit analysis—was criticized for failing to take account of long-term factors such as health care costs for victims of environmentally caused illnesses and long-term energy savings due to recycling.[153] The council was considered a friend to business interests that had lost before Congress, the agency, and the OMB—interests that were "now given a fourth bite at the apple behind closed doors."[154] Quayle was said to be covertly interfering with the regulatory process on behalf of the business lobby, and was quoted as saying in a speech to business leaders, "Now is your chance. Come and tell us what regulations and what rules are burdening the business sector."[155] Some criticized the council for being secretive and abrogating the public process of agency rulemaking. Claiming executive privilege, Quayle and his staff refused to respond to Freedom of Information Act requests or to testify before committees overseeing the agencies whose rules the council reviewed.[156] President Clinton retained White House oversight of agency regulatory proposals after defeating Bush and Quayle in 1992, but public disclosure rules ended the backdoor lobbying practices.[157]

The council had seven permanent members, including the vice president, the secretary of the treasury, the attorney general, the secretary of commerce, the director of the OMB, the chairman of the Council of Economic Advisors, and the White House chief of staff.[158] Richard Thornburgh, attorney general from 1988 to 1991, would go on to join the board of advisors for the Federalist Society's Criminal Law and Procedure Practice Group.[159] His successor, William Barr, was a champion of the unitary executive theory in the Office of Legal Counsel prior to becoming attorney general.[160] The theory (discussed in more detail in Chapter 6) gives constitutional support for an expansion of presidential power relative to Congress.[161] The council itself was in fact said to be the most "visible expression" of the unitary executive theory in action theory during the Reagan and Bush Sr. administrations.[162] Barr is a frequent Federalist Society panelist and participant.[163]

Quayle's staff, led by David McIntosh, handled the day-to-day activities of the council. And McIntosh, a firm believer that regulations could be characterized as takings of private property, set to work.[164] McIntosh fought regulation of wetlands. Bush Sr.'s revisions to the 1989 federal wetlands delineation manual meant that approximately half of all wetlands in the United States would potentially lose wetland status, removing their regulatory protections and thus freeing them up for development.[165] At the time, McIntosh joked to Quayle, "This land is your land (except as otherwise provided by government regulations)."[166] Ultimately, the wetland designation guidelines remained unchanged.[167] But McIntosh would take this issue up again as a congressman and as chairman of the Subcommittee on National Economic Growth, Natural Resources, and Regulatory Affairs during the Clinton administration. At a 1997 subcommittee hearing entitled *Wetlands: Community and Individual Rights v. Unchecked Government Power*, McIntosh urged participants to "look at this from the perspective of preserving our civil rights, because one of the rights that our Constitution guarantees is that the Federal Government will not take private property without paying just compensation, even if it is for the best public use."[168]

McIntosh's deregulation campaign continued into his congressional career. In 1995, when a journalist pointed out a FDA-mandated nutritional label on a bottle of ketchup, McIntosh responded:

> Say somebody did research and found that ketchup reduced cancer. You couldn't put that on the label until the FDA approved the cancer study. And you couldn't write, 'Low Cholesterol,' because you'd be deceiving people into thinking it was low fat. . . . My view is to give consumers accurate and true information, but don't be paternalistic. Let them decide what they want to eat, especially since the regulatory process is not up on the latest information and the whole system is so slow.[169]

In Congress, McIntosh sponsored bills seeking to reduce tariffs, increase oversight of agency rulemaking, and reduce environmental protections. H.R. 3521, the Congressional Accountability for Regulatory Information Act of 2000, sought to resurrect, in part, the role of the Council for Competitiveness—establishing a congressional committee with oversight of agency regulatory activity and requiring agency action to be analyzed for potential costs and benefits as well as alternative regulatory approaches.[170] McIntosh also introduced H.R. 2221, entitled the Small Business, Family Farms, and Constitutional Protection Act, which sought to foreclose federal funding of the implementation of Kyoto targets until the Senate had given its advice and consent to ratification. As well as seeking to forestall regulation and inquire into whether the EPA had legal authority to regulate CO_2, this bill also sought to block any possibility that Kyoto might be ratified by congressional-executive agreement, a fast-track means of conducting international agreements that many conservatives consider unconstitutional.[171] The bill stated, "The most effective way for members of the Congress to protect United States competitiveness, small businesses, and family farms from the regulatory excesses of a possible future climate treaty is to declare their unequivocal and unqualified opposition to the Kyoto Protocol."[172]

McIntosh was at the forefront of resistance to the EPA's designation of carbon dioxide as a pollutant, a stance that Epstein has also advocated for.[173] A report by the Department of Energy that McIntosh commissioned found that it was too costly to regulate CO_2 emissions. This report was said to have convinced President George W. Bush to walk away from his campaign pledge to seek cuts in emissions of carbon dioxide.[174]

PUBLIC INTEREST LAW FIRMS AND PROPERTY RIGHTS ACTIVISM

A number of Federalist Society members have waged a long antiregulatory campaign from inside public interest law firms. In many instances, they have found litigants and brought cases to defeat property regulation at the state and federal level using legal arguments grounded in Epstein's theory of the takings clause—partial takings, ending the "nuisance exception," and judicial takings. They and others have fought government on how redevelopment authorities have defined "blight," seeking to narrow its definition in order to weaken the government's ability to take private property for broader public use. These lawyers have also forged new ground in protecting economic liberties like the right to earn a living, often litigating under state constitutions, which generally offer more protections for individual rights than the federal constitution. This section explores some of the major figures and organizations, explains their ideas and legal arguments, and some of their key victories in shaping the law to protect individual economic liberties.

Clint Bolick, a leading conservative legal theorist and practitioner on issues as diverse as school choice, school vouchers, and affirmative action, has spent a considerable amount of his career advocating for individual economic rights. Bolick cofounded the Institute for Justice with William "Chip" Mellor with the help of the Koch brothers in 1991.[175] The IJ is a nonprofit law firm "dedicated to defending the essential foundations of a free society: private property rights, economic and educational liberty, and the free exchange of ideas."[176] The IJ is also "committed to the principle that '[i]ndividual freedom finds tangible expression in property rights' and that such rights are imperiled by arbitrary use of the power of eminent domain for the benefit of private interests." Bolick and Mellor have dedicated their professional lives to these ideas. Both men, and the organizations they have become involved with, have enjoyed considerable success in litigating takings claims and invalidating laws that restrict economic rights.

Bolick designed a legal strategy to restore judicial recognition of economic rights that resulted in several rulings invalidating regulatory barriers to enterprise. His strategy focused on small business owners—often sympathetic, blue-collar plaintiffs who were simply seeking to earn a living but found themselves confronted with regulations that presented a barrier to entry to a certain profession (for example, licensing requirements) or subjected them to criminal or civil sanctions for undertaking an occupation without state approval. For example, Bolick represented JoAnne Cornwell, who was arrested in California for practicing African hair braiding without a cosmetology license. The license not only required 1,600 hours of formal training, but no cosmetology school offered training in the type of hair braiding that Cornwell practiced, and the cosmetology exam did not test the technique. Bolick filed suit, alleging the California law was unconstitutional. The federal judge agreed with Bolick that the state law was not rationally related to a legitimate state interest, and that it infringed on Cornwell's civil right to practice an occupation. Bolick called the decision "a blow to protectionist government regulations across the country."

Bolick also challenged cosmetology regulations in Washington, D.C., representing defendants Taalib-Din Uqdah and Pamela Ferrell, co-owners of Cornrows & Co., who were fined $1,000 for operation of a beauty salon and training program without a cosmetology license.[177] With the defendants facing a one-year jail sentence after the D.C. board of appeals upheld the fine, Bolick took the case to federal court, arguing that the licensing requirements violated due process and equal protection rights.[178] The court ruled in favor of the District of Columbia. But while Bolick was appealing the court's decision, the D.C. City Council amended the law, in line with Bolick's policy arguments, and deregulated entry into the cosmetology profession.[179] Bolick later said that regardless of the loss in court, favorable media coverage "demonstrate[d] the efficacy of arguing in the court of public opinion."[180] In the same vein, the IJ has brought litigation to deregulate the limousine business in Las Vegas, dismantle Arizona's cosmetology regime, and defeat a public bus monopoly in New York, a cab monopoly in Colorado, and a "government-imposed cartel on casket sales" in Tennessee.[181] Although Bolick focuses, in many instances, on small business owners, his deregulatory campaign benefits businesses of all sizes.

Another thread of Bolick's strategy has been to litigate under state constitutions that often provide greater protections for individual rights than the federal constitution.[182] The idea of seeking refuge under state constitutions was promoted by Supreme Court Justice Brennan, who wrote in 1977 in the *Harvard Law Review* of his fear that the protections for individual rights and civil liberties forged in the Warren Court was coming to an end.[183] He urged liberal activists to litigate under state constitutions.

Bolick took up Brennan's call, but to further a conservative agenda. For example, Bolick has contrasted the loss of a private home in *Kelo*—a takings case under the federal constitution—with the outcome for an Arizona business owner, Randy Bailey, who prevailed against the local government in takings litigation in state court and kept his business. Bolick explained that the Arizona Court of Appeals found that its *state* constitution prohibited a taking in Bailey's case.[184]

Bolick's IJ had a hand in a similar success under the Michigan Constitution. In *County of Wayne v. Hathcock*, the Michigan Supreme Court considered whether it was permissible under the Michigan Constitution for private homes to be condemned in order to make way for a proposed business and technology park that the local government hoped would reinvigorate the county's struggling economy.[185] As in *Kelo*, at issue was the definition of the "public use" requirement of the takings clause. The IJ and the Pacific Legal Foundation submitted amicus briefs in support of the plaintiff homeowners. The PLF urged the court to overturn its own eighteen-year-old precedent, which held that the terms "public use" and public purpose" were synonymous.[186] It argued that if any generalized public benefit such as job creation or tax revenues could satisfy the "public use" limitation on takings, then any successful business that *turned a profit* could satisfy that limitation.[187] Citing to the *Federalist Papers* and various writings by James Madison, the PLF cautioned the court that the framers created a government to protect people "from theft or oppression by others," and that allowing the state to redistribute property from one person to give to another would be a "despotic power."[188] The IJ argued that the court's earlier opinion had conflated the narrow idea of "public use" with the much broader "public purpose." On that basis, the current state of the law allowed private parties to be the recipients of private land redistribution. The IJ argued, like the

PLF, that an indirect public benefit like "bolstering the economy" was insufficient to satisfy the public use requirement.[189]

In ruling for the plaintiff homeowners that the taking was unconstitutional, the Michigan Supreme Court agreed with the IJ and the PLF, conceding that generalized economic benefit did not satisfy the "public use" requirement. The court further held that to allow government to transfer property from one private party to another was as good as removing all constitutional restrictions on the government's exercise of its eminent domain power. In the aftermath of *Wayne County*, Chip Mellor noted that it was a "great day for property rights nationwide."[190] The choice of public interest law firms to spend precious resources on the Michigan controversy seems sensible when one considers that three of the seven sitting justices of the Michigan Supreme Court at the time, including the chief justice, were on the board of visitors of the Federalist Society's Michigan chapter. In fact, of the twenty-two members of the board, fourteen were state or federal judges.

Another thread of Bolick and Mellor's strategy to elevate the status of economic rights is urging the Supreme Court to overturn one aspect of the *Slaughter-House Cases*, an 1873 decision that upheld the State of Louisiana's award of a butchering monopoly to a private company.[191] There, the court narrowly construed the privileges and immunities clause of the Fourteenth Amendment, which prevents the various states from making or enforcing any law that would abridge the "privileges or immunities of citizens of the United States," limiting it to the benefits of federal rather than state citizenship.[192] On that basis, the court ruled that the granting of a state monopoly to one citizen and foreclosing that economic advantage to another did not run afoul of the clause. Like the butchers in the *Slaughter-House Cases*, Bolick and Mellor argue that the right to earn a living is in fact a privilege of state citizenship that the Fourteenth Amendment was designed to protect. Bolick and Mellor criticize the *Slaughter-House Cases* for eviscerating protections for economic rights and for giving too much deference to the legislature.

Bolick has also joined Epstein's call for judicial activism to keep federal and state governments in check. On the heels of 2007's *Massachusetts v. EPA*, where the Supreme Court invalidated part of the Bush administration's avoidance strategy regarding global warming and forced the EPA to decide if carbon dioxide was a pollutant and whether it should regulate its emission, Bolick criticized the court in the *Wall Street Journal* for exercising legislative and executive powers by giving a regulatory agency broad lawmaking authority.[193]

Bolick acknowledged that "judicial activism" was generally a criticism that conservatives leveled at liberals. Bolick argued, however, that worse than judicial activism is "judicial nonfeasance." He criticized the modern Supreme Court for allowing certain clauses in the Constitution—which he argues protects individual rights—to remain largely ignored. Specifically, the contracts clause of Article I, which prohibits the states from retroactively passing laws that inhibit contract rights, and the privileges and immunities clause of the Fourteenth Amendment.[194]

Conservative public interest law firms devoted to the strengthening individual rights have litigated on behalf of farmers, small businesses, and homeowners; they have also sought less traditional alignments. Roger and Nancie Marzulla's group, Defenders of Property Rights (DPR), conceived of a strategy in the mid-1990s to advance the libertarian ideals of individual freedom and small government by encouraging tobacco company Philip Morris to take up the same ideals in their effort to reduce government regulation of tobacco products. In an October 1995 letter, a DPR policy advisor informed Craig Fuller, the senior vice president of corporate affairs for Philip Morris, that its current initiatives to restrict underage smoking had potentially opened the door to greater regulation of its messaging to youth, requiring the company to work "against its own market interests" and forcing it to "unilaterally give ground on a constitutional right—the right to own and use property."[195] DPR's solution was to change the messaging to youth, educating them on the inadvisability of smoking while extolling the principles of "individual freedom, personal responsibility and decision-making." The basis of this imperative, according to DPR, was that property and economic liberty are indelibly intertwined, and that the federal government (presumably in restricting tobacco sales and advertising) was "taking" property of the retail and advertising industries in the name of the public good, without just compensation.

The Marzullas are currently engaged in private practice, specializing in environmental, property rights, and water law.[196] In 2001, Roger Marzulla described the aim of his campaign to the *ABA Journal* thus: "[T]o look at property in its broadest definition, to identify cases that extend to more forms of property. We've set out consciously to build a bridge between all the land-based cases and more intangible property."[197] The same article described Marzulla as "rooting for" Philip Morris, Inc., which was (along with other tobacco companies) then seeking to block a Massachusetts law requiring disclosure of cigarette ingredients on the basis that it was a taking of its trade secret recipes that would require just compensation.[198] The tobacco companies won.[199]

THE NEXT FRONTIER OF TAKINGS JURISPRUDENCE

The next frontier of takings advocacy is the theory of a judicial taking—the notion that the judiciary, as much as the executive or legislature, can "take" constitutionally protected property rights, requiring compensation. Under the theory, outlined by Epstein in *Takings*, a court may be said to have taken property if it makes a property law ruling that radically departs from settled principles of common law or abandons prior precedent.[200] The debate as to the legitimacy of the doctrine of judicial takings can be characterized as follows: On the one hand, the takings clause, on its face, does not apply specifically or exclusively to a particular branch of government. On the other hand, the judicial takings doctrine may allow property owners to take a second bite at the apple—after losing in state court, litigants could potentially characterize not only the initial legislative act but the judicial decision that upheld it as a taking.

In a June 2010 decision, *Stop the Beach Renourishment v. Florida Department of Environmental Protection*, the Supreme Court rejected the claim of Florida Panhandle property owners that the Florida Supreme Court had judicially "taken" their private property when it upheld a state-authorized plan to pump sand onto the beach in an attempt to stop erosion, which had the effect of turning the owners' water "front" property into water "view" property.[201] On these particular facts, the court did not find a taking. The ruling held promise for the property rights movement, however, because Justices Scalia, Roberts, Thomas, and Alito went out of their way to state in an accompanying plurality opinion that potentially, a state court ruling *could* constitute a taking that would require compensation from state government. In 1967, Justice Potter Stewart proposed that a judicial taking could be identified as "a sudden change in state law, unpredictable in terms of relevant precedents." This approach was explicitly rejected by Scalia, Roberts, Thomas, and Alito: "What counts is not whether there is precedent for the allegedly confiscatory decision, but whether the property right allegedly taken was well established." This statement was foreshadowed by Scalia, dissenting in the mid-90s, when he wrote that "[n]o more by judicial decree than by legislative fiat may a state transform private property into public property without just compensation."[202] As a result of the plurality opinion in *Stop the Beach Renourishment*, the theory of judicial takings is now on the table in the jurisprudence of the Supreme Court.

CONCLUSION

According to Steven Calabresi, the takings clause initiative is a key example of how the society and its members have advanced a facet of conservative ideology, despite disparate views on the subject. "Robert Bork and Antonin Scalia . . . were very hesitant about expanding the Takings Clause. Then there were people like Richard Epstein who thought everything was a taking."[203] While acknowledging that the society's current position is not the position of either extreme, Calabresi says that the takings clause has been expanded during the lifetime of the Federalist Society. "Having conservatives and libertarians . . . debating this issue and fleshing it out, and having members listen to it" has been one of the means by which a radical legal theory like Epstein's *Takings* has been brought into the mainstream of legal thought. This theory, once ill-received by conservatives and liberals alike, has found life in takings jurisprudence, the legislature and the executive branch, judicial training, law school debate, and legal scholarship. It is one of the great successes of the Federalist Society and the property rights movement.

3

REGULATION OF
PRIVATE PROPERTY

Access to Justice

It is a settled and invariable principle, that every right, when withheld, must
have a remedy and every injury its proper redress.

—*John Marshall*[1]

In a decision ripe with symbolism about access to justice in the age of terror,
the Supreme Court announced on Monday that visitors to its courthouse will
no longer be allowed to enter through the front door.

—*Adam Liptak*[2]

In the last chapter, we described how Federalist Society members have attempted to use the takings clause to oppose regulation of private property. In
this chapter, we explore a different strategy for combating regulation—limiting
access to the courts. Over the past twenty-five years, conservatives have employed
a variety of strategies and doctrines to create obstacles to lawsuits that demand
changes in public policy or that have a regulatory impact on private business.[3]
These strategies furthered conservative values—a preference for policy to be enacted
by legislatures rather than courts, and a preference for the free market, rather than
the government, to regulate the economy.

Arguments to limit access to the courts found a receptive audience in the
Rehnquist Court. As Professor Andrew Siegel has written, that court "expressed a
profound hostility to litigation" in "case after case and in wildly divergent areas of
the law."[4] Siegel concludes, "[H]ostility to litigation has been, in the end, the most
historically significant and all-encompassing theme of the Rehnquist era."[5] The
theme has continued in the Roberts Court.

Cases that raise issues of the regulation of business practices arise in a variety
of settings. For example, a customer signs up with a cell phone provider that promised "free" phones, and then gets billed for the sales tax on the phones. The contract
with the company requires arbitration, but does not permit a class of customers
to have a joint arbitration. Or a hospital patient suffers serious injuries because of
defects in a medical device employed in her treatment. She wants to bring a suit
against the manufacturer to get compensation for her increased future medical
expenses, but the company claims it cannot be sued because the Food and Drug
Administration (FDA) approved the device. Or male employees subject a female

employee to sexual harassment and the company is unresponsive to her concerns. She wants to file a lawsuit, but her employment contract specifies that all disputes must be resolved through arbitration.

Lawsuits intended to change public policy face a variety of obstacles. Procedural hurdles have grown higher in the last thirty years, including the doctrines of standing (whether the plaintiff has suffered a significant enough injury to challenge the policy), ripeness (whether there is a controversy sufficiently immediate to warrant action by the court, and whether all other remedies that must be exhausted first have been tried), and mootness (whether the controversy at issue is still alive). Government officials are frequently able to claim either absolute or qualified immunity from actions for damages, with the result that the plaintiff's complaint is dismissed at the outset of proceedings.[6] The number of cases dismissed on immunity grounds has grown significantly in recent years. Other doctrines make it difficult for citizens suing the government to get access to the information necessary to challenge government policy. These include executive privilege (which protects communications between the president and his advisors), state secrets privilege (which protects sensitive information that might endanger national security), law enforcement privilege (which protects techniques and strategies that government agents use to investigate crime), and a privilege that protects government informants. The Bush administration used these doctrines very effectively to make it difficult to challenge antiterrorism programs that threatened civil liberties. The Obama administration has continued to make many of the same arguments in ongoing litigation.

In other cases, the door to the courthouse is closed when the Supreme Court narrowly interprets the underlying substantive law on which a claim might be made. The court has cut back on the circumstances in which private parties (as opposed to the government) may bring actions under federal regulatory statutes, for example in *Central Bank of Denver v. First Interstate Bank of Denver* (no private claims for aiding and abetting under § 10(b) of the Securities and Exchange Act of 1934), and in *Alexander v. Sandoval* (no private right of action to enforce disparate impact regulations under Title VI of the Civil Rights Act of 1964).[7] The court often refuses to recognize a cause of action based directly on the Constitution, such as in the case of *Correctional Services Corp. v. Malesko* (no constitutional cause of action for a prisoner against a private correctional facility for violations of the Eight Amendment).[8] At other times, the court narrowly interprets the scope of a constitutional right or a statutory remedy and concludes that there is no remedy for an alleged violation by way of a civil suit. For example, Oliverio Martinez filed a civil rights suit after he was blinded, paralyzed, and at risk of dying after having been shot by police officers, and then questioned by a police sergeant in a hospital emergency room over the objections of medical personnel. The Supreme Court dismissed his claim based on the alleged illegal questioning, ruling that the Fifth Amendment right to remain silent protects a suspect only against the use in court of his statements; it does not protect him from the coercive interrogation itself.[9] Or, in a different case we discuss later in this chapter, investors lost much of the original value of their stock as a result of a fraudulent conspiracy between the company they bought stock in and other companies. The Supreme Court narrowly interpreted the securities laws to limit the suit to the company whose shares the investors owned, barring the case against the other wrongdoers.[10]

Our principal focus in this chapter is on the strategies and doctrines that create obstacles for civil claims by persons injured by dangerous products and by consumers aggrieved by corporate practices, or what some conservatives call "regulation by litigation." A successful lawsuit by a person harmed by a drug or by one who has been overcharged by a credit card company may establish a precedent that operates as a legal rule that will affect future cases. In this way, litigation can amount to a form of regulation. That is how the common law developed in this country and in England. Some authors use the term "regulation by litigation" in a more narrow sense, to refer to lawsuits filed in order to create rules that govern how companies must do business in the future.[11] Such rules may result from contested proceedings in which courts issue injunctions ordering defendants to follow certain rules, or they may result from lawsuits that are settled between the parties, where defendants agree to rules binding their conduct in the future. In that event, the court may enter a "consent decree" that gives the parties' agreement the force of a court order. Margaret A. Little harshly criticizes regulation by litigation:

> What a fascinating story it is, this business of regulation by litigation, using litigation and the courts to achieve and enforce regulatory regimes against entire industries without having to go through the expense, uncertainty, or trouble of securing legislative or rule-making authority for such regulation. And a business it most certainly is—when wielded by private lawyers, it is the most lucrative new field of practice in the legal market purchasable by a law license and friends in high places.[12]

In this chapter, we explore the preemption doctrine, the civil justice reform and tort reform movements, and the expansion of arbitration as a substitute for litigation, as examples of how Federalist Society members have opposed both the broad and narrow forms of regulation through litigation. In addition, we look at recent developments with respect to securities litigation in order to demonstrate how conservatives have limited available remedies for investors who claim to have been dealt with unfairly. Federalist Society members from several practice groups have been active in these areas.[13] In addition, these matters are frequently discussed in the Federalist Society publications *State Court Docket Watch* and *Class Action Watch*.

THE PREEMPTION DOCTRINE

In the last several years, Federalist Society members have aggressively used the preemption doctrine to foreclose the ability of injured parties to bring tort claims for compensation in state courts. A "tort" is a civil wrong by one person that causes harm to another. For example, Jones drives his car negligently and collides with

Smith, who suffers a broken leg. Or a doctor carelessly fails to recognize the symptoms of a tumor, with the result that the patient dies, although with proper care she could have been saved. Tort claims may be brought against manufacturers, for example, who make products that are unreasonably dangerous, or who market drugs with labels that fail to warn consumers of dangerous side effects. In a tort action, the plaintiff—the injured party who files the suit—asks the court to award damages against the defendant, the alleged wrongdoer. Compensatory damages are intended to reimburse the plaintiff for her losses—for example, medical expenses, lost income, and pain and suffering. In some states, punitive damages are also available. Punitive damages are not intended to compensate the plaintiff, even though the plaintiff receives the money awarded, but rather to punish the defendant for particularly egregious conduct and to deter the defendant and others from causing harm in similar ways in the future.

The preemption doctrine is based on the supremacy clause of the Constitution, which provides that courts are bound by the federal constitution and laws passed by the federal government, even if the laws of the states are to the contrary.[14] For example, the Constitution gives the federal government the power to regulate interstate commerce; thus, federal statutes and federal agency regulations concerning commerce take precedence over state law. States may regulate commerce, but if there is a conflict between federal law and state law, federal law prevails.

The Supreme Court has recognized two broad categories in which the preemption doctrine requires federal law to override state law. "Express preemption" is applicable where the text of a statute explicitly defines to what extent Congress intends for federal law to trump state law in the area regulated by the statute. Alternatively, the courts will find "implied preemption" where Congress has not expressly declared that a federal statute was intended to rule out any state regulation, but the courts infer that Congress had such intent. There are two types of implied preemption. "Conflict preemption" is found where "compliance with both federal and state regulations is a physical impossibility, or where state law stands as an obstacle to the accomplishment and execution of the full purposes and objectives of Congress."[15] Some authors refer to the latter circumstances as "obstacle preemption." "Field preemption" exists where "the scheme of federal regulation is so pervasive as to make reasonable the inference that Congress left no room to supplement it."[16]

Congress is often imprecise about its intentions, even when it expressly states that a federal statute preempts state law. In such cases, the courts must determine the scope of the circumstances in which Congress intended to preempt state law. The controlling issue in all preemption cases is congressional intent. When the Constitution gives Congress the power to regulate a given area, the supremacy clause allows Congress to monopolize the field if it chooses. On the other hand, Congress may permit the states to regulate and frequently does. The fundamental question in any preemption case is whether the particular regulation in question is one that Congress intended to allow the states to enact.

State tort law may be viewed as a form of regulation. Where federal statutes preempt regulation by the states, they typically provide that state "requirements" or "prohibitions" in addition to those provided by the federal law are preempted. A straightforward example would be a state statute that required more information on the label of a consumer product than mandated by federal regulations. In a different example, if an injured person successfully sued the manufacturer of a product in state court, claiming that the product was negligently designed, a judgment for the plaintiff may be seen as imposing regulatory requirements with respect to the safety standards for that product.[17] Those who favor broad preemption contend that where a product is in compliance with the federal statute and regulations that cover it, states should not be permitted to impose tort liability against the manufacturer in lawsuits filed by private parties. A defendant in a civil suit in state court who claims the benefit of the preemption doctrine will ask the court to dismiss the case at the outset of proceedings.

Opponents of the preemption of tort claims point out that federal regulations do not satisfy one of the primary purposes of tort law—providing compensation to persons who have been injured by the wrongful behavior of others. If tort suits are dismissed because they are preempted by federal regulations, injured individuals are left to bear the costs of the other party's negligence. Courts should be cautious about assuming that Congress intended that result. In a tort suit, the plaintiff's lawyer investigates the cause of a specific injury and thus, for example, in a product liability claim, may discover defects in a product or its labeling that did not come to the attention of a regulatory agency. Moreover, once agencies approve products and allow them to enter the market, they rarely review the products' subsequent performance to determine if additional changes to the product or additional warnings might be necessary. According to this view, it is better to view federal regulations as supplying only minimum safety standards, leaving it to the states to determine whether stricter standards may be required.

The pro-preemption argument creates a conflict between traditional conservative values. Conservatives tend to prefer action by state and local governments to regulation by the national government, particularly with respect to the exercise of the "police powers" of the states to ensure the health, safety, and welfare of their citizens. Conservatives also argue that a principal advantage of our federal system is that the states are able to function as laboratories for experimentation in social regulation. The preemption doctrine undermines these values by taking regulation out of the hands of the states and giving it to the national government.

Many conservatives, including members of the Federalist Society, nonetheless favor preemption of state tort remedies by federal regulation. As a practical matter, manufacturers and sellers perceive that regulation by federal agencies imposes less onerous burdens on them than state tort law. Indeed, at the same time the George W. Bush administration was arguing that corporate defendants were protected from suit by the preemption doctrine, it was also making administrative changes "designed to reduce the burden of federal regulation on American business."[18]

Daniel Troy is a Federalist Society member who was chief counsel of the FDA under President George W. Bush and the architect of the FDA's assertion of preemption in product liability cases during that time. Speaking on a panel at the 2006 National Lawyers Convention, he acknowledged the conflict that preemption poses for conservative values and admitted that Federalist Society members could be accused of hypocrisy on the issue.[19] He argued, however, that the concept of limited government was best served by preempting fifty levels of state regulation in favor of one regime of federal regulation.

Kenneth Starr also recognizes the conflict between competing conservative values, but he resolves it more ruthlessly, at least rhetorically. Starr believes that judges should "vigorously protect states' ability to experiment in their core areas of responsibility," but that "the Commerce Clause should be taken equally seriously, as should the never-ending demands of our national economic union." He favors preemption because regulation in one state has an undesirable effect on manufacturers outside that state, and because he believes business is suffering from a combination of a "litigation explosion and resulting tort crisis," "opportunistic trial lawyers," and "the abuses of aggressive state attorneys general." Starr says, "[W]e must sink or swim together in the waters of commerce. Today those waters are beginning to teem with ravenous sharks bearing the beguiling markings of the several states. Judges and justices should stand ready to harpoon these sharks as soon as they surface."[20]

Tort Reform

At the Federalist Society panel mentioned above, Troy recognized that some people had labeled the approach to preemption by the George W. Bush administration "stealth tort reform."[21] Commentators have used this term to suggest that the Bush administration took up the preemption strategy after more direct approaches to limiting tort claims had been less successful than conservatives desired. The use of the preemption doctrine to limit civil claims is in fact the most recent strategy of the tort reform movement.

Organized resistance to regulation of dangerous business practices through litigation began after an August 1971 confidential letter by Lewis Powell to the head of the Education Committee of the U.S. Chamber of Commerce.[22] Powell, then a corporate lawyer, described a "broad attack" on the U.S. economic system by a variety of leftist and liberal forces. The culprits included, among others, "bright young" Yale graduates who favored "the politics of despair," attorney William Kunstler, Yale law professor Charles Reich (author of *The Greening of America*), and Ralph Nader. Powell accused the business community of indifference to the attack and advocated the formation of a broad and aggressive campaign that would include lobbying and litigation on behalf of business interests. Appreciating the political significance of ideas, Powell identified "the campus" as "the single most dynamic source" of the problem. Two months after this letter, President Nixon appointed Powell as a justice on the Supreme Court. Influenced by Powell and others, the Chamber of

Commerce and conservative philanthropists began to support and fund precisely the sort of effort Powell had advocated, including, eventually, the Federalist Society.

In the 1980s, one of the most significant pro-business lobbying efforts was the "civil justice reform" movement, including the demand for "tort reform."[23] The campaign accused Americans of being unreasonably litigious and argued that court awards and the rising costs of litigation were driving up prices for products and insurance premiums, even bankrupting legitimate businesses. Conservative advocates complained of a wave of frivolous tort claims and vexatious class actions. Professors Michael Rustad and Thomas Koenig have explained that the purpose of this movement was to "produce a dominant discourse that [would] predispose legislators, judges, legal academics and the general public to support liability-limiting tort doctrines."[24] They identified the influence of the Olin Foundation and the Federalist Society on legal education and scholarship as particularly important in the movement.

In 1988, Republican candidate for president George H. W. Bush campaigned on a platform of civil justice reform. His administration established the Council on Competitiveness, nominally headed by Vice President Dan Quayle but administered by Federalist Society founder David McIntosh.[25] The council formed the Federal Civil Justice Reform Working Group, which was chaired by Solicitor General Starr and included, among others, Jay Bybee from the Office of White House Counsel, as well as McIntosh, all then or eventual Federalist Society members. It issued a report, *Agenda for Civil Justice Reform in America*, in August 1991. The report began with a hyperbolic account of the supposed damage that litigation had done to the U.S. economy, including the assertion that "the average lawyer takes $1 million a year from the country's output of goods and services."[26] The report's primary recommendations were for procedural mechanisms designed to lower the cost of lawsuits.

Substantively, the council recommended that punitive damages should be limited to the amount of compensatory damages awarded, that the loser of a lawsuit should be required to pay the winner's attorneys' fees and costs, that there be a moratorium on attorneys' fees awarded under federal fee-shifting statutes that provided for fees to victorious plaintiffs but not defendants, and that courts encourage greater use of alternative dispute resolution (ADR). With respect to ADR, the report encouraged the private sector to use contract provisions requiring nonjudicial means of dispute resolution. The contractual approach to requiring arbitration has taken off. At present, as a result of form contracts that corporations present to individuals who have no realistic opportunity to negotiate terms, workers and consumers are routinely forced into arbitration and denied access to court for disputes with those corporations. Credit card contracts, cell phone agreements, and many employment contracts, for example, provide that all disputes between the individual and the company must be settled by arbitration.

Despite the activities of the Council on Competitiveness, the George H. W. Bush administration did not succeed in passing any significant federal civil justice reform legislation. The tort reform movement, however, had considerably greater success in state legislatures. Between 1986 and 2002, forty-five states and the District of Columbia enacted limitations on tort claims.[27] They included rules favoring defendants in medical malpractice cases, caps on punitive damages, limitations on joint and several liability, and restrictions on the collateral source rule. Joint and several liability means that where a plaintiff recovers a judgment for injuries caused by the combined actions of two or more defendants, each defendant is liable for the full amount of the judgment. A plaintiff may not collect more than the amount of the judgment, but he or she can collect it all from one defendant if he or she chooses. In that event, the defendants must sort out among themselves their proportions of the damages. Plaintiffs prefer joint and several liability because it increases the chances that they can collect the full amount of the judgment, even if some of the defendants have no funds. Defendants dislike the doctrine because they would prefer to be liable only for their own proportionate share of the harm they caused. The collateral source rule provides that a plaintiff is entitled to collect damages for all harms she suffered from the defendant, even if she has already received reimbursement for losses from other sources, such as insurance. Those other sources are usually able to recover the sums they paid from the plaintiff. Defendants dislike the collateral source rule because they would prefer to have the damages they must pay reduced by the amount the plaintiff has already recovered.

The trend in the law over the first seventy-five years of the twentieth century had been to expand the availability of tort remedies. In products liability claims, for example, courts were motivated by a desire to compensate consumers harmed by dangerous products, to share the burden of the cost of injuries more widely, and to provide an incentive for manufacturers to make safer products. In the 1980s, however, massive advertising campaigns by insurance companies and business interests attacked tort law across the board. Calls for "tort reform" were successful in convincing Americans that there were too many frivolous claims and that awards by juries were too high, and that as a result the public was suffering from higher prices for products and insurance. There was little hard evidence for these claims, but the public campaigns exploited and sometimes distorted anecdotal accounts of unusual individual cases that were presented as typical.

Professor Sandra Gavin uses the expression "stealth tort reform" to refer to this campaign to change public opinion about tort law. She is a harsh critic, concluding, "Stealth tort reform operates to manipulate public perception about the state of the law without regard to truth or logic." She analyzes the tort reform campaign's use of "assertive rhetoric," a "passion-based method of persuasion" designed to ensure "that only one side of the question gets a hearing."[28] The techniques the reformers favored included "crisis labeling" and "fear mongering," and the use of myths and urban legends and the corresponding identification of "demons" (the lawyers, the victims, and the juries). Their presentations were dramatic, employing the rhetorical devices of "fright, the focus on personalities, and the significance of the vivid example."[29] Despite serious questions about the legitimacy of the tactics of this campaign, there is no doubt that it was effective—the public's appreciation of the work done by lawyers and courts soured.

Federalist Society members and allies supported these campaigns with scholarship that legitimated the claims of a crisis. For example, when the American Bar Foundation (ABF) published a study that concluded that special interest groups had manufactured the "tort crisis," the Federalist Society's publication *ABA Watch* attacked the ABF for failing to find empirical evidence that the United States was suffering from a litigation crisis.[30] Publications on basic tort reform issues included, among other topics, criticism of plaintiffs' lawyers,[31] attorneys' fees,[32] class actions,[33] products liability,[34] punitive damages,[35] limits on noneconomic damages,[36] rules of procedure,[37] and the general subject of regulation by litigation.[38] Mark A. Behrens, the cochair of the Tort and Product Liability Subcommittee of the Litigation Practice Group's executive committee, has written over 140 articles that touch in some way on the tort system and the need for tort reform.[39] In addition, some law school casebooks have taken a more conservative direction.[40] As the battle over tort reform continues, some state courts have held limitations on tort recoveries to be unconstitutional under various state constitutional provisions. The Federalist Society has provided a platform for critics of those rulings.[41]

Federalist Society members coordinated their tort reform efforts in the alliance Lawyers for Civil Justice, consisting of a variety of other conservative groups, such as the U.S. Chamber of Commerce, the Defense Research Institute, and the American Tort Reform Association.[42] Theodore ("Ted") H. Frank, a member of the Executive Committee of the Federalist Society's Litigation Practice Group, is the founder and president of the Center for Class Action Fairness. Walter Olson, a senior fellow at the Cato Institute, has been described by the *Washington Post* as the "intellectual guru of tort reform" and is a frequent speaker at Federalist Society events such as "Is Overlawyering Overtaking Democracy?"[43]

During the Clinton administration, Newt Gingrich, Speaker of the House of Representatives following the Republican success in the midterm election of 1994, became his party's principal spokesperson for the civil justice reform movement. The movement's concerns were expressed in the "Contract for America," particularly in the proposed federal Common Sense Legal Reforms Act (CSLRA). This document "embodied the core principles animating the conservative critique of civil justice in the United States, as refined over a decade."[44]

Preemption doctrine first appeared as a strategy for civil justice reform at this time. The CSLRA articulated rules governing liability and damages in products liability cases and provided that the federal law would preempt state law with respect to the subjects of regulation covered by the federal law. Among other provisions, the proposed law would have limited the liability of sellers of defective products in several ways and would have put limits on punitive damages.[45] Gingrich failed, however, to get this bill enacted into law. The next step was "stealth tort reform" and the preemption strategy.[46]

The George W. Bush Administration

During the George W. Bush administration, advocates of the preemption strategy operated on three fronts. In Congress, they sought to add preemption language to regulatory statutes, without much success. In administrative agencies, they had greater success in adding preemption language to administrative regulations and the preambles to regulations, in part because Bush appointed tort reform advocates to important positions in the Department of Justice and federal agencies.[47] In court, they sought a broad interpretation of preemption language in order to dismiss state tort claims.

Aside from preemption, the Bush administration did not succeed in getting other significant tort reform on the federal level, with one exception, the Class Action Fairness Act of 2005.[48] That act expanded federal jurisdiction over class actions where the damages sought exceeded a total of five million dollars and there are more than one hundred members in the class.[49] There are exceptions to the act that would leave some cases in state courts, but the primary purpose of the act was to allow defendants to remove cases to federal court when plaintiffs originally file them in state court.[50] This was intended to defeat the ability of lawyers for plaintiffs to "forum shop" (i.e., to choose plaintiffs in class actions who reside in a state court jurisdiction that has a reputation for favoring the type of claim being filed). The act also provided for greater scrutiny of plaintiffs' attorneys' fees in "coupon settlements," where the amount of recovery for individual class members is small and they receive coupons to purchase products. Conservatives and business interests were in favor of the act.[51]

Before the George W. Bush administration, federal agencies had only rarely argued in favor of preemption in court.[52] The chief counsel of the FDA under President Clinton, Margaret Jane Porter, had stated, "FDA's view is that FDA product approval and state tort liability usually operate independently, each providing a significant, yet distinct, layer of consumer protection."[53] But under President Bush, federal agencies actively pushed for preemption. The Federalist Society members who served as solicitor generals in the Bush administration, Ted Olson and Paul Clement, filed numerous briefs urging the Supreme Court to find that federal statutes or regulations preempted tort actions.[54] They did so even in cases where the U.S. government had previously taken the position that the statute or regulation in question did not preempt such suits.[55]

As we have noted, federal agencies in the Bush administration added preemption language to their regulations. The American Association for Justice conducted a survey based on Freedom of Information Act requests to the government and found that seven agencies had issued over sixty rules with preemption language in the preamble.[56] For example, the Consumer Product Safety Commission adopted a rule that its new federal standard for fire resistant bedding preempted "inconsistent state standards and requirements, whether in the form of positive enactments or court created requirements."[57] The National Highway Traffic Safety Administration (NHTSA) included preemption language in several regulations, such as in head restraint requirements.[58] It originally proposed regulations regarding roof crush resistance for automobiles that would have preempted state regulation, but after a storm of protest from consumer groups and others, it withdrew the preemption language from its proposed regulations.[59] The FDA, the Federal Railroad Administration, the Department of Homeland Security, the Pipeline and Hazardous Materials Safety Administration, and the Office of the Comptroller of the Currency also added preemption provisions to their regulations or otherwise took the position that their regulations preempted state law.[60]

The Food and Drug Administration

The FDA provides a prime example of the preemption strategy of the George W. Bush administration. Bush appointed Daniel Troy as chief counsel of the FDA. Beginning in 2002, Troy filed amicus briefs on behalf of the government in several cases in the lower federal courts and state courts supporting defendants' arguments that tort claims were preempted by federal regulations. Indeed, Troy asked pharmaceutical companies to advise the FDA of cases in which amicus briefs from the government would be helpful.[61] This strategy had very limited success.[62] In January 2006, the FDA augmented the preemption strategy by adding preemption language to the preamble of drug-labeling regulations.[63] Although the regulations were generated by an administrative agency and not by Congress, the argument would be made that courts should give deference to the judgment of the agency that Congress had intended for the statute to have a preemptive effect. The FDA preemption strategy was met with approval by Federalist Society members and friends. Victor E. Schwartz characterized the FDA interpretation of the scope of implied preemption as "a logical, perhaps inevitable, step toward meeting its congressional mandate as the federal agency responsible for regulating drugs."[64]

In addition to the 2006 drug-labeling regulations preamble, the FDA took the position that a variety of other regulations had preemptive effect. Professor Catherine Sharkey accused the FDA of "bait-and-switch" tactics, citing a number of examples where it had initially characterized proposed rules as having no federalism implications or effect on the states, and then later inserted preemptive language.[65]

Troy reprised his arguments in favor of FDA preemption in a 2007 collection of essays by Richard Epstein and Michael Greve.[66] He wrote that when state courts and juries conduct their own risk-benefit analyses of drugs without the FDA's expertise, they undermine the mission of the FDA. He argued that the FDA approves drugs when the benefit of making the drug available outweighs the risk of harm, not when the drug is risk-free, and that jurors might not appreciate this point. According to Troy, the FDA attempts to strike a balance between providing sufficient information about risks in drug labels and refraining from providing so much information that the consumer either may not read it or may be discouraged from taking a drug that would in fact be beneficial. Thus, he views FDA standards as both a floor and a ceiling for regulation. Troy was concerned that juries might deviate from what he viewed as the optimal balance struck by the FDA. As a result, a jury verdict that provides compensation to one plaintiff might have severe and unintended consequences for other potential users of the drug. For example, a jury might find a defendant liable for failing to warn of a rare side effect of a drug, in a case where the plaintiff suffered harm from that side effect. Troy argued that the FDA might have judged it better to forego that warning, because it might discourage too many patients who need the drug and would not suffer the side effect from taking it. Overall, Troy claimed that tort liability stifles innovation in the pharmaceutical industry, reduces the availability of drugs, causes higher drug prices, and encourages manufacturers to engage in indiscriminate and prolix labeling of risks. Troy's case depended in part on whether his assertion was true that "the FDA is ideally placed to make the risk-benefit determinations required for effective pharmaceutical regulation."[67]

The FDA had traditionally not taken the position that Troy adopted. For example, previous FDA chief counsel Porter had written:

> FDA regulation of a device cannot anticipate and protect against all safety risks to individual consumers. Even the most thorough regulation of a product such as a critical medical device may fail to identify potential problems presented by the product. Regulation cannot protect against all possible injuries that might result from use of a device over time. Preemption of all such claims would result in the loss of a significant layer of consumer protection, leaving consumers without a remedy for injuries caused by defective medical devices.[68]

Troy's critics argued that the FDA preapproval process is not effective in identifying all risks of drugs because its testing does not detect "side effects that occur relatively rarely, have long latency periods, or adversely affect subpopulations (like children and the elderly) that were not represented in the premarket testing." They submitted that the problem is not solved by post-market surveillance by the FDA, because its program in that regard "has been chronically starved for resources."[69] In their view, the tort system is often better than the regulatory agencies at uncovering the dangers of products, including the drugs and the medical devices licensed by the FDA. Tort lawyers devote substantial resources to examining how a particular product caused harm in a specific real world situation. They are able to subpoena documents and testimony from employees of manufacturers that the companies did not make available to administrative agencies. A jury determines whether a product is unreasonably dangerous after adversary presentations on the issue, guided by legal instructions from the trial judge.

One factor that raises skepticism about the preemption argument is the "revolving door" practice of lawyers who move back and forth between the representation of major corporations and the government agencies that regulate them. Troy is a good example, and not a unique case. He represented pharmaceutical companies before he became chief counsel at the FDA. After he left the government, he went to the law firm Sidley Austin, once again representing pharmaceuticals, now armed with the preemption arguments he had advanced at the FDA. While in office, Troy's practice of repeatedly filing briefs on behalf of the FDA to support the position of drug companies in litigation caused Rep. Maurice Hinchey of New York to offer an amendment to an appropriations bill to strip $500,000 from the chief counsel's budget, to rein him in.[70] Troy was paid over $358,000 by Pfizer in the year before he went to the FDA; then, within four months of arriving at the FDA, he filed an amicus brief on behalf of the government supporting Pfizer's defense in a Zoloft suicide case in the Ninth Circuit Court of Appeals.[71] Troy left the FDA at the end of 2004. Five months later, he filed an amicus brief in the Supreme Court on behalf of the Pharmaceutical Research and Manufacturers of America in support of an unsuccessful petition for certiorari by Warner-Lambert Co., asking the court to reverse a punitive damages award against the company.[72] In 2007, he filed a brief in the Supreme Court directly on behalf of Warner-Lambert Co., now owned by Pfizer, arguing that another suit against the company by a Michigan resident was preempted.[73] To complete the circle, Solicitor General Clement filed a brief in that case on behalf of the U.S. government supporting Warner-Lambert's position.[74] The Federalist Society also published an article that Troy wrote about the issue.[75] Troy is now the senior vice president and general counsel of GlaxoSmithKline PLC.

The Supreme Court ultimately rejected the FDA's preemption arguments concerning drug labeling in *Wyeth v. Levine* in 2009.[76] Diana Levine sued Wyeth, the manufacturer of a nausea medication, for a failure to adequately warn of the dangers of administering the drug intravenously through the "IV-push" method. That method of administration caused Levine to suffer gangrene, the amputation of her arm, and the loss of her career as a professional musician. Wyeth's warning had received FDA approval. Wyeth argued the claim was preempted.

The court first rejected Wyeth's argument that it was not possible to change the label once it learned of problems with the IV-push method. It then declined to adopt Wyeth's argument that the state tort claim created an unacceptable obstacle to congressional objectives. The court found no evidence that Congress intended for the FDA to establish both a floor and a ceiling for regulation. Congress had not enacted an express preemption provision in the Federal Food, Drug, and Cosmetic Act (FDCA). The court inferred that Congress had determined that state tort claims provided appropriate relief for injured consumers, noting that the FDA has limited resources to monitor the eleven thousand drugs on the market and that tort suits uncover unknown hazards. Finally, the court concluded that the preemption language in the FDA's 2006 amended preamble to the regulations did not control the issue, in part because it was a dramatic change in the FDA's longstanding position that preemption was not appropriate without a reasoned explanation. The court's conclusion—that state tort law provided a form of drug regulation that complemented the FDA—in effect ratified the contentions of critics of Troy's arguments.

The amicus briefs by Federalist Society members in *Wyeth* illustrated the contradiction we have noted between the goal of reducing government regulation, on the one hand, and the preference for state and local government over the national government, on the other. Ted Frank filed an amicus brief on behalf of economists and law and economics professors supporting Wyeth's preemption claim.[77] It was based primarily on theoretical arguments that the FDA has an incentive to err on the side of the overregulation of prescription drugs. It argued that state tort suits exacerbate that problem by imposing additional requirements on pharmaceutical companies. On the other hand, Thomas W. Merrill, former chairman of the Administrative Law Practice Group's executive committee, filed an amicus brief opposing preemption, on behalf of a consumer welfare organization. He argued that "unless Congress has expressly delegated authority to preempt, agency statements of opinion about the preemptive effect are entitled to no deference by courts."[78] Merrill's brief labeled Wyeth's position, and the support it received from several amici and the federal government, as part of a "broader movement in which federal administrative agencies have joined forces with regulated industries to urge preemption of state tort and consumer protection laws."[79]

President Barack Obama reversed the course of the Bush administration's preemption policy. On May 20, 2009, Obama issued a memorandum to the heads of executive departments and agencies, noting that states and local governments have frequently protected health, safety, and the environment more aggressively than the national government.[80] The memo instructed department heads not to include statements of preemption in regulations and their preambles unless justified by appropriate legal principles, including those discussed in President Clinton's "Federalism" executive order of August 4, 1999. That order had emphasized the importance of respecting the policymaking discretion of the states. It specifically provided that federal agencies should preempt state law only "to the minimum level necessary to achieve the objectives" of relevant federal statutes.[81] Professor Sharkey has concluded, based on her empirical research, that President Obama's memorandum prompted serious internal review in the majority of the agencies she surveyed. The most pronounced policy shifts in rule making and litigation has occurred at the NHTSA and the CPSC. She found it more difficult to evaluate the extent of change at the FDA.[82]

Supreme Court Decisions

Conservatives have had mixed success in winning preemption arguments in the Supreme Court. Because the preemption analysis begins with an attempt to determine the intent of Congress in each case, one cannot expect Supreme Court decisions to be consistently in favor of preemption or against preemption. Even taking that into account, however, many commentators find Supreme Court jurisprudence in this area to be disconcertingly inconsistent.[83]

Ted Olson has been a major figure in Supreme Court preemption litigation, during his tenure as solicitor general, and as a private lawyer before and after his government service.[84] In addition to appearing as counsel for one of the parties before the court, he has authored a number of amicus briefs. In *Riegel v. Medtronic, Inc.*, which Olson argued in 2007, the Supreme Court held that a lawsuit by Charles Riegel and his wife, for injuries sustained when a Medtronic catheter ruptured in his coronary artery during heart surgery, was preempted by the FDA's premarket approval process under the Medical Device Amendments of 1976 (MDA). Unlike the Federal Food, Drug, and Cosmetic Act that the court would review the following year in *Wyeth v.*

Levine, the MDA included an express preemption provision. The court ruled that the common law tort claim would impose a "requirement" different from the premarket approval requirements imposed by the FDA under the MDA.[85] *Riegel* was a significant victory in the campaign to use federal regulations to preempt state tort claims. The case also demonstrates the intricacies of preemption analysis.

The *Riegel* opinion distinguished a 1996 case in which Medtronic had lost its preemption argument, *Medtronic, Inc. v. Lohr*.[86] In that case, the court held that claims by Lora Lohr and her husband, based on the failure of her Medtronic pacemaker, were not preempted. Justice Scalia's majority opinion in *Riegel* explained the difference between the cases on the ground that the federal manufacturing and labeling requirements in *Lohr* were not specific to the device in question, the pacemaker, but were generic concerns about device regulation generally. Even more technically, the FDA approved the pacemaker in *Lohr* as a device "substantially equivalent" to another device that was on the market before the MDA was passed, and therefore exempt from premarket approval (under the "§ 510(k) process"). In *Riegel*, Scalia explained that even though substantial equivalence review under § 510(k) is device-specific, that type of approval process does not impose device-specific "requirements," but determines "a qualification for an exemption rather than a requirement."[87] The catheter in *Riegel*, on the other hand, was subjected to a premarket approval process at the FDA, which does impose "requirements."

Riegel also demonstrates how the inquiry into congressional intent with respect to preemption often leads to conflicting interpretations, thus leaving room for the justices' individual views about regulation, the tort system, and preemption, to influence their decisions. Justice Ginsburg dissented in *Riegel* and would have found no preemption. She began her analysis by citing the "presumption against preemption," a venerable doctrine found in many preemption opinions, but one whose strength has waned in recent years. The presumption is based on the argument that Congress does not supersede the historic police powers of the states unless Congress has demonstrated a clear and manifest purpose to do so. Ginsburg added that this presumption is heightened "where federal law is said to bar state action in fields of traditional state regulation."[88] (Here we should note that the internal conflict of constitutional values in preemption cases afflicts liberals as well as conservatives. In other types of cases, the liberals tend to sustain assertions of federal regulatory power and dismiss the conservatives' complaints about "states' rights."[89] It was ironic for Justice Ginsburg to dissent from a Justice Scalia opinion on the ground that he was trenching on the special domain of the states.)

Ginsburg concluded that Congress did not intend for the MDA to preempt state tort claims. She argued that the absence of a federal compensatory remedy for consumers in the MDA suggests that Congress did not intend to preempt state common law claims, because it is "difficult to believe that Congress would, without comment, remove all means of judicial recourse" for injured consumers of defective medical devices.[90] Scalia responded to this by saying, "[T]his is exactly what a pre-emption clause for medical devices does by its terms."[91] Thus, he found there was a purpose to preempt, based on the text of the statute. The disagreement be-tween Ginsburg and Scalia is certainly influenced by their views on the importance of defending tort remedies. How slippery the congressional intent piece can be is illuminated best in the concurring opinion of Justice Stevens. He concluded that the significance of the preemption provision in the MDA was not "fully appreci-ated until many years after it was enacted." The statute's "text and general objective cover territory not actually envisioned by its authors." Thus, "it is ultimately the provisions of our laws rather than the principal concerns of our legislators by which we are governed."[92] Stevens agreed with Ginsburg that Congress did not intend pre-emption, but nonetheless concluded that the text of the statute compels it.

Eight months after the Supreme Court's decision in *Riegel*, Ted Olson ar-gued *Altria Group, Inc. v. Good*, claiming that the Federal Cigarette Labeling and Advertising Act (FCLAA) preempted a lawsuit under the Maine Unfair Trade Practices Act (MUTPA). Smokers alleged that a tobacco company's claims that its cigarettes (Marlboro Lights and Cambridge Lights) were "light" and had "lowered tar and nico-tine" were fraudulent misrepresentations. This time Olson and the company lost. The FCLAA has an express preemption provision, and in 2001, in *Lorillard Tobacco Co. v. Reilly*, the court had ruled that the federal statute preempted Massachusetts regu-lations regarding the location of cigarette advertisements. Massachusetts had argued that the federal statute governed only the content of the advertisements, not their location, and that the federal law preempted only regulations relating to "smok-ing and health," whereas the Massachusetts regulations were motivated by concerns about juveniles. The court rejected these arguments. Altria argued that the decision in *Lorillard Tobacco* compelled a decision in favor of preemption in its case.

This time the majority opinion, written by Justice Stevens, began with the pre-sumption against preemption, and the corollary that when the text of a preemption clause is capable of more than one reading, the court should use the reading that disfavors preemption. The court concluded that the purpose of Congress in enact-ing the FCLAA was twofold—to adequately warn the public about the hazards of cigarette smoking, and to protect the national market in cigarettes by preempting nonuniform regulations by the states. It then concluded that neither purpose would be served by limiting the states' ability to prohibit deceptive statements in ciga-rette advertising. Altria argued that enforcement of state fraud rules would lead to nonuniform regulations. The court rejected that argument, however, on the ground that fraud claims rely on a uniform standard: falsity.

After concluding that congressional purpose did not require preemption, the court turned to the question of whether the text of the statute required it nevertheless. Here the court had to reckon with its 1992 decision in *Cipollone v. Liggett Group, Inc.*, where a plurality opinion had concluded both that a fraudulent misrepresentation claim was not preempted (because it was based on a duty not to deceive, not a duty based on smoking and health) and that a "warning neutralization" claim in the case was preempted. The court rejected Altria's argument that the alleged violation of the Maine statute was more like "warning neutralization" than it was like deceit. The court concluded that "the phrase 'based on smoking and health' fairly but narrowly construed does not encompass the more general duty not to make fraudulent statements."[93] Chief Justice Roberts and Justices Thomas, Scalia, and Alito dissented.

A significant issue in preemption cases, one that was implicated by the Bush administration's "preemption by preamble" strategy, is how much weight the courts should give to administrative agency determinations. The agencies may express conclusions not only about congressional intent, but also about whether a given state regulation conflicts with the purpose of federal regulations. In 2011, in *Williamson v. Mazda Motor of America*, the court held that Federal Motor Vehicle Safety Standard 208 does not preempt state tort claims.[94] The issue was whether the standard, which gave manufacturers a choice about what sort of seat belt to install on a rear inner seat, would preempt a tort suit in which a successful claim by the plaintiff would have denied manufacturers that choice by imposing liability on those who installed a simple lap belt. Paul Clement filed an amicus brief on behalf of automobile manufacturers and dealers' associations, arguing that the case was controlled by the court's 2000 decision in *Geier v. American Honda Motor Co.*, finding preemption based on the same regulation.[95] But in *Williamson* the court found no preemption, relying on the statements of the Department of Transportation (DOT) and the arguments of the solicitor general, which asserted that the DOT believed that giving a manufacturer the choice of which belts to use *did not* further significant regulatory objectives. The court distinguished *Geier* on the ground that in 2000 the agency had indicated that giving the manufacturer a choice with respect to restraints *did* further regulatory objectives.[96]

Williamson suggests that in future preemption cases the court may pay more attention to the views of the administrative agencies responsible for the regulations.[97] That may be, and if so, it may somewhat simplify Supreme Court jurisprudence in this area. It would not, however, inhibit those who seek to minimize regulation through the tort system from lobbying agencies to favor preemption. At least for the foreseeable future, we can expect preemption cases to be a battleground where disputes about the extent to which the government may regulate private industry will be waged.

ARBITRATION CLAUSES

As we noted above, one method corporations employ to limit the ability of consumers and workers to bring lawsuits is the use of contractual provisions that require disputes with the company to be arbitrated. Congress passed the Federal Arbitration Act (FAA) in 1925. It provides that arbitration agreements in contracts "shall be valid, irrevocable, and enforceable, save upon such grounds as exist at law or in equity for the revocation of any contract."[98] The statute was passed in the teeth of judicial hostility to arbitration agreements in the early twentieth century, but in the current era the Supreme Court has repeatedly held that the statute requires the enforcement of arbitration provisions, including in employment contracts.[99]

The Supreme Court held in *Circuit City Stores, Inc. v. Adams*, in 2001, that the FAA governs employment contracts.[100] The statute excludes "contracts of employment of seamen, railroad employees, or any other class of workers engaged in foreign or interstate commerce."[101] That provision could be read to exclude employment contracts for all workers in interstate commerce, as Justice Stevens did in his dissent, making a strong argument based on the legislative history of the statute. The attorneys general of twenty-one states filed an amicus brief urging that the exception be given a broad meaning, so that state policies that restricted or limited the availability of arbitration in the labor context could be enforced.[102] The court, however, limited the exception to transportation workers.

Eight years later, in *14 Penn Plaza LLC v. Pyett*, employees in the building services industry in New York City claimed they had been demoted as a result of their age: night lobby watchmen and similar workers had been reassigned to jobs as night porters and light duty cleaners when a subcontractor was hired to provide security personnel.[103] Their union filed a grievance, but then withdrew the age discrimination claim from arbitration because in the meantime it had consented to the contract for the new security personnel. The demoted employees responded by filing an age discrimination claim with the EEOC and then a lawsuit. The employer sought dismissal of the case on the ground that the collective bargaining agreement required union members to arbitrate claims under the Age Discrimination in Employment Act. The Supreme Court, in a decision written by Justice Thomas, held that the contract's arbitration provision was enforceable. The decision means that even statutorily protected civil rights can be deemed waived by a collective bargaining agreement that provides for arbitration.

The most restrictive arbitration clauses prohibit arbitration by a class of people who have similar disputes with a company, requiring each individual to make his claim in a separate proceeding. Initially, several state and lower federal courts ruled that the provisions prohibiting classwide arbitration were unenforceable. The issue took over two decades to be resolved in the U.S. Supreme Court. As the controversy over this issue was pending, Federalist Society members weighed in to urge that provisions foreclosing classwide arbitration should be enforced. Erika Birg, a special advisor to the Executive Committee of the Litigation Practice Group, argued that there was no substantive or inalienable right to bring a class action, and that the parties' contractual agreement should control the matter. If an agreement does not provide for classwide arbitration, the courts should not allow it.[104]

In April 2011, the Supreme Court ruled in *AT&T Mobility LLC v. Concepcion*, in a majority opinion written by Justice Scalia, that the FAA preempted California law with respect to a waiver of class action arbitration proceedings in cell phone contracts.[105] The AT&T contract provided for arbitration of disputes between the company and its customers, but prohibited arbitration on behalf of a class of consumers. The Concepcions had signed up for cell phone service in response to advertisements that promised free phones, but to their surprise AT&T charged them $30.22 in sales tax for the phones. They filed suit and their complaint was consolidated with a class action that alleged AT&T had engaged in false advertising and fraud by promising "free phones" but charging sales tax. AT&T moved to compel arbitration of the Concepcions' individual claim. The district court denied the motion, based on California law, and the case ultimately came to the Supreme Court.

The California Supreme Court had held that an arbitration clause in such contracts was unenforceable unless it permitted arbitration on behalf of a class of consumers affected by the provision. That court held such contracts were "unconscionable," a well-recognized ground for voiding contracts. The term is employed when a contract is so unfair to one party that the court will refuse to enforce it. The court reasoned that in a consumer contract where the consumer has no realistic opportunity to negotiate the terms of the contract, where disputes predictably involve small amounts of damages, and where "it is alleged that the party with the superior bargaining power has carried out a scheme to deliberately cheat large numbers of consumers out of individually small sums of money," a waiver of classwide relief would exempt the more powerful party from responsibility for its own fraud.[106] The Concepcions argued that AT&T knew that most customers would not seek arbitration of the $30.22 sales tax and that, absent a class action, AT&T would reap a huge illegal windfall based on its own fraud.

Although the FAA permits contracting parties to waive their rights to file lawsuits and thus be limited to arbitration for resolving disputes, the act includes a provision that such agreements may be declared unenforceable "upon such grounds as exist at law or in equity for the revocation of any contract."[107] The Supreme Court recognized that unconscionability was such a ground, but nonetheless held that in this setting, a requirement of "classwide arbitration interferes with fundamental attributes of arbitration and thus creates a scheme inconsistent with the FAA."[108] In other words, the court imposed conflict preemption. Justice Scalia argued that classwide arbitration would be less informal, slower, more costly, and more likely to generate procedural morass, than individual arbitration.

Federalist Society members supported the preemption argument made by AT&T. Ted Frank and Brian P. Brooks, cochair of the Class Actions Subcommittee of the Litigation Practice Group, filed an amicus brief on behalf of the Center for Class Action Fairness.[109] According to the brief, the center "represents consumers by objecting to unfair settlements that do not provide meaningful relief to class members and by seeking court rulings that protect consumers from class action attorneys." Frank and Brooks provided a general critique of class actions, arguing that they are frequently a "poor vehicle for the vindication of consumer rights," and that arbitration is a superior remedy in many cases. They reasoned that class actions are slow, involve high transaction costs and frequently result in returning only "pennies on the dollar" to class members.[110] The authors took the position that consumers were harmed by conflicts of interest with their lawyers, and by the large fees that class action lawyers collect on settlements, citing, among others, articles and speeches by Federalist Society members and friends R. Ted Cruz (director of the Office of Policy Planning in the Federal Trade Commission during the Bush administration) and Professors Brian Fitzpatrick, Jonathan Macey, and Geoffrey Miller. The center's brief concluded, largely on the basis of theory and some polling, that consumers prefer arbitration to litigation, and thus the Ninth Circuit Court of Appeals, which had held that the suit was not preempted, was incorrect when it reasoned that customers would not file individual arbitration claims. The brief did not mention that between 2003 and 2007, only 170 of AT&T's seventy million customers filed arbitration claims.[111] Another major omission from the brief was any argument about what would motivate companies like AT&T to avoid this type of fraudulent scheme in the first place in the absence of any potential for class action relief.

The center made an economic argument that if class actions were superior, the market would make them available. This argument was based on two theoretical propositions. The first proposition was that if classwide arbitration were more efficient at providing consumer relief, companies would adopt it, because "the perceived quality of a company's process for resolving customer complaints is reflected in brand image and loyalty, and thus a more efficient process leads to increased demand and the ability to command above-market prices." The second proposition put forward the assumption that companies would theoretically pass the savings from reduced arbitration transaction costs along to consumers, and that the consumers would "choose companies offering efficient complaint resolution mechanisms in order to capture these cost savings," in the words of Professor Stephen J. Ware, faculty advisor to the Federalist Society at Kansas University Law School.[112] The reader can assess the validity of this argument by asking, first, whether he or she knew there was an arbitration clause in the cell phone contract at the time he or she signed it, and second, whether the arbitration clause was the reason he or she chose that cell phone company. In any event, choice in such matters is probably no longer available, insofar as the Supreme Court's decision in *Concepcion* provides an incentive for every major company selling consumer goods to adopt contracts with arbitration clauses that rule out class action relief.

The Federalist Society was well represented by other amicus briefs in *Concepcion*, including one by Paul Clement on behalf of CTIA-The Wireless Association®,[113] a brief by Kevin C. Newsom, cochair of the Role of the Courts Subcommittee of the Federalism and Separation of Powers Practice Group, on behalf of DRI-The Voice of the Defense Bar,[114] and a brief on behalf of "Distinguished Law Professors" Randy E. Barnett, Richard Epstein, Michael I. Krauss, Gregory E. Maggs, and Stephen B. Presser, among others.[115] Of course, given its importance of the case, numerous other groups filed amicus briefs on both sides of the question.

Professor Brian T. Fitzpatrick analyzed the *Concepcion* decision in the Federalist Society's *Class Action Watch*. He concluded that "the decision could lead to the end of class actions against businesses across most—*if not all*—of their activities."[116] Fitzpatrick explained that the only significant class actions currently filed against businesses are by people that the companies can require to sign arbitration agreements, including waivers of class arbitration. Fitzpatrick's empirical research demonstrated that shareholders, employees, and consumers file over 75 percent of class actions. In Fitzpatrick's opinion, there is nothing in the decision in *Concepcion* or in federal law that would prohibit companies from requiring all these classes of plaintiffs to consent to arbitration of disputes and a waiver of class arbitration.

LIMITING REMEDIES FOR SECURITIES VIOLATIONS

The case of *Stoneridge Investment Partners v. Scientific-Atlanta, Inc.*, decided by the Supreme Court in January 2008, is a paradigmatic example of Federalist Society concerns with respect to the litigation of securities violations.[117] In this case, investors who lost money after they purchased stock in Charter Communications, Inc., a cable operator, sued Charter, its auditor, Arthur Andersen, and two other corporations, Scientific-Atlanta, Inc., and Motorola, Inc., alleging a fraudulent scheme to inflate the price of Charter's stock. As the fraud was revealed, the stock price fell from $4.06 per share on July 18, 2002, to 78 cents per share on October 11, 2002.[118]

The plaintiffs claimed that Charter agreed to pay Scientific-Atlanta twenty dollars over the ordinary price for each digital cable converter box it bought, with the understanding that Scientific-Atlanta would return the overpayment by purchasing $6.73 million in advertising from Charter. In Motorola's case, Charter contracted to purchase 540,000 converter boxes by December 31, 2000, even though it had no need for them and no intention of buying them, and to pay Charter twenty dollars in damages for each box it did not purchase by the specified date. In return, Motorola agreed to purchase $10.8 million in advertising from Charter. The advertising rates charged to both companies were four to five times higher than those paid by other advertisers. There was no economic substance to these transactions, and the companies agreed to backdate the purchase agreements for the boxes to create the false impression that the converter box transactions were unrelated to the advertising contracts. The fraudulent scheme allowed Charter to report approximately seventeen million dollars in phony advertising revenue and operating cash flow. This allowed its quarterly reports to meet Wall Street expectations for cable subscriber growth and operating cash flow and inflated its stock price.

The plaintiffs sued under a provision of the 1934 Securities Exchange Act that prohibits "any manipulative or deceptive device or contrivance" "in connection with the purchase or sale of any security."[119] Rule 10b-5 of the Securities Exchange Commission (SEC) enforces the statute by making it unlawful to employ any fraudulent device, scheme, artifice, act, practice, course of business, or untrue statements in connection with the purchase or sale of any security. The act does not explicitly provide that private parties can enforce it through a lawsuit, but the Supreme Court held in 1971 that the right to do so was implied by the words of the statute and the implementing regulation.[120] Such lawsuits are a very important vehicle for redress for investors victimized by fraudulent practices.

The issue in *Stoneridge* was whether the investors could sue Scientific-Atlanta and Motorola for their part in the fraudulent scheme, in addition to suing Charter. The court, in a 5–3 decision, ruled they could not. Justice Kennedy wrote the majority opinion, joined by Chief Justice Roberts and Justices Scalia, Thomas, and

Alito. Justice Stevens wrote a dissenting opinion, joined by Justices Souter and Ginsburg. Justice Breyer did not participate in the case.

Kennedy's opinion concluded that the investors' suit could not reach the customer/supplier companies Scientific-Atlanta and Motorola because the investors had not relied on any statements or representations those companies had made. Kennedy based the decision on a 1994 case, *Central Bank of Denver v. First Interstate Bank of Denver*, which held that a § 10(b) action could not be filed against parties who merely aided and abetted the fraud of the principal defendant.[121] Following *Central Bank*, there were calls for Congress to amend the statute to provide for liability in private suits against aiders and abettors, but it had not done so. Instead, Congress provided that the SEC could prosecute aiders and abettors. Based on *Central Bank*, Kennedy argued that reliance by the investor on a defendant's own deceptive acts is an essential element of the § 10(b) cause of action, and that in this case the deceptive acts of Scientific-Atlanta and Motorola had not been communicated to the public and hence had not been relied on by the investors.

Kennedy took a narrow view of the law. As Stevens concisely put it at the outset of his dissent, "Investors relied on Charter's revenue statements in deciding whether to invest in Charter and in doing so relied on [Scientific-Atlanta's and Motorola's] fraud, which was itself a 'deceptive device' prohibited by § 10(b) of the Securities Exchange Act of 1934." The dissenters concluded that was a sufficient basis for liability.

The majority did not accept the argument that investors rely not only on the public statements relating to a security but also on the transactions those statements reflect. Employing the slippery slope reasoning often used to limit regulation, Kennedy concluded that basing liability on underlying fraudulent transactions "would reach the whole marketplace in which the issuing company does business."[122] Stevens responded that the kind of sham transactions alleged in this case are isolated departures from the ordinary course of business and that Kennedy's stated concern for the whole marketplace was hyperbole. He argued that legitimate businesses would be protected by the fact that liability could be imposed only on those transacting companies whose own conduct violated § 10(b).

Kennedy concluded that the fraudulent actions of Scientific-Atlanta and Motorola were too remote from the investors for the investors to have relied on them. He reasoned that their actions had not made it *necessary* or *inevitable* for Charter to misrepresent the transactions in its statements. The more important point, however, is that Scientific-Atlanta and Motorola made it *possible* for Charter to misrepresent the value of its stock and it was perfectly *foreseeable* to them that Charter would do so. That, after all, was the point of the scheme.

The broader themes in this case reflect the agenda of many Federalist Society members. Kennedy cautioned that if the cause of action were extended to this sort of conduct, "there would be a risk that the federal power would be used to invite litigation beyond the immediate sphere of securities litigation and in areas already governed by functioning and effective state-law guarantees."[123] This is a "states' rights" argument. In other words, ruling for the defendants here had the effect of restricting the power of the federal courts to monitor deceptive transactions on which securities fraud might be based, leaving those issues to the states to regulate. States, of course, may or may not engage in such regulation and may have difficulty enforcing their securities laws. Taking enforcement out of the hands of the parties injured by securities fraud makes regulation less likely to be effective. Kennedy's states' rights argument was ironic, given that thirty-five states (plus eighteen state and local employees' retirement plans) had joined in amicus briefs arguing that the federal courts had jurisdiction over Stoneridge's claim.

Kennedy also concluded that recognizing the cause of action against these transacting companies would "undermine Congress' determination that this class of defendants should be pursued by the SEC and not by private litigants."[124] This was a "judicial activism" argument, in which Kennedy argued that the courts ought not to be making law, a prerogative of Congress. Indeed, Kennedy suggested that by recognizing an implied cause of action not intended by Congress, the court would be expanding the jurisdiction of the federal courts in violation of the Constitution.

Stevens rejected the premise of Kennedy's argument that the plaintiffs were "expanding" the previously recognized cause of action, and argued that imposing liability for transactions that caused misrepresentations was well within the regulation Congress intended. The fact that Congress did not restore liability for mere aiding and abetting after the Supreme Court's decision in *Central Bank* does not mean that it wanted to exempt from liability companies whose own conduct was deceptive and violated § 10(b). Moreover, Stevens argued that it was historically the business of judges to fashion a remedy for the violation of a law designed to protect a class of citizens, and that given that history it was wrong to conclude that Congress did not intend to permit suits under the circumstances of this case when it passed the Securities Exchange Act in 1934.

By restricting the power of the federal government vis-à-vis the states, by restricting the power of the federal judiciary vis-à-vis Congress, and by limiting the ability of injured parties to bring private actions to enforce regulatory statutes, the decision in *Stoneridge* substantially undermined the ability of investors to obtain redress for securities fraud.

The Stoneridge case attracted enormous attention in the business and legal communities. Thirty-one groups filed amicus curiae briefs in the Supreme Court, including the federal government and most of the major financial associations on behalf of the defendants, and a wide variety of public and private investors and retirement plans on behalf of the plaintiffs. The brief filed on behalf of thirty-two states characterized the case as "probably the most important legal issue for the securities industry in a generation."[125] The brief filed on behalf of a coalition of seven unions, Change to Win, called attention to the recent losses suffered by workers' pension funds and argued, "The view that those crafty enough to benefit from participating in a securities fraud can escape liability by carefully avoiding a public statement directly conflicts with the broad language and purposes of the antifraud provisions. Indeed, it is precisely with respect to such secret schemes that the antifraud provisions are needed the most."[126]

The Federalist Society had a great deal of interest in the case. In October 2007, the society sponsored a symposium and a debate about the case at Case Western Reserve University School of Law, featuring presentations by lawyers and professors on both sides of the dispute.[127] On October 9, 2007, the day of the Supreme Court oral argument, Professor Richard Epstein published an Internet column predicting victory for the corporate defendants. He acknowledged that it was anomalous to allow secondary violators like Scientific-Atlantic and Motorola to escape liability when primary wrongdoers like Charter were subject to suit. His solution to the discrepancy, however, would be to eliminate all private actions against even primary offenders, on the ground that private suits over deter wrongful conduct, cause a "temporary imbalance in the markets" that "far exceeds the social losses from the underlying chicanery," and impose "harsh penalties" that "induce firms to remain silent lest they incur huge liabilities for modest misstatements." Among the specific problems with liability for secondary offenders, according to Epstein, is that it "chews up huge social losses in litigation costs that detract key executives from their major jobs."[128] One might argue, however, that protecting the public from harm caused by corporate fraud is part of the job for key executives.

Several Federalist Society members and allies participated in amicus briefs at the Supreme Court. The solicitor general, Paul Clement, filed a brief on behalf of the United States in which he argued that allowing liability in this case "would constitute a sweeping expansion" of the § 10(b) private right of action, "potentially exposing customers, vendors, and other actors far removed from the market to billions of dollars in liability when issuers of securities make misstatements to the market." He submitted that such a "radical expansion of liability is a task for Congress, not the courts."[129] Ken Starr filed an aggressive brief on behalf of the conservative Washington Legal Foundation in which he argued that the principal issue of fraud the case presented had "little to do with" the fraud perpetrated by Charter, but that the "real question" of fraud was the danger of "potentially abusive litigation enabled by subjective liability standards." Starr articulated his concern that the court might become "distracted" by the arguments by Stoneridge and its supporters and "overlook" the burdens that abusive litigation puts on the investing public.[130] Starr further argued that recognizing the claim against Scientific-Atlanta and Motorola in this case would undermine the international competitiveness of U.S. public securities markets, because our "public markets are losing their position as global leaders in large part due to the growing international perception that the United States' legal system is costly, unpredictable, and out of control."[131]

These arguments, typical of the positions taken by Federalist Society members, severely curtail access to justice for private citizens injured by corporate securities fraud. Following the court's decision, Larry Obhof, in an article published both in *Engage* and *Class Action Watch*, reviewed the details of the Kennedy opinion, pleased with the fact that the court in *Stoneridge* "prudently declined to extend the private right of action."[132] On this issue, Federalist Society members have been very successful in limiting government regulation of business practices.

— 4 —

RACE AND GENDER DISCRIMINATION

The way to stop discrimination on the basis of race is to stop discriminating on
the basis of race.

—John Roberts[1]

A racially discriminatory act is, quite simply, an action taken on the basis
of race.

—Lino A. Graglia[2]

One of the most controversial legal issues with respect to race is whether
government may take race into account to benefit minority groups that
have traditionally been discriminated against. Historically, when civil
rights lawyers litigated against racially discriminatory government policies, they argued that decisions should not be made on the basis of race. They said that members of minority groups deserved to be treated as individuals and judged on their
merits. Today, many civil rights advocates believe that in many areas, race must be
considered to overcome the vestiges of previous discrimination. Conservatives argue, however, that the Constitution does not permit a double standard, and that
any use of race in decision making by the government is illegal and harmful. These
are important questions of constitutional law and government policy that should be
considered in each instance in the historical context in which they arise.

In *Parents Involved in Community Schools v. Seattle School District No. 1*, the
court struck down voluntary school integration plans in Seattle, Washington, and
Jefferson County, Kentucky.[3] The court held that the plans violated the equal protection clause of the Fourteenth Amendment, on the ground it was unconstitutional for these school districts to take race into account in making decisions about
school assignments. The decision was a major triumph in a long-standing, well-
organized, and well-funded conservative campaign to abolish race-conscious decision making by the government. Influential members of the Federalist Society have
been heavily involved in this campaign. Federalist Society members were crucial
participants in *Parents Involved*, as they had been in numerous earlier cases. Lead
counsel for the parents challenging the school assignment plans in the Supreme
Court was Harry J. F. Korrell, an executive board member of the Federalist
Society's Puget Sound lawyers chapter and a member of its Labor and Employment
Practice Group's national executive board. Paul Clement, solicitor general of the
United States, filed an amicus brief supporting the parents on behalf of the federal

government. Other Federalist Society members filed amicus briefs on behalf of a variety of conservative groups.

This chapter begins by describing the arguments that Federalist Society members have developed over the past three decades to oppose affirmative action plans that rely on racial or gender classifications. These arguments formed the basis of the court's decision in *Parents Involved*. Federalist Society critic Lee Cokorinos says it is the goal of the Federalist Society "to undermine the idea of a public commitment to diversity."[4] Conservatives believe, however, that it is not appropriate for the government to promote racial balance. The essence of the conservative position is that there is no legal difference between considering race or gender for purposes of *exclusion* and considering race or gender for purposes of *inclusion*. They argue that both are harmful and make racial problems worse. On the other hand, many civil rights advocates believe that because our history has been one of the systematic exclusion of racial minorities and women from social, political, and economic institutions and from positions of power and influence, the conservative view leads to the continuation of exclusion and retards society's ability to move toward inclusion.

The major issues in this debate, which are interrelated, are identified here and then discussed at some length. Some of the points raise technical constitutional issues, which will be explained. The principal conservative arguments are:

- The courts must review all racial classifications made by the government, including for purposes of affirmative action, under the standard of "strict scrutiny."
- The only compelling government interest that meets the strict scrutiny requirement and justifies racial classifications is providing a remedy for previous intentional discrimination by the government unit in question.
- The government may not use racial classifications to remedy "social discrimination."
- The Fourteenth Amendment's equal protection clause guarantees equal opportunity, not equal results.
- The Fourteenth Amendment's equal protection clause secures the rights of individuals, not groups.
- Affirmative action unfairly penalizes innocent individuals with no responsibility for discrimination.
- Racism has been largely overcome in the United States.
- The equal protection clause of the Fourteenth Amendment to the Constitution requires that government action be colorblind, rather than color conscious.
- With respect to gender, excessive concern about equality for girls and women has resulted in neglecting and oppressing males, particularly boys and young men.

After analyzing these principles, the chapter describes how Federalist Society members have attempted to implement them. This has included participating in conservative public interest law firms, supporting litigation to strike down affirmative action plans, working on public campaigns to restrict affirmative action programs, and securing key posts in government, including the judiciary.

THE PRINCIPLES

Clint Bolick is one of the society's most influential members on the topic of affirmative action. Ed Meese has repeatedly praised Bolick and exhorted others to adopt his strategies.[5] Bolick began writing about affirmative action in his law school newspaper when he attended U.C. Davis (King Hall) in the late seventies and early eighties:

> It is irresponsible to promote unqualified students. It is, further, a cruel hoax to send graduates into the legal world who cannot communicate effectively or represent clients competently. . . . The most effective way to inhibit disqualification is to screen applications more carefully. In our frenzy to increase the number of minority students, we should—in fairness to the applicants, community-at-large, and King Hall students—admit only those who are clearly qualified. King Hall must not, and cannot, be a remedial institution for those who have been disadvantaged. It is too late in the educational process for such an effort.[6]

It may seem ironic that Bolick is criticizing a "frenzy" to admit minority students at a law school named after Dr. Martin Luther King Jr. Bolick, however, has always claimed that his colorblind approach to constitutional issues is faithful to King's vision.

Bolick couples his opposition to affirmative action with his libertarian philosophical opposition to government regulation of the economy. As discussed in Chapter 2, he represents small business owners who file suit challenging local regulations that restrict their ability to operate. Bolick's prototypical client is someone like Ego Brown, an African American and a "darned good shoeshine artist" who sued to attack the District of Columbia's regulation of shoeshine vendors.[7] Bolick is in favor of "empowering" the African American community to engage in business and to advance its economic well being through the market, rather than by taking government handouts. In his view, this strategy "by definition *expands* opportunities, as opposed to contemporary civil rights policies that merely redistribute rights."[8]

Federalist Society members and other conservatives argue that using race preferences as a method of affirmative action is both legally wrong and bad government policy. For example, Gerald A. Reynolds, then the president of the Center for New Black Leadership, argued in the Civil Rights Practice Group newsletter, "Racial preferences offend basic notions of fairness and divide society along racial lines."[9] Robert Woodson, the founder and president of the National Center for Neighborhood Enterprise and a resident fellow at the American Enterprise Institute, asserted that affirmative action does not help low income African Americans, but only professionals and unionized workers. He believes that the expectation of help from the government is self-defeating. He argues that in the past,

African Americans were denied an opportunity to achieve by law, but now they are discouraged from competing, "because they were victimized in the past by the existing system and now all they have to do is sit back and wait to be given a gift for past suffering."[10] Woodson preaches self-reliance: "We must say to the victims that racism and discrimination may have knocked them down, but it is the victim who must get up."[11]

Bolick's philosophy emphasizes the importance of individual self-determination. He believes that affirmative action and excessive government regulation have the same negative consequences. He argues that both "a quota that keeps a young Asian student out of a state university" and "a government regulation that keeps an unemployed black man from starting his own business" result in "[reducing] individual autonomy in equal measure."[12]

Bolick believes that civil rights have their origin in natural law as understood by John Locke and Sir William Blackstone in the seventeenth and eighteenth centuries; they believed that individual liberty and the right of private property are equally inviolable. He submits that this is what the framers of the Constitution believed, and that it was also the concept of individual rights that motivated the creation of the Thirteenth, Fourteenth, and Fifteenth Amendments to the Constitution and civil rights legislation after the Civil War.

For Bolick, belief in laissez-faire economics flows directly from this natural rights understanding. He rejects as "manifestly incorrect" Justice Oliver Wendell Holmes's dissent from the majority's decision in the landmark *Lochner* case in 1905, where the Supreme Court held unconstitutional a New York law that protected workers in bakeries by imposing a limitation on the number of hours they could work in a week.[13] The court held that such statutes interfered with "freedom of contract." Holmes had famously written, "[A] constitution is not intended to embody a particular economic theory, whether of paternalism and the organic relation of the citizen to the state or of laissez-faire. . . . The Fourteenth Amendment does not enact Mr. Herbert Spencer's Social Statics."[14] Holmes's view was ultimately adopted by the Supreme Court in 1937 when it stopped striking down wage and hour statutes and began sustaining New Deal legislation. This historic turning point in constitutional law is anathema to Federalist Society members. Bolick contends that Holmes was wrong and that Spencer's natural law philosophy in *Social Statics* did parallel the views of the framers of the Constitution and the Fourteenth Amendment.[15]

Bolick also asserts that civil rights advocates during the first half of the twentieth century (including Martin Luther King Jr. and Thurgood Marshall, during the latter's days as a lawyer for the NAACP) shared this natural law and individual rights conception of civil rights.[16] From that, Bolick argues that the pleas that civil rights advocates made for colorblindness during the years of state-sponsored segregation articulated an absolute principle: that individual liberty requires that government cannot make racial classifications. Chief Justice Roberts made the same argument in *Parents Involved*, which he based in part on the oral argument of the schoolchildren's attorney Robert L. Carter before the Supreme Court in *Brown v.*

Board of Education. Carter had argued, "We have one fundamental contention which we will seek to develop in the course of this argument, and that contention is that no State has any authority under the equal-protection clause of the Fourteenth Amendment to use race as a factor in affording educational opportunities among its citizens."[17] Roberts claimed, "There is no ambiguity in that statement."[18] Thus, Roberts argued that the court's decision in *Parents Involved* was "faithful to the heritage of *Brown*."[19]

Roberts's attempt to dragoon the civil rights lawyers who argued *Brown* into his camp was immediately controversial. The day after the Supreme Court announced the decision in *Parents Involved*, the *New York Times* reported that the plaintiffs' lawyers from *Brown* who were still alive rejected Roberts's characterization of their views. Jack Greenberg called it "preposterous," William T. Coleman Jr. said it was "dirty pool," and Carter himself, then a senior judge of the U.S. District Court in New York, said it stood their argument on its head.[20] Remarkably, Judge Carter had predicted this development in his article "Brown's Legacy: Fulfilling the Promise of Equal Education" in the *Journal of Negro Education*, published three days after the *Parents Involved* opinion on July 1, 2007, but obviously written before the case was decided. Carter described the court challenges to the integration plans in Jefferson County and Seattle and wrote, "These cases illustrate that there are those who seek to have the principles established in Brown used against the cause of equal educational opportunity, ironically seeking to prohibit race-conscious remedies of the continuing effects of a pervasive, historic, and ongoing racism in this country."[21] He explained, "If Brown had been interpreted as requiring integration, as the legal team responsible for it had envisioned and understood it to mean, then perhaps today we might not face a situation where so many Black children are still attending low quality schools with almost exclusively minority student-bodies. Instead, Brown is now widely and incorrectly understood only to require desegregation or the mere removal of the formal legal barriers to integration." He submitted that it is a "watering down and twisting" of the principles behind *Brown* to argue that legislative powers cannot be used "to improve the quality of education for minority students."[22]

Strict Scrutiny

Whenever the Supreme Court reviews legislation to determine whether it is constitutional, it must first decide what standard of review to employ. Our system of separation of powers permits the courts to strike down legislation that violates the Constitution, but also requires the courts to respect the legislature as a coequal branch of government. The issue is how much deference the court should accord the legislature's judgment—specifically, how rigorously the court should review the legitimacy of the legislature's purpose and the efficacy of the means chosen to achieve it. The most lenient standard, the one that applies to most legislation, is "rational basis review." Under it, the court must find a statute constitutional if the purpose of the law was within the powers granted to the legislature by the

Constitution, and if the legislature could have had any rational basis for concluding that the statute would achieve its purpose.

With respect to certain categories of legislation, the court has concluded that the risks of unconstitutional action by the government justify a more rigorous review. The most exacting standard is "strict scrutiny." Under it, legislation must serve a "compelling" (not merely permissible) government purpose and must be "narrowly tailored" to achieve that purpose. "Narrow tailoring" requires that the means must specifically address the ends to be achieved, and not burden the rights of citizens substantially more than necessary to further the government's compelling interest. It is very rare for the court to uphold legislation as constitutional once it subjects the law in question to strict scrutiny.

The Supreme Court first planted the seed of strict scrutiny with respect to racial classifications in *Korematsu v. United States* in 1944 when it reviewed the placement of Japanese Americans in internment camps during World War II.[23] Although the court purported to subject the government's race-based internment policy to "the most rigid scrutiny," it shamefully held that it was constitutional. By the 1960s, a general agreement developed that racial classifications that oppress or disadvantage a historically disfavored class should be reviewed under the strict scrutiny standard.

It is still hotly debated, however, whether strict scrutiny is appropriate when racial classifications, such as affirmative action measures, purport to be for the advantage of a previously disadvantaged class. A majority of the Supreme Court concluded that strict scrutiny was the appropriate test for all racial classifications in *City of Richmond v. J.A. Croson, Co.*, in 1989 (with respect to local and state government action), and in *Adarand Constructors, Inc. v. Pena*, in 1995 (with respect to federal government action).[24] These cases involved requirements or incentives for setting aside a percentage of jobs for racial minorities in the construction industry. The majority followed these precedents in *Parents Involved* and subjected the school districts' plans to strict scrutiny. Chief Justice Roberts argued that strict scrutiny is justified in all cases where there are racial classifications, in part on the ground that it is too difficult to distinguish between invidious uses of racial criteria to harm specific groups and benign uses to help them.

The dissenting Justices Breyer, Stevens, Souter, and Ginsburg, however, disagreed. They argued that given the purpose of the Fourteenth Amendment "to bring into American society as full members those whom the Nation had previously held in slavery," the framers of the amendment "would have understood the legal and practical difference between the use of race-conscious criteria in defiance of that purpose, namely to keep the races apart, and the use of race-conscious criteria to further that purpose, namely to bring the races together."[25]

Even though a majority of the Supreme Court has settled this issue, many federal court judges and constitutional law specialists continue to argue that racial classifications for the purpose of affirmative action should be reviewed under a lower level of scrutiny. Justice Stevens argued that it is untenable to assume there is no significant difference between a decision by the majority to impose a special burden on the members of a minority and a decision by the majority to provide a benefit to that minority despite its incidental burden on some members of the majority. He concluded, "There is no moral or constitutional equivalence between a policy that is designed to perpetuate a caste system and one that seeks to eradicate racial subordination."[26]

Justice Ginsburg concluded that "consistency," with respect to the standard of review, regardless of the purpose for which racial classifications are employed, would only be fitting "were our Nation free of the vestiges of rank discrimination long reinforced by law."[27] She emphasized, however, that "the effects of centuries of law-sanctioned inequality remain painfully evident in our communities and schools."[28] She underscored the relevance of social discrimination in employment, access to health care, and residential housing to diminished educational opportunity.[29]

Roberts's view, on the other hand, is that strict scrutiny is required because racial classification in and of itself is "odious to a free people whose institutions are founded upon the doctrine of equality." In his view, government actions based on race "promote notions of racial inferiority and lead to a politics of racial hostility."[30]

Justice Thomas agrees with Roberts. In his concurring opinion in the *Adarand* case, Thomas concluded that "there is a 'moral [and] constitutional equivalence,' . . . between laws designed to subjugate a race and those that distribute benefits on the basis of race in order to foster some current notion of equality."[31] He finds that "racial paternalism and its unintended consequences can be as poisonous and pernicious as any other form of discrimination." In his view, "benign discrimination" teaches that minorities cannot compete without "patronizing indulgence," and such programs may make minorities dependent on them at the same time they breed resentment among others who believe they have been wronged by affirmative action.[32]

Courts of Appeals judges Alex Kozinski in the Ninth Circuit and Michael Boudin in the First Circuit argued that affirmative action programs were not "aimed at oppressing blacks," were "certainly more benign than laws that favor or disfavor one race, segregate by race, or create quotas for or against a racial group," and were "far from the original evils at which the Fourteenth Amendment was addressed."[33] In *Parents Involved*, Justice Thomas concluded that the opinions of Kozinski and Boudin were "inimical to the Constitution and to this Court's precedents."[34]

It may be argued that the criticism that affirmative action racial classifications "stamp minorities with a badge of inferiority," as Thomas puts it, is misleading. It draws attention away from the more significant problem, which is the underlying historical assumption of African American inferiority that has always driven issues of race in America. For example, in *Parents Involved*, Roberts argues that the Supreme Court in *Brown* "held that segregation deprived black children of equal educational opportunities regardless of whether school facilities and other tangible factors were equal, because government classification and separation on grounds of race themselves denoted inferiority."[35] His analysis stops there. This view, however, takes *Brown* out of its historical context. Abstract characterization of the consequences of classification ignores the reality in which *Brown* was decided—the social system that had begun with slavery and was perpetuated with nearly a century of legally enforced apartheid, in which the institutions of the Jim Crow South were designed to reinforce the notion of African American inferiority and defend white privilege and power. As Justice Breyer put it in his dissenting opinion, "segregation policies did not simply tell schoolchildren 'where they could and could not go to school based on the color of their skin'; they perpetuated a caste system rooted in the institutions of slavery and 80 years of legalized subordination."[36]

An assumption of African American inferiority has been deeply rooted historically in our nation's racial consciousness and social institutions. This assumption was not created by the law. Judge A. Leon Higginbotham Jr. has explained that the social assumption of inferiority is the dominant principle that drove jurisprudence with respect to race. Other precepts of slavery jurisprudence were different. For example, the master's property rights in his slaves were eliminated once the law abolished slavery. Property rights were created by the law and could be dissolved by the law. In contrast, the assumption of inferiority "spoke to the state of the mind and the logic of the heart. It posed as an article of faith that African Americans were not quite altogether human." Law did not create this concept of inferiority, because the colonists were prepared to regard Africans as inferior from the moment they first arrived as slaves. The Thirteenth Amendment could abolish slavery, but not the precept of inferiority. Later, "when the law abolished state-enforced racial segregation, it still did not eliminate the precept."[37]

This suggests that challenging underlying assumptions of African American inferiority requires equal access to education through programs that address the reality of historical discrimination. Thus, Judge Higginbotham favored affirmative action plans.[38]

The purpose of the Fourteenth Amendment was to guarantee liberty and the benefits of citizenship to the class of African Americans recently freed from slavery. Therefore, many scholars and jurists conclude that the Fourteenth Amendment prohibits *subordination* based on race, but not all *classifications* based on race. Stanford law professor Pamela Karlan, for example, has criticized the *Parents Involved* Court for requiring a symmetrical reading of the equal protection clause. She does not agree that all race-conscious government action, whether it serves to segregate or to integrate civic institutions, is equally suspect.[39] She argues that the vice that originally concerned the Supreme Court in *Brown v. Board of Education* "was neither the provision of inferior tangible facilities nor the simple separation of groups. It was subordination."[40] Karlan criticizes Chief Justice Roberts for characterizing *Brown* as an anticlassification decision, noting that "all of the ringing language in the Court's [*Brown*] opinion sounded in antisubordination."[41] Yale law professor Stephen L. Carter says:

> [T]o say that two centuries of struggle for the most basic of civil rights have been mostly about freedom from racial categorization rather than freedom from racial oppressio[n] is to trivialize the lives and deaths of those who have suffered under

racism. To pretend . . . that the issue presented in *Bakke* [a challenge to affirmative action by a white applicant to medical school] was the same as the issue in *Brown* is to pretend that history never happened and that the present doesn't exist.[42]

Focusing on racial classification obscures the fact that racism is not merely a system that distinguishes one race from another, but more importantly one that allocates power to the white race and denies power to minority races. Focusing on racial subordination as the fundamental evil at which the equal protection clause is aimed would lead to the conclusion that it is not necessary to subject all racial classifications to strict scrutiny.

Compelling Government Interests

When strict scrutiny is used as the standard, racial classifications by the government must serve a "compelling government interest" to be constitutional. In recent cases, the Supreme Court has recognized only two interests as compelling: (1) remedying past intentional discrimination by the government body regulated by the classification, and (2) diversity, broadly defined, in higher education.

The Supreme Court has limited the circumstances in which remedying prior discrimination can be invoked to justify racial classifications, as *Parents Involved* demonstrates. Chief Justice Roberts concluded that past discrimination did not justify the use of racial classifications in the school assignment plans. In his view, the history of each community did not demonstrate that the purpose of racial classifications was to provide a remedy for past intentional discrimination. In Seattle, there had never been a judicial determination that the city maintained a system of legally required separation of the races in schools (*de jure* segregation). With respect to Jefferson County, a federal court had found in 1973 that the county maintained a segregated school system. The system operated under a desegregation decree of the federal court until 2000, when the court closed the case, concluding that the county had achieved "unitary status" by eliminating "to the greatest extent practicable" the vestiges of the prior policy of segregation. Thus, the historic *de jure* segregation of schools in Jefferson County was deemed remedied by the federal court decree that was terminated in 2000.

Many Federalist Society members do not believe that diversity can ever be a compelling justification for racial classifications. Federalist Society members and their allies have bombarded the federal courts with briefs arguing that diversity is not a compelling government interest ever since Justice Powell raised the issue in the *Bakke* case in 1978, discussed below.[43]

Nonetheless, the Supreme Court recognized that diversity in higher education, defined as "all factors that may contribute to student body diversity," was a compelling interest in *Grutter v. Bollinger* in 2003, a decision upholding the affirmative action plan of the University of Michigan Law School.[44] The plan considered race only as one of several diversity contributions given substantial weight in admitting students. On the same day, the court struck down the plan employed by the University of Michigan's College of Literature, Science, and the Arts, because it automatically awarded "plus points" to members of minority groups in making admissions decisions. This failed the narrow tailoring test, because of its exclusive reliance on race. In both cases, however, the court recognized diversity in higher education to be a compelling government interest.

In *Parents Involved*, Roberts limited the diversity justification for race-conscious measures to higher education. Only Justices Scalia, Thomas, and Alito joined this portion of the Roberts opinion; thus, it was not approved by a majority of the court. Dissenting justices Breyer, Stevens, Ginsburg, and Souter found that increasing diversity in high schools and elementary schools, including for the purpose of avoiding racial isolation, was a compelling government interest. Justice Kennedy wrote a separate concurring opinion in which he agreed that the plans in this case were unconstitutional because they were not narrowly tailored. He concluded, however, that "[d]iversity, depending on its meaning and definition, is a compelling educational goal a school district may pursue."[45] Thus, a majority of the justices in *Parents Involved* concluded that diversity in education before college might be a compelling government interest, although the parameters of when Kennedy would recognize it to be so were not clearly spelled out.

Roberts limited diversity as a compelling interest to higher education by arguing that in *Grutter* the court "relied upon considerations unique to institutions of higher education, noting that in light of 'the expansive freedoms of speech and thought associated with the university environment, universities occupy a special niche in our constitutional tradition.'"[46] Roberts provided little explanation for why diversity would not be as important in high school or elementary school as in a university. In an earlier landmark case, *Swann v. Charlotte-Mecklenburg Board of Education* (1971), the Supreme Court had suggested that as a matter of "educational policy" it would be within the "broad discretionary powers of school authorities" to conclude "that in order to prepare students to live in a pluralistic society each school should have a prescribed ratio of Negro to white students reflecting the proportion for the district of a whole."[47] Roberts rejected this language from *Swann* as mere dicta (legal pronouncements not necessary to the actual decision of a case and hence technically not binding on later decisions). The dissenters, on the other hand, relied heavily on this principle and argued that, although dicta, it had achieved "wide acceptance in the legal culture."[48]

Seattle and Jefferson County argued that "educational and broader socialization benefits flow from a racially diverse learning environment." Because they were specifically seeking racial diversity—not the broader diversity at issue in *Grutter*—they argued that "it makes sense to promote that interest directly by relying on race alone."[49] The chief justice rejected these arguments. He distinguished the purpose of these plans—to have the racial balance of individual schools mirror the racial balance of the district as a whole—from a purpose to maintain a particular level of diversity required to obtain the asserted educational benefits. Roberts concluded that whatever merit the latter approach might have, the former sought racial balance "pure and simple," an illegitimate goal. He reasoned that racial balancing runs counter to the notion that equal protection requires the government to treat citizens as individuals rather than as members of a class. He predicted that accepting racial balancing as a permissible government goal

> would "effectively assur[e] that race will always be relevant in American life, and that the 'ultimate goal' of eliminating entirely from governmental decisionmaking such irrelevant factors as a human being's race" will never be achieved.[50]

When the school districts argued that their compelling government interests were racial diversity, avoidance of racial isolation, and racial integration, Roberts said that all those interests amounted to simple racial balancing and rejected the districts' argument.

The dissenting Justices Breyer, Stevens, Souter, and Ginsburg took the position that the Constitution permits local governments to adopt desegregation plans even where it does not require them to do so. They argued that the goal of integration and the avoidance of racial isolation in schools was a compelling government interest that justified the plans in this case. The dissenters also argued that "the distinction between *de jure* segregation (caused by school systems) and *de facto* segregation (caused, *e.g.*, by housing patterns or generalized societal discrimination)" was "meaningless" in the context of this case.[51]

The compelling interest in integration recognized by the dissenting opinion has three elements:

> First, there is a historical and remedial element: an interest in setting right the consequences of prior conditions of segregation. . . . Second, there is an educational element: an interest in overcoming the adverse educational effects produced by and associated with highly segregated schools. . . . Third, there is a democratic element: an interest in producing an educational environment that reflects the "pluralistic society" in which our children will live.[52]

The dissenters argued that the court should give deference to the school districts' decisions that the plans were an appropriate means to achieve integration. Justice Thomas, however, said the deference argument was equivalent to the approach the "segregationists" had taken in *Brown*.[53] Thomas also accused the dissenters of replicating the arguments from *Plessy v. Ferguson* (the 1896 decision regarding segregated railroad cars that approved the doctrine of separate but equal) that the segregationists made in *Brown*.[54] Thomas's friend Clint Bolick has also frequently argued that affirmative action proponents are no better than segregationists.[55] He claims that "the left has keep the flickering flame of *Plessy* alive" by embracing the notion that race is a "reasonable" basis on which to make distinctions.[56]

Thomas also argued that the racial balancing programs of the school districts were motivated only by "an interest in classroom aesthetics and a hypersensitivity to elite sensibilities."[57] Here Thomas echoes a common conservative criticism of affirmative action—that it is driven by the agenda of the liberal academic elite. Federalist Society member Lino A. Graglia, one of the most conservative and outspoken academics in the United States, categorically rejects the diversity rationale for affirmative action. He concludes, "Race is not a proxy for anything relevant to higher education. . . . What whites and Asians are most likely to learn or think they learn from the presence of less qualified blacks in their class is that even the most advantaged blacks tend not to be fully academically competitive."[58] He argues that the recognition in the *Bakke* case that diversity might justify race-conscious admissions policies was explained by the fact that "[r]ace preferences, however, were, then as now, so strongly favored by liberal academic opinion, the usual basis of Supreme Court constitutional rulings, as to make a total prohibition unlikely."[59]

Graglia's explanations for why liberal academics favor racial preferences run from misguided altruism to selfish motivations. In one article, he writes that "high-minded and self-sacrificing" academics are incapable of understanding that racial preferences and quotas can never be made acceptable to the majority of Americans who are motivated by self-interest.[60] Elsewhere, he suggests that the purpose of racial preferences in higher education "is not to benefit blacks but to relieve the distress that being part of a nonblack institution would cause liberal white administrators and faculty."[61]

Graglia also contends that "[r]ace preference programs in higher education are simply attempts to hide or ignore, rather than have to admit and face, the fact of an 'immense racial gulf in cognitive skills.'"[62] He says that "we have 'diversity' programs only because blacks as a group are not academically competitive with whites and Asians."[63] He concludes, "The reality at the root of race preference programs in higher education is that very few blacks meet the ordinary admission standards of elite schools, and this is seen by liberal academics as both unchangeable and politically and ideologically intolerable."[64]

Whether or not he is accurate in his characterization of liberal academics, Graglia himself has suggested that racial group differences may be innate: "It may be that we will have to accept that there may be racial group differences that we cannot eradicate and, more important, that we have no need to eradicate. We have no need, for example, to equate personal worth with academic aptitude."[65]

Social Discrimination

Some advocates of affirmative action have sought to use race-conscious means to remedy the underrepresentation of minorities that has resulted from social discrimination, although the institution where they would be enrolled or employed has no provable history of intentional discrimination. They argue that a complex matrix of historical discrimination in a variety of social institutions and practices leads to the underrepresentation of minorities in schools and jobs. They contend that it is impossible to address the consequences of diffuse social discrimination by assessing schools and employers individually and requiring proof of overt culpable misconduct.

Conservatives argue that when the rationale for using racial classifications is previous discrimination, there must be proof of intentional discrimination by the institution in question. Limiting government's role in addressing societal discrimination appeals to conservatives both because of their analysis of race and because in general they prefer small government. Rejecting societal discrimination as a justification for race-conscious government action has long been a priority for conservatives. In the government's amicus brief in the 1986 Supreme Court case of *Wygant v. Jackson Board of Education*, President Reagan's solicitor general argued in favor of a mandatory "last hired, first fired" policy, opposing Jackson, Michigan's policy of protecting the jobs of recently hired minority teachers from layoffs.[66] The federal government dismissed the city's concerns about societal discrimination, underrepresentation of minority teachers, and the need to supply role models for minority students as a "casual waving aside" of fundamental Fourteenth Amendment principles. The signers of the brief included Federalist Society members William Bradford Reynolds, Charles J. Cooper, Michael Carvin, and Samuel A. Alito Jr., who had become a justice of the Supreme Court by the time of the *Parents Involved* decision. Along the same lines, in one of its 1988 reports to the attorney general, the Office of Legal Policy underlined that the equitable powers of the federal courts to achieve desegregation should be limited to remedies for "specific violations," not for "broad and systemic social problems."[67]

The conservative argument has prevailed in the Supreme Court. Thus, racial imbalance in a school that results from something other than intentional discrimination by that school district is not a problem that can be addressed by the explicit use of race in student assignment decisions. Racial imbalance in a government workforce cannot be addressed by taking race into account in hiring, unless there has been intentional discrimination by that government employer.

Chief Justice Roberts broadly concluded in *Parents Involved* that "remedying past societal discrimination does not justify race-conscious government action."[68] This means that much of our social history is deemed irrelevant to whether race may be taken into account in fashioning a remedy for the underrepresentation of minorities in a particular institution. In *Parents Involved*, for example, the school districts sought to employ racial classifications to address underrepresentation in the schools caused by residential housing segregation. The court held that this was unconstitutional.

Limiting past behavior that can be addressed by race-conscious remedies to *intentional* discrimination leaves much discrimination without a remedy. The court's current doctrine does not permit the use of racial classifications to remedy problems of what may be termed institutional racism. By that, we mean systems that predictably result in racial imbalance through deeply ingrained, although frequently unconscious, patterns of perception, classification, affinity, and associations. Contemporary scholarship demonstrates that the most significant causes of discrimination in the United States today are of this institutional and unconscious nature.[69]

The Fourteenth Amendment's Equal Protection Clause
Guarantees Equal Opportunity, Not Equal Results

In almost every case where affirmative action is proposed, it is necessary to ask how "equal protection of the law" should be measured. Is it sufficient that members of minority groups are given the right to apply for admission to schools or to apply for jobs? Or should compliance with the equal protection clause be determined by whether the students are admitted and the job applicants actually hired?

Conservatives criticize affirmative action programs because they seek equality with respect to results and not merely with respect to opportunity. For example, Professor Lino A. Graglia has written, "The tragedy of the Civil Rights Act of 1964 is that it fell into the hands of bureaucrats and judges who saw the total abolition of racial discrimination by government and business as much too limited a goal, and saw proportional representation by race in all institutions and activities as a more desirable objective."[70] Clint Bolick opined that the Left had abandoned any "claim to moral leadership in the field of civil rights" by seeking equal results over equal opportunity. "The Left," he said, "learned all too well the lesson of the white supremacists it earlier had so bitterly opposed: that government's power to discriminate is awesome once unleashed, and that it can confer enormous tribute upon its beneficiaries."[71] For these conservatives, "equal opportunity" is achieved once intentional, overt discrimination has been eliminated. Only formal equality of opportunity matters. It is not necessary to determine whether social discrimination, poverty, environmental distractions, and the phenomenon of white privilege have undermined true equality of opportunity.

Affirmative action proponents argue that results are one significant measure of whether opportunity has been equal in fact and not merely in form. The conservative response is that unequal results are to be expected, in part echoing the social Darwinism of late nineteenth- and early twentieth-century philosophers. Bolick goes further back and cites Thomas Paine in support of his argument that equality of rights does not guarantee equality in outcomes. Paine wrote, "That property will ever be unequal is certain. Industry, superiority of talents, dexterity of management, extreme frugality, fortunate opportunities, or the opposite, or the means of those things, will ever produce that effect."[72] On the bench, Justice Thomas agrees that only equal opportunity, not equal results, is constitutionally guaranteed. In the *Adarand* case, he concluded, "Government cannot make us equal; it can only recognize, respect, and protect us as equal before the law."[73]

The Fourteenth Amendment's Equal Protection Clause
Secures the Interests of Individuals, Not Groups

In *Parents Involved*, Chief Justice Roberts emphasized that the equal protection clause of the Fourteenth Amendment "protect[s] *persons*, not *groups*," citing the court's opinion in *Adarand*.[74] The notion that the Fourteenth Amendment protects only individuals is an essential element of the conservative understanding of the equal protection clause. It limits both the scope of discrimination that can be considered as a justification for affirmative action measures, and the scope of who may benefit from such measures. This argument suggests that only a person who has personally suffered discriminatory treatment is entitled to a remedy. The fact that African Americans have been historically underrepresented at a school or in a work place does not give an African American applicant any greater entitlement to a place at the school or to a job than a white applicant has. It follows that race-conscious measures are inappropriate remedies for the underrepresentation of a minority group as a class.

Civil rights advocates argue that the focus on individual rights ignores the fact that the Fourteenth Amendment was enacted to assist the freed slaves as a class. They submit that the civil rights movement and its judicial successes in the mid–nineteenth century were intended to benefit the entire minority population. Slavery and state sponsored apartheid were institutions designed to oppress the minority races and to benefit the dominant white race as a class, not discrete acts directed at individuals. Hence, the civil rights advocates argue that remedies for a class of victims of discrimination are appropriate under the equal protection clause.

Affirmative Action Unfairly Penalizes Innocent Individuals with No Responsibility for Discrimination

A corollary of the argument that the Fourteenth Amendment protects only individuals is the argument that whites or males who do not get admitted to schools or offered jobs because of affirmative action plans suffer unfairly as innocent victims. Indeed, Alan Bakke, Cheryl Hopwood, Barbara Grutter, and Jennifer Gratz, the white plaintiffs in the "reverse discrimination" cases discussed in this chapter, argued that their Fourteenth Amendment rights as individuals entitled to equal protection of the law were violated by affirmative action programs.

Perhaps whites and males who do not get into schools or accepted for employment are "innocent" in the sense that they did not create or control the mechanisms of discrimination that led to the underrepresentation of minorities and women. Nonetheless, it can be argued that whites and males are the historical beneficiaries of privileges that centuries of discrimination have created, and that they approach the application process for schools and jobs with a head start.

Racism Has Largely Been Overcome in the United States

In 1998, Federalist Society member Roger Clegg reviewed *America in Black and White* by Stephan and Abigail Thernstrom in the newsletter of the Civil Rights Practice Group.[75] He wrote, "The most interesting conclusion to be drawn from it is the enormous progress achieved by blacks—economically, socially, and legally—well before the passage of the civil rights statutes, and certainly before the use of pro-minority racial preferences became institutionalized." As to ongoing racial problems, Clegg adopted the Thernstroms' view that African Americans themselves are largely to blame: "'No issue so poisons relations between the races as that of black crime,' stress the Thernstroms. 'If the African American crime rate suddenly dropped to the current level of the white crime rate, we would eliminate a major force that is driving blacks and whites apart and is destroying the fabric of black urban life.'"

Other authors in Federalist Society publications explain racial imbalance in various sectors of American life as something other than a consequence of racism. Conservative author and former American Enterprise Institute fellow Dinesh D'Souza departs from fellow conservatives who argue that colorblindness alone will achieve equitable results in American society. D'Souza believes that both equality of rights for individuals and equality of results for groups are important. He acknowledges that equality of rights for individuals will not lead to equality of results for groups, but argues that this is not the result of racism. He concludes, "The real problem is that African-Americans are not competitive with other groups in our society."[76] D'Souza claims to reject arguments based on genetic or biological inferiority. Instead, he contends that African Americans have suffered from: a cultural breakdown, characterized by excessive reliance on government; virtual paranoia that racism is to blame for all their problems, including personal ones; hostility to academic achievement, which is very often dismissed as a form of "acting white"; a call to violence; and the normalization of illegitimacy in the inner city.[77] In D'Souza's view, it is time to abandon the tenets of cultural relativism that hold that all cultures are equal. Instead, he argues that what is needed is "a concerted and direct effort to raise the cultural standards of all groups and particularly that of blacks."[78]

Brian W. Jones, a director of the Center for New Black Leadership and the former editor of the Federalist Society Civil Rights Practice Group newsletter, blamed liberal critics of the Supreme Court for the fact that as of 1999 less than 4 percent of the justices' clerks had been Hispanic or African American. Jones argued that liberal critics had "responded furiously to the Court's restrained civil-rights jurisprudence in recent years and have savaged those who would dare to agree with the Court's approach." Thus, he concluded, "Given the civil-rights left's concerted effort to poison the well of conservatism, does it not stand to reason that the pool of minority students seeking to clerk for the justices might perhaps be more limited than it otherwise might be in a world where genuine diversity is appreciated?"[79]

The extent to which one believes racism remains a serious problem in the United States depends in part on how racism is defined. Conservatives tend to limit the definition of racism to conscious discrimination based on race. For example, in 1996, frequent Federalist Society speaker and honoree Judge Laurence H. Silberman of the D.C. Circuit Court of Appeals objected to the wide-ranging inquiries undertaken by the Judicial Council's Task Force on Gender, Race, and Ethnic Bias. He argued that the term "bias" should be limited to discrimination or unequal treatment.[80] Judge Silberman dismissed as an excess of political correctness the idea that there might be a more subtle relationship between gender or race bias and decision making. He was particularly offended by the suggestion that gender or racial bias might affect the substantive outcomes of cases. He argued that this was an inappropriate matter for the Task Force to investigate.

The view that racism is manifested only through conscious discrimination underlies the currently accepted doctrine that to prove a violation of the equal protection clause when a government policy does not make explicit racial classifications, one must demonstrate not only a disparate impact on a minority, but an underlying intent to discriminate. The Supreme Court adopted this principle in 1976 in *Washington v. Davis*, where it held that it was not sufficient to prove that a written entrance examination for the police department excluded African Americans at a rate more than four times greater than the rate for whites, and that the test had not been shown to be job related.[81] The court held that to establish a constitutional violation, the African American recruits would have to prove the test was adopted with the intent to discriminate against them.

Federalist Society members have long believed that requiring proof of intentional discrimination, not merely disparate impact, should be required to establish a violation of the equal protection clause. In *Report to the Attorney General: The Constitution in the Year 2000*, the Office of Legal Policy in the Reagan administration devoted a chapter to the question "Will the Supreme Court define discrimination in terms of 'disparate impact' and thereby use the Equal Protection Clause to require race and gender 'affirmative action' policies?"[82] Noting that some civil rights advocates had argued for eliminating the intent requirement and using a disparate impact analysis in constitutional claims, the authors concluded, "This debate goes to the very heart of how our society will define 'civil rights' and 'discrimination' in the future."[83] The authors noted that a disparate impact analysis would affect any government policy that affects minority groups in a disproportionate statistical manner, including imposition of the death penalty, government testing, voting procedures, housing policies, veterans' preferences, school desegregation, economic legislation, tax policy, and "affirmative action programs that burden non-minorities." They predicted that an effects test in constitutional cases would raise the question of whether "the government's failure to act to remedy general societal discrimination violates equal protection guarantees."[84]

A broader understanding of racism, however, perceives that discrimination is "deeply ingrained in our society's institutions and culture," "often sustained through institutional structures, implicit categorization and processing, and historical dimensions of racial inequality," and "subconscious."[85] Indeed, this was the understanding of the Seattle School District. Its efforts to explore the issue of institutional racism were bitterly criticized by conservatives in the blogosphere and elsewhere. The district's website had included a definition of "cultural racism" as "[t]hose aspects of society that overtly and covertly attribute value and normality to white people and whiteness, and devalue, stereotype, and label people of color as 'other,' different, less than, or render them invisible."[86] Andrew Coulson, director of the Cato Institute's Center for Educational Freedom, attacked this definition as "ideologically charged," "left of center," and "incredibly polarizing."[87]

In a similar vein, in *Parents Involved* Chief Justice Roberts highlighted an assertion by Seattle's director of equity and race relations that the district website was not intended "to hold onto unsuccessful concepts such as melting pot or colorblind mentality"; Roberts contrasted this with "Our Constitution is color-blind and neither knows nor tolerates classes among citizens," John Marshall Harlan's famous statement of dissent in *Plessy v. Ferguson*.[88]

Judge Robert L. Carter, one of the plaintiffs' lawyers in *Brown v. Board of Education*, rejects the rose-colored version of racial progress that conservatives have proclaimed:

> Some Whites claim to labor under the outrageous belief that because the Supreme Court declared Blacks to be entitled to equal treatment under the law, any continued racial disparity must be a result of Blacks' own failure to take advantage of the opportunities afforded them. Such views do not take into account the actual availability and accessibility of those supposed equal opportunities. . . . However, the application of free market principles to low-income minority communities assumes a certain level of mobility and access to information that does not take account of current realities. This supposition by policymakers ignores the continued lack of resources and discrimination experienced by large segments of Blacks in this country.[89]

Justice Thurgood Marshall also criticized the assumption that racial discrimination was "largely a phenomenon of the past." He did not believe that this country was "anywhere close to eradicating racial discrimination or its vestiges."[90]

Government Action Must Be Colorblind, Rather Than Color Conscious

Conservatives maintain that the Constitution is colorblind. The most frequently cited source for this principle is Justice Harlan's dissent from the separate but equal doctrine in *Plessy v. Ferguson*, where he famously declared,

> The white race deems itself to be the dominant race in this country. And so it is, in prestige, in achievements, in education, in wealth, and in power. So, I doubt not, it will continue to be for all time, if it remains true to its great heritage, and holds fast to the principles of constitutional liberty. But in view of the constitution, in the eye of the law, there is in this country no superior, dominant, ruling class of citizens. There is no caste here. Our constitution is color-blind, and neither knows nor tolerates classes among citizens.[91]

Despite this passage's iconic position as an early rejection of *de jure* discrimination, it is also noteworthy for Harlan's assumption that the social and economic superiority of the white race could be permanent. As Professor Jamin Raskin has noted, colorblindness was presented by Harlan as a principle of formal neutrality, "perfectly compatible with the perpetuation of white supremacy in the economic field, in the political field, and in the cultural field."[92]

Moreover, as Professor Goodwin Liu has explained, the "colorblind" reference follows Harlan's elucidation of the fact that "the law" allows "no superior, dominant ruling class" and no "caste."⁹³ Liu concludes that the phrase "our Constitution is color-blind" "does not clearly state a categorical principle against classification by race," but rather restates the principle of the preceding sentences that "the Constitution does not permit government to validate or perpetuate a race-based system of social hierarchy."⁹⁴ He argues that Harlan did not endorse colorblindness as Roberts employs the term. He notes that in several cases Harlan tolerated discrimination against Chinese immigrants, and that he limited his vision of racial equality to the civil rights that are fundamental to citizenship in a republican government. Indeed, Harlan either wrote or joined other legal opinions that sanctioned discrimination against African Americans.⁹⁵

Chief Justice Roberts relied on Harlan's opinion in *Parents Involved* to argue for a colorblind interpretation of the Constitution. Justice Kennedy, however, said that Harlan's observation that the Constitution is colorblind was justified in the context of *Plessy*, and that "as an aspiration, Justice Harlan's axiom must command our assent." Nonetheless, he concluded, "In the real world, it is regrettable to say, it cannot be a universal constitutional principle."⁹⁶

Boston University economics professor Glenn C. Loury, writing in the Federalist Society's *Harvard Journal of Law and Public Policy*, concluded that, "establishing the colorblind principle is the only way to secure lasting civil equality for the descendants of slaves."⁹⁷ Philosophically, Loury believes that "the most important challenges and opportunities confronting any person arise not from his racial condition, but from our common human condition."⁹⁸ Human beings can transcend racial differences because they are "identical in essentials, different only in details."⁹⁹ On the other hand, "unless individualism is truly exalted, multiculturalism descends into crass ethnic cheerleading."¹⁰⁰ Loury argues that by racializing politics, blacks have become dependent on left-wing policies that expand the welfare state, increase taxes, promulgate more regulations, and give blacks political representation only in gerrymandered electoral districts. In so doing, they have ignored the "white rightward drift" in the country and failed to grasp opportunities to make alliances with conservatives. To overcome the problem, Loury proposes "that we suppress as much as possible the explicit use of racial categories in our discourses about public affairs."¹⁰¹

Speaking at the same symposium, Raskin rejected Loury's suggestion that "racial thinking somehow began on the left" and noted that our basic documents were cast in racial terms, citing the description of Native Americans in the Declaration of Independence as "merciless Indian Savages" and the structural protection of slavery in the Constitution.¹⁰² He argues, "In the real world today, the only alternative to multiculturalism is a return to cultural and political white supremacy."¹⁰³ Raskin views multiculturalism "as the contemporary expression in America of what Hegel called the 'human struggle for recognition.'" He continues, "People who have been locked out, disenfranchised, and silenced finally enter the public space. They want to be seen. They demand to be heard."¹⁰⁴

Gender and Affirmative Action

Federalist Society publications have provided a forum for harsh criticism of affirmative action based on gender. Civil Rights Practice Group newsletter articles criticized Title IX of the Education Amendments of 1972 on the ground that it established a "quota system" for male and female participation in college athletics. The argument is that men and boys are hapless victims of feminist extremism. For example, Kimberly Schuld, the director of Play Fair, a project of the Independent Women's Forum, complained, "The control that feminist political leaders wield over our college campuses and K-12 education policy has systematically pushed men and boys to the fringes of the systems."[105] Melinda Sidak, a member of the National Advisory Board of the Independent Women's Forum, charged that the "new quota system" resulting from the courts' interpretations of Title IX would "force colleges to cut sports participation opportunities for men."[106] She explains that Title IX has not been amended to remedy this problem because "most members of Congress of both parties are utterly spineless when it comes to standing up to feminist demands, no matter how contrary to common sense or to the real interests and desires of ordinary American women."[107] Jennifer Cabranes Braceras, a member of the Civil Rights Practice Group, criticized the Title IX regulations as having "created a vast and rigid quota system."[108]

Christina Hoff Sommers provided a critique of Title IX at a student Federalist Society meeting at Suffolk University Law School in October 2009.[109] Sommers, a resident scholar at the American Enterprise Institute and the author of several books, including *Who Stole Feminism?* and *The War against Boys*, spoke on the topic "When Bad Things Happen to Good Law: The Truth About Title IX."

Sommers's principal theme was that efforts to create parity for women have driven men from the playing field, both in sports and in higher education generally. Boys are "languishing" behind girls, and in almost every activity in schools, girls are "in charge." She noted that women now constitute a majority of the students in college and in a large number of graduate schools. This is true, but research demonstrates that this is a very complex issue that exists in most developed countries and impacts people of different ages and from different classes and races differently.[110] Sommers simply argued that young men perceive college as a "hostile environment" where no one cares about them. The "number one reason" boys drop out of college is because "I just felt like nobody wanted me there." The reality, however, is that boys and girls graduating from high school enter college at almost the same rate. The gender gap is explained in part by the fact that among older students returning to college after having been in the work force, women outnumber men almost 2 to 1.[111]

The "paradox of the evening" according to the speaker was the question of how to get boys to go to college. Her answer—football. More schools need to have teams, because 20 to 30 percent of boys are "sportsoholics" who don't even care if they get to play. They are happy to sit on the bench; they just want to be near the game. Based on her assertion that 95 percent of the participants in "fantasy football" leagues are male, Sommers concluded that greater interest in sports on the part of males was "something very deep in human nature." The problem, she stated, is that more schools cannot start football teams because of Title IX.

Sommers blamed an "advocacy gap" for the fact that society was indifferent to the problems of boys. This claim is typical of the strategy of contemporary conservatives to grossly understate their own power and influence in order to argue for more. Noting that there were 112 advocacy groups for women, she charged that "there are no groups that represent a different point of view that have any impact in Washington." Sommers evidently hoped the audience would ignore her own affiliation with the American Enterprise Institute and the fact that the gathering itself was a meeting of the Federalist Society, which has extraordinary influence in Washington. Along the same lines, she bemoaned the fact that when former Harvard University president Lawrence Summers had spoken of differences in aptitude between men and women, the criticism he received had been "career annihilating." Again, the speaker ignored the fact that Summers became the director of the White House National Economic Council and retained his professorship at the John F. Kennedy School of Government at Harvard.

Sommers criticized participants at an Obama White House conference on women's issues for their intention to campaign for greater inclusion of women in science and engineering. She asked, "Can you imagine what this country would be like if it had no male engineers?" Arguing that it was men, after returning from fighting World War II, who built the strength that the United States has today, Sommers raised the specter of the United States losing its competitive advantage in the global economy if male participation in higher education continues to decline.

The criticisms that Schuld, Sidak, Braceras, and Sommers make of Title IX misrepresent the law in this area. Title IX, enacted in 1972, states, "No person in the United States shall, on the basis of sex, be excluded from participation in, be denied the benefits of, or be subjected to discrimination under any education program or activity receiving Federal financial assistance."[112] The statute is not limited to athletics, but sports have proven to be an important area of enforcement.

The Office for Civil Rights (OCR) of the Department of Education interpreted Title IX in 1979 to permit institutions to demonstrate compliance with the statute with respect to sports in any one of three ways: (1) by showing that the ratio of women to men in the intercollegiate athletic program is substantially proportional to the ratio of women to men in the student body; (2) by demonstrating a history and continuing practice of program expansion responsive to the interests and abilities of an underrepresented sex; or (3) by showing that the interests and abilities of the members of the underrepresented sex are fully and effectively accommodated by the present program. With regard to the third method, the burden of proof is on complainants to prove that there is unmet demand, not on a university to prove that no such demand exists.[113]

Schuld, Sidak, and Sommers claim that Title IX is enforced only through the proportionality test and thus is a quota system. Schuld, for example, argued that the second test would not avail schools that had already expanded women's programs to the maximum and that the third test was "functionally useless." Thus, Schuld contended, schools were left only with the proportionality test, which in effect requires cutting men's sports where there is a budget shortfall for athletics programs. As she put it, "Feminist leaders are out to destroy one of the last bastions of maleness—the varsity team."

Schuld's argument that the "unmet demand" criterion is functionally useless is based on her reading of the district court opinion in *Cohen v. Brown University*, an influential Title IX case in 1992. She argues that the court rejected proof of no unmet demand on the ground that the OCR had provided no vehicle for measuring compliance under that standard. This is simply not true.[114] Women athletes sued Brown because it had demoted women's gymnastics and volleyball teams from university-funded varsity status to donor-funded intercollegiate club status, which Brown officials acknowledged was a "step down." The court found that Brown had not fully accommodated women because it had denied varsity status to the teams despite interest and ability to perform on the varsity level. The court noted that if there were no other women who wanted to compete on varsity teams, or if Brown had attempted to create new women's varsity teams but there was no interest or ability to participate, or if women had not asked Brown to establish any new varsity teams, the university would have a defense to the Title IX complaint. Brown, however, had not offered such evidence. On appeal, the First Circuit Court of Appeals held that Brown had violated Title IX because there was interest and ability for women's varsity sports not being met by its current program.[115] The court repeatedly stressed that Title IX was not a quota program and that the proportionality inquiry was only the first step of the analysis and was not determinative of whether a school was in compliance with the statue.

F. Carolyn Graglia, an attorney who chose to leave her legal career to work as a housewife—she is married to Lino Graglia—also makes harsh criticisms of affirmative action law with respect to gender. She describes affirmative action as something "upon which feminism later capitalized to make alleged victimhood profitable."[116] She criticizes feminism for driving women into the workplace and for bringing about a "sea-change in men" with the result that "many males accepted the new androgyny that feminism had helped engender and capitulated to feminist demands that impaired men's earning abilities."[117]

Writing in the Civil Rights Practice Group newsletter, Anita K. Blair, the executive vice president and general counsel of the Independent Women's Forum and the author of its amicus brief in *United States v. Virginia*, criticized the Supreme Court's decision in that case, which mandated the admission of women to the Virginia Military Institute(VMI).[118] She argued the decision "effectively prohibits states from treating individuals differently on the basis of sex." Virginia was represented in the Supreme Court by the prominent Federalist Society lawyer Ted Olson, who defended the exclusion of women from VMI.

IMPLEMENTING THE AGENDA

Federalist Society members have advanced the foregoing principles in a wide variety of forums since the early 1980s. The 2012 Executive Committee of the Civil Rights Practice Group included representatives from conservative institutions and conservative public interest law groups, including Roger Clegg, the Center for Equal Opportunity; William Maurer, the Institute for Justice; Curt A. Levey, the Committee for Justice; Sharon L. Browne, the Pacific Legal Foundation; and Todd F. Gaziano, the Heritage Foundation.[119]

The Civil Rights Practice Group published a newsletter between 1996 and 2000. Of the thirty articles included in the newsletter during those years, twenty-four related in some way to criticism of affirmative action involving racial classifications. Another defended a voucher program in Florida that had been sued by the ACLU and the NAACP, and one gave a critical review to a favorable biography of Jesse Jackson.[120] It would not be an exaggeration to say that, at least judged by the published material, the "Civil Rights Practice Group" is primarily the "Anti-Affirmative Action Practice Group."

The Reagan Administration

The Reagan administration provided a launching pad for the conservative campaign against affirmative action and for the careers of a large number of Federalist Society members who would become prominent participants in it. In addition to Ed Meese, there were Carolyn Kuhl and Michael McConnell, who would be appointed as Court of Appeals judges by George W. Bush; Charles J. Cooper, director of the Office of Legal Counsel; T. Kenneth Cribb Jr., Meese's counselor and now a member of the Board of Directors of the Federalist Society; Michael Carvin, now senior advisor to the Civil Rights Practice Group and a cofounder of the Center for Individual Rights; Linda Chavez, staff director at the U.S. Commission on Civil Rights in Reagan's first term and later the founder and chair of the Center for Equal Opportunity; and Roger Clegg, now the president and general counsel of the Center for Equal Opportunity.[121]

Gerald A. Reynolds, then president of the Center for New Black Leadership, heralded the major change that the Reagan administration brought to affirmative action in the Civil Rights Practice Group newsletter, in that "no [previous] administration had ever mounted a sustained campaign against the use of racial preferences."[122] In 2000, Meese reflected that "[o]ne area of litigation in which the Reagan Administration was most successful in returning to constitutional principles was in the area of discrimination on the basis of race and sex through quotas and preferences."[123] The principal architect of the Reagan administration's policies was William Bradford Reynolds as head of the Civil Rights Division of the Justice Department. He is now a member of the Board of Visitors of the Federalist Society.

Gerald Reynolds argued that it was a different worldview, not racial animus, that caused William Bradford Reynolds (no relation) to disagree with the civil rights establishment. He wrote, "Reynolds was well aware of the lingering effects of slavery and invidious discrimination. However, he did not believe that it was legal or proper to implement policies that compensate blacks, as a group, at the expense of whites. Reynolds believed that the Civil War Amendments and anti-discrimination laws were intended to protect the rights of individuals, not remedy historical wrongs inflicted upon racial and ethnic minorities."[124]

William Bradford Reynolds's actions as head of the Civil Rights Division were so controversial that his nomination to the position of associate attorney general was rejected by the Senate Judiciary Committee, despite the fact that it was led at that point by Republicans. Critics claimed that he "had refused to enforce civil rights laws and ignored court rulings with which he disagreed."[125] Republican senator Arlen Specter "accused Reynolds of giving misleading testimony, 'disregarding the established law,' and 'elevating [his] own legal judgments over the judgments of the courts.'"[126]

Clarence Thomas was chairman of the Equal Employment Opportunity Commission (EEOC) from 1982 to 1990. The direction of the EEOC under President Reagan was determined by the 1980 EEOC transition team that included committed conservatives Jay Parker, the chair; Thomas; Hugh Joseph Beard Jr., later counsel to the Center for Equal Opportunity; Andrew W. Lester, former membership director of the Civil Rights Practice Group; and William Keyes. Chairman Thomas waged "a counterattack on the received wisdom of the civil rights community."[127] Thomas turned the EEOC away from the sweeping enforcement activities that had been focused on goals, timetables, and the use of tests and other hiring requirements disadvantageous to minorities. Instead, he focused on individual claims of discrimination. Thomas argued, "Law enforcement, not social engineering, was the proper mission of the agency."[128]

Clint Bolick went to work for Clarence Thomas at the EEOC during President Reagan's second term. Bolick eventually developed a "deep and abiding" relationship with Clarence Thomas.[129] Bolick asked Thomas to be the godfather to his second son.[130] According to Nina Easton, Bolick "learned to spin the debate" from Ricky Silberman, the vice chair of the EEOC, by avoiding terms like "affirmative action," "goals," or "timetables" and using instead "quotas" and "racial preferences." At that time, Bolick described the civil rights community as "complacent, elitist, patronizing, and increasingly detached from the needs of its claimed constituency."[131] Thomas raised the question of whether "state and local laws and regulations [were] preventing people of color from becoming entrepreneurs instead of welfare dependents."[132] After working for the EEOC for one year, Bolick moved to the Civil Rights Division of the Justice Department.

As Lee Cokorinos has explained, lawyers in the Reagan administration framed the attack on affirmative action "as a return to a 'color-blind' Constitution—with desegregation efforts cast as racism in reverse."[133] For example, the government made the argument that the Constitution should be colorblind to the Supreme Court in *Wygant v. Jackson Board of Education* in 1986, asserting that its argument in that case was true to *Brown v. Board of Education*.[134]

In another case, the United States had filed suit in *Local 28, Sheet Metal Workers v. EEOC* in 1971 against a union for discriminating against nonwhites. In 1986, after the union was held in contempt for violating court orders, the EEOC argued in the Supreme Court against the minority workers. It claimed that the district court's order, which required the union to reach a minimum percentage of minority members, was illegal both because it established a quota and because it provided relief to minority workers who had not themselves been the victims of discrimination.[135] The government criticized the district court for employing "racially discriminatory means" and "[d]isregarding the impact [of the order] on white members and applicants for membership."[136]

The NAACP filed suit in Alabama in *United States v. Paradise* in 1972 because there had been no black state troopers in the thirty-seven year history of the state patrol. The United States was joined as a party plaintiff. After many years of litigation, blacks were still underrepresented in the officer ranks and the district court entered an order requiring the promotion of one black for each white Alabama state trooper promoted. The United States opposed that order and in 1987 it sought Supreme Court review of the one-for-one remedy.[137] It argued that "this quota requires discrimination against innocent white state employees for no independently justifiable remedial purpose." The government accused the district court of "holding innocent white state troopers hostage."[138]

The signers of the government's briefs in *Wygant, Local 28,* and *Paradise* included several current and former influential members of the Federalist Society's Civil Rights Practice Group: William Bradford Reynolds, Michael A. Carvin, Roger Clegg, Clint Bolick, Charles J. Cooper, Samuel A. Alito Jr., and Carolyn B. Kuhl. They had a partial victory in *Wygant*, but the Supreme Court upheld the affirmative action policies in *Local 28* and *Paradise*, based on the documented history of racial discrimination against minorities in each instance.

The Reagan years closed, however, with a major success for Federalist Society members and their allies. In 1989, in *City of Richmond v. J.A. Croson, Co.*, they were successful in establishing that all racial classifications by state and local governments must be judged under the strict scrutiny standard.[139] The Supreme Court overturned a minority set aside program for construction firms that Richmond, Virginia, had voluntarily adopted. The Solicitor General's Office filed an amicus brief in the case supporting the attack on the constitutionality of Richmond's affirmative action plan. The signers included William Bradford Reynolds and Roger Clegg.

Public Interest Law Firms and Advocacy Organizations
Federalist Society members have worked in and with numerous conservative public interest law firms on affirmative action issues, including the Institute for Justice, the Center for Equal Opportunity, the Center for Individual Rights, the Pacific Legal

Foundation, and the Landmark Legal Foundation.[140] Federalist Society members have also worked with other conservative groups that have been active opponents of affirmative action, such as the American Civil Rights Institute, the Center for New Black Leadership, and the Independent Women's Forum.[141] Such groups deepened their relationships over the course of the 1990s through the efforts of Federalist Society members Ed Meese at the Heritage Foundation and Roger Clegg at the Center for Equal Opportunity.[142] Lee Cokorinos provides a rich account of the interlocking leadership, history, litigation activities, and funding of these groups in *Assault on Diversity*.[143]

Representative Cases

In the years following the Reagan presidency, Federalist Society members continued to be very active in litigation in the employment discrimination area and have continuously moved the law in a conservative direction. Title VII of the Civil Rights Act of 1964 prohibits discrimination on the basis of race and gender in employment. Congress is entitled, for public policy reasons, to afford victims of discrimination greater rights than those strictly required by the Constitution, and Title VII does so. A 1971 decision by the Supreme Court in *Griggs v. Duke Power Co.* recognized two discrete theories under which aggrieved employees could prove discrimination by their employer.[144] Under a "disparate treatment" theory, an employee can establish discrimination by showing that his employer treated him differently on the basis of his race, with the intent to discriminate against him. Under a "disparate impact" theory, employees can establish discrimination by showing that an employment practice had a disparate impact on a class of people protected by Title VII, even though they have no evidence that the employer intended to discriminate. The disparate impact theory is applicable to statutory claims brought under the Civil Rights Act, but is not sufficient to prove a constitutional violation under the equal protection clause. Under this theory, if employees are able to show that a challenged employment practice has a discriminatory impact, the employer must justify the practice for nondiscriminatory business reasons to avoid liability for discrimination. Ed Meese characterized the decision in *Griggs* as "insidious" and argued that it would force employers to adopt racial quotas to avoid the expense of defending disparate impact claims.[145]

The 1989 decision by the Supreme Court in *Wards Cove Packing, Inc. v. Atonio* involved the details of what must be proven by the two parties at various stages of a case brought under the disparate impact theory.[146] Although the case did not involve an affirmative action plan that employed racial classifications, Federalist Society members used it as an opportunity to warn of the dangers posed by "quotas."

In *Wards Cove*, nonwhite employees in salmon canneries in Alaska complained that they were discriminated against on the basis of race. The case involved two categories of jobs. "Cannery jobs" were on the line where workers packed the fish into cans and cooked them, and were classified as unskilled labor. "Noncannery jobs" included a variety of positions and were classified as skilled labor. The cannery jobs were filled predominantly by nonwhite workers, Filipinos and Alaska natives, and the noncannery jobs predominantly by white workers. Although it would ultimately rule in favor of the employers, the Supreme Court acknowledged that "[v]irtually all of the noncannery jobs pay more than cannery positions. The predominantly white noncannery workers and the predominantly nonwhite cannery employees live in separate dormitories and eat in separate mess halls."[147] Justice Stevens put it more pointedly in his dissenting opinion: "Some characteristics of the Alaska salmon industry described in this litigation—in particular, the segregation of housing and dining facilities and the stratification of jobs along racial and ethnic lines—bear an unsettling resemblance to aspects of a plantation economy."[148] The cannery workers complained of a variety of employment practices that contributed to these disparities, including nepotism, a rehire preference, a lack of objective hiring criteria, separate hiring channels, and a practice of not promoting from within the cannery ranks to noncannery positions.

The Supreme Court adopted several arguments that Federalist Society members had made in amicus briefs. The case originally came to the Supreme Court at the end of the Reagan administration. The Solicitor General's Office filed a brief supporting the position of the employer, signed by Charles Fried as solicitor general, and William Bradford Reynolds and Roger Clegg from the Attorney General's Office, among others.[149] The brief encouraged the court to rule, as it ultimately did, that the plaintiffs' intra-workforce statistics did not establish a disparate impact claim and that comparison with the relevant labor market would be required to do so; that the cause of any disparate impact must be proven with respect to specific hiring selection practices (not on the employer's overall employment policies, or other practices, such as segregated housing); that the standard for judging whether employment practices were justified by nondiscriminatory reasons should be whether there are "legitimate business reasons," with the emphasis on reasonableness; and that the ultimate burden of proof in these cases remains on the plaintiff and does not shift to the defendant.[150] Clint Bolick filed an amicus brief on behalf of the Landmark Legal Foundation Center for Civil Rights, supporting the same arguments.[151] The court's rulings altered the law under Title VII and made it more difficult for plaintiffs to prove employment discrimination on a disparate impact theory.

The Supreme Court held that the fact that the cannery workers were predominantly nonwhite and the noncannery workers were predominantly white did not constitute relevant statistical proof of disparate impact. The court reasoned that it was inappropriate to compare the number of nonwhites in one category of employees with the number of nonwhites in another category. The appropriate comparison, according to the court, was between the percentage of nonwhites who were cannery workers with the percentage of nonwhites in the labor market for those positions, and between the percentage of nonwhites who were noncannery workers with the percentage of nonwhites in the labor market for those positions. The court concluded that only in this way could it be determined whether there was discrimination against workers actually qualified and willing to take the more desirable noncannery jobs.

Moreover, the court ruled that it would not be enough for plaintiffs to show that there was a statistical disparity between nonwhites in the noncannery positions and nonwhites in the labor market for those positions. Plaintiffs would also have to prove a causal relationship between one or more of the employment practices they were complaining about (nepotism, rehire preference, etc.) and the disparity, specifically showing that *each* challenged practice had a significantly disparate impact on employment opportunities for whites and nonwhites.

What is the broader significance of these seemingly technical matters regarding statistical proof and causation on which the court's opinion focused? A different analysis might have considered the totality of the evidence presented, including such matters as the stratification and stereotyping employed by this entire industry in Alaska, the seasonal nature of the work, the arbitrary nature of the qualifications actually imposed for noncannery jobs, the significant race-labeling that the evidence disclosed ("the Native crew," "the Oriental bunkhouse," and the like), and whether the employers had manipulated the labor pools by seeking employees for different categories of jobs from different geographical areas.[152] Justice Stevens's dissenting opinion, on which he was joined by Justices William J. Brennan Jr., Thurgood Marshall, and Harry Blackmun, concluded that taking into account the context in which the case arose, particularly that a requirement for employment was "availability for seasonal employment in the far reaches of Alaska," the evidence comparing racial compositions within the workforce was more probative than general population statistics.[153]

What, then, did the amicus briefs by Federalist Society members and the court conclude was the evil in this broader approach? They raised the specter of quotas. With respect to the intra-workforce statistical analysis, the court warned that the risk of being sued for a racially imbalanced workforce and the attendant cost of such litigation would drive employers to adopt racial quotas as a defensive measure.[154]

With respect to causation, Clint Bolick argued that plaintiffs in disparate impact cases must be required to prove the causative effects of "isolated" decision-making practices, in order to disallow "broad, nebulous claims" that would require employers to adopt "illegal and pernicious 'quotas and preferential treatment [policies].'"[155] Bolick found it unacceptable that the employees had "attempted at trial to show that one or more of about sixteen challenged employment practices, either separately or together, violated Title VII."[156] It is unclear what advice Bolick would give workers whose employer actually does employ numerous direct and indirect practices to discourage minorities from seeking jobs traditionally held by whites. Justice Stevens's dissent provided the obvious answer to Bolick and the ruling of the court:

Although the causal link must have substance, the [challenged] act need not constitute the sole or primary cause of the harm. . . . Thus in a disparate-impact case, proof of numerous questionable employment practices ought to fortify an employee's assertion that the practices caused racial disparities.[157]

After discussing the plaintiffs' burdens, the court addressed what the employer's burden was with respect to justifying its employment practices. Previous Supreme Court decisions had stated that the employer would have to show that the employment practices in question were required by "business necessity" or "essential to job performance."[158] In *Wards Cove*, however, the court watered down this standard and said that although it would not be enough for an employer to proffer "a mere insubstantial justification," there was no requirement that the challenged practice be "essential" or "indispensable" to the employer's business. The solicitor general's brief had raised the issue of quotas on this point as well, urging the court to adopt the lower standard because a standard that required a hiring practice to be essential to the business "would threaten to put pressure on employers to avoid disparate impact liability by adopting quotas or otherwise turning their attention away from job qualifications and toward numerical balance."[159]

Who has the ultimate burden of proof is crucially important in close cases. The language in previous court decisions had suggested that the ultimate burden of proof on the business justification for employment practices shifted to the employer in disparate impact cases, but the *Wards Cove* decision rejected that proposition. The court held that if an employer does offer evidence that an employment practice served legitimate business goals, the burden remains on the employee to disprove that the practice was based solely on a legitimate neutral consideration. The dissenting justices argued that the legitimate business practice defense constituted an affirmative defense, and that the employer should have the ultimate burden of proof on this point.

Two years after the decision in *Wards Cove*, Congress amended Title VII in the Civil Rights Act of 1991.[160] The act reversed the Supreme Court's interpretations of the statute and made it easier for plaintiffs to win disparate impact cases. Congress explicitly recognized the disparate impact theory of recovery; permitted plaintiffs to demonstrate that the elements of an employer's decision-making process are not capable of separation for analysis, and in such cases to analyze them as one employment practice; required employers to demonstrate that a challenged practice is job related for the position in question and consistent with "business necessity"; and placed the ultimate burden of proof on the defendant with respect to establishing business necessity. The act did not, however, clarify what type of statistics would constitute sufficient proof in the disparate impact context.[161]

With regard to certain technical matters, the conservative victory in *Wards Cove* was short-lived as a result of congressional action. On the other hand, the decision reflected the strength of aspects of the conservative critique of antidiscrimination law and affirmative action. First, the court's decision demonstrated the power of the "quota phobia." The case did not involve quotas and the court was not review-ing an affirmative action program that included race preferences. Nonetheless, the court bought the argument that high standards for employers with respect to em-ployment practices that have a disparate impact on minorities should be avoided because they may cause employers to adopt quotas to avoid the costs of litigation or the necessity of defending business practices in court.

Second, the decision showed that the court was turning away from an analy-sis that takes into account the history of segregation and racism to understand the power of practices that have a discriminatory impact.[162] Justice Blackmun was so upset by the court's failure to consider the overt and institutionalized discrimi-nation in the salmon industry that he famously remarked in his dissent, "One wonders whether the majority still believes that race discrimination—or, more ac-curately, race discrimination against nonwhites—is a problem in our society, or even remembers that it ever was."[163]

Race preferences, a background issue in *Wards Cove*, were the principal issue in the 1996 Fifth Circuit Court of Appeals decision in *Hopwood v. Texas*.[164] The court ruling made the use of race in university admissions illegal in the Fifth Circuit (which includes the states of Louisiana, Mississippi, and Texas). Cheryl Hopwood was denied admission to the University of Texas Law School. She and three other rejected white students filed suit, claiming that they were qualified for admission and had only been rejected because of their race. They argued that the law school's affirmative action program denied them their right to equal protection of the law. The attorneys for the plaintiffs included a former vice chairman of the Civil Rights Practice Group, Michael Rosman of the Center for Individual Rights, and Ted Olson. *Hopwood* shut down the use of race in admissions decisions in a good part of the South until 2003, when the Supreme Court decided in *Grutter v. Bollinger* that diversity concerns could justify the consideration of applicants' race.[165]

The *Hopwood* Court applied strict scrutiny to determine whether the use of racial classifications violated the Constitution. While *Hopwood* was pending and before it was decided, the Supreme Court ruled in another affirmative action case, *Adarand Constructors, Inc. v. Pena*, that all racial classifications by all levels of gov-ernment must be reviewed under strict scrutiny.[166] *Adarand* was filed and argued by the conservative public interest law firm Mountain States Legal Foundation. The *Adarand* decision by the Supreme Court compelled the Fifth Circuit to use strict scrutiny in *Hopwood*.

With strict scrutiny in place as the standard, the *Hopwood* Court rejected the law school's argument that diversity was a compelling government interest that could satisfy the standard. The law school had relied on the previous opinion of Supreme Court Justice Lewis Powell in the well-known 1978 *Bakke* case, where a white applicant to medical school had challenged the affirmative action plan of the University of California.[167] Under Powell's conception, an affirmative action pro-gram that considered multiple diversity factors, including race, would be constitu-tional. Although no other justices had joined Powell's opinion in *Bakke*, his views had been widely accepted as authority for the proposition that diversity in education, broadly defined, was a legitimate goal for government to pursue. The Fifth Circuit declined to adopt Powell's endorsement of an approach to diversity that included race as a factor and suggested that Powell's opinion did not reflect the views of the Supreme Court.

In applying strict scrutiny and rejecting diversity as a compelling government interest, the *Hopwood* decision adopted many of the principles that Federalist Society members and other conservatives had advocated with respect to affirmative action. The court reasoned that the labeling of a racial classification by the government as "benign" or "remedial" is meaningless. It emphasized that the rights protected by the Fourteenth Amendment are guaranteed to *the individual*, not to classes of people. The opinion argued that the use of race in admissions for diversity purposes would foster, rather than minimize, the use of racial classifications by the government, and might promote improper racial stereotypes and fuel racial hostility. It concluded that the only compelling government interest that permitted the use of racial classifications was remediation of previous discrimination. In that respect, the court held that racial classifications could not be employed to remedy societal discrimination, nor could racial classifications at the law school be employed to remedy discrimination at the elementary and secondary school level in Texas.

The University of Texas Law School had refused to admit African American students until the Supreme Court struck down its *de jure* segregated policy in 1950.[168] The *Hopwood* Court found that any other discrimination by the law school ended in the 1960s. The court ruled that historical discrimination by the law school could not justify its current affirmative action program and rejected as irrelevant the district court's factual findings that the law school had a "lingering reputation in the minority community, particularly with prospective students, as a 'white' school," and that it was perceived as "a hostile environment for minorities."[169]

The *Hopwood* Court borrowed language from the Fourth Circuit Court of Appeals on the weight to be given to racial history: "The case against race-based preferences does not rest on the sterile assumption that American society is untouched or unaffected by the tragic oppression of its past. . . . Rather, it is the very enormity of that tragedy that lends resolve to the desire to never repeat it, and find a legal order in which distinctions based on race shall have no place."[170] The opposing argument, of course, is that racial discrimination cannot simply be brought to a screeching halt without any need to be conscious of race in fashioning remedies for the harm previously caused.

Ironically, the courts ultimately decided that Cheryl Hopwood and the other white plaintiffs were not qualified for admission to the University of Texas Law School. When the court of appeals decided that race was an improper factor in the admissions decision, it ruled the plaintiffs would be entitled to damages unless the University of Texas proved that they would have had no reasonable chance of being admitted to the law school under a race-blind system. It sent the case back to the district court for fact-finding on that issue. The district court ruled that the white plaintiffs would have been rejected even under a race-blind system and thus denied them damages. That finding was affirmed on appeal.[171]

The Supreme Court declined to review either of the Fifth Circuit opinions in *Hopwood* and the case generated a storm of controversy across the country until the Supreme Court reviewed the affirmative action plans of the University of Michigan in *Grutter v. Bollinger* and *Gratz v. Bollinger* in 2003.[172] White applicants who had been denied admission challenged the law school's affirmative action plan in *Grutter* and the college's plan in *Gratz*. The Supreme Court held the college's plan unconstitutional because it awarded one-fifth of the number of points required for admission to all African American, Hispanic, and Native American applicants, solely on the basis of their race. At the same time, the court held the law school's plan constitutional because it required individualized review of applicants and considered race as only one of several factors that contribute to diversity. Both cases were decided by 5–4 margins, with Justice Sandra Day O'Connor providing the swing vote, approving the law school's program but rejecting the program of the college. Contrary to the Fifth Circuit's opinion in *Hopwood*, Justice Powell's views on diversity in *Bakke* were definitively endorsed by a majority of the Supreme Court.

The court held in both Michigan cases that broadly defined diversity in the student body of an institution of higher education was a compelling government interest that justifies the use of race as a factor in making admissions decisions. The undergraduate program was held unconstitutional, however, because it did not provide for the individual consideration of applicants, awarded special points to all members of the specified minority groups, and awarded such a large number of points that race was a deciding factor for virtually every minimally qualified applicant from these groups. The court ruled that the program was not narrowly tailored to achieve permissible diversity.

Federalist Society members were extremely active in the Michigan cases. The *Hopwood* plaintiffs' lawyer, Michael Rosman from the Center for Individual Rights, represented the white plaintiffs in both cases. Ted Olson, who worked with Rosman on *Hopwood* as a private lawyer, had been appointed by President George W. Bush as the solicitor general of the United States by the time these cases reached the Supreme Court. He appeared and argued in that capacity in support of the white students. He was joined on the government's brief by Brian W. Jones, a former vice chairman of the Civil Rights Practice Group whom President George W. Bush had appointed general counsel of the Department of Education. Numerous other Federalist Society members and friends filed amicus briefs challenging these affirmative action programs. On the other side, a large number of liberal groups filed amicus briefs supporting Michigan's programs. Although the conservatives took some satisfaction in striking down the college's plan, the court's decision upholding the law school's plan was a major blow to the positions that many Federalist Society members had taken.

The Supreme Court applied strict scrutiny in assessing Michigan's affirmative action plans. Justice O'Connor, however, pointedly emphasized that the use of strict scrutiny does not automatically result in invalidating a government program that uses racial classifications.[173] She argued that context matters, and placed great weight on the fact that these cases arose in the context of higher education. Indeed, the court's opinion explicitly deferred to the law school's "educational judgment that . . . diversity is essential to its educational mission."[174] The court explained that the educational benefits of diversity are substantial: promoting cross-racial under-standing, helping to break down racial stereotypes, and enabling students to better understand persons of different races.[175] The court cited amicus briefs from business and military leaders that underlined the importance of diversity in preparing people to participate in the global marketplace and in developing a racially diverse officer corps.

The *Grutter* Court ruled that the law school's program was narrowly tailored because it did not amount to a quota system, but rather considered race or ethnicity along with all other pertinent elements of diversity in an individualized consideration of each applicant for admission. The court specifically found that the law school's goal of admitting a "critical mass" of underrepresented minority students did not create a quota program.[176]

Despite recognizing diversity as a compelling government interest in higher education, the Grutter opinion did reinforce several themes that many Federalist Society members espouse. The court agreed with Justice Powell's decision in *Bakke* with respect to the following propositions: the goal of reducing the historic deficit of a traditionally disfavored minority in a profession, standing alone, amounts to unlawful racial balancing; remedying societal discrimination is not a compelling government interest because it risks placing unnecessary burdens on "innocent third parties" who are not responsible for the harm the beneficiaries of the program have suffered; and even if increasing the number of professionals who will practice in underserved communities were a compelling interest, affirmative action in the selection of graduate students is not geared to promote that goal.[177]

Moreover, the court concluded that a "core purpose of the Fourteenth Amendment was to do away with all governmentally imposed discrimination based on race," and thus "race-conscious admissions policies must be limited in time."[178] Justice O'Connor predicted, "We expect that 25 years from now, the use of racial preferences will no longer be necessary to further the interest approved today."[179]

The conservative justices bitterly dissented in *Grutter*. Justice Scalia wrote that "the University of Michigan Law School's mystical 'critical mass' justification for its discrimination by race challenges even the most gullible mind. The admissions statistics show it to be a sham to cover a scheme of racially proportionate admissions."[180] Justice Thomas concluded that previous racial disparities in admissions were caused by the fact that Michigan chose to maintain an "elite" law school and suggested that the state's stake in diversity was little more an interest in "classroom aesthetics."[181] Thomas concluded that such affirmative action programs are *per se* harmful and do not benefit minority students.[182]

The conservatives' victory in *Wards Cove* had been overturned by Congress when it passed the 1991 Civil Rights Act, and *Grutter* was a major setback. But by the time the Supreme Court held the school assignment plans unconstitutional in *Parents Involved*, Federalist Society members and their allies had succeeded through litigation in severely limiting the use of racial classifications in affirmative action plans.[183]

Debates and Presentations

The focus of the Federalist Society's founders on affirmative action dates back to their days as Yale undergraduates; as leaders of the Yale Political Union, David McIntosh, Steven G. Calabresi, Peter D. Keisler, and Lee Liberman sponsored a debate on the topic "Resolved: That Yale should abolish affirmative action."[184] At the 2009 Federalist Society National Lawyers Convention, the panel "Civil Rights: Affirmative Action in the Obama Era" was moderated by Ninth Circuit Judge Carlos T. Bea. The panel included two affirmative action proponents: Shirley J. Wilcher, executive director of the American Association for Affirmative Action, and Columbia law professor Theodore M. Shaw, former director-counsel and president of the NAACP Legal Defense and Educational Fund.[185]

The affirmative action critics were Linda L. Chavez, former staff director of the U.S. Commission on Civil Rights during the Reagan administration and currently chair of the Center for Equal Opportunity, and Peter N. Kirsanow, a commissioner on the U.S. Commission on Civil Rights and chairman of the Center for New Black Leadership's board of directors. Kirsanow, a conservative loyalist, was appointed to the commission by President George W. Bush and testified in the Senate on behalf of the appointments of Chief Justice Roberts and Justice Alito to the Supreme Court. The panel consisted entirely of Hispanic and African American speakers, but it appeared that the only person of color in the audience of approximately two hundred people was a young black man operating the AV system.

Chavez opened her remarks by announcing she had been compelled to throw out her prepared remarks after watching the Army chief of staff, General George Casey, on television the previous Sunday. General Casey had described the recent killing of soldiers at Fort Hood, Texas, as a tragedy, and expressed concern about diversity in the armed forces becoming a casualty of the incident. Chavez said, "Gen. Casey should be fired for his statements, but he will not be fired because the whole premise behind his statements suggests how pervasive and pernicious the whole concept of diversity at any cost has become. If what Casey says is true, then protecting diversity has become more important than protecting lives and the world has gone mad."[186]

Chavez went on to criticize President Obama's appointment of Thomas Perez as assistant attorney general in charge of the Civil Rights Division. She was particularly scornful of an equal protection claim made by the federal government against the Department of Correction in Massachusetts on behalf of women challenging the department's physical abilities test, which Chavez claimed measured applicants' abilities to perform duties required by the job. The suit alleged that the test was not job related and unnecessarily excluded women from jobs for which they were qualified. Chavez's criticism of the litigation was consistent with her overall theme that "[w]e have become inured to the idea that diversity at any cost is offensive."[187]

Peter Kirsanow also abandoned his prepared remarks, after spotting his friends Stephan Thernstrom and Roger Clegg in the audience. Kirsanow said that although "originally maybe a lot of us thought affirmative action was a worthy goal," now it has "stolen a base." The problem is that affirmative action is no longer about "equal opportunity," but about "equal results." Kirsanow criticized President Obama for not supporting the Michigan Civil Rights Initiative when he was in the Senate. The ballot initiative would have amended the state constitution to prohibit discrimination based on race, including affirmative action, and was nearly identical to the California Civil Rights Initiative (Proposition 209).

Kirsanow asserted that affirmative action is not achieving results. Citing Thernstrom's research on bar exam passage rates, he concluded that beneficiaries of affirmative action in law school have a greater likelihood of failing. Referencing data on the increasing gap between white and black children in high school, Kirsanow concluded that the problems are getting worse after forty years of affirmative action. He attempted no analysis of these issues, but attacked the prevalence of racial preferences.

Public Campaigns

Despite considerable success in litigation, conservatives are dissatisfied with the failure of the judicial branch to eliminate affirmative action completely. They are equally concerned that elected politicians have not and probably will not completely reject affirmative action. Roger Clegg evaluated President George W. Bush's record on affirmative action as one marked by inaction, which he blamed on his political opponents:

> Indeed, if the Administration could have avoided saying anything at all about the subject of racial preferences—if it could have simply made the issue go away—it would have done so eagerly. This is probably because, on the one hand, its lawyers and policy advisers thought such discrimination difficult or impossible to defend, but its political experts were reluctant to court attacks from race-baiting Democrats and the civil rights establishment.[188]

As a result of their dissatisfaction, Federalist Society members and other conservatives turned in the mid-1990s to ballot initiatives to ban racial classifications in affirmative action measures. The campaign began in California and, in November 1996, the state's voters passed the California Civil Rights Initiative (CCRI), Proposition 209, which barred all use of race and sex preferences in government contracting, employment, and education, including in affirmative action programs.

This "direct democracy" measure required big money. The group Yes on Proposition 209 raised $5,239,287 and spent $4,396,572 to get it passed.[189] Other groups and individuals spent additional hundreds of thousands of dollars.[190]

The Civil Rights Practice Group newsletter provided a platform for supporters of the proposition. Tom Wood, a coauthor of the CCRI, characterized it in the newsletter as the "hottest battle in the race/sex-based affirmative action wars."[191] Clint Bolick was actively involved in the campaign to pass the CCRI. Nina Easton described a memo Bolick circulated to CCRI organizers in July 1996, reminding them that "vocabulary matters." He urged organizers to avoid saying that the CCRI would ban "affirmative action," because a slight majority of people favor "affirmative action," although they oppose "racial preferences."[192] Easton described Bolick's participation in a celebration of the success of the CCRI at the home of a law professor in Southern California, where he toasted the volunteers, saying, "I never thought this day would come. . . . Let me quote my favorite revolutionary, Tom Paine: 'We have the power to begin the world over again.'"[193]

Affirmative action proponents challenged the constitutionality of the CCRI in court. Federalist Society lawyers and their allies defended it. Amicus briefs were filed by Ted Olson for the Independent Women's Forum, Clint Bolick for the Institute for Justice, Sharon L. Browne for the Pacific Legal Foundation, and G. Michael German for the conservative gay organization Log Cabin Republicans of California.[194] The conservative U.S. Justice Foundation also filed an amicus brief, which was signed by Gary G. Kreep and Kevin T. Snider.[195] The Center for Individual Rights intervened in the case to argue for the measure's constitutionality.[196] On the other side, well-known liberal lawyers and professors filed briefs arguing that the measure was unconstitutional. Ultimately the Ninth Circuit Court of Appeals held that the CCRI was constitutional.[197]

Hans Bader, associate counsel at the Center for Individual Rights, reported on this litigation in the Civil Rights Practice Group newsletter.[198] Bader argued against the ACLU's position that a statewide ban on racial preferences unconstitutionally distorted the political process by precluding local governments from adopting them. Bader disparaged the motives of liberals who challenged the CCRI, charging that "[t]he ACLU and the denizens of California's vast 'diversity' industry have too great a stake in institutionalized racial divisions to allow California's experiment with colorblindness to survive."

After the success of the CCRI, Ward Connerly created the American Civil Rights Institute (ACRI) to "carry this message of equal opportunity to other states and to Washington, D.C.," announcing his plans in the Civil Rights Practice Group newsletter.[199] The mission of the new organization would be to educate the public about the problems with race and gender preferences and to lobby for a federal civil rights initiative.[200] ACRI's intent was to "openly challenge the organizations and people in our nation who believe that equal opportunity means equal results." ACRI belatedly filed financial disclosure forms in the summer of 2011 for the years 2008, 2009, and 2010. They revealed that Connerly's annual salary at ACRI was between $1.2 million and $1.5 million per year, more than half the organization's annual revenue.[201]

Civil rights activists criticized Connerly for announcing the formation of the new group on January 15, the birthday of Dr. Martin Luther King Jr. In the newsletter, he responded, "[W]hat better day to unveil a new organization dedicated to achieving a colorblind society—the kind that Dr. King dreamed of—than Dr. King's own birthday?" Connerly criticized "modern day leaders" like Jesse Jackson who "don't want a colorblind society. They want a color-conscious society."

Connerly succeeded in getting CRI ballot measures passed in Washington State in 1998, Michigan in 2006, Nebraska in 2008, and Arizona in 2010. Voters rejected a similar initiative in Colorado in 2008. Signature-gathering campaigns to put the initiative on the ballot were unsuccessful in Missouri and Arizona in the same year, and Connerly withdrew the initiative in Oklahoma in the face of challenges to the signatures gathered there.

The success of CCRI led to an effort to enact a federal statute, the Civil Rights Act of 1997, that would have proscribed race and gender preferences along the same lines. The proposed statute had ninety-five cosponsors. Representative Charles T. Canady (R-FL), the author of the bill, articulated his reasons for supporting it in the Civil Rights Practice Group newsletter.[202] He argued that "the present system of discriminatory preferential treatment for a select group of Americans based upon race and gender is the opposite of civil rights." The House Judiciary Committee tabled the bill and it was never passed.

The ballot initiative campaign is ongoing. Connerly reflected on his efforts in a 2009 article in the *Harvard Journal of Law and Public Policy*. He argued, "With respect to the matter of equal treatment before the law, representative government at all levels has become totally unresponsive to the people, who clearly support the principle of 'colorblind' government."[203]

Capturing Important Government Posts

One of the Federalist Society's greatest successes was the nomination of Clarence Thomas to the Supreme Court of the United States. Lee Liberman was "a key architect behind Clarence Thomas's narrow confirmation to the U.S. Supreme Court."[204] Clint Bolick worked hard to promote the appointment and was embittered by the attacks on Thomas during the hearings.[205]

As described above, Thomas has written significant opinions critical of affirmative action. These opinions are informed by his narrow view of how racism manifests itself in the United States. For example, in *Parents Involved*, Thomas suggested that the "racial theories" of the Seattle School Board raised a "question whether school boards should be entrusted with the power to make decisions on the basis of race."[206] Thomas mocked both the school board's website's definition of "cultural racism" and the fact that the school district sent a delegation of students to a conference on the topic of white privilege. One conference participant defined white privilege as "an invisible package of unearned assets which I can count on cashing in each day, but about which I was meant to remain oblivious. White Privilege is like an invisible weightless knapsack of special provisions, maps, passports, codebooks, visas, clothes, tools, and blank checks."[207] On the one hand, it is perhaps surprising that an African American Supreme Court justice would deride an educational system for exploring the often invisible nature of the advantages that whites enjoy as a consequence of our nation's history of slavery and nearly a century of state-mandated apartheid throughout the South. On the other hand, Thomas's views are completely consistent with an understanding of racism that holds it is manifested only by individual and intentional acts motivated by subjective race prejudice.

Federalist Society members have been active in opposing the appointments of prominent liberals. Clint Bolick was instrumental in defeating President Clinton's nomination of Lani Guinier to head the Civil Rights Division of the Justice Department. Bolick wrote an op-ed piece headlined "Clinton's Quota Queens" in the *Wall Street Journal* on April 30, 1993, criticizing Guinier and another nominee the day after Clinton announced Guinier's nomination. Later, Bolick reviewed her writings with his contacts in the press. He called her "breathtakingly radical" and claimed her theories promoted "tyranny of the minority . . . the most radical notion of government I've seen presented in my lifetime."[208] Clinton pulled her nomination on June 3. Bolick, collaborating with Roger Clegg and Ed Meese, also successfully organized senators to oppose President Clinton's nomination of Bill Lann Lee as the head of the Civil Rights Division of the Justice Department, with the result that Lee was not confirmed and was forced to serve out his term as the acting head of the division.[209]

Federalist Society members have recently occupied important positions on the U.S. Commission on Civil Rights. The mission of the commission is to investigate complaints of discrimination; to study, collect, and serve as a national clearinghouse for information relating to discrimination; to appraise federal laws; to issue public service announcements; and to submit reports, findings. and recommendations to the president and Congress.[210] President George W. Bush appointed Gerald Reynolds of the Center for New Black Leadership as chairman of the commission.[211] The center was devoted to "developing and promoting a market-oriented, community-based vision of public leadership for black communities in Americas and abroad."[212]

Bush also appointed a well-known conservative critic of affirmative action, Abigail Thernstrom, an adjunct scholar at the American Enterprise Institute, as vice chair of the commission, and Peter N. Kirsanow and Jennifer C. Braceras as commissioners. University of San Diego law professor Gail Heriot, chairman of the Civil Rights Practice Group, and Todd F. Gaziano, a special advisor to the Civil Rights Practice Group and director of the Center for Legal and Judicial Studies of the Heritage Foundation, received congressional appointments to the commission in 2007 and 2008.[213] Appointments are for six-year terms and the president may remove a commissioner only for neglect of duty or malfeasance in office.

Before the Bush appointees took control, the commission favored affirmative action measures.[214] The Bush appointees radically changed the orientation of the commission, as demonstrated by a 2007 briefing report regarding affirmative action in American law schools.[215] The findings and recommendations in the report, which the Bush appointees and Federalist Society members unanimously endorsed, were based on testimony from just four witnesses.[216] The commission criticized the ABA standard that requires law schools to "demonstrate by concrete action a commitment to providing full opportunities for the study of law and entry into the profession by members of underrepresented groups, particularly racial and ethnic minorities, and a commitment to having a student body that is diverse with respect to gender, race, and ethnicity."[217] The commission concluded that law schools might have to use racial preferences to meet the standard.

The report recommended voluntary disclosure by law schools, including to potential applicants, of data on "academic performance, attrition, graduation, bar passage, student loan default, and future income disaggregated by academic credentials." In other words, schools were to publish statistics on what a student's grades, loan repayments, and income are likely to be, based on his or her LSAT score and college GPA. The report also urged states to require bar admissions authorities to disclose bar passage rates disaggregated by academic credentials.

Finally, the report called on the ABA Council to eliminate the accreditation requirement that law schools demonstrate a commitment to diversity, and recommended that any compliance with the council's standard not be judged by the diversity results actually achieved by law schools. The conservative majority members of the commission had previously attempted to persuade the Department of Education to remove the ABA as the accrediting agency for law schools unless it withdrew this standard.[218]

Commissioners Arlan D. Melendez (Democrat, appointed by Senate Minority Leader Harry Reid in September 2005) and Michael J. Yaki (Democrat, appointed by Congress in February 2005) dissented from every recommendation. They criticized the commission for relying on informal briefings rather than formal investigative hearings and for issuing reports "containing predetermined findings and recommendations."[219] They accused the commission of a lack of serious scholarship, noting that it had made no attempt "to assess the consensus positions of the scientific or legal community" on the relevant issues, had done no independent research, and had not performed a comprehensive review of others' research.[220] They wrote, "We fear the Commission majority has lost touch with the agency's mission to carefully and thoughtfully investigate and report on the country's civil rights challenges, rising above narrow partisan politics."[221] In a separate dissent, Michael Yaki said that the current commission was "a pale shadow of its formal self" and "dominated by an ideology that rejects the fundamental premise that America today, though far different than 50 years ago, is still an America where the promise of true equality remains unfulfilled for many people of color."[222]

Melendez and Yaki faulted the report for failing to address "the real obstacles to minorities more successfully entering the legal profession—lack of early educational opportunities comparable to white classmates, financial hardship, and discrimination."[223] They recommended that individual schools make decisions about disclosures of data in light of their particular circumstances, and raised concerns about the phenomenon of "stereotype threat"—the risk that the performance of minorities on academic testing is "substantially affected by negative expectations a student is aware of in his social environment."[224] They concluded, "It is upsetting that the United States Commission on Civil Rights has come to the point where all it does is try to discredit race-conscious policies."[225]

The April 2007 briefing report is consistent with the commission's other actions critical of racial classifications and affirmative action. It vigorously sought to eliminate consideration of race for diversity or inclusion goals across a wide variety of government activity.[226] On August 4, 2008, the commission wrote to President Bush, urging review of Department of Transportation guidelines with respect to its Disadvantaged Business Enterprise program. The commission argued that this program should be employed only where there has been a finding of discrimination in the local highway contracting industry.[227]

On July 21, 2009, the commission wrote to Senator Ray Miller of Ohio, to discourage the State of Ohio from directing educational institutions in the state to comply with minority business enterprise set-aside requirements:

> You may well be presented with evidence of racial *disparities* in contracts awarded by Ohio's community colleges, state community colleges, technical colleges, and university branches. Such evidence must be viewed with an appropriate degree of skepticism, especially if it is presented by interested parties who stand to benefit financially from the implementation of so-called 'remedial' racial set-asides.[228]

In other words, the U.S. Civil Rights Commission urged state officials to be skeptical of claims by victims of discrimination. It predicted expensive and costly litigation if the state were to make any effort to employ racial classifications to remediate prior discrimination. The commission letter adopted Chief Justice Roberts's language from *Parents Involved*; "The way to stop discrimination on the basis of race is to stop discriminating on the basis of race."[229]

On October 9, 2009, and again on December 11, 2009, the commission wrote to President Obama and several congressional leaders, complaining that the health care bills H.R. 3200 and H.R. 3590 contained racially discriminatory provisions.[230] The commissioners disapproved of provisions in the bills that would give preferences in contracts and grants to medical training facilities that have a demonstrated record of training individuals from underrepresented minority groups or disadvantaged backgrounds. It should be noted that the legislation neither required nor endorsed the use of racial classifications in admitting students to such institutions.

On January 25, 2010, the commission wrote to the chairman of the Securities and Exchange Commission (SEC) to gather information about the SEC's new regulations, which required corporate boards to disclose their diversity policies. The commission's letter sought virtually all the internal and external communications of the SEC regarding the adoption of the regulations.

Those who would prefer to see the Civil Rights Commission return to its historic role of protecting the rights of people who have traditionally been the victims of discrimination were appalled by the change in emphasis. As Ted Shaw asked, "Why devote so much of one's time, money, resources, indeed life's energy to fighting so passionately against affirmative action when so much racial inequality, as a consequence of our nation's long history of white supremacy, remains intact?"[231]

Conclusion

What remains on the conservative agenda? The question of affirmative action in university admissions is back on the docket of the Supreme Court in a challenge by a rejected white applicant to the admissions policy of the University of Texas at Austin.[232] It is conceivable that the court could overrule its decision in *Grutter*, which upheld the affirmative action program at Michigan Law School. Several conservative groups filed amicus briefs in support of the white student's petition for the Supreme Court to take the case.[233] Beyond that, Roger Clegg addressed the conservative agenda in his article in the *Harvard Journal of Law and Public Policy* where he evaluated the record of the Bush administration on affirmative action.[234] He identified the following goals:

- Challenge the constitutionality of the Voting Rights Act of 2006
- Continue filing lawsuits to challenge the use of racial preferences in government contracting
- Seek a decision holding that although remedying past discrimination in government contracting is a compelling governmental interest, it is impossible for the use of racial preferences to be narrowly tailored
- Make all federal programs race-blind and race-neutral
- Monitor whether local school districts are complying with the decision in *Parents Involved* striking down the use of racial classifications with respect to school assignments
- Monitor the use of race classifications in university admissions
- File ballot initiatives state by state to render the use of race classifications in university admissions unconstitutional
- Chip away at the Supreme Court's decision in *Grutter*, limiting the circumstances that establish a compelling interest in preferences or constitute a narrowly tailored program; ultimately seek a decision from the Supreme Court holding the use of race preferences in university admissions unconstitutional

- Seek to end the use of non-admissions race classifications—for example, in summer programs, internships, and scholarships—at the university level
- Oppose arguments that diversity justifies the use of racial classifications in employment and seek a Supreme Court decision that bars the use of racial classifications even to remedy manifest racial imbalances in a traditionally segregated job category unless there is a showing of relatively recent discrimination that cannot otherwise be remedied
- Repeal, or strike down through litigation, regulations that enforce Executive Order No. 11,246, which requires companies that do a minimum level of contracting work with the federal government to have an affirmative action plan with goals and timetables to address the underrepresentation of minorities and women in their workforces

The agenda remains ambitious, and the commitment of Federalist Society members to carrying it out has not wavered.

5

The Jurisprudence of Personal Sexual Autonomy

Many Americans do not want persons who openly engage in homosexual conduct as partners in their business, as scoutmasters for their children, as teachers in their children's schools, or as boarders in their home. They view this as protecting themselves and their families from a lifestyle that they believe to be immoral and destructive. The Court views it as "discrimination" which it is the function of our judgments to deter. So imbued is the Court with the law profession's anti-anti-homosexual culture, that it is seemingly unaware that the attitudes of that culture are not obviously "mainstream" [and] that in most States what the Court calls "discrimination" against those who engage in homosexual acts is perfectly legal.

—Antonin Scalia[1]

It was the summer of 1969. Norma McCorvey, a twenty-one-year-old unskilled worker living in Texas, learned that she was pregnant. Single, unable to obtain an abortion in her home state, and unable to afford to travel to a state where she could procure one, she gave birth. Without means to provide for the child, her third, McCorvey sought the services of an adoption agency. In the process, she met two young lawyers who undertook to challenge the constitutionality of the Texas abortion law. Norma McCorvey became Jane Roe.[2]

The stormy confluence of personal decisions related to the fundamentals of human existence and identity, and the meaning and force of the laws that we as citizens impose on one another, are felt nowhere more keenly than in the jurisprudence of personal sexual autonomy. This chapter focuses on the landscape of abortion law and policy. Because the rights of access to contraception, of private consensual homosexual conduct, and of marriage equality are linked to abortion by intertwined constitutional jurisprudence—and resisted to varying degrees by conservatives—these issues are presented as context for the abortion narrative.

We examine how members of the Federalist Society have promulgated conservative ideology in abortion law and policy. As in other areas of law, Federalist Society members' contributions include the development of legal theory and strategy, publishing and popularizing their ideas in legal journals and public forums, working in coalitions, holding key government positions, promoting legislation, representing parties in court, and filing amicus briefs on important issues. Symbolic of their influence, members of the Federalist Society have presented the oral argument to the Supreme Court in every significant abortion case since 1992.

The chapter first identifies the links between the Federalist Society and the most prominent individuals and groups in the antiabortion and "family values" movements. We explain the influence that Federalist Society members had over government policy toward abortion in the administrations of Ronald Reagan, George H. W. Bush and George W. Bush. After outlining the jurisprudence of intimate personal liberties in Supreme Court cases leading up to *Roe v. Wade*, we discuss the prescient constitutional analysis regarding abortion and same-sex marriage outlined by young conservative lawyers in the Reagan Justice Department.[3] We then analyze how Federalist Society members' ideas and tactics have shaped abortion law and jurisprudence since *Roe*, shining a light on the success that conservatives have had chipping away at the right to make abortion decisions.

We note that Federalist Society members and other conservatives do not universally share the substantive arguments against a constitutional right to choose an abortion. Of the broad group of viewpoints that make up the conservative spectrum, moral issues present perhaps the greatest ideological and social divide. A libertarian may favor only minimal regulation of abortion, while a social conservative may prefer a complete ban. Studies have shown that the greatest social divides among lawyers of the right are between economic conservatives and abortion opponents, and between libertarians and those devoted to traditional family values.[4]

THE FEDERALIST SOCIETY AND THE FAMILY VALUES MOVEMENT

The Federalist Society shares membership—and leadership—with a swath of politically mobilized Christian advocacy groups within the family values movement. These groups seek to promote traditional Christian values and morality in actions "that reflect God's design," such as defending the sanctity of life and defining marriage as between one woman and one man.[5] These groups are active in policy, politics, and the law, seeking to propagate their vision of the Constitution as a protector of God's will. The major players in the abortion arena over the last twenty years include Focus on the Family, the Christian Coalition, Americans United for Life, the Legal Life Defense Foundation, the Family Research Council, and the National Right to Life Committee. Many of these groups predate the Federalist Society and conduct their campaigns for law and policy change in a much more overt manner. As discussed in more detail below, many senior members of these giants of Christian conservatism are also leaders in the Federalist Society. This enables the sharing of broad access to networks, resources, and intellectual capital.

These Christian advocacy groups share a number of foundational tenets with the Federalist Society—individual liberty, the separation of powers, and religious freedom. They have extraordinary influence, and they have contributed significantly to bringing cases and submitting amicus briefs to oppose gay rights and reproductive rights, assert parental rights (for example, regarding visitation, school prayer, and home schooling), fight the legalization of assisted suicide, and urge a halt to stem cell research.[6]

Although the Federalist Society and Christian advocacy groups are aligned in many ways, they are not in total agreement. In the abortion context, Joan Crawford Greenberg best described the relationship: Social conservatives, for whom abortion is simply immoral, care more about *results*—laws that restrict access to abortion and, ideally, that counsel against it. Judicial conservatives, who probably make up a larger percentage of the Federalist Society and its leadership, care more about *process*—they are more concerned about judicial restraint and originalist constitutional interpretation. They argue that unenumerated rights deserve little protection from courts, and that to the extent they constitute social policy, such policy should be determined by state legislatures.[7]

Within the Federalist Society, the home of efforts to limit or overturn the constitutional rights related to personal sexual autonomy is the Religious Liberties Practice Group. The group's name reflects the libertarian, individual rights–based view that pervades the society. It also suggests the view that state or federal laws advancing gay rights, access to contraception, and abortion offend the religious liberty of those who disagree. Such laws amount, some have argued, to "government-backed persecution."[8] The society's Free Speech and Election Law Practice Group also concerns itself (although to a lesser extent) with the abortion issue. There, debate rages over whether abortion-related speech (such as protests outside abortion clinics, or requirements that physicians provide warnings to women considering abortion) is unduly restricted in comparison to other equivalent forms of speech.

Just as the Federalist Society does, the groups and individuals associated with the family values movement preach originalism as the correct method of constitutional interpretation, decrying liberal activist judges who, they believe, legislate from the bench, creating social policy that offends the conservative worldview. Focus on the Family, for example, expressly ties originalism to its family values agenda. It lobbies against judicially created privacy rights that have "mandated new social policies, such as the right to abortion, the right to homosexual sex, the right to publish obscenity, as well as trampling on First Amendment religious freedoms," as "unconstitutional and ungodly."[9]

Many of these individuals and groups also take what might be considered a narrow view of which Christian values are basic to the United States. Few focus on notions of equality, sacrifice, or common welfare. This approach has been encouraged by Robert George, a senior advisor to the Religious Liberties Practice Group. He suggested to a gathering that included a number of bishops in Washington, D.C., in 2009 that the church should devote less energy to issues of social justice, and concentrate more on "moral social" issues such as same-sex marriage, stem cell research, and abortion, where principles attributable to natural law and Gospel principles were unequivocal.[10] He had no objection to the bishops "making utter nuisances of themselves" about poverty and injustice generally, but argued that they should not support economic policies tied to social justice, such as minimum wage laws or progressive taxation, which he cast as "matters of public policy upon which

Gospel principles by themselves do not resolve differences of opinion among reasonable and well-informed people of good will."[11]

Before describing the most influential members of the Religious Liberties and Free Speech Practice Groups, it is worth noting that Leonard Leo, executive vice president of the society, has for decades been firmly entrenched within powerful Catholic lobbying organizations. As Catholic strategist for the George W. Bush White House and the Bush-Cheney reelection campaign, Leo lobbied Catholic groups nationwide in support of Bush's election to a second term in 2004. Leo has been a voice for the United States in a number of international forums, including many with ramifications for religious freedom. During George H. W. Bush's administration, Leo served as a delegate to the UN Commission on Human Rights and participated in two World Health Organization delegations. George W. Bush appointed him to lead the U.S. Commission on International Religious Freedom in 2007 and 2008 (he was reappointed in 2010 by the Republican Senate minority leader). He has also served on the U.S. National Commission to UNESCO and the World Intellectual Property Organization.[12] Leo is a director of Liberty Central, the Tea Party–affiliated group launched by Justice Clarence Thomas's wife, Virginia. In 2010, this group campaigned against the construction of Cordoba House, an Islamic community center to be located near the former World Trade Center site in New York. Leo's opposition to abortion was reflected in his praise of the courage of unsuccessful Supreme Court nominee Harriet Miers for seeking, as president of the Texas State Bar Association, to alter the ABA's pro-abortion stance.[13]

The Religious Liberties Executive Committee reads like a "who's who" of Christian conservative advocacy. The *New York Times* called Robert George this country's "most influential conservative Christian thinker."[14] His role as a thought leader for Christian conservatism is difficult to overstate, as is his influence in litigating abortion and other reproduction issues, as well as same-sex marriage. George is credited with persuading President George W. Bush to restrict embryonic stem cell research. Justice Antonin Scalia has acknowledged that George is one of the most talked-about thinkers in conservative legal circles.[15] During his run for the Republican presidential nomination in 2011, Newt Gingrich mentioned George as a potential Supreme Court nominee. George is the chairman emeritus of the National Organization for Marriage, which the *Washington Post* has called the "preeminent" national organization formed to protect marriage as a heterosexual union.[16] George also founded the American Principles Project, a grassroots organization dedicated to, among other things, "the sanctity of human life and the integrity of marriage and the family."[17] Not long after its formation, the group called for the removal of Kevin Jennings, an education official in the Obama administration who had been a founder of the Gay, Lesbian and Straight Education Network. George claimed that Jennings's intent was, "in defiance of the wishes of parents, to use our elementary schools to teach pro-sexual-liberationist, pro-homosexualist propaganda."[18] The Catholic publication *Crisis* once noted, "If there really is a vast right-wing conspiracy, its leaders probably meet in George's kitchen."[19]

Professor Hadley Arkes, a special advisor to the practice group, has been a particularly influential figure in the development of the law with respect to abortion. He is the champion of the incrementalist strategy. This approach is designed to chip away slowly at access to abortion through state and federal legislation and litigation, rather than challenging *Roe* head-on, either in court or in the court of public opinion. Incrementalists attempt to determine where the "moral threshold" is—that is, where abortion becomes unpalatable to people who might otherwise be pro-choice, and then to move that threshold, in small steps, toward the pro-life position. For example, they challenge people to consider whether a certain type of abortion procedure or abortion for certain reasons (such as gender preference, physical deformity, or genetic illness) should be legal. Arkes has described it thus: "One step, modestly framed, may follow another; each one draws wide support in the public; and step by step people become accustomed again to the notion that it is reasonable to deliberate about the grounds on which abortions may be justified and unjustified. And what is more, the judgments that people arrive at in this way may be enacted now, in legislatures, with the force of law."[20] The most successful embodiments of this strategy to date are the Federal Born-Alive Infants Protection Act of 2002 and the Federal Partial-Birth Abortion Ban Act of 2003. Arkes was the chief architect of the Born-Alive Infants Act, which sought to offer a "modest first step" via legislation designed to protect the life of a child that has survived an abortion.[21]

Senior Religious Liberties Practice Group leaders also include William L. Saunders, a vice president of legal affairs at Americans United for Life (AUL). AUL was founded in 1971 and was the first national pro-life organization in the United States.[22] AUL's mission is to "defend human life through vigorous legislative, judicial, and educational efforts, on both the state and national level."[23] Robert George and Hadley Arkes are also on its board. Saunders is also a longtime fellow at the Family Research Council (FRC) and former director of its Center for Human Life and Bioethics.[24] The FRC's early leadership was stacked with former Reagan White House officials. Once a division of Focus on the Family, the FRC has been described as the successor to the Christian Coalition, and it was instrumental in the passage of the Federal Partial-Birth Abortion Ban Act of 2003. The act's passage was certainly easier because Republicans controlled Congress. But then–attorney general John Ashcroft acknowledged the FRC's contribution to the act's passage to a three-hundred-person crowd soon thereafter: "If you don't believe you have an impact in this city, take a look at the vote in the United States Senate yesterday and then go 16 blocks down Pennsylvania Avenue and think about the fact that the president has indicated he will sign that legislation."[25]

Kevin Hasson, founder of the Becket Fund for Religious Liberty, served in the George H. W. Bush White House under then–deputy assistant attorney general Samuel Alito, as an advisor on, among other constitutional issues, church-state relations.[26] Hasson was the chair of the practice group in 2007.

James Bopp, perhaps his generation's most prolific anti-abortion litigator, has been a longtime leader of the Federalist Society's Free Speech and Election Law

Practice Group. Bopp got his start in conservative activism when he headed the Indiana University chapter of Young Americans for Freedom, the group started by William F. Buckley. In 1978, at the age of twenty-nine, Bopp became the first general counsel of the National Right to Life Committee (NRLC)—a position he still holds.[27]

The NRLC is a "federation" of fifty state-based right-to-life organizations and the United States' largest pro-life group. It was founded in direct response to the Supreme Court's decision in *Roe v. Wade.* The NRLC has eight state directors, based primarily in the South, and it focuses on educating and legislating in the areas of euthanasia, assisted suicide, infanticide, and abortion.[28] Since the early 1990s, after *Planned Parenthood v. Casey* first held certain restrictions on abortion (such as mandatory waiting periods and regulation from the time of conception) to be constitutional, the NRLC has drafted model abortion legislation designed to make abortion less accessible.[29] The NRLC works with state legislators to develop and then defend its anti-abortion legislation against lawsuits brought by reproductive rights organizations, "so activist judges can't easily tie a good law up for years in court or strike it down completely."[30] Douglas Johnson of the NRLC is credited with coining the phrase "partial-birth abortion"—a term not found at the time in medical textbooks.[31] His phrase has subsequently been used in numerous state laws, and in the Federal Partial-Birth Abortion Ban Act. This act was signed into law in 2003 by President George W. Bush, and upheld by the Supreme Court three years later in *Gonzales v. Carhart.* Douglas's rhetoric became a powerful tool in attracting support for a law that criminalized a specific type of abortion and, for the first time, contained no exception permitting the procedure when necessary to protect the health of the mother.

Bopp is also a founder and general counsel of the James Madison Center for Free Speech, an organization dedicated to securing freedom of political speech under the First Amendment.[32] Early in his career, Bopp participated in the distribution of voter guides in support of Reagan's presidential bid in 1980. He went on to defend numerous challenges to voter guides by the Federal Election Commission, including on behalf of the Christian Coalition, after which he was described by Ralph Reed as a "bulldog litigator."[33] He has been at the helm of the bulk of challenges funded by major Republican donors and interest groups to laws that restrict the extent to which corporations can contribute to political campaigns, in particular the McCain-Feingold Act of 2002.[34] It has been said that Bopp's work in *Federal Election Commission v. Wisconsin Right to Life, Inc.* (in which the Supreme Court held that issue ads, paid for by corporate interests, could not be banned during the months preceding a primary or general election) laid the foundation for the *Citizens United v. Federal Election Commission* victory three years later, the biggest free speech case of Bopp's career.[35] There, the Supreme Court held that corporations, unions, and nonprofit groups have a right of free speech that includes unlimited spending in supporting or opposing the election of a candidate. This decision led to the creation of Super Political Action Committees (Super PACs) that enable groups supporting political candidates to raise and spend monies for political advertising with impunity. The power of these groups and the vitriolic messages they produced became a feature of the 2012 presidential race. Bopp shepherded *Citizens United* through the lower courts. Federalist Society member Ted Olson argued it before the Supreme Court.[36]

Bopp's abortion and political speech work are connected. Before his breakthrough in *Citizens United*, he expressed despair about what he perceived to be the Supreme Court's hyperprotection of the unenumerated abortion right in the face of the court's supposed lack of protection for the enumerated free speech right. Bopp has written extensively about the relationship between pro-life advocacy and freedom of speech. Because of the history of protest near abortion clinics, countless cities and towns have passed ordinances that restrict speech and association outside abortion clinics. Pro-life campaigners such as Bopp argue that these rules are not written or enforced evenly and that—more often than not—they quash pro-life speech.

In addition to his tenure of more than thirty years with the NRLC, Bopp also serves as special counsel to Focus on the Family.[37] As described later in this chapter, Bopp has authored nearly twenty Supreme Court amicus briefs for anti-abortion lobbying groups (including the NRLC), for individual interested persons (such as women who have undergone abortions but later believed they had not been provided the facts necessary to make an informed choice), and for collections of elected officials. He has been credited with persuading the Supreme Court to "uphold restrictions on abortion funding, the ban on partial-birth abortions, and requirements for informed consent."[38]

Donald Hodel, a Reagan-era secretary of the interior and member of the Federalist Society's board of visitors, served as president of Focus on the Family from 2003 to 2005. Focus has been called a "powerhouse of the religious right" and is perhaps the most powerful voice within the movement.[39] Founded by James Dobson in 1970, Focus has grown into an international organization with over one thousand employees and with revenues in excess of one hundred million dollars annually.[40] Focus spends more than thirty million dollars on an annual basis on broadcast and print materials, reaching more than two hundred million people in over one hundred countries via radio and television broadcasts.

In the realms of public policy and legislation, Focus has, since 2006, concentrated its efforts on the definition of marriage as between one man and one woman, and "the sanctity of human life in all its forms."[41] In 2010, Focus spent nearly six million dollars on these issues. In addition, it made over forty grants of ultrasound machines and/or training to abortion clinics across the nation, reportedly for "pregnancy medical care."[42] These gifts are part of "Option Ultrasound" which seeks to increase the probability that a pregnant woman will view the fetus before making the abortion decision, presumably on the basis that seeing the image will have a deterrent effect. This effort has run in parallel with a host of state legislative efforts either to mandate the ultrasound or to require physicians to offer an ultrasound before an abortion, under the guise of "informed consent." Since its inception in 2004, Option Ultrasound has provided over five hundred grants to organizations in all fifty states for ultrasound machines or sonogram training.[43] As of August 2012, twenty-one states have inserted an ultrasound requirement into the abortion process:

- Two states require a pre-abortion ultrasound *and require* that the provider show and describe the image to the patient.
- Six states require a pre-abortion ultrasound and require the provider to *offer* to show and describe the image to the patient.
- Nine states require that if a pre-abortion ultrasound is performed, the patient be given an opportunity to view it.
- Five states require that a patient be provided with the opportunity to view a pre-abortion ultrasound image.[44]

Jay Sekulow, a close friend of the Federalist Society who has frequently spoken at its meetings, was one of the "four horsemen"—along with Leonard Leo, C. Boyden Gray, and Edwin Meese—who guided President George W. Bush's judicial nomination strategy.[45] Sekulow is general counsel to the American Center for Law and Justice (ACLJ), which was founded by Pat Robertson in 1990. It now boasts over a million members. *Time Magazine* named Sekulow one of the twenty-five most influential evangelicals in America and called the ACLJ "a powerful counterweight" to the American Civil Liberties Union.[46]

Robertson, along with Federalist Society member Ralph Reed, founded the Christian Coalition in 1989 following Robertson's unsuccessful campaign for president. Robertson and Reed met at a dinner given by Students for America during President George H. W. Bush's 1989 inauguration.[47] Reed was just twenty-eight years old at the time. Reed and Robertson envisioned the coalition as a grassroots organization, connecting people at a local level rather than focusing on large national issues. The group campaigned against abortion by advocating for state restrictions such as requirement of parental consent for minors, and it actively supported "partial-birth abortion" bans at the state and federal levels. The coalition's influence waned in the late 1990s, however, and the prominence it enjoyed when George H. W. and George W. Bush consulted it when seeking the presidency has not returned.

Federalist Society leaders were active both as leaders of the Christian Coalition and as advocates for the organization in court. Hodel served as president from 1997 to 1999 and oversaw Robertson's transition out of the organization. Bopp represented the coalition in 1999 in *Federal Election Commission v. Christian Coalition*, a suit by the FEC to enjoin alleged violations of federal campaign financing laws. Bopp obtained dismissal of several claims, but the district court ruled that in Georgia the coalition had violated the "express advocacy" limitation on corporate campaign expenditures by urging voters to vote for Newt Gingrich for Congress as a "Christian Coalition 100 percenter." It also held that the coalition had violated federal law by making a valuable mailing list available to the campaign of Oliver North for Senate in Virginia in 1994.[48]

THE SUPREME COURT JURISPRUDENCE OF PERSONAL SEXUAL AUTONOMY

The Constitution does not mention marriage and family, nor does it say anything about abortion or the rights of homosexuals. The Constitution guarantees "liberty," and the framers left it to the courts to determine the specific content of that term. In the last hundred years, the Supreme Court has recognized a variety of rights that provide constitutional protection to individual interests in family relationships, marriage, procreation, the termination of pregnancy, and intimate relations. The court has vacillated with respect to the constitutional foundations for these rights, and there has been much disagreement among the justices and the wider legal and political community with respect to them. A thorough analysis of the doctrinal developments in this area would take us far beyond the limitations of this book. A brief outline of the jurisprudence is essential, however, to understanding the positions of Federalist Society members in the relevant debates.

Early Supreme Court cases dealing with liberty issues articulated the relevant rights in terms that protected the family. In 1923, in *Meyer v. Nebraska*, the court held unconstitutional a Nebraska law that forbade teaching in any language other than English, and also forbade the teaching of any foreign language to a pupil below the eighth grade.[49] The court held the Nebraska law violated both the teacher's right to pursue his occupation as a German-language teacher and the rights of the child's parents to hire the teacher to instruct their children, both protected by the liberty guaranteed under the Fourteenth Amendment. Two years later, in *Pierce v. Society of Sisters*, the Supreme Court held unconstitutional an Oregon statute that required children between ages eight and sixteen to attend public rather than private schools. The court found that the statute unreasonably interfered "with the liberty of parents and guardians to direct the upbringing and education of children under their control."[50]

In *Stanley v. Illinois*, in 1972, the court held that an unwed father had a due process right to a hearing before he could be deprived of the custody of his children after their mother's death. The court declared that "the interest of a parent in the companionship, care, custody, and management of his or her children" was substantial enough that the Constitution required such a hearing.[51] In 1977, in *Moore v. City of East Cleveland*, the court struck down a municipal ordinance that limited the occupants of a single-dwelling unit to a "family" and defined "family" narrowly. Mrs. Inez Moore had been charged criminally because she lived with her son and with two grandsons who were cousins rather than brothers. The court held that "the Constitution protects the sanctity of the family precisely because the institution of the family is deeply rooted in this Nation's history and tradition," making clear that "family" included extended families.[52] In *Santosky v. Kramer*, in 1982, the court held that the rights of natural parents may not be terminated without clear and convincing evidence. It acknowledged its "historical recognition that freedom of personal choice in matters of family life is a fundamental liberty interest protected by the Fourteenth Amendment."[53]

Other decisions recognized a specific constitutional right to procreate. In *Skinner v. Oklahoma*, in 1942, the court held unconstitutional a statute that allowed state courts to order the involuntary sterilization of a person convicted of two or more crimes of "moral turpitude."[54]

The court afforded the marital relationship constitutional protection in *Loving v. Virginia*, in 1967, when it nullified a Virginia statute under which Mildred and Richard Loving had been criminally prosecuted for their interracial marriage. In this decision, based both on the equal protection clause and on substantive due process grounds, the court declared, "Marriage is one of the 'basic civil rights of man,' fundamental to our very existence and survival."[55]

None of the foregoing decisions was based on a right of privacy.[56] But in 1965, in *Griswold v. Connecticut*, a right of privacy was finally recognized when the Supreme Court struck down a Connecticut statute that criminalized the use of contraceptives for the purpose of preventing conception.[57] In his opinion for the court, Justice William O. Douglas concluded that the statute violated the right of marital privacy, which right he found in the "penumbras" of various enumerated rights in the Bill of Rights that created zones of privacy. Douglas's creative argument, which proved to have no future in Supreme Court jurisprudence, resulted from his distaste for the doctrine of substantive due process, because of the way that doctrine had been employed during the *Lochner* era to strike down progressive social and economic legislation.[58] Other justices in *Griswold* recognized privacy as an element of liberty protected by substantive due process and by the language of the Ninth Amendment safeguarding "additional fundamental rights, protected from governmental infringement, which exist alongside those fundamental rights specifically mentioned in the first eight constitutional amendments."[59] In any event, the focus of the case was on the marital relationship. As Douglas put it, "Would we allow the police to search the sacred precincts of marital bedrooms for telltale signs of the use of contraceptives? The very idea is repulsive to the notions of privacy surrounding the marriage relationship."[60]

The court provided protection for the use of contraceptives by single people in *Eisenstadt v. Baird*, in 1972. It held that under the equal protection clause of the Fourteenth Amendment, there was no rational basis for treating married and unmarried persons differently with respect to the use of contraceptives. *Eisenstadt* transformed the law with respect to decision making about intimate issues, moving the focus from the family or the marital unit to the individual. Justice Brennan wrote:

> Yet the marital couple is not an independent entity with a mind and heart of its own, but an association of two individuals each with a separate intellectual and emotional makeup. If the right of privacy means anything, it is the right of the individual, married or single, to be free from unwarranted governmental intrusion into matters so fundamentally affecting a person as the decision whether to bear or beget a child.[61]

One year later, in *Roe v. Wade*, the court concluded that this series of cases, together with others, demonstrated that the Constitution protected a right of privacy that included personal rights that are "fundamental," or "implicit in the concept of ordered liberty."[62] This right of privacy "is broad enough to encompass a woman's decision whether or not to terminate her pregnancy." As with other personal rights, the court concluded that although the right is fundamental, it is not absolute. It used pregnancy's trimester framework as a means of balancing a woman's right to decide to terminate her pregnancy against the state's right to regulate the procedure for the purposes of safeguarding the health of the pregnant woman, maintaining medical standards, and protecting the potential life of the fetus.[63]

The foregoing history describes the essential outlines of the jurisprudence of individual rights in the intimate spheres of life as it existed when Reagan assumed the presidency in 1981. Shortly after the beginning of his second term, in 1986, the Supreme Court decided *Bowers v. Hardwick*, upholding the constitutionality of a Georgia sodomy law in a 5–4 decision.[64] Meese considered this case the Reagan administration's biggest victory of the Supreme Court's 1985 term, even though the U.S. government was not a party to the case and did not file an amicus brief: "We don't have to be in a case to get our view across. The point of view that we've been making—that the Court should not supersede its judgment for the judgment of the states—was vindicated in that case."[65] Professor Laurence Tribe explained that Meese regarded the decision as a significant victory because the majority opinion of the court adopted the same theory the Reagan administration had advanced for overruling *Roe v. Wade*—namely, that "such un-enumerated rights as privacy really do not deserve much protection."[66]

In *Bowers*, Justice Byron White distinguished between a "right of homosexuals to engage in acts of sodomy" and the protections the court had previously afforded to family, marriage, and procreation, finding no connection between them. He was unwilling to extend the guarantee of liberty in the Fourteenth Amendment to homosexual conduct, concluding that history and tradition proscribed—rather than protected—homosexuality.

PUBLICATIONS OF FEDERALIST SOCIETY MEMBERS

As we described in Chapter 1, the founders of the Federalist Society obtained significant positions in the Department of Justice after they graduated from law school. They and other conservatives, under Attorney General Meese, authored a series of reports that were published by the DOJ's Office of Legal Policy (OLP) near the end of President Reagan's second term. In *Report to the Attorney General: The Constitution in the Year 2000*, published in 1988, the OLP laid out the potential future conflicts it foresaw on the Supreme Court with respect to abortion and homosexual rights, as well as in other areas of constitutional law. The authors considered whether the right to abortion would be expanded or restricted, whether a constitutional right of sexual preference would be used to invalidate laws that disadvantaged homosexuals, and whether a broad definition of the right of privacy would invalidate state laws that promote public morality.[67]

The OLP analyzed issues within abortion jurisprudence that it believed were likely to surface in the coming years, many of which remain areas of concern for anti-abortion groups today. These issues included the extent to which states may require parental consent for minors' abortions, whether a state's refusal to subsidize the abortions of indigent women would violate the equal protection clause, and whether an expansion of privacy rights would prevent the federal government from imposing anti-abortion restrictions on foreign aid programs.[68] The OLP also questioned whether *Roe* might be expanded to include the right to abortion for the purposes of fetal experimentation, stating that the court "might expand the concept of 'health' broadly enough to cover fetal experimentation on the ground that the mother may receive an economic reward or a psychic gratification."[69]

The report outlines what in effect became the strategy championed by Hadley Arkes, in which states incrementally narrowed the right to choose an abortion through various means. The OLP predicted state laws requiring women to receive information prior to obtaining an abortion, including the potential physical and psychological consequences of the decision, available alternatives, and even information on the potential moral consequences of the decision. The report noted, "The vast majority of women seeking an abortion would perhaps be unlikely to alter their choices as a consequence, but the community would at least be able to impress upon the citizenry in general, and those seeking to have abortions in particular, the gravity of this decision."[70] Reflecting the philosophical divide over the appropriate judicial role, the OLP noted that "the debate over Roe is not just about abortion issues, but about who will decide those issues—the people through their elective representatives or the courts."[71]

With respect to the rights of homosexuals, the OLP questioned whether the Supreme Court would identify the right of privacy as encompassing all private, consensual sexual conduct, including that of homosexuals, and whether classifications relating to homosexuality would be subjected to heightened scrutiny by the court under the equal protection clause of the Fourteenth Amendment. Such heightened scrutiny, it noted, could lead to the invalidation of laws excluding homosexuals from the armed services and sensitive government positions, and to the invalidation of state laws discriminating against homosexuals with respect to child custody and adoption. Affirmative action programs, it noted, might be expanded to include homosexuals. The report counseled that it was not "far-fetched" to imagine that strict scrutiny of classifications based on sexual preference would lead to the recognition of homosexual marriages.[72] It concluded that virtually "all . . . government regulation of homosexuals and homosexual conduct would be open to question."[73] Indeed, the OLP mused whether the equal protection clause could be used to invalidate programs designed to prevent the spread of AIDS on the basis that they impermissibly discriminate against homosexuals.[74]

The report was written in a balanced tone, but the "parade of horribles" that it predicted would follow an expansion of homosexual rights certainly sent a clear message to conservative readers. Moreover, the conservative bias against judicial recognition of unenumerated rights was manifested in the report's conclusion that were the Supreme Court to overrule *Bowers*, the court "would likely then impose its own solution in an area where the states are currently debating and resolving the issues."[75]

The most interesting section of the report dealing with privacy issues is chapter 4, where the authors discuss how the right of privacy might be defined in the future. On the one hand, the right of privacy could be tied to "traditional family values," such as family integrity, parental rights, marriage, and procreation. On the other, it could be defined more expansively in terms of notions of individual autonomy. *Bowers* represents the former approach; *Roe*, the latter. The authors concluded that to the extent the expansive definition was taken, it would call into question whether public morality alone would ever be a sufficient justification for legislation that interferes with individual liberty.

The OLP identified a radical series of consequences that could follow from an expansive definition of the right of privacy. They included: the invalidation on constitutional grounds of laws regulating sexual activities between consenting adults, including adultery, bigamy, prostitution, incest, and those limiting marriage to heterosexual couples; greater independence of children from their parents, to the point of eliminating all legal distinctions between children and adults; and the invalidation of criminal laws prohibiting the use of drugs. The report also discussed the possible effect on laws with respect to suicide and euthanasia; the possibility that individuals might have a right to possess and use obscene materials outside the home; and the possibility that seat belt and motorcycle helmet laws could be struck down.

Slippery slope arguments, such as the OLP's list of potential consequences, can be (and often have been) overstated to make an underlying argument that rests on policy grounds. The radical consequences that the OLP predicted might follow from a definition of the right of privacy based on individual autonomy are far from inevitable. The Supreme Court never defines individual rights as absolute, whether they are enumerated in the Constitution or unenumerated. Even when rights are recognized as "fundamental," the government may still enact laws and regulations that compromise such rights, where there is a compelling government interest and the means chosen to achieve that interest are narrowly tailored. Regulation of the extreme consequences of the recognition of privacy is not difficult where the government or social interest is real.

The OLP was correct, however, in predicting that the central question with respect to a right to privacy would be whether it is based in traditional family values or in individual autonomy. And the report correctly apprehended that a judicial recognition that the right of privacy is based on individual autonomy would undermine the argument that state regulation of individual rights may be justified solely by considerations of socially prevailing morality.

The question of what the basis is for a constitutional right of privacy continues to be controversial. Some of the recent decisions of the Supreme Court, however, are premised more on the need to protect and nurture individual autonomy than on traditional family values. In *Planned Parenthood of Southeastern Pennsylvania v. Casey*, in 1992, the Supreme Court declined to overrule *Roe v. Wade* and reaffirmed a woman's right to choose an abortion, although it abandoned the trimester formulation and altered the standard for when government regulation would be justified. In their plurality opinion for the court, Justices O'Connor, Kennedy, and Souter reiterated the emphasis on the rights of the *individual* to make decisions about procreation recognized twenty years earlier in *Eisenstadt v. Baird*. They went on to say:

> These matters, involving the most intimate and personal choices a person may make in a lifetime, choices central to personal dignity and autonomy, are central to the liberty protected by the Fourteenth Amendment. At the heart of liberty is the right to define one's own concept of existence, of meaning, of the universe, and of the mystery of human life. Beliefs about these matters could not define the attributes of personhood were they formed under compulsion of the State.[76]

Similarly, in *Lawrence v. Texas*, in 2003, the Supreme Court overruled *Bowers v. Hardwick* and held unconstitutional a Texas law that had made it a crime for two persons of the same sex to engage in consensual acts of sodomy. In his majority opinion for the court, Justice Kennedy began by saying, "Liberty presumes an autonomy of self that includes freedom of thought, belief, expression, and certain intimate conduct. The instant case involves liberty of the person both in its spatial and in its more transcendent dimensions."[77]

Federalist Society members who are at the forefront of anti-abortion efforts have published prolifically.[78] Their ideas, raised in academic and policy forums, have taken hold in arguments raised before the Supreme Court. For example, in a 1998 article, James Bopp recited many of the arguments eventually submitted (by him and others) to the Supreme Court in support of the constitutionality of partial-birth abortion bans.[79] Bopp essentially argued that abortion precedent could not be properly applied to the laws, because abortion law concerned the unborn, and partial-birth abortion bans concerned the "partially born." Hadley Arkes has published scholarly articles on a number of subjects, including constitutional interpretation, morality and law, and abortion.[80] In the *University of St. Thomas Journal of Law and Public Policy* (whose board of advisors includes Michael Paulsen and Robert Delahunty), Arkes posited in 2007 that partial-birth abortion bans were compatible with *Roe v. Wade*, just as Solicitor General Paul Clement, also a society member, had suggested at oral argument in *Gonzales v. Carhart* in 2006.[81]

Robert George has written and lectured extensively on the immorality of abortion, premised on the fact that upon fertilization, a new and distinct organism, an individual human embryo, comes into existence, and to abort that embryo (or at later development, a fetus) constitutes the killing of a human being, "a whole living member of the species homo sapiens, the same kind of entity as you or I, only at an earlier stage of development."[82] This premise forms the basis of the first principle of the Manhattan Declaration, released in 2009 and coauthored by George, which

affirms "the profound, inherent, and equal dignity of every human being as a creature fashioned in the very image of God, possessing inherent rights of equal dignity
and life."[83] The declaration, subtitled "A Call of Christian Conscience," advocates
resistance, including civil disobedience if necessary, to laws that allow abortion or
same-sex marriage, and to laws that restrict religious freedom. To date, the declaration has gathered nearly half a million signatures.[84]

Federalist Society founder Steven Calabresi sketched out a campaign plan
for pro-life groups in "How to Reverse Government Imposition of Immorality:
A Strategy for Eroding Roe v. Wade." He suggests learning from previous moral-
constitutional campaigns, such as those against racial segregation and capital punishment. He recommends, first, the use of "shrewd" litigation strategy to erode
the precedential value of Roe, leading to its eventual overturning, and second, a
campaign to turn public opinion against abortion. Calabresi suggests incremental
law change: banning abortion for sex selection; banning any form of abortion that
might cause pain to the fetus; prohibiting partners or family members from exert-
ing pressure on a woman to obtain an abortion; and a mandatory waiting period,
to be applied nationally. To sway public opinion, Calabresi suggests comparing
"abortion providers, like Planned Parenthood, to big tobacco companies. The comparison is fair: both are entities that exist to make money by encouraging vice."
Fundamentally, Calabresi posits that the U.S. law's recognition of a constitutional
right of women to have abortions is "deeply" and "profoundly" immoral. By making the legality of abortion "a matter of individual constitutional right," the legal
system has "put its highest moral imprimatur on a loathsome procedure that ought
to be at least discouraged by the law if not forbidden altogether."[85]

ABORTION LAW AFTER ROE

In 1973, immediately after Roe, opponents of the holding mobilized against the
newfound constitutional right to abortion. Although the Catholic Church had
been battling against liberalization of state abortion laws during the 1960s, it had
not been a fight on the national stage.[86] One commentator has suggested that the
suddenness of the decision caused a more powerful response than if the states had
simply continued to quietly and disparately liberalize abortion laws.[87] An early law
review article written by pro-life academic Charles Rice—who had also authored an
amicus brief in Roe for AUL, and is affiliated with the Federalist Society—argued
that the 1973 decision "did the same thing to the child in the womb that the Dred
Scott case did to the slaves. Where the right to life or liberty depends on the existence of personhood, it violates elementary natural justice to deny that status to
certain classes of human beings while granting it to others."[88]

In Congress, various constitutional amendments were introduced, supported
by people who would later join the Federalist Society. They proposed to restore the
states' power over abortion regulation by authorizing legislatures to protect human
life at every stage of biological development and defining the fetus as a "person"

within the meaning of the Fifth and Fourteenth Amendments, such that it possessed a constitutional right to life.[89] These efforts were grounded in the *Roe* Court's refusal to "resolve the difficult question of when life begins," on the basis that experts in medicine, philosophy, and theology could not find consensus and therefore the judiciary "at this point in the development of man's knowledge, is not in a position to speculate as to the answer."[90] Many hundreds of amendments have been introduced since *Roe*—a few illustrative examples follow. Just one made it to a Senate vote, but it failed to attract the two-thirds majority vote required by the Constitution.

In 1981, the National Right to Life Committee drafted the NRLC Amendment, with the help of constitutional scholars and consultants.[91] According to James Bopp, it met all eleven "vital objectives for a full and proper reversal of *Roe*" and sought to fully restore legal protection to the unborn.[92] It declared that the word "person" in the Fifth and Fourteenth Amendments applies to all human beings, including the unborn, at every stage of their biological development, including fertilization. It permitted only those medical procedures that were required to prevent the death of either the pregnant woman or her unborn offspring. It was introduced in the Senate by Jesse Helms.[93]

Senator Orrin Hatch introduced the Human Life Federalism Amendment (HLFA) into the 97th Congress in 1981.[94] It specifically provided that a right to abortion is not secured by the Constitution. Hatch withdrew the HLFA from consideration by the full Senate in September 1982. A truncated version emerged from committee to a full Senate vote in June 1983. It was defeated by 50 votes to 49.[95]

In addition to this flurry of activity in Congress, within thirty years of *Roe*'s first arguments, more than a dozen states had called for state constitutional conventions to consider a human life amendment.[96] With just one amendment going to a Senate vote in the twenty years following *Roe*, however, pro-life advocates realized that their odds of success in obtaining legal protections for the unborn through a change in the federal constitution were practically zero.[97] They moved the battleground to the states. Legislation was enacted to restrict abortion funding, to ban certain abortion procedures, and to place certain restrictions around the abortion procedure, such as mandatory waiting periods, mandatory pre-procedure informational materials, parental consent, and clinic licensure and inspection regimes. More recently, states have considered human life amendments to their constitutions in order to limit access to abortion and birth control; others have sought to narrow the window in which a woman can obtain an abortion based on fetal pain or the detection of a fetal heartbeat, and to limit insurance coverage of the procedure.[98] Some of these measures have come before the Supreme Court, and significantly altered the landscape of abortion law.

In 1980, the court heard *Harris v. McRae* and upheld the Hyde Amendment, severely limiting the use of federal funds to reimburse the cost of abortions under the Medicaid program.[99] The court held that states that participated in Medicaid were not required to fill the funding shortfall due to the amendment even for medically necessary abortions.[100] To this day, in fact, the Hyde Amendment is a rider to the annual Labor, Health and Human Services, and Education appropriations bill, and it prevents Medicaid and any program within any of these departments from funding abortion, with limited exceptions. 1981's *H. L. v. Matheson* confirmed this post-*Roe* shift in the court's view of the abortion right.[101] There, a five-justice majority held that the constitution did not compel states to "fine-tune" their laws to encourage or facilitate abortion.[102]

These were the first chinks in *Roe's* armor. And with each case brought to the Supreme Court, pursuant to Hadley Arkes's incrementalist strategy, *Roe's* rigidity has been softened, and the court's interpretation of what states may do to regulate or restrict abortion has generally favored the pro-life movement. In 1992, the court abandoned *Roe's* trimester framework for determining when the state could ban abortion and replaced it with "viability," the moment when a child can survive outside the mother. Before viability, the state cannot create "undue burdens" to a woman's right to choose an abortion. After viability, the state may restrict abortions if it provides exceptions for pregnancies that endanger a woman's life or her health. It also ruled that states may restrict the use of public funds or facilities for nontherapeutic abortions, and that they can require mandatory waiting periods, notification of affected parties, and distribution of certain information prior to an abortion, primarily under the guise of informed consent. Perhaps most importantly, the court has backed away from holding abortion to be a "fundamental" right.

In 1983, the court heard *City of Akron v. Akron Center for Reproductive Health, Inc.*, which concerned an abortion-regulating ordinance passed by the city of Akron, Ohio. The ordinance required all second-trimester abortions to be performed in a hospital, parental consent for minors under fifteen, the distribution of certain materials to the woman prior to the abortion, a twenty-four-hour waiting period, and the disposal of fetal remains in a certain way.[103] *Akron* was the first of the Reagan administration's two opportunities to weigh in on a Supreme Court abortion case. It was the first time that the federal government filed an amicus brief where a state abortion law was being challenged. In fact, no president before Reagan—who was the first serious presidential candidate to support a human life amendment—had sought to advance the pro-life position while in office.[104] Reagan published an essay on *Roe's* ten-year anniversary entitled "Abortion and the Conscience of a Nation," which discussed the arguments against "abortion-on-demand." Reagan described his efforts to assist Congress to "reverse the tide of abortion," specifically through the Human Life Bill introduced by Jesse Helms, which was the vehicle for Senate hearings in 1981, and the Respect Human Life Act, sponsored by Henry Hyde and Roger Jepsen, which sought to prohibit the federal government from "performing abortions or assisting those who do so, except to save the life of the mother." Infanticide, Reagan warned, "flows inevitably from permissive abortion as another step in the denial of the inviolability of innocent human life."

The government's amicus brief in *Akron* was primarily authored by Solicitor General Rex E. Lee and approved by Attorney General William French Smith and advisors to the president Jim Baker and Ed Meese. At oral argument, Lee explicitly stated he did not seek a reversal of *Roe*, but that state legislatures should be left to make determinations about abortion law and that the issue ought not be in the court's purview.[105] Three years after his oral argument in *City of Akron*, Lee would say that his positions as solicitor general before the Supreme Court had a "special weight" because they were "regarded as representing not merely the political views of the Administration but the broad interests of the nation."[106]

The second case of the Reagan presidency was *Thornburgh v. American College of Obstetricians and Gynecologists* in 1986. The court reviewed a Pennsylvania statute that required a woman seeking an abortion to listen to a form speech delivered by her physician about the gestational age of the child, unforeseeable detrimental physical and mental effects of abortion, the medical risks of the procedure versus carrying a child to term, available benefits for prenatal care, childbirth, and neonatal care, and the fact that the father is legally required to financially support the child.[107] Printed materials were to be made available to the woman, including statements such as "There are many public and private agencies willing to help you carry your child to term" and "The Commonwealth of Pennsylvania strongly urges you to contact them before making a final decision about abortion."[108] The act also restricted the method by which a post-viability abortion could be performed and contained detailed reporting requirements that purported to be private, but would be available to the public for copying, including the name of the physician and the age, race, marital status, and political registration of the woman, as well as the number of her prior pregnancies.[109]

Charles Fried, who had succeeded Lee as solicitor general, now urged the court to overturn *Roe*. Samuel Alito, a lawyer in the Justice Department at the time, helped prepare Fried to argue the case. In a memo to Fried, Alito argued that not urging the court to overturn *Roe* in *City of Akron* had been a mistake. Alito noted that the Civil Division of the DOJ and the OLP, which included the young Federalist Society lawyers, recommended amicus participation in support of the constitutionality of the Pennsylvania abortion statute at stake in *Thornburgh*.[110] Alito characterized the "informed consent" information and materials as "accurate, factual and non-inflammatory."[111] He argued that abortion invoked a moral choice that *Roe* had taken from state lawmakers and given to pregnant women and, for that reason, pregnant women should have at their disposal "at least some of the same sort of information that we would want lawmakers to consider."[112] Making the argument that the recordkeeping requirements passed constitutional muster, Alito criticized the lower court's conclusion that reporting would increase the costs of abortion—a fact that both parties in the case had agreed on, and had actually stipulated to—and that the recordkeeping requirement would lessen physicians' willingness to perform abortions.[113] Alito began, "I would hate to have to compile a list of all the federal, not to mention state and local, recordkeeping and reporting laws. Many of these laws increase the cost of goods and services. . . . Does this mean that these recordkeeping and reporting laws are unconstitutional? . . . If we focus just on the abortionist, why single out reporting requirements? Why not all regulation that increases his costs of doing business and thus his fee?" Alito surmised that what presented an obstacle to physicians was not the thought of writing abortion reports or the "wildly unlikely prospect of criminal prosecution for an abortion-related offense, but the thought of a visit from an IRS agent investigating tax shelters."[114]

Alito's suggested strategy was one of incrementalism: make the point that even after *Akron*, "abortion is not unregulable"; "nudge" the court toward having greater recognition of the states' interest in protecting the unborn *throughout* pregnancy; and dispel the "mystical faith" in the physician performing the abortion "that supports *Roe* and the subsequent cases."[115] Alito advised that this incremental strategy was preferable to a frontal assault on *Roe*, evidently sensing that the court would not overturn *Roe* in *Thornburgh*. "When the court hands down its decision and *Roe* is not overruled, the decision will not be portrayed as a stinging rebuke. We also will not forfeit the opportunity to address—and we will not prod the Court into summarily rejecting the important secondary arguments outlined above."[116] This approach would not concede *Roe*'s legitimacy; instead, it would signal that the government believed the issue was "live and open."[117] In a personal statement authored when he applied for the role of deputy assistant to Attorney General Meese, Alito had written that he personally believed and was "particularly proud" of his contributions in recent cases "in which the government has argued in the Supreme Court . . . that the Constitution does not protect a right to an abortion."[118]

James Bopp also contributed two amicus briefs in *Thornburgh*. His NRLC brief focused on just one section of the Pennsylvania law.[119] It argued that it was a reasonable exercise of the state's power, grounded in its compelling interest in viable unborn life, to require the physician to use the abortion procedure most likely to result in a live birth unless there existed a significant increase in the risk to maternal life or health (not to include the potential psychological or emotional impact on the mother of the child's survival). The NRLC argued that the court's previous decisions supported the position that maternal health should be construed more narrowly in the post-viability context, where the state's interest in protecting the potential life becomes stronger. This contradicted the holding of *Doe v. Bolton*, the companion case to *Roe*, where the Supreme Court stated that the factors relating to maternal health included the "physical, emotional, psychological, familial, and the woman's age."[120]

Bopp also authored an amicus brief on behalf of three women who had decided to have abortions, "without being adequately informed of the nature of the abortion procedure, the medical risks involved, or the alternatives to abortion."[121] Bopp argued that neither the form speech nor the content of available printed materials were objectionable. He wrote that it was "unrealistic to rely on abortion providers to willingly provide information" otherwise required by the Pennsylvania law, and that it was disingenuous (and incorrect, under *Doe*) to argue that information about the fetus's development was not medically relevant to the abortion choice.

The court summarily rejected these amici's arguments. Writing for the majority, Justice Blackmun noted that since *Akron*, a number of states and municipalities had adopted measures seemingly designed to prevent a woman from exercising her freedom of choice.[122] He stated that the states were not free, "under the guise of protecting maternal health or potential life, to intimidate women into continuing pregnancies." Blackmun further criticized the "extreme" recordkeeping provisions, stating that identification of women who had obtained an abortion was their "obvious purpose."[123] Blackmun read his opinion, a confirmation of his intent to protect the abortion right, from the bench, something justices tend to do only when they wish to make a forceful point about their decision. Although Blackmun's response was terse, an increased number of justices dissented in *Thornburgh*, an indication of *Roe*'s declining strength.

Although President Reagan was vocal about his anti-abortion views, he did not make abortion jurisprudence or policy a priority, by some accounts. He appointed anti-abortion Justice Scalia to the court, but his administration has been criticized for failing to appoint serious pro-life persons to positions within the administration, for failing to unite the myriad pro-life organizations regarding strategy, and for failing to make a real dent in the *Roe* framework.[124] The two Bush administrations, however, more vigorously opposed the right to choose an abortion; Federalist Society stalwarts Kenneth Starr and Paul Clement served Bush Sr. and Bush Jr. respectively as solicitor general, and the stage was set outside government by conservatives such as James Bopp, who had had established himself as counsel to the leading pro-life organizations.

In 1989, the court heard *Webster v. Reproductive Health Services*. This was the second time that the court examined a statute that utilized the incrementalism tactic of restricting the abortion right by limiting or eliminating state funding. In *Webster*, the court upheld a Missouri law that forbade the use of state monies or facilities to encourage or counsel a woman to have an abortion declared in its preamble that life begins at conception, and allowed an abortion after twenty weeks only if the fetus was not "viable."[125] The fact that there was no majority opinion demonstrated the fractured abortion views of the justices and exposed *Roe*'s vulnerability. The only issue that all the justices agreed on subsequently became moot.[126] Justice Scalia stated that he believed the plurality opinion effectively overruled *Roe*, but that he would do it more "explicitly." Rehnquist, who had dissented in *Roe*, used *Webster* as an opportunity to criticize *Roe* on the basis that its underpinnings— trimesters and viability—were not found in the text of the Constitution. He made clear that he believed the state's interest in protecting potential human life was as compelling before viability as it was after. The court declined to determine whether the preamble, which stated the "life of each human being begins at conception," was constitutional. This was, they said, simply a value judgment on the part of the state. The court upheld the statute's prohibition of the use of state facilities or personnel to perform or assist in an abortion, because a woman could still procure an abortion privately, because the Constitution contained no right to state aid, and because the allocation of public resources was an appropriate way for the state to impose its value judgment on its citizens.[127]

Nearly eighty amicus briefs were submitted in *Webster*, a huge leap from *Thornburgh*'s thirty. Bopp again penned two amicus briefs, one for the NRLC, the other for the American Academy of Medical Ethics. The NRLC brief, for the first time, urged the court to reverse *Roe*.[128] Bopp argued that confronting what was the proper standard of review for abortion regulations would solve the problem of "interminable litigation of the subject of abortion in this and other courts."[129] Bopp criticized *Roe* as an exercise in legislation and social policy making by its majority, founded in medical determinations that were certain to evolve. He also showed the court the extent to which abortion jurisprudence was in turmoil, citing the 113 federal district court opinions, 45 federal appellate decisions, and 14 cases in the Supreme Court relating to abortion that had occurred in the seven years after *Roe*, and the 22 abortion cases heard by the court between 1980 and 1989. Relying heavily on the court's 1986 opinion in *Bowers v. Hardwick*, holding there was no fundamental right to homosexual sodomy, Bopp argued that the right of privacy did not extend to the abortion decision and that the court should analyze state restrictions on abortion under the most deferential, rational basis test.[130] Bopp argued that the *Bowers* Court undertook a more rigorous review of this nation's history and traditions than had the *Roe* Court, when determining that there was no fundamental right to the activity at issue. Bopp criticized the *Roe* Court for an approach that suggested that "a shift of opinion, in favor of abortion, among selected elites and in a few states" was constitutionally significant.

Bopp's second brief was for the American Academy of Medical Ethics, a lobbying group with twenty thousand physician members who are "ethically opposed to the practice of abortion (except to save the life of the mother) and the involvement of physicians in referring for the procedure."[131] Bopp argued that the language of the Missouri statute was sufficiently clear, that prohibiting public funding for "encouraging and counseling to have an abortion" did not violate the First Amendment, and that the same prohibition was not, as the Court of Appeals had held, "an obstacle in the path of women seeking full and uncensored medical advice about the alternatives to childbirth." Referring to *Harris v. McRae*, which declared that "while a state may not erect obstacles in the path of a woman seeking abortion, it need not remove those not of its own making," Bopp noted that indigency was one of the obstacles not of state making.[132] Missouri's refusal to fund "encouraging and counseling" to have an abortion (he termed it "abortion advocacy") for women who could not afford to hear such "advocacy" elsewhere, Bopp argued, is the fault of their indigency, and not of the state.[133]

In 1992, the court, now including George H. W. Bush's appointees Clarence Thomas and David Souter, and without Justices Brennan and Marshall, revisited the abortion issue in *Planned Parenthood of Southeastern Pennsylvania v. Casey*. *Casey* was the first of the major modern abortion cases in which at least one Federalist Society member argued before the court, defending the abortion-restricting law in question. In *Casey*, a Pennsylvania statute regulated abortions by requiring a twenty-four-hour waiting period, requiring physicians to inform women of the availability of educational information about the fetus, requiring spousal notification before abortions, requiring parental consent for abortions for unmarried minors, and requiring reporting and recordkeeping.[134]

Nearly thirty amicus briefs were submitted. James Bopp, author of the amicus brief of the NRLC, urged the court again to use the opportunity to overturn *Roe v. Wade* and return the issue to state legislatures.[135] Additionally, the NRLC argued for a more deferential review of state abortion laws (mirroring then-Judge Samuel Alito's dissent in the Third Circuit Court of Appeals' review of the Pennsylvanian legislation, and Bopp's argument in *Webster*).[136]

Bopp also authored the amicus brief of the Life Issues Institute (LII).[137] There, the LII set up and then rebutted an equal protection argument protecting the abortion decision. Bopp argued that laws restricting abortions distinguish between men and women because women get pregnant and men do not. Therefore, the classification between men and women is predicated on the *differences* between men and women, and does not raise the specter of an equal protection violation. Thus, abortion regulations should be subject only to the rational basis test. Bopp further argued that the Ninth Amendment, invoked by several justices in *Griswold v. Connecticut* to demonstrate that a privacy right existed in the Constitution, neither provided constitutional protection for the right to abortion nor stood in the way of overturning *Roe v. Wade*.

Kenneth Starr, then solicitor general, authored a brief for the United States as Amicus Curiae Supporting Respondents in support of the abortion law.[138] Starr stated that *Roe* should be overturned on the basis that there is no fundamental right to abortion found in the Constitution, in particular because no right to abortion can be found in the history and traditions of the United States. Starr explained that the *Roe* Court referred to a line of cases that recognized a right to privacy encompassing certain activities involving marriage and procreation, but that the court was wrong to place *Roe* in that lineage because *Roe* involved the taking of a human life.

The court did not use the rational basis standard in *Casey*, as pro-life advocates had hoped. It did, however, displace *Roe's* trimester framework with the so-called undue burden standard in evaluating abortion restrictions before viability—a lower standard than in *Roe* and one that seemed likely to allow more abortion-restriction statutes and regulations to pass constitutional muster. The court determined that the spousal notification requirement was a violation of Fourteenth Amendment due process because it imposed an undue burden on the woman's right to choose to have an abortion. However, in a victory for the NRLC, IIL, Bopp, Starr, the Bush administration, and the right-to-life movement in general, the informed consent, mandatory twenty-four-hour waiting period, reporting requirements, and parental consent provisions were upheld, even if the purpose behind them was to persuade a woman to choose childbirth over abortion.[139]

Of the remaining three major abortion cases that the Supreme Court heard in the ensuing years, two dealt with bans on the intact dilation and extraction (D&X)

method of abortion—that is, "partial-birth abortion."[140] In a 1998 article, Bopp recited many of the arguments eventually submitted (by him and others) to the Supreme Court in support of the constitutionality of such bans.[141] He argued that abortion precedents did not apply to the bans because abortion law concerned unborn rather than partially delivered persons, characterizing intact D&X abortions as "infanticide"; that lawmakers had clearly defined and limited what abortion procedure they sought to prohibit and that courts have a duty to construe a statute to be constitutional if it is possible to do so; and that courts ought to review the bans only to ensure they are rationally related to a legitimate state interest. Bopp called the bans the "final frontier" of the court's abortion jurisprudence, because they concerned procedures undertaken when pregnancy was significantly advanced.[142] He clearly recognized the potential value of this kind of ban for the pro-life movement, noting that it "forced the pro-abortion camp to publicly defend a particularly visible and gruesome practice."[143]

In 2000's *Stenberg v. Carhart*, the court considered whether a Nebraska statute that criminalized the intact D&X method was constitutional.[144] *Stenberg* contributed to an already-simmering conflict within the pro-life lobby. Incrementalists, who supported the ban, faced off against those (for example, advocates of "personhood" amendments to the federal and various state constitutions) who did not, on the basis that when a human life is at stake, mere limitation of the abortion procedure is inadequate.

The extent of the involvement of Federalist Society members in *Stenberg*— advocating for the partial-birth abortion ban—was considerable. Society member Donald Stenberg, the attorney general of Nebraska, argued the case for his state. James Bopp filed three briefs on behalf of various amici, including one with William Pryor. Alan Lance, the attorney general of Idaho, also a member of the society, filed an amicus brief on behalf of his state jointly with various officials of a number of different states. David McIntosh, in his role as a congressman from Indiana, joined in a brief with other members of Congress.

Bopp's three amicus briefs strategically attacked the law from separate angles. First, in an amicus brief on behalf of certain members of Congress, Bopp sought to reassure the court that the state law was sufficiently narrow, seeking to ban only the controversial intact D&X procedure and not any other more conventional abortion method.[145] Bopp also sought to have the Nebraska law reviewed under the rational basis test, rather than under Casey's higher "undue burden" standard. In taking this approach, Bopp had to concede that an abortion right did exist (unlike the arguments he had made in *Casey*). The trade-off was that by doing so, he could argue that the abortion right was related to an *unborn* child, not to a *partially born* child; since the Nebraska statute affected the rights of a *partially born* child, by definition it did not put the abortion right at stake, so the rational basis test was the proper standard of review. In a second brief—authored with Pryor, among others—on behalf of several states, the governors of Rhode Island and West Virginia, and the State Legislature of New Jersey, Bopp made a federalism argument.[146] Bopp and

Pryor urged the court to preserve the principles of federalism and separation of powers by construing the statute narrowly and by not finding it unconstitutional if there was "any fair interpretation of the statute by which it can be saved."

Third, Bopp wrote for the NRLC, the Christian Legal Society, Concerned Women for America, the Southern Center for Law and Ethics, and Focus on the Family.[147] This brief stated that the right to decide to terminate a pregnancy was not unqualified, and that it did not include the right to choose the abortion method. It asked the court to construe the law as banning a certain form of "feticidal conduct" rather than an abortion method.

In its ruling, the court refused to adopt the language or positions of the amici discussed above and determined that the Nebraska partial-birth abortion ban was unconstitutional, because it lacked an exception permitting the procedure when the health of the mother was otherwise at risk, and that it was written so broadly it could be construed to ban other abortion methods.[148] This was a stinging defeat for Federalist Society members and allies, but they would have an opportunity to defend another partial-birth abortion ban just seven years later.

In 2006's *Ayotte v. Planned Parenthood of Northern New England*, a number of abortion providers organized to challenge a New Hampshire law that required a parent or guardian to be notified at least forty-eight hours before a minor (or a woman for whom a guardian or conservator had been appointed) obtained an abortion.[149] Violation of the law brought both criminal and civil penalties. Planned Parenthood argued that the notification requirement was an undue burden, in the parlance of *Casey*. Its challenge hinged largely on the fact that the law provided no exception to the notification requirement, where a forty-eight-hour delay might result in serious physical harm to the pregnant minor (for example, the consequence of never being able to have children unless the abortion was performed on an emergency basis). Planned Parenthood brought the suit not as a party harmed by the law, but on the basis that the law, regardless of its application, was unconstitutional (termed a "facial" challenge).

A unanimous court, extremely rare in the abortion context, upheld the law. Acknowledging that the New Hampshire statute would be unconstitutional as applied to the small number of minors for whom an emergency abortion might be needed to protect them from serious physical harm and for whom the forty-eight-hour period was simply too long, Justice Ginsburg, writing for the court, stated that the proper solution (rather than ruling the entire law unconstitutional) was for New Hampshire's lower courts simply to issue an injunction prohibiting "only the statute's unconstitutional application." The decision demonstrated the court's preference for partial rather than facial rejection of abortion laws, and a further relaxation of the strictures of *Roe*.

The attorneys for the parties were Kelly Ayotte, as the New Hampshire attorney general, and Jennifer Dalven for Planned Parenthood. In addition, society member Paul Clement, then U.S. solicitor general, argued before the court on behalf of the United States in support of New Hampshire's abortion regulation. Society member

R. Ted Cruz, then solicitor general of Texas, was counsel for the amicus brief on behalf of eighteen states.[150] Peter D. Keisler, a cofounder and leader of the society, joined the amicus brief for the United States as the assistant U.S. attorney general.

James Bopp authored an amicus brief for the Horatio R. Storer Foundation, an Oklahoma-based nonprofit "organized to provide the public with educational materials on fetal development, abortion, persons with disabilities, and euthanasia; to educate the general public to respect all human life, and to provide positive alternatives to the solution of social, emotional, medical, and personal problems of women."[151] Bopp sought dismissal of the case, arguing that the abortion providers were not harmed and therefore had no standing to challenge the law. The brief of Clement and Keisler argued that the court should apply the extremely high *Salerno* "no set of circumstances" standard (from a 1987 opinion authored by Justice Rehnquist), whereby a plaintiff challenging a law as facially unconstitutional must show that there exists no set of circumstances under which the law would be valid.[152]

Ted Cruz, as counsel of record for an amicus brief of eighteen states, offered no argument as to the substance of the New Hampshire law.[153] Instead, as Clement and Keisler had, Cruz urged the court to apply the strict *Salerno* test to this and similar challenges to other regulations in the abortion context, rather than the "large fraction" test articulated by the three-justice joint opinion in *Casey* (and the lower court in the present case). In *Casey*, the court had ruled that the spousal notification requirement was an undue burden and therefore invalid because in a "large fraction of the cases where [it] is relevant, it will operate as a substantial obstacle to a woman's choice to undergo an abortion."[154]

The arguments raised by Cruz, Keisler, and Clement were well received by the court. In *Ayotte*—as the amici had urged—the court changed the frame of reference of facial challenges that *Casey* had previously set forth.[155] The controlling class in *Casey*'s "large fraction" test was not all women, and not even all pregnant women, but all women for whom the spousal notification requirement would be a relevant restriction. Everything else being equal, a smaller denominator produces a larger fraction and a greater showing of an undue burden. In *Ayotte*, the court did not actually use *Casey*'s large fraction test, but as part of its calculus, it considered the proportion of possible unconstitutional applications to possible constitutional applications by using all pregnant minors seeking abortions as its controlling class. This broader categorization (i.e., not all pregnant minors seeking abortions for whom the forty-eight-hour delay would be a relevant restriction) necessarily produced a larger denominator than the calculation in *Casey* had, producing a smaller fraction and a significantly diminished likelihood of showing an undue burden.[156]

Undertaking review of a second regulation of a partial-birth abortion ban in 2007, the court, in *Gonzales v. Carhart*, considered a challenge to the Federal Partial-Birth Abortion Ban Act of 2003, which was strikingly similar to the Nebraska law upheld by the court in *Stenberg* in 2000.[157] The act was conceived by the NRLC, and its supporters sought not only to ban the practice, but to "plant[]

precedents for legislating further restrictions on abortion."[158] The NRLC had enjoyed success in Congress just one year earlier, with the passing of the Born-Alive Infants Protection Act of 2002. Hadley Arkes called that act a measure that could become "the most powerful and serviceable lever available to the pro-life side." The act, which President George W. Bush by statement of administration policy, "strongly support[ed]," simply provided that for purposes of federal law, "the words 'person,' 'human being,' 'child,' and 'individual,' shall include every infant member of the species homo sapiens who is born alive at any stage of development."[159] The essential goal of the act was to protect newborns who had survived an abortion procedure. It included neither mandates nor penalties, serving more as a policy statement than anything else.

In drafting the Federal Partial-Birth Abortion Ban Act of 2003, Congress "deliberately sought to remedy the deficiencies identified by [the Supreme Court] in the Nebraska statute at issue in *Stenberg*."[160] The act prohibited the *intentional* use of the intact D&X procedure, which along with another D&X method, represented less than one percent of all second-trimester abortions.[161] The act was deemed unconstitutional by federal courts in the Eighth Circuit in the *Carhart* case, and by courts in the Ninth Circuit in a parallel case brought by Planned Parenthood in California.

The Supreme Court agreed to hear the case, in which Dr. Leroy Carhart and three other physicians who performed late-term abortions sued to stop the act from going into effect. Carhart argued that the act was too vaguely written and could be interpreted to prevent more common abortion procedures, which would prevent most post-first-trimester abortions from occurring. This, according to Carhart, constituted an undue burden on the right to obtain an abortion. The plaintiffs also argued that the lack of a health exception for the pregnant woman rendered the law unconstitutional (despite congressional findings underpinning the act that partial-birth abortions are never necessary and thus would never need to be performed to protect the health of the mother).

The case attracted nearly fifty amicus briefs. The American Center for Law and Justice filed two amicus briefs with Jay Sekulow as lead counsel.[162] In its first brief, the ACLJ sought to demonstrate flaws in the factual basis underpinning abortion jurisprudence. First, the ACLJ argued that the oft-stated claim, repeated by Planned Parenthood in this case, that the risk of death associated with childbirth is some multiple higher than the risk associated with abortion, was irrelevant and wrong.[163] A second brief—submitted by the ACLJ, seventy-eight members of Congress, and the Committee to Protect the Ban on Partial-Birth Abortion—argued that a law enacted to prevent "infanticide" ought not be judged under the court's abortion jurisprudence, and that the court should defer to congressional fact finding regarding the medical evidence underpinning the act.[164]

Hadley Arkes submitted a brief on behalf of himself and the Claremont Institute Center for Constitutional Jurisprudence at Chapman University School of Law.[165] The counsel of record for Arkes on the brief was Ed Meese. There, amici argued that while the states might more properly enact a ban such as this, the commerce clause was an appropriate source of federal power and the act should be upheld.[166] Arkes noted that Congress had not sought to overturn *Roe* by passing and supporting the act, and neither did amici seek such an overruling. Rather, "[o]ur own judgment, deepened by our own hope, is that this Court will accept this gentle offer to enter into a conversation on the contours of the right to abortion it has unilaterally recognized."[167]

William Saunders authored an amicus brief as of counsel for the Family Research Council and Focus on the Family in conjunction with Notre Dame Law School.[168] The brief urged the court to defer to the factual findings of Congress—that there is a "disturbing similarity" between the banned procedure and "killing a newborn infant"—and to uphold the ban.[169] Concerned Women of America, the Pro-Life Legal Defense Fund, and the Thomas More Society all joined various amicus briefs, in some instances more than one. It was the strongest showing of amici in a major abortion case since *Webster*, nearly twenty years earlier.

James Bopp, in an amicus brief for the Storer Foundation, also framed the law as properly prohibiting infanticide (as he had in *Stenberg* and many publications).[170] He argued that the government's compelling interests in protecting the "partially born" fetus ought to prevail over the diminished liberty or privacy interest of the mother in choosing to terminate a pregnancy in this manner. In effect, Bopp argued that as a child became "more born," its constitutional rights as a person increased, as its mother's privacy right proportionally decreased: "To the degree that the fetus has emerged from the maternal body is also to the degree that any claim to a 'right to privacy' or personal liberty to abortion diminishes."[171] Bopp further argued that no health exception to the ban was necessary because the number of abortions actually affected by this act was very small and that the burden on the pregnant woman's health (as a result of the continued pregnancy) was essentially zero, because by the time the act actually takes effect, the pregnancy is essentially over. Bopp noted that the act required proof of intent to partially deliver the fetus and then kill it, which "obviously" precluded application to other abortion methods.[172]

The United States' appellate brief, authored by Paul Clement as solicitor general in the *Planned Parenthood* companion case, argued that the court should uphold the ban because it advanced "vital state interests" in protecting human life and in preventing a rarely used procedure "that resembles infanticide."[173] Clement urged the court to defer to Congress's factual findings that the procedure was never necessary to preserve the health of the mother, and that the lack of a health exception therefore did not present an undue burden to a woman seeking an abortion. Clement pointed out that the federal act, unlike the Nebraska statute in *Stenberg*, featured very specific language, which made it clear to both physicians and women what procedure the act forbade.

The court upheld the Federal Partial-Birth Abortion Ban Act in a 5–4 decision. Writing for the majority and reflecting many of Clement's and Bopp's arguments, Justice Kennedy concluded that the act was sufficiently specific as to what it prohibited and therefore did not constitute an undue burden on a woman's right to abortion, that the act furthered legitimate congressional purposes, and that the lack of a health exception did not render the act facially unconstitutional. The court distinguished but did not overrule *Stenberg v. Carhart*, because the language of the Nebraska abortion ban at issue in *Stenberg* was broader than the wording in the Federal Partial-Birth Abortion Act. Kennedy, noting that the doctors who brought a facial challenge had a more difficult task of proving the law unconstitutional than if the challenge had been brought by a woman whose health was actually at risk because of it, remarked that the case "should not have been entertained in the first instance."[174] He went on to explain that the court's ruling would not preclude subsequent so-called "as applied" challenge to the federal ban. Justice Thomas filed a terse, four-sentence concurring opinion, in which Justice Scalia joined. They stated that they joined the majority opinion because it accurately applied the court's abortion jurisprudence, and they restated their view that this line of cases, which included *Roe* and *Casey*, "has no basis in the Constitution."[175]

Gonzales was a considerable victory for Bopp, Arkes, pro-lifers in general, and in particular, incrementalists. The dissent, however, authored by Justice Ginsburg, and joined by Justices Stevens, Souter, and Breyer, greatly concerned Bopp. He saw reason to worry that the court, as then constituted, might find a constitutional right to abortion based on what Ginsburg had long advocated, an "equal protection" analysis under the Fourteenth Amendment. Citing Ginsburg, Bopp wrote:

> "[L]egal challenges to undue restrictions on abortion procedures do not seek to vindicate some generalized notion of privacy; rather, they center on a woman's autonomy to determine her life's course, and thus to enjoy equal citizenship stature." If this view gained even a plurality in a prevailing case, this new legal justification for the right to abortion would be a powerful weapon in the hands of pro-abortion lawyers that would jeopardize all current laws on abortion, such as laws requiring parental involvement for minors, waiting periods, specific informed consent information, and so on.[176]

CONCLUSION

Nowhere else in the western world does the abortion issue attract as much public angst, legislative energy, political attention, and judicial resources as in the United States. The constitutional right to make the abortion decision first recognized by the Supreme Court in 1973 was, and remains, repugnant to conservatives both in substance and because it came from the judicial branch. Members of the Federalist Society, as litigators, legislators, strategists, lobbyists, and judges, working with the groups and individuals that make up the family values movement, have worked around *Roe* to limit the abortion right in hundreds of ways. Their work, and the work of those who share their vision, have significantly reduced access to the procedure, in particular for the poor. Since the mid-1980s, states' abortion restrictions have increased exponentially, and more such laws were passed in 2011 (ninety-two laws in twenty-four states) than any other year.[177] Consider the following:

- *Roe* did not address whether state law could require that a woman seeking an abortion must be provided with certain kinds of information—by way of pre-abortion procedures, reading materials, or physician's advice—even though they are designed to discourage abortion. As of 2012, thirty-four states require that women be given information about the specific procedure; eleven of those require information on the ability of a fetus to feel pain.[178] Additionally, twenty-one states regulate the provision of ultrasound by abortion providers. Eight of them mandate an ultrasound prior to an abortion, and require the physician to offer the woman the opportunity to view it.[179] Eleven states require that a woman be given information, either orally or in writing, on accessing ultrasound services.[180]

- Whether parental or spousal consent could be required prior to an abortion was not at issue in *Roe*. As early as 1974, state legislatures began to enact laws requiring such consent; as of 2012, thirty-seven states require some type of parental involvement in a minor's decision to have an abortion.[181]

- *Roe* did not consider at what age "personhood" begins. Currently, efforts are underway in a handful of states to modify their constitutions to confer personhood at conception.[182] In 2011, fourteen state legislatures introduced twenty-six personhood measures that would ban all abortions on the basis that life begins at fertilization.[183]

- Specific abortion procedures were not at issue in *Roe*. As of 2012, in addition to the federal law, thirty-one states have enacted bans on so-called partial-birth abortions.[184]

- *Roe* did not address how an abortion might be paid for, or whether a nurse or physician might object on religious or moral grounds to participating in an abortion procedure. As of 2012, because Medicaid funds have been cut off for abortion, only seventeen states provide funding for medically necessary abortions to low-income women, while thirty-four provide funding where the woman has been a victim of a sexual crime.[185] Forty-six states allow individual health care providers to refuse to participate in an abortion on moral grounds, and forty-four give institutional providers the same right of refusal.[186]

These incremental steps, taken across the various states over many decades, have created a new landscape of abortion law and policy. Women seeking an abortion now face a thicket of prohibitions limiting their right to choose to terminate a pregnancy. Although the Supreme Court has not overruled *Roe*, the woman's right to self-determination it has come to stand for has been substantially undermined.

◆ 6 ◆

AMERICAN EXCEPTIONALISM, SOVEREIGNTY, AND INTERNATIONAL LAW

It is our true policy to steer clear of permanent alliances with any portion of the
foreign world; so far, I mean, as we are now at liberty to do it; for let me not
be understood as capable of patronizing infidelity to existing engagements.
I hold the maxim no less applicable to public than to private affairs, that
honesty is always the best policy. I repeat it, therefore, let those engagements
be observed in their genuine sense. But, in my opinion, it is unnecessary and
would be unwise to extend them.

—*George Washington*[1]

In 2000, Peter Spiro described what he termed the "new sovereigntists" in *Foreign Affairs*. Acknowledging that the United States has historically been wary of
participation in global governance, for fear of compromising its freedom of action, Spiro identified a growing band of influential conservatives who could not be
regarded as pure isolationists because they were amenable to international law and
institutions, but only to the extent that the law and institutions suited the interests
of the United States. He called this "international law à la carte."[2]

Many of these new sovereigntists have found a home in the Federalist Society.
They share a realist view of foreign relations—that in an anarchic world community, each country will act to advance its own interests. They believe that as the
hegemonic power within that community, the United States may pick and choose
which international organization it supports, which treaty it ratifies, which international agreement it follows, and whether its own military action requires international support.

There is no such thing as a single "conservative" approach to international law
and institutions, nor is there a cohesive policy that the Federalist Society as a group
subscribes to. This chapter does not purport to describe a concise ideology or program designed to rebuff the influence of international law, norms, and institutions
on U.S. law. Rather, it discusses how members of the Federalist Society, and the organization itself, have steered the conversation about America's place in the world.

Conservative academics, policymakers, lawyers, government officials, and
members of the judiciary—many of whom have ties to the Federalist Society—
have produced volumes of scholarship, speeches, amicus briefs, court decisions, and

memoranda. These works reveal a number of core ideas around which this chapter is structured.

This chapter begins with an introduction to American Exceptionalism, and then explores the ideology of the new sovereigntists, who believe in American self-determination above all. This ideology incorporates:

- *A realist view of "sovereignty."* This is a rejection of international law and international institutions to the extent that they interfere with the United States' absolute right of self-determination. In comparison, the idealist view of sovereignty embraces cooperation via alliances, treaties, and the rule of international law as a means to promote greater prosperity and stability for the entire system of nations.

- *The rule of domestic law.* This holds that (1) international law (for example, the Geneva Conventions or the decisions of international courts) and (2) foreign law (for example, a foreign court's ruling on the meaning of a principle of international law, or of a clause within its own Constitution) are irrelevant to the interpretation of constitutional questions in the American legal system.

- *A belief in a strong unitary executive.* This theory is justified by an original-ist interpretation of the Constitution. In the foreign policy arena, it combines the vesting clause in Article II, Section 1 of the Constitution, which states that "[t]he executive power shall be vested in a President of the United States of America," with the president's role as commander in chief. It holds that the president may override legislation if it conflicts with the president's agenda pertaining to war or foreign policy. It also holds that the president is the ultimate arbiter of whether the United States' actions are "legal" under domestic or international law.

There are myriad means by which these ideas have been transformed into law and policy. Notable academics, including Steven Calabresi, Jeremy Rabkin, and Michael Paulsen, have produced abundant scholarship reflecting conservative and originalist ideas on American Exceptionalism, the meaning of sovereignty, the influence of foreign law on Supreme Court jurisprudence, and the force of international law on American foreign policy and domestic law. Members of the Federalist Society old guard such as Don Hodel have orchestrated long-term, widespread lobbying efforts to defeat ratification of human rights treaties. The Federalist Society's Special Project on Sovereignty and International Law and its International and National Security Law Practice Group have provided a stage for conservative views on the meaning of sovereignty and the reasons to resist the influence of foreign law and international institutions. Global Governance Watch, a monitoring organization backed by the Federalist Society and the American Enterprise Institute, is dedicated to delegitimizing nongovernmental organizations (NGOs) and global governance, which many in the Federalist Society consider to be antidemocratic. Federalist Society members John Yoo and Jay Bybee had considerable influence in the Office of Legal Counsel in the Department of Justice on both domestic and foreign policy in the late 2000s, in particular pertaining to war on terror issues. John Bolton, who has held high-level positions in the Departments of Defense and State, and was formerly U.S. ambassador to the United Nations, had a direct role in shaping isolationist policies at the United Nations and successfully resisting U.S. ratification of certain human rights treaties.

The chapter closes with a brief history of the use of foreign and international law in the Supreme Court and discusses the ideas and influence of Federalist Society members, who reject the notion that international or foreign law should influence constitutional law decisions. Their ideas spawn debates that concern the preeminence of the Constitution, the separation of powers, and the realities of existing in a globalized world: what is the true nature of our Constitution, and can (and should) U.S. courts truly operate in isolation?

AMERICAN EXCEPTIONALISM

Frenchman Alexis de Tocqueville is said to have first coined the phrase "American Exceptionalism" in his work *Democracy in America*, published in 1835. "The situation of the Americans," wrote de Tocqueville, "is entirely exceptional, and there is reason to believe that no other democratic people will ever enjoy anything like it."[3] De Tocqueville used the term in a relative sense, comparing the young democracy, and the forces that shaped and preserved it, with the older societies of Europe, in particular, France. He marveled most at the equality that permeated American society. He observed that America was born from a single revolution and lacked the heavy burdens of feudalism, bully kings, and aristocracy that had handicapped France's long march toward egalitarianism. He cited America's puritanical origins, vastness, and geography, formal separation of church and state, and individual rights culture as some of the many reasons why the young nation was able to leapfrog past the societies of the old world toward the inevitable goal (as he saw it) of social equality.[4]

John Winthrop's rousing speech to the colonists in Massachusetts in 1631 that they "shall be as a city upon a hill" is a touchstone of American Exceptionalist imagery used in presidential speeches from Kennedy to Reagan. Winthrop's vision of America as God's chosen country was said to be the providential motivation behind Woodrow Wilson's League of Nations.[5] American Exceptionalism, as invoked by presidents in the twentieth- and twenty-first century, describes the United States as a beacon of freedom and democracy to the world, conveying ideas about the innate goodness, righteousness, and civilization of this nation. In his 1901 autobiography, Theodore Roosevelt wrote that the United States' history of expansion was due "solely to the power of the mighty civilized races which have not lost the fighting instinct, and which by their expansion are gradually bringing peace into the red wastes where the barbarian peoples of the world hold sway."[6] This reflected the ideas of the poet Frederick Jackson Turner, who wrote that American Exceptionalism was born in the advance westward along the frontier, as immigrants with European sensibilities met, and overcame, the harsh realities of the American interior.[7] In the immediate aftermath of the September 11, 2001, terrorist attacks on U.S. soil, President George W. Bush told the nation that "America was targeted for attack because we're the brightest beacon for freedom and opportunity in the world."[8] In a commencement address at West Point in 2002, he told the assembled graduates and their families that "[w]e are in conflict between good and evil, and America will call evil by its name," evoking President Reagan's description of the Soviet Union as the "evil empire."

The 1776 Declaration of Independence laid the political and institutional groundwork for America's Exceptionalism. The founders, in breaking with the British Empire, believed that sovereignty rested not with a monarch but with the people, who gave their government certain limited powers to protect their freedom. One of the "truly innovative aspects" of the newly established American polity was that the government existed only with the consent of the people.[9] The Constitution further secured America's distinct system of rights against the government. Its unique features included the dissociation of legislative and executive power, the superior power of the Constitution over all lawmaking and lawmakers, the existence of an independent judiciary to decide matters under the Constitution, and the ultimate power in the people to abolish, alter, or amend the Constitution. In *Federalist* No. 53, published in 1788, James Madison wrote: "The important distinction so well understood in America between a Constitution established by the people, and unalterable by the government; and a law established by the government, and alterable by the government, seems to have been little understood and less observed in any other country."

De Tocqueville's term has been applied to countless developments in American society, culture, foreign and domestic policy, and legal traditions in the 170-odd years since he coined it. The term has been offered to describe and defend a wide range of inherent individual and state behaviors that demarcate the United States as unique, even among other relatively young western democracies. Internally, neither socialism nor a welfare state ever really took hold. The United States clings to an archaic system of feet and inches while most of the rest of the Western hemisphere uses the metric system of measurement. Externally, American ideals about liberty and democracy have been exported around the world and its Constitution has served as a model for many emerging states. American Exceptionalism is invoked as a rationale for the United States' erratic treaty behavior. The United States will provide considerable input during the drafting and negotiation processes, but it has a low frequency of ratifying the treaties once finalized.

Exactly how exceptional the United States remains, in an increasingly interconnected world, is part of the debate as to the proper role of foreign or international law in the Supreme Court's deliberations. Students of U.S. foreign policy argue over the same question. To what extent does U.S. involvement in international organizations erode this nation's power of self-determination (and in doing so, make America less exceptional)? In a sense, the argument about America's place in the world order is waged over just how exceptional the United States is. Therefore, we begin this chapter with a discussion of how effective the organized Right has been in propagating the idea that American Exceptionalism is a reason to remain apart from the rest of the world.

John Bolton is a friend of the Federalist Society, who served as undersecretary of state for arms control and international security affairs and the United States' permanent representative to the United Nations during the George W. Bush administration. He holds out American Exceptionalism as a rationale for American unilateralism.[10] After President Obama's election, Bolton criticized the new president for implementing foreign policy that places too much emphasis on multilateralism and not enough on advocating American interests. Bolton called the president's first address to the United Nations "a post-American speech by our first post-American President" and implied that the president wished to run American foreign policy through the United Nations.[11] In an October 2009 speech at the University of Chicago, Bolton accused Obama of "not believ[ing] in American Exceptionalism."[12]

Steven Calabresi posits that because Americans believe the United States is an exceptional nation, which by definition should have exceptional laws, it is simply not "appropriate" to apply European or Canadian law to domestic judicial decision making.[13] He points out the United States was shaped by republicans like Jefferson and Franklin, who saw America as part of God's design and who likened the birth of this nation to the delivery of the Israelites from slavery in Egypt. He points out that the Great Seal of the United States bears the expression "Novus Ordo Seclorum"—"a new order for the ages"—demonstrating the founding fathers' quasi-religious belief in the creation of a true "new world."[14] Calabresi's version of American Exceptionalism is grounded in American ideals in liberty, religious freedom, and patriotism, and is conjured from scholarship that explores Americans' unique combination of optimism, libertarian economics, religious fervor, moralistic views, individualism, and philanthropic and conservative tendencies.

Calabresi places Ronald Reagan firmly in the center of modern American Exceptionalism, as "arguably the most dominant politician of the last sixty years" and "our greatest leader of the last half century." He cites then-Governor Reagan's speech at the 1974 Conservative Political Action Conference:

> And how stands the city on this winter night? More prosperous, more secure, and happier than it was eight years ago. But more than that: After 200 years, two centuries, she still stands strong and true on the granite ridge, and her glow has held steady no matter what storm. And she's still a beacon, still a magnet for all who must have a freedom, for all the pilgrims from all the lost places who are hurtling through the darkness, toward home.

Calabresi anchors American Exceptionalism in the Constitution, as does Michael Paulsen, another founding member of the Federalist Society at Yale Law

School and a former attorney in President George W. Bush's Department of Justice. Paulsen has said that American Exceptionalism is a misnomer—that in fact, in the context of international law at least, American Exceptionalism is in fact American constitutionalism.[15] In Paulsen's view, the Constitution is what preserves the United States' freedom of action from the constraints of international law. Paulsen posits that "the constitutional power to interpret, apply, and enforce international law for the United States is not possessed by, is not dependent upon, and can never authoritatively be exercised by actors outside the constitutionally recognized Article I, Article II, and Article III branches of the U.S. government."[16]

These two prominent Federalist Society members, along with other conservative mavens like Rabkin and Bolton, have long argued that the Constitution is the unique creed that will always set the United States apart from the rest of the world. As we will see later in the chapter, they and others have achieved considerable success in invoking American Exceptionalism to justify unilateral action in U.S. foreign policy, and in shielding domestic law from the influence of foreign and international law.

In contrast, Michael Ignatieff, a legal scholar, former Harvard professor, and leader of the Canadian Liberal Party, has gathered four different explanations for American Exceptionalism, particularly as it relates to the United States' behavior in the realm of international human rights: (1) a realist explanation, that as the hegemonic power in the world system, the United States can get away with negotiating and promoting human rights treaties and accords but then refusing to ratify them; (2) a cultural explanation, where this country seeks to defend its distinctive rights culture through its treaty behavior; (3) an institutional explanation, incorporating (i) the inertia in the U.S. legal system due to its emphasis on precedent and judicial review, and (ii) the lack of incentives to stabilize its institutions with foreign treaties or an overarching legal system (compared with, for example, Europe, which has faced centuries of political instability); and (4) a political explanation, accounting for a growth in the strength of American conservatism, which surged in reaction to the height of American liberalism in the civil rights era of the sixties and continues to be vital today. Just as conservatives made states' rights arguments against the use of federal power to desegregate the south, they now make national sovereignty arguments to prevent the importation of international human rights regimes into domestic U.S. law and policy.[17]

Ignatieff identifies three main threads of American Exceptionalism as demonstrated in the context of international law: (1) exemptionalism (supporting international treaties as long as Americans are exempt from them); (2) double standards (criticizing others for not heeding the findings of international human rights bodies, but ignoring what these bodies say of the United States); and (3) legal isolationism (the tendency of American judges such as Antonin Scalia and other constitutional originalists to ignore law and legal norms from other jurisdictions).

Harold Hongju Koh is a former dean of Yale Law School and a human rights scholar who has served in the Reagan, Clinton, and Obama administrations.

Compared to Ignatieff, he is less certain of America's exceptionalism. Koh argues that America is less of an outlier than Ignatieff suggests.[18] Koh defines American Exceptionalism as comprising four things: (1) the Constitution's distinctive rights structure (for example, the fact that the Constitution comprises mostly "negative rights" that protect citizens' individual rights against governmental violations, and America's fierce protection of freedom of speech, including hate speech, for which much of Europe and Asia offers little protection); (2) distinctive terminology (for example, America's human rights vernacular, which makes our attitude toward certain issues seem more nonintegrationist than it actually is); (3) treaty ratification behaviors (many countries adopt a strategy of ratification without compliance; in contrast, the United States has adopted the "perverse" practice of human rights compliance without ratification); and (4) the United States' proposals that a different rule should apply to itself than what applies to the rest of the world.[19] Examples of this behavior include the practice started by President George W. Bush, and continued under President Obama, of securing "Article 98" agreements, which shield U.S. citizens from prosecution by the International Criminal Court, and the United States' refusal prior to 2005 (when the Supreme Court struck it down) to outlaw the juvenile death penalty, despite it having disappeared from most developed legal systems many years prior.[20]

Justice Antonin Scalia has grounded some of his written opinions in the idea of American Exceptionalism. When writing for the majority in *Printz v. United States*, a 1997 case that had federalism issues at its core, Scalia wrangled with the dissent's comparison of European federalist structures: "We think such comparative analysis inappropriate to the task of interpreting a constitution, though it was of course quite relevant to the task of writing one."[21]

Justices Scalia, Rehnquist, and Thomas have propagated the idea that America is so exceptional as to render foreign or international law, or international human rights norms, entirely inapplicable to any constitutional question presented to the Supreme Court. This resistance is explained later in the chapter, but preliminarily, Scalia has derided human rights law on the basis that there is little "sameness" within the world community that could make any norm or standard either legitimate or applicable to an exceptional America: "Human Rights are important, right? These are questions of morality. There must be right answers. Some answers are right and some answers are wrong, and the right answers are written in the sky." Scalia argued that justices around the world are looking for these answers, and to find them, "they cite us; we cite them. But this is an absolutely crazy system."[22] Scalia, of course, does not think that the right answers have some independent existence, in the sky or anywhere else. Nor does he believe that the right answers depend on some consensus of what enlightened jurists around the world believe. In Scalia's view, the only legitimate source for determining what the U.S. Constitution requires is the Constitution itself.

While the new sovereigntists exalt American Exceptionalism, others are more wary. Certainly, American Exceptionalism has "both good and bad faces."[23]

Unilateral military action and a refusal to join international agreements preserve an ultimate power of self-determination, but at a cost. A state may have difficulty enforcing certain rules and norms for its own benefit if it has declared itself immune from them.[24] The international regimes that the United States refuses to be constrained by may be lost to it as tools to shape its national interests.

GLOBAL GOVERNANCE: INTERNATIONAL LAW AND INSTITUTIONS

Leonard Leo has said that those on the right consider international law in the same light as they saw the treatment of constitutional law in the Supreme Court during the Warren era: "The empty vessel into which liberals would pour all sorts of concepts that they couldn't get through the political process."[25] John Bolton has said that global governance advocates "have found themselves unable to prevail in a fair fight within America's system of representative government, so they now seek international forums to argue their positions, where their collectivist proclivities find greater sympathy among foreign governments and NGOs."[26] The United Nations is a target-rich environment among friends and members of the Federalist Society. Robert Bork, who was Bolton's law professor at Yale, has said that UN resolutions are fundamentally illegitimate because they are not created by democratic processes and therefore do not express the will of the citizens of member states. Expressing dismay at a political environment where small, despotic nations have an equal voice with the United States, Bork has said, "It is not just that the United Nations is useless . . . it is, in fact, almost entirely detrimental to the interests of the United States."[27] Bolton has called the one-nation-one-vote system "as fraudulent an analogy to real democracy as has ever been made—[that] completely dominates U.N. program, budget, and management decision-making, almost entirely to the detriment of the United States."[28]

To be sure, there has been debate over the extent to which the United States should involve itself in world affairs since the earliest days of the Republic.[29] In his farewell address, George Washington warned his successors to "steer clear of permanent alliances with any portion of the foreign world," notwithstanding the handful of trade treaties in existence at the time.[30] The unease with foreign entanglements felt by the framers was woven into the text of the Constitution and reflected in the structure of the republic. For example, the individual states were afforded no treaty-making power, and the power of the president to conduct treaties with foreign nations requires a two-thirds vote in the Senate. This requirement tasked the Senate with a role as protector of states' rights, and the responsibility of weighing the threat to those rights against the national interest served by ratifying a particular treaty.

Bolton worked hard at the United Nations to undo the policy preferences he said the Clinton administration had shared with NGOs. Bolton asserted the United States' right to unilateral action in a manner not seen before, railing against what he calls the way "leftist groups such as Greenpeace and Human Rights Watch had successfully worked to 'isolate' the United States on the Kyoto Protocol, the Rome Statute, and the Ottawa Land-mines Convention."[31] Bolton was also dismayed at the way he said these groups used the same tactics concerning domestic issues like the rights of children, the death penalty, and gun control.

Another common objection to international agreements asserted by the new sovereigntists is that an agreement with an internal mechanism to allow parties to alter its terms after ratification is said to be an unconstitutional delegation of law-making power to a supranational body. For example, the Kyoto Protocol, which the United States was heavily involved with negotiating, but did not ultimately ratify, became a lightning rod for the domestic debate over the United States' role in global environmental governance. Those opposed to the protocol argued, with considerable success, that a loss of sovereignty follows from signing agreements that have a built-in amendment process. And article 20 of the protocol, if consensus cannot be reached on a proposed amendment, directs that "the amendment shall as a last resort be adopted by a three-fourths majority vote of the Parties present and voting at the meeting."[32] The argument goes that the ability of a supermajority vote of ratifying parties to make post-ratification changes to Kyoto targets is tantamount to a supranational body promulgating U.S. environmental regulations. The claim is that this poses a threat to U.S. sovereignty because it erodes the right of a democratic people to self-govern.[33]

Another reason offered by the new sovereigntists to remain apart from the system of global governance is the involvement of NGOs in the decision-making and implementation processes. Bolton derides NGOs as part of "presumptively named civil society." In describing his defeat of NGOs over the UN light weapons and small arms treaty, he accused NGOs of "[e]xpropriating the term 'civil society' from the national context." Bolton appeared displeased that "at U.N. meeting after U.N. meeting, there would be delegations from member governments, and then delegations from 'civil society,' as if 'civil society' existed outside of nation-states."[34] In a similar vein, David Rivkin blames "activist NGOs" for a thirty-year campaign attempting to phase out the term "enemy combatant."

Global Governance Watch (GGW) is a joint project between the Federalist Society and the American Enterprise Institute. The project's mission is to "raise awareness about global governance, to monitor how international organizations influence domestic political outcomes, and to address issues of transparency and accountability within the United Nations, related intergovernmental organizations (IGOs), and other non-state actors."[35] GGW asserts that NGOs in developed democracies often usurp legitimate government and by their terms are antidemocratic. First, they purportedly interfere in government negotiations over trade and other international agreements through advocacy work and mobilizing public opinion. Second, they criticize business and corporate interests for acting without regard for the public interest. Perhaps ironically, GGW does not acknowledge that (1) AIE and the Federalist Society are themselves NGOs, organized primarily to influence the political and legal process, and (2) there are many multinational enterprises, including for-profit corporations, also without elected constituencies, who wield more power on the international stage than some states.

Application of International Law to Individuals

GGW is organized into four pillars—human rights, environment and health, law and sovereignty, and economics and development.[36] GGW's pillar on law and sovereignty posits that IGOs and NGOs are attempting to use international law and the international system of courts to hold corporations and individuals accountable for violations of international law, which it says "technically applies" only to states. This view of international law, shared by the new sovereigntists, is archaic at best and misleading at worst. "Historically applied" might be a more precise definition. The idea that international law applied exclusively to states only prevailed up until the early twentieth century. Hugo Grotius, a Dutch scholar considered to be the father of international law, wrote in *De Jure Belli ac Pacis* (The Law of War and Peace) in 1625 that international law is defined as "[e]thical notions that constrain the actions of nations in pursuit of their own advantage." The "law of nations" that Chief Justice Marshall referenced in 1900 in *The Paquete Habana* considered only state actors to be accountable to, and therefore capable of violating, international law. This state-centric notion of international law was in place at the time of the founding of the United States. International law now, however, is broadly accepted as a creator of rights and obligations for individuals as well as state actors. At its most inclusive, modern international law is said to comprise customary international law or *opinion juris* (rules that become entrenched as "law" because of consistent state behavior, such as the universal prohibitions against genocide, torture, and slavery); treaties, such as the Geneva Conventions, the North American Free Trade Agreement (NAFTA), or the United Nations Framework Convention on Climate Change (UNFCCC); and general principles of law or *jus cogens* (where the internal legal systems of states share widely recognized principles such as "fairness"). With the rise of international tribunals, a body of precedent has developed from these judicial decisions that, although not binding, is considered by some also to be a part of the fabric of international law.

The extension of the applicability of international law to individuals began at the close of World War II. The United Nations' Universal Declaration on Human Rights, adopted by the UN General Assembly on December 10, 1948, was the first treaty to enshrine individual human rights under an international regime. The rights expressed in the declaration included freedoms of thought, conscience, opinion, expression, and religion; the right to a trial before an impartial body; the right to participate in government; and the idea that all persons are entitled to a social and international order in which the rights and freedoms set forth in the declaration can be fully realized. The obligations set forth imparted the notion that all humans are endowed with reason and conscience and should act toward one another in a spirit of brotherhood.[37]

The declaration followed closely on the heels of the end of World War II and the Nuremberg Trials, which began in 1945 with the prosecution of Herman Goering for war crimes, crimes against peace, crimes against humanity, and conspiracy. The American William Chanler, a friend of U.S. Secretary of War Henry Stimson, had suggested that the activities of the Nazis ought not be treated as a criminal plot, arguing instead that the waging of a war of aggression was a crime against international law and should be prosecuted as such.[38] Stimson, a Republican, insisted on proper judicial proceedings against Nazi war criminals, arguing that legal justification for them lay in the Kellogg-Briand Pact of 1928 that had outlawed war.[39] Stimson led the U.S. Department of War in drafting the first proposals for an international tribunal. Former officers of the Reich, including Rudolph Hess, Joachim von Ribbentrop, and Albert Speer, were tried before this tribunal, on charges including war crimes and crimes against humanity. Robert Jackson, who later became a U.S. Supreme Court justice, was the chief prosecutor at Nuremberg. In his opening remarks, he stated that "[t]his trial represents mankind's desperate effort to apply the discipline of the law to statesmen who have used their powers of state to attack the foundations of the world's peace and to commit aggressions against the rights of their neighbors."[40] His words reflected the sentiment of the tribunal—a recognition that individuals were subjects of international law:

> These defendants were men of a station and rank which does not soil its own hands with blood. They were men who knew how to use lesser folk as tools. We want to reach the planners and designers, the inciters and leaders, without whose evil architecture the world would not have been for so long scourged with the violence and lawlessness, and wracked with the agonies and convulsions of this terrible war. . . . The charter recognizes that one who has committed criminal acts may not take refuge in superior orders nor in the doctrine that his crimes were acts of states.[41]

The principle that international law creates rights and obligations in individuals has been recognized in decisions of permanent international courts, temporary international tribunals, and U.S. courts. The International Court of Justice justifies the principle as an "elementary consideration of humanity." In the prosecution of Duško Tadić, the appeals chamber of the International Criminal Tribunal for the former Yugoslavia held that the former president had committed crimes against protected persons under international humanitarian law.[42] In April 2012, the Special Court for Sierra Leone found Charles Taylor, the former president of Liberia, guilty of crimes against humanity, violations of the Geneva Conventions, and other violations of international humanitarian law.[43] In the United States, the Second Circuit Court of Appeals in New York expanded the notion of the "law of nations" to include international human rights in the seminal case of *Filartiga v. Pena*. There, the court held that state-sanctioned torture "violates established norms of the international law of human rights, and hence the law of nations."[44] In 2004, the Supreme Court also held that the law of nations no longer applied only to state actors, in *Sosa v. Alvarez-Machain*; "For two centuries we have affirmed that the domestic law of the United States recognizes the law of nations. . . . It would take some explaining to say now that federal courts must avert their gaze entirely from any international norm intended to protect individuals."[45]

AMERICAN EXEMPTIONALISM: U.S. TREATY BEHAVIOR

Despite broad acceptance of international law's application to individuals, demonstrated by international human rights agreements and the pronouncements of U.S. courts, the new sovereigntists continue to push back in the name of American sovereignty. In 2001, President Clinton signed the Rome Statute, which established the International Criminal Court. Senator Jesse Helms (R-NC), then chairman of the Foreign Relations Committee, called the decision "outrageous" and "inexplicable." Helms argued that Clinton's signature was an assault on American sovereignty and derided the court as a kangaroo court. He professed that he would "gladly stand with James Madison, and the rest of our Founding Fathers, over that collection of ne'er-do-wells in Rome any day."[46]

Clinton's successor George W. Bush famously "unsigned" the treaty, agreeing with his conservative base that the idea of an international criminal court that could prosecute American citizens for war crimes was an affront to U.S. sovereignty and self-determination. John Bolton physically "unsigned" the treaty for the United States, while working in the Department of State. He called it "[m]y happiest moment at State" and recollected that "only sundry High Minded Europeans cared even slightly (about the unsigning), which was simply further evidence that unsigning was the right thing to do."[47] He added that he regretted not unsigning more "bad treaties," like the Kyoto Protocol and the Comprehensive Test Ban Treaty. In addition to unsigning the Rome Statute, the United States began a process under President George W. Bush that continues under President Obama, of concluding legally binding bilateral Article 98 agreements with foreign governments that prohibit the surrender of U.S. citizens to the International Criminal Court.[48]

Studies show that U.S. treaty ratification has been especially strong when there is a proponent of the treaty in the White House or a Democratic majority in the Senate. Human rights treaties in particular have suffered under Republican majorities in the Senate.[49] But U.S. treaty behavior is not an area where the split between the Left and the Right is firm. America's haphazard pattern of treaty ratification (and nonratification) and involvement (and noninvolvement) in international institutions is a behavior that underpins American Exceptionalism and defies partisanship.[50] The United States played an enormous role in the creation of the United Nations, but has often criticized it as a bureaucratic monster undeserving of American support. Similarly, the United States contributed considerable resources (and in some instances, rights embodied in its own constitution) to UN treaties, including the Convention on the Rights of the Child, the Kyoto Protocol, the Rome Statute, and the Convention on the Elimination of All Forms of Discrimination against Women. It has ratified none of these treaties.

Examples of America's inconsistent relationship to treaty ratification abound. Woodrow Wilson, a Democrat, ardently supported the United States joining the League of Nations, but a Republican-dominated Senate was too strong for him to overcome and the United States never became a member. Harry Truman, also a Democrat, ushered in ratification of the UN Charter and the NATO pact and signed the Genocide Convention. The Senate Foreign Relations Committee rejected the Genocide Convention, and after a similar false start under Richard Nixon, the Senate finally ratified it under Ronald Reagan's watch.[51] Under Truman's Republican successor, Dwight Eisenhower, the Senate ratified the Nuclear Test Ban Treaty and negotiated the International Labor Organization's treaty on forced labor and the Supplemental Slavery Convention. John F. Kennedy sent the Convention on the Political Rights of Women, the International Labour Office (ILO) Convention on the Abolition of Forced Labor, and a supplement to the 1926 UN Slavery Convention to the Senate in 1963.[52] The Senate took years to act on them: the Supplementary Slavery Convention was ratified in 1967, the Convention on the Political Rights of Women was ratified in 1975, and the ILO Convention was ratified in 1991. In 1983, Ronald Reagan directed all federal agencies to comply with all the provisions of the Law of the Sea Treaty except the one concerning deep-sea mining. Although Reagan objected most to treaty provisions requiring technology and wealth transfers from developed to underdeveloped countries as being "out of step with the concepts of economic liberty," he did take steps toward embracing a treaty considered one of the most significant environmental and trade treaties of the modern era.[53] President George H. W. Bush sent NAFTA to the Senate for ratification, but NAFTA's side agreements concerning labor and environmental standards, which alienated his Republican base, held the treaty up. In 1994, President Clinton ushered in the Convention against Torture, the International Convention on the Elimination of All Forms of Racial Discrimination, and NAFTA. The United States ratified the UN Convention on Civil and Political Rights under President George W. Bush, but as mentioned earlier, he unsigned the Rome Statute and began the Article 98 agreement process. The UN Convention on the Elimination of All Forms of Discrimination against Women (CEDAW) and the Convention on the Rights of the Child (CRC) languished during the terms of both Presidents Clinton and G.W. Bush. President Bush refused to sign and submit the CRC to the Senate.[54] Under the new Democratic administration of President Obama, thus far the United States has not ratified either of these treaties. The Obama administration also refused to send the Land Mine Treaty to the Senate for ratification.

Although partisan political lines regarding treaty ratification are sometimes blurred, the Federalist Society has amplified the voices of those opposed to U.S. ratification of human rights and environmental treaties, those opposed to trade agreements that incorporate nonmarket mechanisms such as labor or environmental side agreements, and those who believe that international alternative dispute resolution mechanisms (such as the WTO system or arbitration agreements contained within investment treaties) are illegitimate and a threat to American values and self-government.

John Bolton explains why: "[G]lobal governance advocates . . . hope to transfer areas of authority traditionally left to national government to supranational bodies, or to constrain nation-states through 'norming,' effectively tying their hands." (Norming is the UN practice of taking a definite position on an issue, despite potentially disparate views on that issue across member states, with the aim of creating international norms of behavior.) Bolton argues that these advocates drag issues such as abortion and family planning, environmental policy, the right to keep and bear arms, and the death penalty into the international arena, "often with the support of the U.S. left." Liberals, according to Bolton, "have found themselves unable to prevail in a fair fight within America's system of representative government, so they now seek international forums to argue their positions, where their collectivist proclivities find greater sympathy among foreign governments and NGOs."[55] During his tenure at the United Nations, Bolton derailed a treaty on the illicit trade of light arms and small weapons. His view was that the real agenda behind the treaty was the restriction of gun ownership by private citizens, and that the treaty on the illicit trade in light arms would eventually lead to future treaties restricting the legitimate gun trade and U.S. citizens' Second Amendment right to gun ownership.[56] Bolton told the General Assembly, "We do not support measures that prohibit civilian possession of small arms. This is outside the mandate for this Conference. . . . The United States will not join consensus on a final document that contains measures contrary to our constitutional right to keep and bear arms."[57]

Human Rights Treaties

The United States' failure to ratify the UN Convention on the Rights of the Child (CRC) is a textbook example of how the organized Right, including the Federalist Society and its members, has mobilized public and political opinion against a human rights treaty that runs afoul of their particular beliefs about religion, social values, and the separation of powers. The CRC entered into force on September 2, 1990, and sets out a child-specific human rights framework in fifty-four articles and two optional protocols that broadly address the often ignored but devastating problems of child soldiers and child prostitutes.[58] The four core principles of the convention are nondiscrimination; the best interests of the child; the right to life, survival, and development; and respect for the views of the child. The particular rights embodied in the CRC include the right to survival; to develop to the fullest; to protection from harmful influences, abuse, and exploitation; and to participate fully in family, cultural, and social life. The CRC is the most broadly and swiftly ratified multilateral treaty in UN history.[59] The newest of the seven major UN human rights treaties, the CRC is also the first legally binding international instrument incorporating the full range of human rights—civil, political, social, economic, and cultural.[60] Currently, all UN members have ratified the convention except for Somalia—a state without a functioning government—and the United States.

Resistance to ratification of the CRC runs deep within Federalist Society circles. In a 1987 memo to then-Assistant Attorney General John Bolton, his deputy Samuel Alito wrote that the convention did not reflect the American dislike for government intervention in parenting or childrearing practices and interfered with state policy matters like child welfare standards and the juvenile death penalty. [61]

Opponents of the CRC assert that the convention erodes sovereignty, interferes with the right of parents to raise their children, can be read as pro-abortion, and unduly requires the United States to adhere to international human rights norms that are contrary to its interests and not part of its domestic legal framework. Some of the organizations at the forefront of promulgating these concerns have been the Christian Coalition, Concerned Women for America, the Eagle Forum, ParentalRights.org, the Family Research Council, Focus on the Family, the John Birch Society, the National Center for Home Education, and the Rutherford Institute. As discussed in Chapter 5, the leaders of many of these organizations have ties to the Federalist Society, in particular its Religious Liberties Practice Group.[62]

Focus on the Family has resisted ratification of the CRC, arguing that it intrudes on national sovereignty and puts children at risk.[63] Focus asserts that the CRC could be used to promote radical agendas and undermine the legitimate authority of parents. Articles of specific concern are Article 24(4)(f), concerning family planning, and Article 16, concerning the right to privacy.[64] Focus warns that that the CRC could be used to allow abortions or sex education for children, against the wishes of their parents.[65]

Focus has propagated the theory that ratification of the CRC, combined with the "last in time" rule, would mean that the CRC becomes part of the "Supreme Law of the Land," on an equal footing with federal law, superior to state law, and superseding all law passed before ratification. The "last in time rule" stems from the Supreme Court's 1888 opinion in *Whitney v. Robertson*, and holds that if a treaty and a statute are inconsistent, the most recent in date will control the other.[66] Through this string of inferences, Focus argues that because the CRC addresses many aspects of juvenile justice and family law that have traditionally been regulated by the individual states, it threatens the separation of powers and would interfere with the ability of state courts to deal effectively with legal issues involving children.[67] In fact, treaties, like all governmental acts, are subject to the Constitution, so any treaty clause that enables government to act in a manner that the Constitution prohibits is void as a matter of domestic law.

Global Governance Watch's opposition to the CRC is partly grounded in the organization's belief that the treaty has the potential to make it easier for pregnant women under the age of eighteen to receive abortions without the permission or knowledge of their parents. GGW also plays into the constitutional rhetoric utilized by many of the Christian conservative groups: "If the United States ratified the CRC, it would give U.N. international courts the power to bypass U.S. local, state, and federal courts and even the Supreme Court. Giving up the power of self-governance for the sake of an unclear and sometimes contradictory document is by no means a good decision for the U.S., for ratifying the CRC could make the U.S. a target of U.N. sanctions."[68] In fact, beyond formal reporting requirements, the CRC provides for no penalties, punishments, or direct criticism of the substance or validity of domestic laws. It simply assumes good faith ratification and compliance.

A second instance of an almost universally adopted human rights treaty that the United States has shunned is the UN Convention on the Elimination of All Forms of Discrimination against Women (CEDAW). CEDAW came into force in 1981. Today there are 186 signatories, including all industrialized nations except the United States.[69] The convention's stated goals are to define discrimination against women and to set up an agenda for national action to end such discrimination. As member states ratified the convention, prominent conservatives expressed hostility to the United States becoming a party. Jesse Helms, then chairman of the Senate Committee on Foreign Relations, resisted a vote by that committee regarding U.S. ratification. He declared that under CEDAW, it would be considered "discrimination" to refuse to provide abortion services to all women.[70] Global Governance Watch warns that "ratification of CEDAW would give U.N. experts control over U.S. domestic policies."[71]

In articles entitled "CEDAW Would Undermine American Sovereignty" and "The Convention on the Elimination of All Forms of Discrimination against Women: A Leading Example of What's Wrong with International Law," the Federalist Society gives a voice to those opposed to U.S. ratification of the treaty. Some familiar trends emerge. CEDAW is touted as a means by which "Americans will lose what remains of their right to govern themselves and define their culture. They will lose their freedom."[72] Specifically, the authors warn that if CEDAW is ratified, the United States will become subject to the scrutiny of a committee composed of persons from ratifying states with poor human rights records such as Indonesia, China, and Cuba; that CEDAW requires "legalizing prostitution," "access . . . to easy and swift abortion," and "redistribution of wealth"; and that feminist, activist lawyers in the United States are preparing to use CEDAW to force "wholesale political and social change."[73] Both articles are replete with anti-UN rhetoric. One author improperly calls members of the CEDAW committee "judges" and refers to opinions issued by the CEDAW committee as "rulings."[74] Another refers to the CEDAW committee as "treaty enforcers" who rule from "their pulpit at the UN."[75] The rhetorical themes evident in this piece of work demonstrate the broader movement that the Federalist Society and its members have successfully supported. These include denigrating persons ideologically opposed to them by labeling them "activist," using fear of upsetting the domestic legal order or the supremacy of the Constitution to rally support against treaty ratification, and accusing human rights agreements of having antimarket and "socialist" sentiments.

Trade Agreements

While the new sovereigntists embrace international trade, they are reticent about international trade agreements that grow limbs featuring regulatory or human rights constraints. The United States is a party to hundreds of treaties and thousands of executive agreements.[76] Two of the most important multinational trade agreements to which it belongs are the General Agreement on Trade and Tariffs (GATT), which is administered by the World Trade Organization (WTO), and, regionally, NAFTA.

Many leading conservatives endorsed NAFTA. At the time of ratification, former secretary of state Henry Kissinger called NAFTA "the architecture of a new international system" and "the most creative step toward a new world order since the end of the Cold War."[77] Ronald Reagan, Margaret Thatcher, and Milton Friedman were also pro-ratification.[78] Congress passed NAFTA with a majority of Republican votes.[79] Those in favor of NAFTA relied on the demonstrated benefits of increased openness to trade and foreign investment that other free trade agreements had brought—increased employment, lower prices, greater access to foreign capital, technology transfer, and better access to global goods and services by domestic firms and consumers.[80]

NAFTA's two side agreements pertaining to minimum standards on labor and the environment, however, were extremely unpopular with many conservatives, who considered them the first step in a slippery slope toward a political union like the European Union.[81] They also considered the side agreements to be an erosion of U.S. sovereignty because the supranational panels overseeing them had the power to pass judgment on the actions of local municipalities, states, and the federal government.[82] Critics accused NAFTA of being yet another example of antidemocratic global governance, where NGOs, accountable to no constituency, have had an inordinate amount of influence in the creation of law and policy.[83] John Bolton has written that the side agreements are a prime example of how NGOs have begun to "crowd into the [international] trade field," attracted by its growth, success, and stability.[84]

Similar criticisms have been leveled at the WTO by conservative commentators and scholars. Jeremy Rabkin accuses the WTO appeals board of "activism" on the basis of its announcement that it would be guided not only by the text of the trade agreements, but by general principles of international law and by guides to treaty interpretation such as the Vienna Convention on the Law of Treaties, which the United States has not ratified. Rabkin, like many of his Federalist Society colleagues, prefers international law as a body of rules setting out the rights and duties of sovereign states in their mutual interactions, and where trade agreements like the GATT allow states to punish other states for noncompliance by withdrawing concessions that had benefited the delinquent state.[85] The GATT, in Rabkin's opinion, was a true system of trade treaties, that were bargains between states, and therefore constituted "proper" international law.

Rabkin's objection to the WTO is that under the guise of freeing up trade, the WTO is creating a system of international laws and regulations—concerning otherwise domestic issues—that acts as a framework around trading rights and actually strangles international trade. According to Rabkin, the WTO has become less about the free exchange of goods and services between sovereign nations, and more about the standardization and proliferation of international regulatory standards, which are an affront to state sovereignty.[86] He concludes, "[W]hat had once seemed a series of trade bargains was now presented as a set of solemn legal duties, embedded in a wider framework of international law."[87] Bolton shares Rabkin's view—that the GATT was good, on the basis that it was a "classic" trade agreement, but that the WTO (like NAFTA's side agreements) proliferates supranational regulations, which are detrimental to U.S. self-determination and sovereignty.[88]

Environmental Agreements

Global environmental agreements have received similar treatment from some high-profile Federalist Society members and affiliates. Rabkin states that environmentalists "sought to speak for the entire earth" with international environmental treaties and accords, starting with the UN Conference on the Human Environment (UNCHE), held in Stockholm in June 1972 and widely considered to mark the beginning of modern political and public acknowledgement of global environmental problems.[89] At the 2008 Federalist Society National Lawyers Convention, Rabkin's cofellow at the American Enterprise Institute, Steven F. Hayward, called Kyoto's targets "the climate change policy equivalent of wage and price controls."[90] John Bolton has called Kyoto another "Globalist project" with an overall objective of "reducing individual nation-state autonomy, particularly that of the United States."[91]

CONGRESSIONAL RESISTANCE TO FOREIGN AND INTERNATIONAL LAW

The United States has a long history of congressional action seeking to shield the United States against the influence of international law and organizations. Attempts at constitutional and statutory amendments evidenced hostility to international law, sought to undermine the legitimacy of international institutions, and embodied the notion that federal judges can and should be censured by the legislature for considering international or foreign law in their deliberations.

In its 1953–1954 term, the Senate considered the Bricker Amendment to the Constitution. It sought to rein in executive agreements—international agreements conducted solely by the president, without the participation (or veto) of the Senate. The amendment's proponents believed that such agreements violated the treaty clause of the Constitution (and left the Senate in many ways impotent with regards to international affairs). The amendment was also crafted as a buttress against the imposition of the values, rights, and duties embodied in the various human rights treaties that had been proposed by the United Nations after the end of World War II (such as the Universal Declaration of Human Rights and the Genocide Convention).

The Bricker Amendment found a vocal supporter in ABA President Frank E. Holman, at a time when the ABA leaned considerably more to the right than it does at the time of this writing. Holman was concerned with communist influence on international organizations. The *ABA Journal* published articles describing an "excessive egalitarianism" growing in the world community.[92] It was in fact the increasing liberalization of the ABA, many years later, that contributed to the formation of the "anti-ABA"—the Federalist Society.

The Bricker Amendment was also a somewhat delayed reaction to the Supreme Court's 1920 decision in *Missouri v. Holland*, which held that Congress can constitutionally ratify a treaty whose subject matter would otherwise be the provenance of the states under the Tenth Amendment.[93] This was controversial because the Tenth Amendment essentially bestows on the states all powers that are not specifically delegated to the federal government.[94] In *Holland*, the state of Missouri argued that the Migratory Bird Treaty Act of July 3, 1918, was unconstitutional because the federal government held no enumerated powers over migratory birds, and therefore, under the Tenth Amendment, that power was reserved to the states. The court found in favor of the federal government, upholding the treaty on the basis that the states had no demonstrated ownership in the migratory birds by their very nature, and that a national interest was involved that could be protected only by national action in concert with another state.

Clearly, the migration of birds is far from a banner conservative issue. But conservatives were eager to overturn judge-made law that broadened the powers of the federal government. And they had other objections to *Holland*. In his opinion, Justice Oliver Wendell Holmes articulated the idea of a "living Constitution"—the idea that the founders understood that they could not possibly have envisioned the forces that would shape the nation in years to come and as a result, the Constitution was written with purposeful ambiguity. Holmes was reflecting the view espoused in 1819 by Chief Justice Marshall in *McCulloch v. Maryland*, where Marshall described the Constitution as "intended to endure for ages to come, and, consequently, to be adapted to the various crises of human affairs."[95] This idea is the antithesis of originalism.

Under Holmes's holding, the United States could constitutionally ratify a treaty whose subject-matter is exclusively the ambit of the states, albeit only if it was an interest of national importance that required agreements with other countries. To this day, it is anathema to those opposed to U.S. ratification of human rights treaties, which tend to include mandates and norms in areas customarily regulated by the states, such as child welfare, adoption, religion, gun ownership, child labor, speech freedoms, and sexual equality. Secretary of State John Foster Dulles made a deal that precipitated the rejection of the Bricker Amendment. He promised that the Eisenhower administration would not send any human rights treaties to the Senate for ratification. This policy would have a lasting, suppressive effect on U.S. treaty behavior.[96]

The Reaffirming American Independence Resolution (RAIR) was passed by the House in May 2004 but stalled in the Senate. It specifically provided that judicial determinations regarding the meaning of the laws of the United States should not be based on "judgments, laws or pronouncements of foreign institutions" unless they "inform an understanding of the original meaning of the Constitution of the United States."[97] The resolution sought not only to formalize the rejection of foreign law in U.S. courts, but also to legislatively mandate originalism as the sole means of constitutional interpretation. This radical resolution was spearheaded by a trio of Republican politicians: Senator John Cornyn (Texas), Representative Tom Feeney (Florida), and Representative Robert Goodlatte (Virginia). The resolution's catalyst was Justice Kennedy's 2003 opinion in *Lawrence v. Texas*, holding that a Texas law criminalizing sodomy between homosexuals violated the liberty interest protected by the due process clause. In overturning a 1986 case, *Bowers v. Hardwick*, which had upheld a Georgia law criminalizing sodomy between any two people, Kennedy wrote: "To the extent Bowers relied on values we share with a wider civilization, it should be noted that the reasoning and holding in Bowers have been rejected elsewhere. The European Court of Human Rights has [not] followed . . . Bowers. . . . Other nations, too, have taken action consistent with an affirmation of the protected right of homosexual adults to engage in intimate, consensual conduct. The right the petitioners seek in this case has been accepted as an integral part of human freedom in many other countries. There has been no showing that in this country the governmental interest in circumscribing personal choice is somehow more legitimate or urgent."[98]

The American Justice for American Citizens Act was introduced in the House by Ron Paul in 2004.[99] It criticized the Supreme Court rulings in *Lawrence v. Texas* and *Atkins v. Virginia* (holding that the executions of mentally retarded criminals are "cruel and unusual punishments" prohibited by the Eighth Amendment) for citing foreign law. The act asserted that constitutional principles designed to be permanent were being transformed into "evolving standards" subject to change by judges, and it sought to prevent federal judges from employing any foreign or international law when interpreting or applying the U.S. Constitution, limiting their interpretive context to law relied on by the Constitution's framers. The act never became law.

The Constitution Restoration Act of 2005 provided in part that judges would be subject to impeachment if they used any foreign source other than English constitutional and common law in interpreting and applying the Constitution. Sources considered impeachable in the act were "any constitution, law, administrative rule, Executive order, directive, policy, judicial decision, or any other action of any foreign state or international organization or agency." The act was filed by two Republican senators from Alabama, Richard Shelby and Robert Aderholt, on March 3, 2005. The act never became law.

AMERICAN CONSTITUTIONALISM AND INTERNALIZING THE MEANING OF INTERNATIONAL LAW

The new sovereigntists' belief that the Constitution limits the United States' amenability to international law reflects a realist view of international relations, which holds that there is no legitimate global governing system that regulates nation-states, and in this anarchic system, nation-states act out of self-interest to preserve their security and sovereignty. This view finds its counterpoint, liberalism, in the European Union, where member states have created a supranational legal structure that is superior to any of their domestic legal frameworks. This includes two courts that have the power to interpret the constitutions of the individual states. The European Court of Human Rights (ECHR) adjudicates human rights claims by individuals against member states, and the European Court of Justice (ECJ) adjudicates matters of community law.

The new sovereigntists reject the European model and the liberal view of international relations. John Bolton, for example, has called the European Union "post-Westphalian, above and beyond the nation-state" and has argued that it is using the United Nations to further its agenda of cloning its model elsewhere. "The UN," writes Bolton, "is a critical venue to achieve full transformation of the EU's institutional form and governance style into global governance, and especially to whip the still unrepentantly Westphalian United States into line."[100] Westphalianism is defined by territorialism and the exclusion of external actors from the domestic realm, holding that no supranational structure of lawmaking or command may exist above the sovereign state.

Michael Paulsen has written that liberal international law scholars gloss over many constitutional imperatives in their efforts to solidify the United States as a fully fledged member of the world legal community.[101] His position is that neither the United Nations nor any other foreign or international body can authoritatively determine the content of international law for the United States. Paulsen also considers two broadly accepted doctrines that arose from seminal Supreme Court cases establishing the relationship between international law and U.S. law to be "misleading" and "unsound."[102]

The first, from a 1900 case, *The Paquete Habana*, is that "international law is part of our law."[103] The second arose from an 1804 case, *Murray v. Schooner Charming Betsy*, and holds that U.S. law should, wherever possible, be interpreted so as to not conflict with international law.[104] Paulsen suggests that the judiciary ought to interpret and apply customary international law only when it is exercising common law or admiralty law powers (because those were in place when the Constitution was framed), and only where no contrary federal law applies.

International Law in Wartime

The new sovereigntists' beliefs that the United States is the ultimate arbiter of international law was manifested in the George W. Bush administration's decision to go to war in Iraq and Afghanistan without the backing or support of the international community or the UN Security Council, its subsequent detainment and interrogation of enemy combatants, and its use of military tribunals to try them.

In a speech to the 2003 Federalist Society National Lawyers Convention, Bolton, who was at that time the undersecretary for arms control and international security, discussed the legitimacy of the U.S. invasion of Iraq. In his address, Bolton dismissed Kofi Annan's statement that "[u]nless the Security Council is restored to its preeminent position as the sole source of legitimacy on the use of force, we are on a dangerous path to anarchy." A state's decision to use military force, according to Bolton, is "the most important decision that any nation-state makes, and transferring this power to another source of authority results in a diminution of sovereignty."[105]

Michael Paulsen has argued that if the president's conduct of military operations (including the capture, interrogation, detention, and military punishment of both lawful and unlawful enemy combatants) otherwise falls within his exclusive constitutional power as commander in chief, then neither the prohibitions contained within the Geneva Conventions (which the United States has ratified) nor any other international agreement can restrict those powers.[106] The United States did in fact ratify the UN Convention against Torture and Other Cruel, Inhuman or Degrading Treatment or Punishment (the "Torture Convention"), which came into force in 1987, but Paulsen argues that the federal legislation that implemented the treaty has only narrow application within the United States. Therefore, if the president determines that the government's treatment of prisoners is not "torture," it is not "torture" under the treaty.[107]

David Rivkin, has written, lectured, and debated extensively on the legitimacy of the Bush administration's use of military commissions to try enemy combatants rather than in the domestic court system. The tribunals differ from domestic courts in many important aspects. The rules of evidence are less strict, appeals are limited, they can be held in secret, and they are essentially operated by one of the parties (rather than an impartial judge).[108] In a nod to customary international law, Rivkin acknowledges that the 1977 Protocol to the Geneva Conventions, which establishes the requirement of using a "regularly constituted court" to try captured enemies, is controlling on the United States. He argues, however, that because the term "regularly constituted" is not defined by the convention or the protocol, and because the International Red Cross's commentary suggests the term was included only to stop "summary justice," the U.S. military commissions are in fact "tribunals established in accordance with the law."[109] Military commissions have historically been convened in wartime; before 9/11, the United States had last used them during World War II.

Rivkin further contends that the military commissions should pass constitutional muster on the basis that their rules of evidence and provisions banning the defendant and his civilian lawyer from proceedings governed past military commissions and mirror the rules of the "leading international criminal tribunals."[110]

Rivkin also defends the "Bush doctrine" of preemptive self-defense as being legal under international law.[111] He agrees with Bolton's assertion that a state should not have to seek permission from any international organization before using force, noting that dozens of other states (including Russia, China, Sweden, Britain, France, and Israel) have used preemptive force and maintained it was legal. He also looks to "centuries-old norms" of customary international law that authorize anticipatory defense.[112]

The UN charter, to which the United States is a signatory, explicitly states that the use of military force is lawful only when a state invoking the right has suffered an "armed attack."[113] It is worth considering whether the framers themselves were immune to the broader norms of the world community. Jeremy Rabkin has quoted Alexander Hamilton in the *Federalist Papers* to support a common criticism of international law: "A law which has no means of enforcement, a law which has no penalty attached, is not a law."[114] And yet, Madison and Hamilton wrote that the lessons of "[e]xperience [were] the oracle of truth; and where its responses are unequivocal, they ought to be conclusive and sacred."[115] In *Federalist* No. 63, Madison advised the people of the new nation to pay "attention to the judgment of other nations" and "the opinion of the impartial world" so that the United States would in turn make decisions that were the "offspring of a wise and honorable policy."[116] This essay also stated that "an attention to the judgment of other nations is important to every government. . . . [I]n doubtful cases, particularly where the national councils may be warped by some strong passion or momentary interest, the presumed or known opinion of the impartial world may be the best guide that can be followed."[117] Thomas Jefferson was enamored with the political ideas of Scottish Enlightenment thinkers, including those of Francis Hutcheson, who celebrated the republican notion of honor, which held a person's actions accountable to the rest of mankind.[118] Even the Declaration of Independence invoked the founder's belief in paying "a decent respect to the opinions of mankind."

THE UNITARY EXECUTIVE THEORY AND THE TORTURE MEMOS

Article II, Section 1 of the Constitution states, "The executive power shall be vested in the President of the United States." The theory of the unitary executive posits that all exercises of executive power must be under the control of the president.[119] Steven Calabresi and Federalist Society affiliates John Yoo, Jeremy Rabkin, and Geoffrey Miller have written prolifically about the theory, in particular as it pertains to the theaters of war making and foreign policy. There, the theory is grounded primarily in the president's enumerated constitutional powers as head of the executive branch and the commander in chief of the military, and in the notion of executive privilege.[120] These scholars argue that the president may override legislation—despite the fact that lawmaking is a congressional function—if it conflicts with the president's agenda pertaining to war or foreign policy. Calabresi characterizes the debate over the force of the theory as a debate between the "presidentialists" and the "anti-presidentialists."[121]

At its most extreme, the theory holds that the president may unilaterally exercise the enumerated executive powers and implied powers that depend on them regardless of the position taken by the other branches of government. In other words, the president can interpret independently the constitutionality of legislation and executive acts. This idea was promoted by Ed Meese during his tenure as attorney general. A so-called signing statement initiative was born in the mid-80s, when Calabresi was working for Meese in the Department of Justice. Its proponents wanted signing statements—the statements the president makes to clarify his constitutional interpretation of bills when signing them—to have the same legal weight as the legislative histories of the bills, which courts rely on when they are interpreting laws.[122] President Reagan issued some 276 signing statements, 71 of which questioned the constitutionality of a statutory provision. The practice continued under Presidents George H. W. Bush (214 statements, 146 constitutional objections) and Bill Clinton (391 signing statements, 105 constitutional objections). In the first six years of his presidency, President George W. Bush issued 125 signing statements, which contained more than 800 constitutional objections—more than those of the previous four presidents combined in the preceding twenty years.[123] Taken further, the theory gives the president the power to override even treaties or norms of international law that the United States has internalized as domestic law (for example, the Geneva Conventions) if he believes that they are in violation of his interpretation of the Constitution.

The idea that the president has the independent power to determine the constitutionality of laws directly contradicts the Supreme Court's landmark 1803 ruling in *Marbury v. Madison*.[124] It was in *Marbury* that the court established its power of judicial review—the power to rule whether legislation passed by Congress or actions taken by executive department officials are constitutional. The court famously held that "it is emphatically the province of the judiciary to say what the law is." The court subsequently affirmed that it is the ultimate arbiter of what the Constitution requires in *Cooper v. Aaron*, enforcing desegregation, and *United States v. Nixon*, rejecting a presidential assertion of executive privilege.[125]

John Yoo, along with society member Jay Bybee and other attorneys in the Office of Legal Counsel (OLC), authored memoranda during the George W. Bush administration stating that the president had the constitutional authority to override both international and federal law. Citing a large number of originalist sources, the OLC lawyers asserted the theory of the unitary executive to justify the president's ability not only to circumvent federal wiretapping laws, but to interpret international law vis-à-vis the detention and interrogation of captured Taliban and al-Qaeda personnel.[126]

These memoranda, a handful of which are described below, include the infamous "torture memos."[127] When they were penned, Bybee was assistant attorney general in the OLC and Yoo was a deputy assistant attorney general in the same office. After leaving the DOJ, Yoo resumed his job as a professor of law at Boalt Hall School of Law at the University of California, Berkeley. Bybee was nominated to the federal bench by President Bush in 2003, and remains a judge on the Ninth Circuit Court of Appeals in San Francisco. Yoo has called himself "the de facto head" of war-on-terrorism legal issues and acknowledged the significant role his counsel played, not just as a lawyer, but as a policymaker. Yoo was part of a small, secretive group of senior administration officials that wielded a considerable influence on antiterrorism policy; its other members were White House Counsel Alberto Gonzales; Deputy White House Counsel Tim Flanigan; the vice president's counsel, David Addington; and Jim Haynes, general counsel for the defense department. The group was known as the War Council.[128]

"Authority for Use of Military Force to Combat Terrorist Activities within the United States," an October 23, 2001, memorandum from Yoo and Delahunty to Gonzales and Haynes, concluded that the Fourth Amendment protections against unreasonable searches and seizures did not apply to "domestic military operations designed to deter and prevent further terrorist attacks."[129] It argued that even if a court later found that the Fourth Amendment did apply, the great threat posed by terrorists in light of the September 11, 2001, attacks would render government searches in that context reasonable, and therefore legal.[130] Citing extensively to the *Federalist Papers*, other founding documents, and early constitutional practice, as well as later views of the executive, judicial, and congressional branches, Yoo and Delahunty counseled that "the President has the independent, non-statutory power to take military actions, domestic as well as foreign, if he determines such actions to be necessary to respond to the terrorist attacks upon the United States on September 11, 2001, and before."[131] The authors stated that the Supreme Court had anointed the notion that "[g]overnment's compelling interests in wartime justify restrictions on the scope of individual liberty."[132] The authors further advised that any information obtained during military actions against foreign terrorists on domestic soil without the ordinary protections of the Fourth Amendment could be used in criminal prosecutions, meaning that evidence against an defendant in a criminal trial can be gathered in a way that existing criminal law would otherwise hold inadmissible.[133]

A January 22, 2002, memo to Gonzales and Haynes entitled "Application of Treaties and Laws to al-Qaeda and Taliban Detainees" was drafted by Yoo and Delahunty but signed by Bybee.[134] Undertaking what could be considered an originalist analysis of the Geneva Conventions, the authors interpreted the conventions' "text and context" when it was ratified by the United States.[135] They advised that that the Vienna Conventions did not apply to al-Qaeda or Taliban operatives because they were nonstate actors who could not be a party to international agreements governing war, and therefore could not be afforded any protections under them.[136] Further, the war being fought did not fit any definition of conflict that the conventions contemplated.[137]

The authors acknowledged that some may take the view that although the conventions might not by their original meaning cover conflicts such as the war on terror or adversaries such as the Taliban or al-Qaeda, the substance of the conventions has risen to customary international law, which, under *The Paquete Habana*, "is our law." They rejected this argument as "seriously mistaken," on the basis that it is not the "law of nations" as contemplated by the drafters of the Constitution, and argued that to elevate it to the level of federal law without amending the Constitution, enacting legislation, or obtaining approval by a two-thirds vote of the Senate would offend the delicate procedures constructed by the founders to create law.[138]

On January 25, 2002, Gonzales provided a memorandum to President Bush, approving the advice that Yoo and others had provided, and recommending that the president should declare that the protections of the Geneva Conventions did not apply to the Taliban and al-Qaeda.[139] This conclusion would "avoid foreclosing options for the future" regarding treatment of other nonstate actors. It would also substantially reduce the risk that U.S. citizens could be prosecuted under the U.S. War Crimes Act for activities related toward Taliban or al-Qaeda operatives. The 1996 law defines a war crime to include a grave breach of the Geneva Conventions, and as Gonzales noted, carries the death penalty.[140]

One of the so-called torture memos, dated August 1, 2002, was signed by Bybee, authored by Yoo, and addressed to Gonzales. It was entitled *Standards of Conduct for Interrogation under 18 U.S.C. §§ 2340–2340A*.[141] In the memo, the lawyers responded to two of President Bush's pressing questions: whether interrogation methods authorized by U.S. statute 18 U.S.C. § 2340 complied with the United States' obligations under the Geneva Conventions, and whether such statutorily authorized interrogation methods could be grounds for prosecution of U.S. personnel by the International Criminal Court.[142] Yoo explained that the reservation the George H. W. Bush administration attached to the Torture Convention enabled the United States to define "torture" as it does in federal law, specifically in 18 U.S.C. §2340.[143] That is, for an act to constitute torture, it must "inflict pain that is difficult to endure. Physical pain amounting to torture must be equivalent in intensity to the pain accompanying serious physical injury, such as organ failure, impairment of bodily function, or even death. For purely mental pain or suffering to amount to torture . . . it must result in significant psychological harm of significant duration, e.g., lasting for months or even years."[144]

Yoo further advised that because the president had determined that the al-Qaeda prisoners were not subject to the Geneva Conventions, and because ill-treatment of these detainees was not akin to a widespread and systematic attack against the civilian population, interrogation of an al-Qaeda operative could not constitute a crime under the Rome Statute.

The memo advised that the Torture Convention and the federal law that implemented it (Sections 2340 and 2340A) prohibited only the "most extreme acts."[145] For support, the authors looked to the ratification history of the Torture Convention in the United States, as well as domestic and international court decisions as to what constitutes torture.[146] The memo detailed the level of intent and harm that might violate the convention and the federal implementing law. It noted in many places that a defendant could argue he did not possess the requisite intent by demonstrating that he had a good faith belief that his behavior would not amount to acts prohibited by the convention or the implementing law.[147] As to harm, the authors noted that the threat of death would not constitute torture under U.S. law, but the threat of *imminent* death would.[148]

Before closing with suggested defenses, the authors essentially advised that there was little the president could not authorize regarding the treatment of al-Qaeda operatives. They argued that even if an interrogation method violated the Torture Convention as adopted in federal law, the convention would be unconstitutional "if it impermissibly encroached on the President's constitutional power to conduct a military campaign."[149]

A memo signed by Patrick Philbin from nearly a year earlier, entitled "Legality of the Use of Military Commissions to Try Terrorists," had concluded that the president possesses inherent constitutional authority, as commander in chief of the armed forces and chief executive, to establish military commissions to try and punish terrorists captured in connection with the September 11 terrorist attacks and military operations in response to the attacks.[150] The OLC lawyer wrote that "a declaration of war (which only Congress has the constitutional power to do, and as yet, has not) is not required to create a state of war or to subject persons to the laws of war, nor is it required that the United States be engaged in armed conflict with another nation. The terrorists' actions in this case are sufficient to create a state of war de facto that allows application of the laws of war."[151]

The Supreme Court rejected this argument in *Hamdan v. Rumsfeld*, in which Salid Ahmed Hamdan, an enemy combatant detained at Guantanamo Bay, Cuba, argued that the military commissions lacked the authority to try him and that their procedures violated basic tenets of international and military law, including the principle that a defendant must be permitted to see and hear the evidence against him.[152] The court ruled that the military commissions were not "regularly constituted courts" within the meaning of the Geneva Conventions and therefore violated the conventions, and that the commissions' procedures, which allowed proceedings in the absence of the defendant and his lawyer, violated the U.S. Uniform Code of Military Justice and the Geneva Conventions. The essence of the court's rationale was that the president was not authorized to establish the commissions without a statute from Congress.

The dissents from Justices Thomas, Alito, and Scalia mirrored the scholarship of the Federalist Society academics and OLC lawyers. Thomas's dissent spoke of a limited role for the courts, in particular with respect to war and intrusion on executive authority.[153] Justice Alito argued that the military commissions satisfied Article 3 of the Geneva Conventions as "regularly constituted tribunals" on the basis that they were appointed in compliance with domestic law.[154] He also argued that the relaxed evidentiary rules of the commission did not violate any international standards in existence, stating that "rules of evidence differ from country to country" and "much of the world does not follow aspects of our evidence rules, such as the general prohibition against the admission of hearsay."[155]

Following *Hamdan*, at the request of the Bush administration, Congress enacted the Military Commissions Act of 2006, which expressly authorized the president to create a system of military commissions.[156] The act stripped federal courts of the jurisdiction to hear habeas corpus claims (where a prisoner claims his detention is illegal) and provided that only the U.S. Court of Appeals for the D.C. Circuit could hear appeals from the commissions. It also codified the president's position, as recommended by Yoo and the other OLC attorneys, that "no alien unlawful enemy combatant subject to trial by military commission . . . may invoke the Geneva Conventions as a source of rights."[157]

FOREIGN AND INTERNATIONAL LAW SOURCES IN THE SUPREME COURT

As we have already discussed, Federalist Society members have been outspoken in their criticism of Supreme Court justices who cite foreign sources. In rejecting "foreign" sources, they sometimes conflate two distinct sources of extra–U.S. law: *international* law (such as treaties and the decisions of supranational courts) and *foreign* law (law from other nation-states' courts). Ed Meese argued that Supreme Court justices who use foreign law in their decisions are simply looking for a result that American legal traditions will not support.[158] Robert Bork condemns what he calls the "internationalization of American constitutional law," calling it "bizarre" that a two-hundred-year-old document might be interpreted with reference to modern decisions from foreign courts or nonbinding resolutions from international organizations.[159]

Nonetheless, standards and norms embodied in foreign and international law have long been examined and incorporated into the domestic law of the United States by both the judiciary and the legislature.[160] The Supreme Court has been citing to foreign and international law since the end of the eighteenth century.[161] Many of the justices appointed to "protect and defend" the Constitution continue to consider the practice of looking to sources of law from other western democracies with similar ethical and moral norms a logical and useful practice.[162]

The court's earliest opinions looked out on a growing body of "customary international law," which comprises legal "norms" that become universally accepted through the process of consistent practices among a majority of nations. These practices are said to ripen over time into principles of international law that create rights and obligations among states. The U.S. early reliance on international norms was perhaps an inevitable by-product of being an emerging nation: young, unsure, not yet the hegemonic world power of today. It is often said that weak states have a greater use (and therefore, support) for international law and institutions, because it is the only way they can constrain more powerful states.

In 1793, the first chief justice of the Supreme Court, John Jay, wrote that "the United States, had, by taking a place among the nations of the earth, become amenable to the laws of nations."[163] Fifteen years later, in *Schooner Exchange v. McFaddon*, the Supreme Court heeded the "usages and received obligations of the civilized world" and ruled that a foreign sovereign vessel in an American port was not subject to the jurisdiction of U.S. courts.[164] In 1804, just fifteen years after the U.S. Constitution was ratified, the U.S. Supreme Court decided *Murray v. Schooner Charming Betsy*.[165] Chief Justice John Marshall determined that the seizure of a Danish vessel from international waters was illegal, using international legal principles that counseled against allowing the seizure of neutral vessels from noncombatant countries. This became known as the *Charming Betsy* canon, which holds that an act of Congress should never be construed to violate international law if there is any other possible interpretation.[166] Just one year later in 1805, in an equally famous case also named for the ship at the center of the controversy, *The Paquete Habana*, Chief Justice Marshall declared, after an extensive examination of the "customs and usages of civilized nations," that U.S. authorities had improperly seized a Cuban fishing boat on the basis that that "international law is part of our law."[167] In 1815, the Supreme Court held in *Thirty Hogsheads of Sugar v. Boyle* that "[t]he decisions of the Courts of every country, so far as they were founded upon a law common to every country, will be received, not as authority but with respect."[168] Even in the infamous *Dred Scott v. Sandford*, where the Supreme Court held that U.S-born descendants of slaves had no constitutional right to citizenship, both the majority and the dissent cited European practices to justify their respective decisions.[169]

According to Steven Calabresi's empirical examination of Supreme Court jurisprudence in the modern era, the court has most frequently looked to the consensus of foreign or international laws where the reasonableness of a law or standard is to be determined.[170] It is certain, however, that justices who are identified as having liberal ideologies are more willing to examine foreign or international law to shed light on concepts of human rights. For example, in 1958, in *Trop v. Dulles*, the court considered whether a soldier could be stripped of his citizenship as a punishment for desertion in the penultimate year of World War II.[171] Albert Trop, a natural-born citizen, had escaped from the stockade on a U.S. base in Casablanca, and lost his citizenship by reason of his conviction and dishonorable discharge for wartime desertion. In support of the conclusion that the penalty was a violation of the Eighth Amendment's prohibition against cruel and unusual punishment, Chief Justice Earl Warren cited a UN study which found that only two out of eighty-four nations surveyed imposed denationalization as a punishment for desertion. Warren stated that at the heart of the Eighth Amendment's prohibition "is nothing less than the dignity of man" and declared that the "civilized nations of the world" reject the idea that statelessness can be imposed as punishment.[172]

The cross-pollination of law and legal structures between the United States and the rest of the world has included both the import and export of ideas. This republic's unique structural features—a written Constitution, a high court with the power to strike down legislation, and a Bill of Rights protecting individual freedoms against government—have been emulated elsewhere, in nations as diverse and distant as South Africa and New Zealand. Moreover, decisions of the Supreme Court have been cited by high courts in countries such as Israel, Japan, Germany, and India.[173] The popularity of the U.S. Constitution as a model for developing countries and the extent to which foreign courts are citing to the U.S. Supreme Court, however, are waning. Adam Liptak of the *New York Times* has suggested that as a model, the Constitution is "frozen in amber," because it is difficult to amend, contains few and narrow guarantees, and is increasingly being interpreted by Supreme Court justices according to its original meaning.[174]

The actual number of Supreme Court cases that have cited to international or foreign law is small. Of the many thousands of decisions handed down over the past two hundred years, less than one hundred have mentioned foreign or international legal sources. Yet, this is an important front for conservatives in the battle to maintain American social and legal values, and resistance to using foreign or international law to inform constitutional issues in Supreme Court jurisprudence is strong. For example, Justices Scalia, Thomas, and Rehnquist have demonstrated, during their respective tenures on the court, hostility to the notion that the determinations of foreign or international courts can somehow inform the decisions of an American court. Justice Scalia has referred to "foreigners" and "members of the so-called 'world community,' . . . whose notions of justice are (thankfully) not always those of our people."[175] Dissenting in *Roper v. Simmons*, Scalia stated that the opinion written by Justice Kennedy indicated that the opinions of Americans were "essentially irrelevant" in a decision that imported the views of other countries and the "so-called international community."[176] He continued, "[T]he basic premise of the Court's argument—that American law should conform to the laws of the rest of the world—ought to be rejected out of hand."[177]

In 2002, the court considered but did not take up a case where the petitioner argued that his twenty-seven-year wait on death row constituted "cruel and unusual punishment." Justice Thomas wrote, "While Congress, as a *legislature*, may wish to consider the actions of other nations on any issue it likes, this Court's Eighth Amendment jurisprudence should not impose foreign moods, fads, or fashions on Americans."[178] Thomas was quoting Justice Rehnquist, who had written that same year, dissenting in a different Eighth Amendment case, that reliance on foreign sources was "antithetical to considerations of federalism."[179] In *Printz v. United States*, Scalia (joined by Thomas and Rehnquist) quoted *Federalist* No. 20, which articulates perfectly his resistance to "wily" influences of international law and institutions:

> The important truth, which it unequivocally pronounces in the present case, is
> that a sovereignty over sovereigns, a government over governments, a legislation

for communities, as contradistinguished from individuals, as it is a solecism in theory, so in practice it is subversive of the order and ends of civil polity.[180]

Scalia has declared that using foreign law to determine constitutional issues in U.S. courts is improper because the United States does not have the same "moral and legal framework as the rest of the world" (and never has).[181] "If you told the framers of the Constitution that we're to be just like Europe," he has said, "they would have been appalled."[182] And yet, Scalia is not entirely immune to looking to foreign experience or law. He joined with Chief Justice Rehnquist's opinion in *Washington v. Glucksburg*, where the court considered the constitutionality of laws prohibiting assisted suicide. Rehnquist noted that other western democracies had made it a crime to assist a suicide and discussed assisted suicide provisions in Spain, Austria, Denmark, Italy, the United Kingdom, the Netherlands, France, and Switzerland.[183]

On the modern Supreme Court, the leading internationalist justice is Anthony Kennedy, a Reagan appointee. As we noted above, he wrote the 2003 opinion holding unconstitutional the Texas sodomy law for homosexuals in *Lawrence v. Texas*. He has said that the use of foreign and international law is a central part of American moral leadership in the world because it can help express a "unified concept of what human dignity means."[184] Two years later, in *Roper v. Simmons*, Kennedy wrote the opinion for the court, in which the court held that sentencing a person to death for a crime that they committed before the age of eighteen violated the Eighth Amendment's prohibition against cruel and unusual punishment. The court's determination, wrote Kennedy, "finds confirmation in the stark reality that the United States is the only country in the world that continues to give official sanction to the juvenile death penalty."[185]

The most recent case to consider the applicability of international law to its constitutional jurisprudence as of this writing is the 2010 decision in *Graham v. Florida*. The Supreme Court held that the Eighth Amendment does not permit a juvenile offender to be sentenced to life in prison for a crime that does not include homicide. Justice Kennedy wrote the opinion for the court and again relied on the law of other nations in concluding that a life sentence for juveniles was a "sentencing practice rejected the world over." He acknowledged that the practice of other countries was "not dispositive as to the meaning of the Eighth Amendment," but said that the court would follow its "longstanding practice in noting the global consensus against the sentencing practice in question."[186]

Graham and a related case provoked several amicus curiae briefs on both sides of the issue.[187] In an amicus brief submitted by an international alliance of bar associations (from Hong Kong, Montreal, Australia, England and Wales, Ireland, the Netherlands, and New Zealand) and human rights groups (including Amnesty International and Union Internationale des Avocats), supporters of the prisoners argued that "the universal prohibition against such a sentence outside of the United States reflects not just customary international law, but a peremptory, non-derogable, jus cogens norm of international law." As evidence of this norm, the amici argued that "no known persons [who had been convicted of a non-homicide crime as a juvenile] are actually serving a life sentence outside the United States."[188]

Ed Meese authored an amicus brief on behalf of the Center for Constitutional Jurisprudence. Meese argued that the court ought not to make policy decisions, because the separation of powers demands that policymaking is the sole ambit of the legislature.[189] Citing Alexander Hamilton, he cautioned that the court—and the federal judiciary in general—"may truly be said to have neither force nor will, but merely judgment."[190] The center has strategically submitted amicus briefs for a host of Supreme Court cases of constitutional significance, where it deems that principles "going to the heart of the founding principles" of the United States are at issue.[191]

Justice Kennedy directly responded to specific positions taken in the amicus briefs. He noted that amici arguing in favor of the constitutionality of the sentence had stressed that no international legal agreement binding on the United States prohibits life without parole for juvenile offenders, and thus the court should ignore the international consensus. Kennedy concluded that such arguments "miss the mark," because the question is not whether international law prohibits the United States from imposing a sentence, but whether that punishment is cruel and unusual. Citing *Roper*, he concluded that in that inquiry, "'the overwhelming weight of international opinion against' life without parole for nonhomicide offenses committed by juveniles 'provide[s] respected and significant confirmation for our own conclusions.'" [192] Kennedy further concluded that the debate in the amicus opinions "over whether there is a binding *jus cogens* norm against this sentencing practice is likewise of no import." He reasoned, "The Court has treated the laws and practices of other nations and international agreements as relevant to the Eighth Amendment not because those norms are binding or controlling but because the judgment of the world's nations that a particular sentencing practice is inconsistent with basic principles of decency demonstrates that the Court's rationale has respected reasoning to support it."[193]

In essence, the battle in the Supreme Court over whether foreign or international law can inform constitutional questions boils down to just how exceptional the justices believe the United States is, and what their definition of exceptional is. Are Americans indelibly linked to the rest of the world by their humanity, or does this nation's history, traditions, and rights culture set us too far apart for the views from beyond our shores to be relevant? Calabresi paints the Supreme Court's use of foreign law as class warfare: "American mass culture is . . . sharply at odds with the Supreme Court's elite lawyerly culture on the issue of whether U.S. courts have a lot to learn from foreign law."[194] Scalia has echoed this sentiment, stating that citing to foreign law allows for legal elites to impose their own moral and social views on American society. Questions of constitutional law, which often involve moral sentiments, according to Scalia, should not be determined by what judges, lawyers, and law students think, but what the American people (as reflected in legislation) think.[195]

Conclusion

In the realm of international law and sovereignty, the Federalist Society has given a voice to the new sovereigntists: scholars, lawyers, judges, and policymakers who would return international law to the time when it applied solely to nation-states, who would empower the president to decide when international law applied to the United States, and when it did not so as to preserve freedom of action, and who would choose not to ratify human rights treaties on the basis that they interfere with exceptionally American values and beliefs. Through its network, its institutional projects, its publications, and its debates, it spreads a realist world view that is hinged on an originalist interpretation of the Constitution and tied to the protection of sovereignty at all costs. This view has taken hold. The United States has not signed on to the CRC or the most recent iteration of the UNFCCC. International and foreign law continues to be largely shunned by the Supreme Court. Presidents have seized on the unitary executive theory as a means to reject international law and to place their constitutional interpretation above all others.

Ultimately, the new sovereigntists' version of American Exceptionalism posits that this country is so exceptional that the global human rights regime—which purports to offer all human beings, regardless of ethnicity, citizenship, religion, or nationality, certain rights and freedoms—is incongruous with the particular rights and freedoms this nation's founders fought for and enshrined in its founding documents.

A BRIEF GUIDE
TO LEGAL CITATIONS

The purpose of this guide is to permit the reader who has not been to law school to locate legal materials cited in the endnotes. At first, the citations may appear indecipherable, but there is a simple logic to them. The citations tell you precisely where the case, statute, regulation, or article in question may be found.

Court opinions in cases are published in volumes known as "reporters." A legal citation includes the name of the case, the name of the reporter where it may be found, the volume of the reporter and the page at which the case is printed, the court that decided the case (unless it is obvious from the name of the reporter), and the year it was decided. For example, the case with which we begin the discussion in Chapter 4 is *Parents Involved in Cmty. Schs. v. Seattle Sch. Dist. No. 1*, 551 U.S. 701 (2007). The name of the case is in italics. The case is printed in the United States Reports, abbreviated "U.S.," which is the reporter for U.S. Supreme Court cases. The volume where the case may be found precedes the name of the reporter; here, it is volume 551. The case is printed at page 701, the number that follows the name of the reporter. Sometimes there is a second page number; for example, the citation might have read, "551 U.S. 701, 712." That would tell the reader that the case begins on page 701, and that the specific quotation or material in the text is found at page 712. The case was decided in 2007. We know that the court that decided the case was the U.S. Supreme Court, because only cases from that court are printed in the United States Reports. When a reporter prints cases from more than one court, the name of the court that decided the case is located, in abbreviated form, inside the parentheses with the date.

Citations to legal articles from law reviews follow a similar format, providing the author of the article, the name of the article, the name and volume number of the review or journal, the page at which the article may be found, and the date of publication. For example, in Chapter 4 we cite the following article: Pamela S. Karlan, *What Can Brown® Do For You?: Neutral Principles and the Struggle over the Equal Protection Clause*, 58 DUKE L.J. 1049, 1052–53 (2009). The article is by Pamela S. Karlan and the name of her article is in italics. *Duke Law Journal* published the article in volume 58, at page 1049, and we have referred to material at pages 1052–1053. The publication date was 2009.

Citations to statutes and regulations follow a similar pattern. In Chapter 4, we cite to the following statute: 20 U.S.C. § 1681. The statute is printed in the United States Code (U.S.C.), volume 20, section 1681. Statutes are located by section number, rather than page number.

Reference librarians in law libraries are usually very friendly people and they will help you find the books you need, should you choose to go to the library to look up any of these references.

FEDERALIST SOCIETY MEMBERS AND ALLIES

Many of the members of the Federalist Society, even those who wield substantial power and influence, are not well known to the general public. For the convenience of the reader, we provide below an alphabetical list and brief biographical information, including their law school and graduation year (where applicable), for significant Federalist Society members or allies we have mentioned. As with many political groups, not all members of the Federalist Society publicly state that they are members. In the text, we have tried to indicate, when possible, those who publicly identify as members of the society. We also frequently refer to "allies," "affiliates," or "friends" of the Federalist Society. Those terms refer to people who frequently speak at Federalist Society meetings and debates, publish in Federalist Society journals, or who work closely with Federalist Society members on lawsuits, amicus briefs, or public issue campaigns. We were unable to determine whether the individuals described by these terms are members of the Federalist Society.

In the paragraphs below, we have not distinguished between members and allies, unless the listing indicates that the person holds a particular position in the Federalist Society. To be clear, we are not saying that everyone listed below is a member of the Federalist Society. These are, however, conservatives, mostly lawyers, who in one way or another are active in pursuing one or more of the goals of many Federalist Society members, and of the society itself.

DAVID S. ADDINGTON, *Vice President for Domestic and Economic Policy, Heritage Foundation*
Chief of Staff and Counsel to Vice President Dick Cheney. Known as "the legal mind behind the war on terror."[1] Worked closely with fellow Federalist Society Members Alberto Gonzales, Timothy Flanigan, and John Yoo—the group was regarded as the engine behind many of the Bush administration's most controversial polices.

Reagan administration: Assistant General Counsel, Central Intelligence Agency; Special Assistant, Legislative Affairs; Deputy Assistant, Legislative Affairs. George H. W. Bush administration: Special Assistant to the Secretary and Deputy Secretary of Defense; General Counsel, Department of Defense. *U.S. News and World Report* described him as "the most powerful man you've never heard of."[2] Republican Staff Director, Senate Intelligence Committee; Republican Chief Counsel, House Intelligence, Foreign Affairs, and Iran-Contra Committees. In 1987, coauthored the *Minority Report* with Cheney, which criticized Congress for unconstitutionally restraining the President's inherent national security powers. Duke University Law School (1981).

SAMUEL A. ALITO JR., *Associate Justice, U.S. Supreme Court*

Nominated by President George W. Bush. Federalist Society Founder Spencer Abraham acknowledged Alito's appointment as "beyond our best expectations."[3] Assistant U.S. Attorney, District of New Jersey, 1977–1981. Assistant to Solicitor General Rex E. Lee, 1981–1985. Deputy Assistant to Attorney General Edwin Meese, 1985–1987. U.S. Attorney, District of New Jersey, 1987–1990. Third Circuit Court of Appeals (nominated by President George H. W. Bush), 1990–2006. Clerked for Leonard I. Garth, Third Circuit Court of Appeals. Yale Law School (1975).

HADLEY P. ARKES, *Edward N. Ney Professor of Jurisprudence and American Institutions, Amherst College*

Author of numerous books, including *Beyond the Constitution, Natural Rights and the Right to Choose*, and *Constitutional Illusions and Anchoring Truths: The Touchstone of the Natural Law*, which focus on the preservation of natural rights doctrines in American jurisprudence and constitutional interpretation. Designed the Born-Alive Infants Protection Act, which passed in 2002. First prepared much of the act for President George H. W. Bush in 1988 as part of a debating kit. Senior Fellow, Ethics and Public Policy Center. Director, Center for the Jurisprudence of Natural Law, Claremont Institute. Scholar, Pacific Research Institute.

JOHN ASHCROFT, *Founder and Chairman, Ashcroft Group*

Served Missouri for nearly three decades as Auditor, Attorney General, two-term Governor, and U.S. Senator. Tough on crime and vehemently opposed to abortion and gun control; became a "darling of religious conservatives."[4] After losing Senate seat, pegged by George W. Bush to become U.S. Attorney General to mollify conservative base. Focused Department of Justice on fighting terrorism; strong supporter of U.S.A. PATRIOT Act and military tribunals to try "enemy combatants." University of Chicago Law School (1967).

RANDY E. BARNETT, *Carmack Waterhouse Professor of Legal Theory, Georgetown University Law Center*

Prosecutor, Attorney's Office of Cook County, Illinois, 1977–1981. Professor of Law, Chicago-Kent College of Law, 1982–1993. Boston University School of Law: Austin B. Fletcher Professor of Law, 1993–2006; Faculty Advisor, Federalist Society chapter. Author of many books and articles, including *The Structure of Liberty* and *Restoring the Lost Constitution*, which advance legal libertarianism, the originalist theory of constitutional interpretation, and constitutional construction based on presumption of liberty. Lead Plaintiffs' Lawyer in *Gonzales v. Raich*, 545 U.S. 1 (2005), where Supreme Court held that federal criminal law preempted California's medical marijuana statute. Set forth a list of ten amendments to the constitution entitled "Bill of Federalism," proposing, among other things, term limits for Congress, increased state power, and originalist constitutional interpretation. Senior Fellow, Cato Institute and Goldwater Institute. Recipient, Federalist Society's Paul M. Bator Award. Harvard Law School (1977).

HUGH JOSEPH BEARD JR., *Delegate to the Rules Committee of the Republican National Conventions, 1976–2000.*

Litigated cases challenging affirmative action policies of law schools as Executive Director of North Carolina Fund for Individual Rights. Reagan administration: Deputy General

Counsel, Department of Education 1981–1984 (where he controversially asserted plans to enact restrictions on education funds for disabled); moved to Department of Justice in 1984 as Special Assistant to Assistant Attorney General for Civil Rights William Bradford Reynolds. President, Equal Opportunity Foundation, 1992–2000. Member, Center for Equal Opportunity, until his passing. Died, 2002.University of North Carolina Law School (1971).

DANA BERLINER, *Litigation Director, Institute for Justice*

Attorney, Institute for Justice, since 1994. Litigates cases primarily involving property rights, economic liberty, and related constitutional issues. Particular focus is eminent domain, on which she has written and been quoted widely. Embarked on lengthy eminent domain campaign by litigating state actions to develop a national strategy, leading up to role as co–lead counsel in *Kelo v. City of New London.* Clerked for Jerry Smith, Fifth Circuit Court of Appeals. Yale Law School (1991).

CLINT BOLICK, *Fellow, Hoover Institution; Director, Goldwater Institute*

Special Assistant to Assistant Attorney General William Bradford Reynolds during Reagan administration. Befriended Clarence Thomas at the Equal Employment Opportunity Commission (EEOC). Worked to change EEOC's focus from adverse impact laws to individual claims of discrimination. Cofounded Institute for Justice with Chip Mellor to litigate school choice voucher programs, property rights, and First Amendment issues. Led nationwide effort to defend school voucher programs. Publications include *David's Hammer* (proposing judicial activism for enforcement of conservative ideals); *The Affirmative Action Fraud: Can We Restore the American Civil Rights Vision?* (criticizing affirmative action); and *Voucher Wars: Waging the Legal Battle over School Choice.* University of California Davis School of Law (1982).

JOHN R. BOLTON, *U.S. Senior Fellow, American Enterprise Institute*

George W. Bush administration: Permanent Representative to the United Nations, U.S. Mission to the United Nations, 2005–2006; Under Secretary of State, Arms Control and International Security, 2001–2005. Senior Vice President, American Enterprise Institute, 1997–2001. Attorney, Lerner, Reed, Bolton & McManus, 1993–1999. Assistant Secretary, International Organization Affairs, 1989–1993. Worked closely with a team of Federalist Society lawyers under Attorney General Edwin Meese as Assistant Attorney General, Department of Justice, 1985–1989. Yale Law School (1974).

JAMES BOPP JR., *Attorney, Bopp Coleson & Bostrom*

Litigation and appellate work focuses on campaign finance and election law and abortion issues. Advised Mitt Romney on family and life issues during 2008 bid for Republican presidential nomination; endorsed Romney in 2012. Editor, *Restoring the Right to Life: The Human Life Amendment.* General Counsel, James Madison Center for Free Speech. General Counsel, National Right to Life Committee, 1978–present. Special Counsel, Focus on the Family. Cochairman, Federalist Society's Election Law Subcommittee, 1996–2005. University of Florida College of Law (1973).

ROBERT BORK, *Fellow, Hudson Institute*

In 1982, appointed Judge for the D.C. Circuit Court of Appeals. Nominated for Associate Justice of the Supreme Court by President Reagan in 1987. The Senate rejected the nomination by a vote of 58 to 42—the largest margin by which the Senate has ever rejected a Supreme Court nomination.

Professor, Yale Law School, 1962–1975 and 1977–1981. Faculty Advisor to initial Federalist Society chapter. Solicitor General during the Nixon administration.

Fired Special Prosecutor Archibald Cox on Nixon's orders in a pivotal role during the "Saturday Night Massacre" in which key Department of Justice resignations made him Acting Attorney General. Resigned seat on Court of Appeals in 1988 to become a Senior Fellow at the American Enterprise Institute. Cochairman, Board of Visitors, Federalist Society. University of Chicago Law School (1953).

JENNIFER C. BRACERAS, *Freelance Writer; Political Commentator*

Appointed by President George W. Bush to a six-year term as Commissioner of U.S. Commission for Civil Rights. Testified in support of John Roberts's nomination to the Supreme Court as Chief Justice. Former Senior Fellow for Legal Policy, Independent Women's Forum. Opposes affirmative action and believes Title IX "created a vast and rigid quota system."[5] Clerked for Ralph K. Winter, Second Circuit Court of Appeals. Harvard Law School (1994).

RACHEL L. BRAND, *Chief Counsel for Regulatory Litigation, U.S. Chamber of Commerce, National Chamber Litigation Center*

Department of Justice: Assistant Attorney General for Legal Policy, 2005–2007; Principal Deputy Assistant Attorney General, 2003–2005. Managed the Justice Department's role in the selection and confirmation of federal judges at all levels. Directed policy and regulatory initiatives on issues such as terrorism and national security, immigration reform, tort reform, identity theft, and drug enforcement. Prepared Chief Justice John Roberts and Associate Justice Samuel Alito for U.S. Senate confirmation hearings. Associate Counsel to the President at the White House, 2001–2002. Member, Board of Advisors, University of Minnesota Institute for Law and Politics. Former Member, Executive Committee, Federalist Society's International and National Security Law Practice Group. Clerked for Anthony Kennedy, Supreme Court, and Charles Fried, Supreme Judicial Court of Massachusetts. Harvard Law School (1998).

JANICE ROGERS BROWN, *Judge, D.C. Circuit Court of Appeals*

Deputy Legislative Counsel, Office of Legislative Counsel, California, 1977–1979. Deputy Attorney General, Criminal and Civil Divisions, California Attorney General's Office, 1979–1987. Deputy Secretary and General Counsel, Business, Transportation, and Housing Authority, California, 1987–1989. Legal Affairs Secretary for Governor Pete Wilson. Appointed to Third District Court of Appeal of California in 1994. Justice, California Supreme Court, 1996–2005.

Democrats stalled President George W. Bush's nomination of Brown to the D.C. Court of Appeals for two years; she was confirmed in 2005. In a speech to the University of Chicago's Federalist Society chapter, she described government as a "leviathan [that] will continue to lumber along . . . crushing everything in its path."[6] Strong proponent of federalism, stating that "[w]hen government moves in, community retreats, civil society disintegrates, and our ability to control our own destiny atrophies."[7] Described Federalist Society as "a rare bastion (nay beacon) of conservative and libertarian thought."[8] UCLA School of Law (1977).

SHARON L. BROWNE, *Principal Attorney, Pacific Legal Foundation Individual Rights Practice Group*

Litigation focused on anti-affirmative action programs in public contracting, employment, and education. Involved in defending and implementing Proposition 209, a California initiative to end affirmative action programs. Member, Board of Directors,

Legal Services Corporation. Special Advisor, Executive Committee, Federalist Society's Civil Rights Practice Group. McGeorge School of Law, University of the Pacific (1985).

SCOTT G. BULLOCK, *Senior Attorney, Institute for Justice*

Joined the Institute for Justice in 1991 at its founding and is the organization's Senior Attorney. Litigates economic and property rights cases in state and federal courts. As Cocounsel, argued *Kelo v. City of New London* in the Supreme Court. With Dana Berliner, secured first state supreme court eminent domain victory after *Kelo* in *Norwood v. Horney*, where Ohio Supreme Court ruled in favor of landowners and against developer and city. University of Pittsburgh School of Law (1991).

JAMES S. BURLING, *Director of Litigation, Pacific Legal Foundation; Principal Attorney, Pacific Legal Foundation Property Rights Practice Group*

Practice areas include land use regulation, regulatory takings, and eminent domain, topics on which he has published extensively. Joined Pacific Legal Foundation in 1983. Former Chairman, Federalist Society's Environmental Law and Property Rights Practice Group. University of Arizona College of Law (1983).

JAY S. BYBEE, *Judge, Ninth Circuit Court of Appeals*

Department of Justice: Attorney, Office of Legal Policy, 1984–1986; Attorney, Appellate staff of the Civil Division, 1986–1989; Assistant Attorney General, Office of Legal Counsel, 2001–2003. Authorized 2002 memo approving use of "enhanced interrogation techniques," including waterboarding and forcing prisoners to stay aware for a week or more.[9] Associate, Sidley Austin, Washington, D.C., 1981–1984. Associate Counsel to President George H. W. Bush, 1989–1991. Professor, Paul M. Hebert Law Center, Louisiana State University, 1991–1999; William S. Boyd School of Law, University of Nevada at Las Vegas, 1999–2001. Nominated by President George W. Bush to Ninth Circuit in 2003. Clerked for Donald S. Russell, Fourth Circuit Court of Appeals. Brigham Young University's J. Reuben Clark Law School (1980).

STEVEN G. CALABRESI, *Professor, Northwestern University Law School*

Cofounded Federalist Society. Served in Reagan and George H. W. Bush administrations, advising Attorney General Edwin Meese and Kenneth Cribb. Wrote speeches for former Vice President Dan Quayle. Prolific author of academic articles; comments on a broad range of historical and constitutional issues; leading originalism scholar. Editor, *Originalism: A Quarter-Century of Debate*; coauthored with Christopher Yoo *The Unitary Executive: Presidential Power from Washington to Bush*; coauthored with Society Members Michael Stokes Paulsen and Michael W. McConnell *The Constitution of the United States* (2010), a law school casebook that is described as emphasizing the text, structure, and history of the Constitution and not merely the Supreme Court's most recent cases. Chairman, Board of Directors, Federalist Society. Clerked for Robert Bork, D.C. Circuit Court of Appeals, and Antonin Scalia, Supreme Court. Yale Law School (1983).

MICHAEL A. CARVIN, *Partner, Jones Day*

Department of Justice: Deputy Assistant Attorney General, Office of Legal Counsel, 1987–1988; Deputy Assistant Attorney General, Civil Rights Division, 1985–1987; Special Assistant to the Assistant Attorney General, Civil Rights Division, 1982–1985. Supported Proposition 209, a California initiative to end affirmative action programs. Argued on behalf of George W. Bush before the Florida Supreme Court in the 2000 election recount controversy. Senior Advisor, Federalist Society's Civil Rights Practice Group. George Washington University Law School (1982).

LINDA CHAVEZ, *Founder and Chairman, Center for Equal Opportunity*
Syndicated Columnist and Fox News Political Analyst. Director, U.S. Commission on Civil Rights, 1983–1985; White House Director of Public Liaison, 1985. Opposes affirmative action. President George W. Bush nominated her for Secretary of Labor, but she withdrew after it was found that she employed an undocumented immigrant in her home. University of Colorado (B.A., 1970).

RICHARD "DICK" CHENEY, *46th Vice President of the United States, 2001–2009*
Joined Donald Rumsfeld's staff in 1969 when Rumsfeld was Director of Office of Economic Opportunity in the Nixon Administration. Ford administration: Deputy Assistant, 1974; Chief of Staff, 1975–1977. Six-term Member of House of Representatives, 1978–1989; elected House Minority Whip.

Secretary of Defense, 1989–1993. Directed invasion of Panama and Operation Desert Storm. After election of President Bill Clinton, became a Fellow at the American Enterprise Institute. In 1995, appointed Chairman of the Board and Chief Executive Officer of Halliburton. Joined George W. Bush as vice presidential candidate in 2000. University of Wyoming (B.A., 1965; M.A., political science, 1966).

ROGER CLEGG, *President and General Counsel, Center for Equal Opportunity*
Department of Justice: Deputy Assistant Attorney General, Civil Rights Division, 1987–91, and Environment and Natural Resources Division, 1991–93; Assistant to the Solicitor General, 1985–87; Associate Deputy Attorney General, 1984–85; Acting Assistant Attorney General, Office of Legal Policy, 1984. Said affirmative action is "unfair and divisive" and that "discrimination against whites . . . in university admissions is overt."[10] Past Chairman, Executive Committee, Federalist Society's Civil Rights Practice Group. Yale Law School (1981).

EDITH BROWN CLEMENT, *Judge, Fifth Circuit Court of Appeals*
Appointed to U.S. District Court for the Eastern District of Louisiana by President George H. W. Bush in 1991. Appointed to Fifth Circuit Court of Appeals by George W. Bush in 2001. Attorney in private practice, undertaking primarily maritime law, in New Orleans, 1975–1991.

On President George W. Bush's short list for Supreme Court nominee. Nomination never materialized because of skepticism from the right regarding lack of judicial opinions on abortion, affirmative action, and gay marriage. Member, Advisory Board, Federalist Society Louisiana chapter. Clerked for Herbert W. Christenberry, U.S. District Court for the Eastern District of Louisiana. Tulane University Law School (1972).

PAUL D. CLEMENT, *Partner, Bancroft PLLC*
Solicitor General, 2005–2008. President Bush named Clement Acting Attorney General after Alberto Gonzales resigned from position. Counsel of Record for Arizona when the Supreme Court heard a challenge to Arizona's immigration law. Defended Defense of Marriage Act, and resigned from King & Spalding in 2011 when the firm dropped the case. Georgetown University Law Center: Adjunct Professor, 1998–present; Senior Fellow, Supreme Court Institute. Argued over fifty-five cases before the U.S. Supreme Court. Clerked for Laurence H. Silberman, D.C. Court of Appeals, and Antonin Scalia, Supreme Court. Harvard Law School (1992).

WARD CONNERLY, *Founder and President, American Civil Rights Institute*
One of the foremost critics of affirmative action; in 2012, was called "the face of the movement to end affirmative action for nearly two decades."[11] Former Member,

University of California Board of Regents. As Chairman of California Civil Rights Initiative Campaign, promoted Proposition 209, a ballot measure to end affirmative action in California. Formed American Civil Rights Institute to support similar ballot initiatives in other states, including Michigan, Washington, and Florida. Sacramento State College (B.A., 1962).

CHARLES J. COOPER, *Founding Member and Chairman, Cooper & Kirk, PLLC*

Joined Civil Rights Division, Department of Justice, in 1981. Appointed to Assistant Attorney General for the Office of Legal Counsel by President Reagan in 1985. Lead Counsel defending Proposition 8, California's initiative to ban same-sex marriage. Clerked for Paul Roney of Fifth (now Eleventh) Circuit Court of Appeals, and William H. Rehnquist, Supreme Court. University of Alabama School of Law (1977).

T. KENNETH CRIBB JR., *Counselor, Federalist Society Board of Directors*

Influential member of the conservative movement during the Reagan administration. Deputy to the Chief Counsel, 1980 Reagan-Bush campaign. Appointed Assistant Director for the Office of Cabinet Affairs in 1981. Assistant Counselor to the President, working directly under Counselor Edwin Meese. Became Counselor to Ed Meese when Meese was appointed Attorney General. In 1987, returned to the White House as Chief of Domestic Affairs for Ronald Reagan. President, Intercollegiate Studies Institute (the oldest conservative student organization in the country), 1989–2011. Former Trustee, Sarah Scaife Foundation; Vice Chair, Fulbright Foreign Scholarship Board; Senior Fellow and Consultant, Heritage Foundation. University of Virginia School of Law (1980).

ROBERT J. DELAHUNTY, *Associate Professor of Law, University of St. Thomas School of Law*

Coauthor of secret and controversial legal opinions after September 11, which included assertions that the Bush administration could use military force domestically without obtaining search warrants, and legal arguments for avoiding jurisdiction of the Geneva Conventions. Department of Justice: Attorney, Civil Rights Division, Appellate Section, 1986–1989; Attorney, Office of Legal Counsel, 1989–1991. Special Assistant to the Solicitor of Labor, 1991–1992. Deputy General Counsel, White House Office of Homeland Security, 2002–2003. Original Member, Federalist Society's student chapter at Harvard. Harvard Law School (1983).

VIET D. DINH, *Founding Partner, Bancroft PLLC; Professor of Law, Georgetown University Law Center*

Drafted and developed legal policy initiatives behind the USA PATRIOT Act as U.S. Assistant Attorney General for Legal Policy, 2001–2003. Director and Chair, Nominating and Corporate Governance Committee, News Corporation, since 2004. Joined Kenneth Starr in 2006 lawsuit challenging constitutionality of a provision of the Sarbanes-Oxley Act. Associate Special Counsel to Senator Pete V. Domenici, impeachment trial of President Clinton. Clerked for Laurence H. Silberman of D.C. Court of Appeals, and Sandra Day O'Connor, Supreme Court. Stated before Senate Judiciary Committee that "I am a member of the Federalist Society, and I do not know, quite frankly, what it stands for."[12] Harvard Law School (1990).

JAMES DOBSON, *Founder and Chairman Emeritus, Focus on the Family*

Influential voice of Christian conservatives. Founded Focus on the Family in 1977 to "nurtur[e] and defend[] the God-ordained institution of the family and promot[e] biblical truths worldwide," and led the organization until 2009.[13] Founded the Family Research Council in 1981. Author of more than thirty books, including *Dare to Discipline*, advocating parental discipline and discussing appropriate corporal punishment of children. Increasingly vocal on non-family related policy issues for Christian conservatives; high-profile opponent of same-sex marriage. In *Marriage under Fire: Why We Must Win This Battle*, proposes that heterosexual marriages are failing because of recognition of homosexual relationships. In 2010, launched radio broadcast, "Family Talk with Dr. James Dobson," to continue his Christian outreach. University of Southern California (Ph.D., psychology, 1967).

FRANK H. EASTERBROOK, *Chief Judge, Seventh Circuit Court of Appeals*

Assistant to the Solicitor General, 1978–1979, and Deputy Solicitor General, 1974–1977. University of Chicago Law School: Professor, 1978–1985; Senior Lecturer in Law, 1985–present. Supported the initial Federalist Society chapter at the University of Chicago. Editor, *Journal of Law and Economics*, 1982–1991. Appointed by President Reagan to the Seventh Circuit in 1985. Member, the American Law Institute and the American Academy of Arts and Sciences. Clerked for Levin Campbell, First Circuit Court of Appeals. University of Chicago Law School (1973).

RICHARD A. EPSTEIN, *Laurence A. Tisch Professor of Law, New York University School of Law*

Influential libertarian scholar, known for his research and writings on a wide range of constitutional, economic, historical, and philosophical subjects. Professor, University of Southern California Law School, 1968–1972; University of Chicago Law School, 1972–present; as of 2011, the Law School's James Parker Distinguished Service Professor Emeritus of Law and Senior Lecturer. Editor, *Journal of Legal Studies*, 1981–1991. Editor, *Journal of Law and Economics*, 1991–2001. Director, John M. Olin Program in Law and Economics, University of Chicago, 2001–2010. Member, American Academy of Arts and Sciences, since 1985. Senior Fellow, Center for Clinical Medical Ethics, University of Chicago Medical School, since 1983. Peter and Kirstin Bedford Senior Fellow, Hoover Institution, Stanford University, 2000–present. Faculty Advisor to the initial Federalist Society law school chapter at the University of Chicago. A "revered figure" among many members of the Federalist Society.[14] Yale Law School (1968).

MIGUEL A. ESTRADA, *Partner, Gibson Dunn & Crutcher*

Cochair of Gibson Dunn's Appellate and Constitutional Law Practice Group. Member of legal team representing Governor George W. Bush in *Bush v. Gore*; represented John Yoo both in a suit brought by convicted terrorist Jose Padilla; and in an internal Department of Justice investigation regarding memos authored by Yoo. Nominated to D.C. Court of Appeals by President Bush; nomination filibustered by Senate Democrats; Estrada withdrew his nomination shortly thereafter. Assistant to Solicitor General, 1992–1997. Before that, served as Assistant U.S. Attorney and Deputy Chief of the Appellate Section, U.S. Attorney's Office, Southern District of New York, and practiced corporate law in New York at Wachtell, Lipton, Rosen & Katz. Clerked for Amalya L. Kearse, Second Circuit Court of Appeals, and Anthony Kennedy, Supreme Court. Harvard Law School (1986).

TIMOTHY E. FLANIGAN, *Partner, McGuireWoods*

Office of Legal Counsel, Department of Justice: Principal Deputy Assistant Attorney General, 1990–1992; Assistant Attorney General, 1992–1993. Private practice,

1993–2001. Member of President George W. Bush's legal team during the 2000 presidential election Florida recount. As Deputy White House Counsel under Alberto Gonzales, 2001–2002, worked with other Department of Justice lawyers to provide a legal rationale for the Bush administration's interrogation, wiretapping, and detention policies after the September 11, 2001 attacks.

Senior Vice President and General Counsel, Tyco International, 2002–2007. Paid by Federalist Society to write biography of Supreme Court Chief Justice Warren E. Burger, for whom Flanigan clerked in 1985–1986. University of Virginia Law School (1981).

CHARLES FRIED, *Beneficial Professor of Law, Harvard Law School*
Solicitor General, 1985–1989. Associate Justice, Supreme Judicial Court of Massachusetts, 1995–1999. Professor, Harvard Law School, 1961–present. Argued the landmark Supreme Court case *Daubert v. Merrell Dow Pharmaceuticals*, 509 U.S. 579 (1993), in which the Court revised the standards for expert evidence in federal courts. Author of numerous articles and books, including *Saying What the Law Is: The Constitution in the Supreme Court* and *Order and Law: Arguing the Reagan Revolution.* First recipient of the Charles Fried Intellectual Diversity Award, an annual award given by the Harvard Federalist Society and the *Journal of Law & Public Policy.* Faculty Advisor in early 1980s to Federalist Society precursor at Harvard Law School, the Harvard Society for Law and Policy Studies. Faculty Sponsor, Federalist Society chapter at Harvard Law School. Columbia University Law School (1960).

TODD F. GAZIANO, *Commissioner, U.S. Commission on Civil Rights; Senior Fellow in Legal Studies, and Director, Center for Legal and Judicial Studies, Heritage Foundation*
Office of Legal Counsel, Department of Justice, 1992–1995. Chief Counsel, House Subcommittee on National Economic Growth, Natural Resources, and Regulatory Affairs, 1995–1997, where Gaziano worked on regulatory reform with Chairman David McIntosh. Joined Ed Meese at the Heritage Foundation as Director of the Center for Legal and Judicial Studies in 1997. Congressional appointee to U.S. Commission on Civil Rights for six-year term, starting February 2008. Has stated that federal hate crime laws are "unnecessary" and "counterproductive" because underlying crimes are being prosecuted at the state level.[15] Special Advisor, Executive Committee, Federalist Society's Civil Rights Practice Group. Clerked for Edith H. Jones, Fifth Circuit Court of Appeals. University of Chicago Law School (1988).

ROBERT P. GEORGE, *McCormick Professor of Jurisprudence, Princeton University*
Founding Director, James Madison Program in American Ideals and Institutions, Princeton University. Senior Fellow, Hoover Institution, Stanford University. Herbert W. Vaughan Senior Fellow, Witherspoon Institute, Princeton, New Jersey. Joined faculty of Princeton University in 1985. Member, U.S. Commission on Civil Rights, 1993–1998. Appointed by President George W. Bush to the President's Council on Bioethics. Member, UNESCO's World Commission on the Ethics of Science and Technology. Called the "country's most influential conservative Christian thinker."[16] Contends that same-sex marriages violate tradition and human reason. Senior Advisor, Federalist Society's Religious Liberties Practice Group. Recipient, Federalist Society Paul M. Bator Award. Harvard Law School (1981).

ALBERTO R. GONZALES, *Doyle Rogers Distinguished Chair of Law, Belmont University*
Appointed Attorney General by President George W. Bush in 2005. Resigned in 2007 because of allegations of perjury and controversial dismissal of eight U.S. Attorneys by

the Justice Department. Senator Harry Reid said Gonzales "lacked independence [and] judgment."[17] An investigation found no evidence of wrongdoing. Secretary of State, Texas, 1997–1999; Justice, Texas Supreme Court, 1999–2001; White House Counsel to President George W. Bush, 2001–2005. Recipient of Department of Justice memoranda authored by John Yoo, Robert Delahunty, and others regarding the legality of interrogation techniques, surveillance and detention of enemy combatants, and advised President George W. Bush accordingly. Visiting Professor, Texas Tech, 2009–2011. Of Counsel, Waller Lansden Dortch & Davis, Nashville, since 2011. Joined faculty of Belmont University in 2012. Harvard Law School (1982).

F. CAROLYN GRAGLIA, *Author*
Worked at Department of Justice before clerking for Warren E. Burger, D.C. Court of Appeals. Married Lino A. Graglia and left legal career to become full-time housewife. *Domestic Tranquility: A Brief against Feminism* contends feminist movement is responsible for demise of the traditional family, spread of sexually transmitted disease, growth of income disparity, and emasculation of men. Columbia University Law School (1954).

LINO A. GRAGLIA, *Dalton Cross Professor of Law Professor, University of Texas*
Worked in the Department of Justice in the Eisenhower administration. Controversially remarked that black and Mexican American students are "not academically competitive" with white students at the nation's top colleges.[18] A proponent of the view that "affirmative action has become simply a deceptive label for racial preferences."[19] Author, *Disaster by Decree: The Supreme Court Decisions on Race and the Schools* (1976). Nominated by President Reagan to judgeship on Fifth Circuit Court of Appeals, but received adverse ABA rating. Columbia University Law School (1954).

C. BOYDEN GRAY, *Founding Partner, Boyden Gray & Associates*
Clerked for Earl Warren, Supreme Court, 1968–1969. Private practice, Wilmer, Cutler & Pickering, 1969–1981. Served Vice President H.W. Bush from 1981–1989 as Legal Counsel to the Vice President, Counsel to Presidential Task Force on Regulatory Relief (chaired by Vice President Bush), and Director of the Office of Transition Counsel. Counsel to President H. W. Bush, 1989–1993. Principal Architect of 1990 Clean Air Act. Returned to Wilmer, Cutler, Pickering, Hale & Dorr, 1993–2005. Ambassador to European Union, 2006–2007. Special Envoy for Eurasian Energy Diplomacy, 2008–2009. Special Envoy for European Union Affairs, 2008–2009. Board of Directors, Federalist Society. University of North Carolina Law School (1968).

KAREN R. HARNED, *Executive Director, Small Business Legal Center, National Federation of Independent Business*
Has been at National Federation of Independent Business since 2002. Represented small businesses and trade associations, specializing in food and drug law, at Olsson Frank Weeda Terman Bode Matz PC, 1995–2002. Assistant Press Secretary to Senator Don Nickles (R-OK), 1989–1993. Advisor, Small Business Issues, Federalist Society's Litigation Practice Group. George Washington University Law School (1995).

KEVIN J. HASSON, *Founder and President, Becket Fund for Religious Liberty*
Served in the Office of Legal Counsel, Department of Justice, under then-Deputy Assistant Attorney General Samuel Alito, 1986–1987, advising the White House and cabinet on church-state relations. Formed the Becket Fund for Religious Liberty in 1994. Chairman-Elect, Executive Committee, Federalist Society's Religious Liberties Practice Group. University of Notre Dame Law School (1985).

ORRIN G. HATCH, *Senator, R-UT*

U.S. Senate since 1976; longest serving Senator in Utah history. Lost bid for Republican presidential nomination to George W. Bush in 2000. Vocally supported Robert Bork's failed nomination to Supreme Court in 1987. Cochairman, Board of Visitors, Federalist Society. Son, Brent Hatch, was Clerk for Robert Bork and is Treasurer of Federalist Society's Board of Directors. University of Pittsburgh Law School (1962).

WILLIAM J. HAYNES II, *Chief Corporate Counsel, Chevron Corporation*

General Counsel, Department of Defense, 2001–2008. General Counsel, Department of the Army, 1990–1993. Partner, Jenner & Block, 1993–1996, 1999–2001. Staff Vice President and Associate General Counsel, General Dynamics Corporation, and General Counsel of General Dynamics Corporation's Marine Group, 1996–1998. Along with John Yoo, Alberto Gonzales, Tim Flanigan, and David Addington, advised President George W. Bush on detainment of "enemy combatants," interrogation methods, and wiretapping. Authored memo to Secretary of Defense Donald Rumsfeld regarding dehumanizing interrogation techniques at Guantanamo Bay. Nomination to Fourth Circuit Court of Appeals by President George W. Bush was unsuccessful. Clerked for James McMillan, U.S. District Court for the Western District of North Carolina. Harvard Law School (1983).

STEVEN F. HAYWARD, *F. K. Weyerhaeuser Fellow, American Enterprise Institute*

Conservative political author and commentator focusing on topics of environmentalism, law, and public policy. Senior fellow of environmental studies at Pacific Research Institute. Environmental documentary, *An Inconvenient Truth . . . Or Convenient Fiction?* was called a "point-by-PowerPoint rebuttal of . . . Al Gore's global warming documentary, *An Inconvenient Truth.*"[20] Author of two-volume book, *The Age of Reagan: The Fall of the Old Liberal Order.* Henry Salvatori Fellow and Bradley Fellow, Heritage Foundation, 1993–1994.

DONALD "DON" P. HODEL, *President, Focus on the Family; Chairman and Senior Vice President, Summit Power Group*

Focus on the Family, a conservative nonprofit group, is an evangelical "Christian ministry dedicated to helping families thrive."[21] Summit Power Group is an "energy and natural resources consulting firm" headed by the Christian Right and well known for opposing environmental regulation. Coauthor of *Crisis in the Oil Patch,* a book promoting the idea that there should be less regulation of American oil companies. Michael Farris's Patrick Henry College has named its new $31 million student life center after Barbara Hodel, a long-time trustee of the college and Don Hodel's wife.

In-House Counsel for Georgia Pacific, a lumber and paper conglomerate. Deputy Administrator of the Bonneville Power Administration, a U.S. government–owned electric utility company. Under Secretary, Department of the Interior, 1981–1982. Secretary, Department of Energy, 1982–1985. Secretary, Department of the Interior, 1985–1988. At Department of the Interior, promoted the selling of public lands for commercial use, nuclear power, and loosening environmental regulations. Former President, Christian Coalition. Member, Board of Visitors, Federalist Society. University of Oregon School of Law (1960).

BRIAN W. JONES, *General Counsel, Strayer University*

General Counsel, Department of Education, 2001–2005. Board Member, Center for Equal Opportunity. Cofounder, Center for New Black Leadership. Former Editor, Federalist Society's Civil Rights Practice Group Newsletter. UCLA School of Law (1993).

EDITH H. JONES, *Chief Judge, Fifth Circuit Court of Appeals*
Practiced at the Houston, Texas, firm Andrews, Kurth, Campbell & Jones from 1974–1985. Nominated to Fifth Circuit by President Reagan in 1985. In *McCorvey v. Hill*, 385 F.3d 846 (5th Cir. 2004), expressed discontent with the Supreme Court's decision in *Roe v. Wade*. Frequently mentioned as potential Supreme Court nominee during George W. Bush administration. Gave 8th Annual Barbara K. Olson Memorial Lecture at Federalist Society, in 2008. University of Texas School of Law (1974).

JOHN VON KANNON, *Vice President and Senior Counsel, Heritage Foundation*
Publisher of opinion journal *The American Spectator*. Increased Heritage Foundation's budget from four million dollars to more than seventy million dollars. Vice President, Pacific Legal Foundation. Member, Board of Directors, Foundation for Research on Economics and the Environment, along with Edwin Meese and Judge Edith Brown Clement. Indiana University (B.A., 1972).

BRETT M. KAVANAUGH, *Judge, D.C. Court of Appeals*
Assistant to the President and Staff Secretary, 2003–2006; Senior Associate Counsel, 2003; Associate Counsel, 2001–2003. Nominated to D.C. Court of Appeals by President Bush in 2003. Associate Counsel for Independent Counsel Kenneth Starr during impeachment investigation of President Clinton. Former Cochair, School Choice Subcommittee, Federalist Society's Religious Liberties Practice Group. Clerked for Walter Stapleton, Third Circuit; Alex Kozinski, Ninth Circuit; and Anthony Kennedy, Supreme Court. Yale Law School (1990).

PETER D. KEISLER, *Partner, Sidley Austin LLP*
Acting Attorney General following resignation of Attorney General Alberto Gonzales in 2007. Joined Justice Department in 2002; confirmed as Assistant Attorney General, Civil Division, in 2003. Defended Bush administration's military tribunals program in *Hamdan v. Rumsfeld* before the D.C. Circuit Court of Appeals. Nominated by President Bush for seats on Court of Appeals for the Fourth Circuit and D.C. Circuit, but never confirmed. Served in President Reagan's White House Counsel's Office between judicial clerkships, overseeing Supreme Court confirmation strategies.

Befriended David McIntosh, Steven Calabresi, and Lee Liberman through Yale College Political Union, leading to creation of Federalist Society. Clerked for Robert Bork, D.C. Circuit Court of Appeals, and Anthony Kennedy, Supreme Court. Member, Board of Directors, Federalist Society, 1983–2000. Yale Law School (1985).

PETER N. KIRSANOW, *Partner, Benesch*
Former Head, Center for New Black Leadership. Wrote that "affirmative action may be one of the greatest scams perpetrated on blacks."[22] Appointed to U.S. Commission on Civil Rights and National Labor Relations Board by President George W. Bush. Cleveland-Marshall College of Law (1979).

HARRY J. F. KORRELL, *Partner, Davis Wright Tremaine, LLP*
Lead Counsel for parents in *Parents Involved in Community Schools v. Seattle Sch. Dist.*, 551 U.S. 701 (2007). Recipient, Federalist Society's Justice Theodore Stiles Award. Member, Executive Board, Federalist Society's Labor and Employment Practice Group; Member, Executive Board, Puget Sound Lawyers Chapter of the Federalist Society. University of Chicago Law School (1993).

ALEX KOZINSKI, *Chief Judge, Ninth Circuit Court of Appeals*
Deputy Legal Counsel, Office of President-Elect Reagan, 1980–1981; Assistant Counsel, Office of Counsel to the President, 1981. Appointed by President Reagan to the U.S.

Court of Federal Claims in 1982, and to the Ninth Circuit Court of Appeals in 1985. Has stated that seeing "Federalist Society" on a resume "tells me you're of a particular philosophy, and I tend to give an edge to people I agree with philosophically."[23] Clerked for Anthony Kennedy, Ninth Circuit Court of Appeals, and for Warren E. Burger, Supreme Court. UCLA School of Law (1975).

CAROLYN B. KUHL, *Judge, Los Angeles County Superior Court*

George W. Bush nominated her to Ninth Circuit in 2001, despite objections from her two home state Senators. Filibustered by Senate Democrats; withdrew nomination in 2004. Department of Justice: served variously as Special Assistant to Attorney General William French Smith, Deputy Assistant Attorney General (Civil Division), and Deputy Solicitor General, 1981–1986. In 1985, as Deputy Assistant Attorney General, urged Supreme Court in *Thornburgh v. American College of Obstetricians and Gynecologists* to overturn the *Roe v. Wade* decision. Partner, Los Angeles law firm of Munger, Tolles & Olson, 1986–1995. Superior Court Judge in California since 1995. Known as a "hard-driving conservative lawyer," actively persuaded the Reagan administration to support tax-exempt status of Bob Jones University, which had been revoked because of its racially discriminatory admissions policies.[24] Clerked for Anthony Kennedy, Ninth Circuit Court of Appeals. Duke Law School (1977).

LEONARD A. LEO, *Executive Vice President, The Federalist Society*

Appointed by President George W. Bush and U.S. Senate to three terms to U.S. Commission on International Religious Freedom. Former Delegate to UN Council, UN Commission on Human Rights, Organization of Security and Cooperation in Europe, and World Health Assembly of the World Health Organization. President Bush's Catholic Strategist in 2004 reelection campaign. Organized coalitions for George W. Bush judicial nominations. Coeditor of *Presidential Leadership: Rating the Best and Worst in the White House.* Cornell Law School (1989).

ANDREW W. LESTER, *Attorney, Lester, Loving and Davies*

U.S. Magistrate Judge, Western District of Oklahoma, 1988–1996. Served on President Reagan's Transition Team for the Equal Employment Opportunity Commission (EEOC), 1980–1981. Adjunct Professor, Oklahoma City University School of Law, since 1988. Appointed by U.S. Commission on Civil Rights to its Oklahoma State Advisory Committee in 2011. Former Member, Executive Committee, Federalist Society's Civil Rights Practice Group. President, Federalist Society's Oklahoma City chapter. Georgetown University Law School (1981).

CURT A. LEVEY, *Executive Director, Committee For Justice*

Former Director, Legal and Public Affairs at the Center for Individual Rights. Headed the Title IX Policy Group, Office for Civil Rights, Department of Education, prior to joining Committee For Justice, a conservative foundation dedicated to "defend[ing] and promot[ing] constitutionalist judicial nominees to the federal courts."[25] Member, Virginia State Advisory Committee, U.S. Commission on Civil Rights. Political activist passionate about affirmative action issues and opposed to "judicial activism." Member, Executive Committee, Federalist Society's Civil Rights Practice Group. Clerked for Richard Suhrheinrich, Sixth Circuit Court of Appeals. Harvard Law School (1997).

MARGARET "PEGGY" A. LITTLE, *Director, Federalist Society Pro Bono Center*

Matches Federalist Society lawyers with pro bono opportunities. Clerked for Ralph K. Winter, Second Circuit Court of Appeals. Yale Law School (1984).

J. MICHAEL LUTTIG, *Executive Vice President and General Counsel, Boeing Corporation*
Judge, Fourth Circuit Court of Appeals, from 1991 to 2006, when he joined Boeing. Hired numerous Federalist Society members as law clerks, and many of them went on to clerk for Supreme Court Justices. Assistant Counsel at the White House under President Reagan and Assistant Attorney General in the George H. W. Bush Department of Justice. Clerked for Antonin Scalia, D.C. Court of Appeals, and Warren E. Burger, Supreme Court. Continued to work as Special Assistant to Chief Justice Burger until joining Davis Polk & Wardell in 1985. University of Virginia School of Law (1981).

STEPHEN J. MARKMAN, *Justice, Michigan Supreme Court*
Assistant Attorney General, 1985–1989; served the Senate for seven years prior, as Chief Counsel of the U.S. Senate Subcommittee on the Constitution, and Deputy Chief Counsel of the U.S. Senate Judiciary Committee. U.S. Attorney, Michigan (nominated by President George H. W. Bush), 1989–1993. Follows an originalist approach to law. Has stated that "[p]roponents of a . . . 'living constitution' aim to transform our nation's supreme law beyond recognition."[26] University of Cincinnati College of Law (1974).

ROGER J. MARZULLA, *Founder and Partner, Marzulla and Marzulla*
Former President, Mountain States Legal Foundation. Joined Department of Justice in 1983 as Special Litigation Counsel under Ed Meese. Subsequently promoted to Deputy Assistant Attorney General and confirmed by Senate in 1987 as Assistant Attorney General in Charge of Environment and Natural Resources Division. In 1991, cofounded with wife (Nancie Marzulla) Defenders of Property Rights, a "nonprofit law firm dedicated exclusively to the protection of constitutionally guaranteed rights in property."[27] Coauthored, with Nancie Marzulla, *Property Rights: Understanding Government Takings and Environmental Regulation* (1997). Marzulla and Marzulla is a law firm based in Washington, D.C., that represents "corporate and business clients in a wide array of environmental and property issues."[28] Senior Advisor, Federalist Society's Environmental Law and Property Rights Practice Group. University of Santa Clara School of Law (1971).

WILLIAM R. MAURER, *Executive Director, Institute for Justice, Washington Chapter*
Lead Attorney for Petitioners in *Arizona Free Enterprise Club's Freedom Club PAC v. Bennett*, 131 S. Ct. 2806 (2011), a Supreme Court case striking down matching funds provision of Arizona's Citizens Clean Elections Act. Writes, teaches, and testifies on free speech issues. Clerked for Richard Sanders, Washington Supreme Court, and Victoria Lederberg, Rhode Island Supreme Court. Member, Executive Committee, Federalist Society's Civil Rights Practice Group. University of Wisconsin Law School (1994).

MICHAEL W. MCCONNELL, *Law Professor; Director, Stanford Constitutional Law Center; Senior Fellow, Hoover Institution*
Judge, U.S. Court of Appeals for the Tenth Circuit, 2002–2009. During Reagan administration, Assistant General Counsel at Office of Management and Budget, and Assistant to Solicitor General Rex Lee. Law Professor at the University of Utah and University of Chicago Law Schools. Author of articles and books on constitutional law, federalism, and originalism. Clerked for J. Skelly Wright, D.C. Circuit Court of Appeals, and William J. Brennan Jr., Supreme Court. University of Chicago Law School (1979).

DAVID M. MCINTOSH, *Partner, Mayer Brown*
Recognized as George H. W. Bush's "Regulation Slayer."[29] Later served as Chairman of the Subcommittee on Regulatory Relief, overseeing environmental, labor, and FDA

regulations, while a U.S. Representative from Indiana from 1995–2001. Befriended fellow Federalist Society cofounders Lee Liberman and Steven Calabresi through Yale Political Union during undergraduate studies at Yale. During Reagan administration, served as Special Assistant to Attorney General Meese and Special Assistant to the President for Domestic Affairs. During George H. W. Bush administration, served as Assistant to the Vice President and Executive Director of the President's Council on Competitiveness. University of Chicago Law School (1983).

WILLIAM "CHIP" MELLOR, *President and General Counsel, Institute for Justice*
Cofounded Institute for Justice with Clint Bolick to litigate school choice voucher programs, property rights, and First Amendment issues. Attorney, Mountain States Legal Foundation, 1979–1983. Served in Reagan administration as Deputy General Counsel for Legislation and Regulations in the Department of Energy. President, Pacific Research Institute for Public Policy, 1986–1991. Coauthored *The Dirty Dozen: How Twelve Supreme Court Cases Radically Expanded Government and Eroded Freedom*, with Robert A. Levy. University of Denver Law School (1977).

EDWIN MEESE III, *Ronald Reagan Distinguished Fellow in Public Policy and Chairman of the Center for Legal and Judicial Studies, Heritage Foundation*
Came to power in government with Ronald Reagan. Governor Reagan's Executive Assistant and Chief of Staff in California, 1969–1974, and also his Legal Affairs Secretary. Counselor to the President, 1981–1985; Attorney General, 1985–1988; Member, Reagan's National Security Council; Chairman of the Domestic Policy Council and of the National Drug Policy Board. Chief of Staff and Senior Issues Advisor, Reagan-Bush Committee.

Professor of Law, University of San Diego, 1977–1981. Distinguished Visiting Fellow, Hoover Institution; Member, Board of Regents, National College of District Attorneys; Distinguished Senior Fellow, Institute for U.S. Studies, University of London. Member of the Boards of Directors for the Capital Research Center, the Landmark Legal Foundation, and the Federalist Society. University of California at Berkeley, Boalt Hall School of Law (1958).

EUGENE B. MEYER, *President, Federalist Society*
Executive Director and CEO, Federalist Society, for more than twenty-five years. The only Executive Director it has had. Responsible for organizing Federalist Society events and organizational operations. Former Board Member, Holman Foundation; Trustee, Philadelphia Society. International Chess Master. Son of Frank Meyer, Founding Coeditor of *National Review.* London School of Economics (M.A., political science, 1976).

MICHAEL B. MUKASEY, *Partner, Debevoise & Plimpton*
Attorney General, 2007–2009, succeeding Alberto Gonzales. Declined to characterize the practice of waterboarding as "torture" in his confirmation hearing. Judge, U.S. District Court for the Southern District of New York, 1987–2006. Heard several cases regarding alleged terrorists and enemy combatants. Began practice in New York as Assistant U.S. Attorney. Joined Patterson Belknap Webb & Tyler in 1976 and returned to the firm after retiring from district court. Justice Advisor, Rudy Giuliani's presidential campaign; administered oath of office for Mayor Giuliani in 1994 and 1998. Member, Board of Visitors, Federalist Society. Yale Law School (1967).

GALE A. NORTON, *Founder, Norton Regulatory Strategies*
General Counsel for Royal Dutch Shell Unconventional Oil, 2007–2010. First woman to hold the position of Secretary of the Department of the Interior, 2001–2006.

Appointed despite strong opposition from environmental groups. Said to have been "more interested in development than conservation."[30] Attorney General of Colorado, 1991–1999. Associate Solicitor for Conservation and Wildlife, Department of the Interior, 1985–1990. Assistant to the Deputy Secretary of Agriculture, 1984–1985. Senior Attorney, Mountain States Legal Foundation, 1979–1983. Member, Board of Visitors, Federalist Society. University of Denver Sturm College of Law (1978).

THEODORE B. OLSON, *Partner, Gibson, Dunn & Crutcher*

Recognized as "one of the leading Supreme Court advocates of his generation."[31] Served as Solicitor General from 2001 to 2004 following decisive victory in *Bush v. Gore.* An originalist, successfully argued *Citizens United v. Federal Election Commission* and countless other prominent Supreme Court cases, prevailing in three-quarters of cases. Distinguished career focused on conservative causes, including federal preemption, litigation against environmental regulation and affirmative action. Attorney for plaintiffs in *Perry v. Brown*, 671 F.3d 1052 (9th Cir. 2012), challenging Proposition Eight, California's ban on same-sex marriage. Private practice exclusively at Gibson, Dunn & Crutcher since 1965. Head, Office of Legal Counsel, Department of Justice, 1981–1984; later defended President Reagan during the Iran-Contra affair. Association with Federalist Society dates back to inaugural meeting. University of California at Berkeley, Boalt Hall School of Law (1965).

LEE LIBERMAN OTIS, *Senior Vice President and Faculty Division Director, Federalist Society*

Started University of Chicago Law School chapter of Federalist Society with David McIntosh. Organized Society's first conference at Yale, second conference at Chicago, and first Lawyers Division chapter in Washington, D.C. Led efforts to incorporate Federalist Society, obtain early funding, recruit permanent staff, and was initially a Founding Director. Awarded Heritage Foundation's Henry Salvatori prize for citizenship for her work with the Society.

Department of Justice: Special Assistant under Attorneys General William French Smith and Edwin Meese; later Associate Deputy Attorney General. Associate Counsel to President George H. W. Bush. Practiced appellate litigation at Jones, Day, Reavis & Pogue. Chief Counsel, Immigration Subcommittee of Senate Judiciary Committee; General Counsel, Department of Energy. Assistant Professor, George Mason University School of Law. Adjunct Professor at Georgetown University Law Center. Clerked for Antonin Scalia, D.C. Circuit Court of Appeals, and again for Scalia after his appointment to Supreme Court. University of Chicago Law School (1983).

PRISCILLA OWEN, *Judge, Fifth Circuit Court of Appeals*

Appointed in 2005. Justice, Supreme Court of Texas, 1994–2005. Partner, Andrews & Kurth, 1974–1994. Member, Board of Advisors, Houston and Austin chapters of Federalist Society. Baylor University Law School (1977).

MICHAEL S. PAULSEN, *University Chair and Law Professor, University of St. Thomas*

University of Minnesota Law School: McKnight Presidential Professor of Law and Public Policy, Briggs and Morgan Professor of Law, and Associate Dean for Research and Scholarship, 1992–2007. Department of Justice: Attorney, Criminal Division, 1985–1986; Attorney-Advisor, Office of Legal Counsel, 1989–1991. Staff Counsel, Center for Law and Religious Freedom, Washington, D.C., 1986–1989. Testified in 2009 before Senate committee that the advice given to President Bush by Office of Legal Counsel

Attorneys Jay Bybee, Alberto Gonzales, and Steven G. Bradbury with respect to interrogation methods was "substantively correct on the merits."[32] By his own admission, "most liberals' nightmare constitutional conservative."[33] Yale Law School (1985).

SHELDON "JAY" PLAGER, *Senior Judge, Federal Circuit Court of Appeals*
Administrator, Office of Information and Regulatory Affairs, Office of Management and Budget, 1988–1989; Associate Director, Office of Management and Budget, 1987–1988; Counselor to the Undersecretary, Department of Health and Human Services, 1986–1987. Nominated to the bench by President George H. W. Bush in 1989. University of Florida College of Law (1958).

ROGER PILON, *Vice President for Legal Affairs, Cato Institute*
Founder and Director, Center for Constitutional Studies, Cato Institute. Office of Personnel Management: Special Assistant to the Director, 1981–1982; Special Assistant to General Counsel, 1982–1984; Senior Professor, Federal Executive Institute, 1984–1986. Director of Policy, Bureau of Human Rights and Humanitarian Affairs, State Department, 1986–1987. Director, Asylum Policy and Review Unit, Department of Justice, 1987–1988. George Washington University School of Law (1988).

RICHARD A. POSNER, *Judge, Seventh Circuit Court of Appeals; Senior Lecturer in Law, University of Chicago Law School*
Appointed in 1981. Influential legal theorist; helped found the law and economics movement. Professor, University of Chicago Law School, since 1969; Associate Professor, Stanford Law School, 1968–1969. Prior to entering academia, served during the Kennedy and Johnson administrations as Assistant to Commissioner Philip Elman of the FTC, Assistant to Solicitor General Thurgood Marshall, and General Counsel of President Johnson's Task Force on Communications Policy. Writer of more than 2,500 published judicial opinions. Prolific author of books and academic articles, many of which focus on the application of economics to law. Founding Editor, *Journal of Legal Studies* and *American Law and Economics Review.* As their professor, supported Liberman and McIntosh, who founded the Federalist Society chapter at University of Chicago Law School. Clerked for William J. Brennan Jr., Supreme Court. Harvard Law School (1962).

WILLIAM H. PRYOR JR., *Judge, Eleventh Circuit Court of Appeals*
Appointed in 2004 by President George W. Bush during congressional recess when 2003 nomination was filibustered. Attorney General of Alabama, 1997–2004; Deputy Attorney General, 1995–1997. Associate, Cabaniss, Johnston, Gardner, Dumas & O'Neal, 1988–1991. Associate, Walston, Stabler, Wells, Anderson & Bains, 1991–1995. Adjunct Professor, Samford University, Cumberland School of Law, 1989–1995. Called *Roe v. Wade* decision "the worst abomination of constitutional law in our history."[34] Clerked for John Minor Wisdom, Fifth Circuit Court of Appeals. Tulane University Law School (1987).

JEREMY A. RABKIN, *Professor of International Law, George Mason Law School*
Renowned scholar in international law and U.S. sovereignty. Professor of Government, Cornell University, 1980–2007. Board of Directors, U.S. Institute of Peace; Board of Academic Advisors, American Enterprise Institute; Advisory Board, *Harvard Journal of Law and Public Policy*; Board of Directors, Center for Individual Rights. Senior Advisor, Executive Committee, Federalist Society's International and National Security Law Practice Group. Harvard University (Ph.D., Government, 1983).

RALPH E. REED JR., *President, Century Strategies; Founder and Chairman, Faith & Freedom Coalition*

Executive Director, Christian Coalition, 1989–1997. Religious-right political activist. At the age of thirty-three, made the cover of *TIME* magazine, which called him "The Right Hand of God" for his unprecedented influence on Christian conservative politics. Executive Director, College Republican National Committee, during Reagan's reelection campaign. Advisor, Bush-Cheney campaigns; Chair, Southeast Region, 2004. Worked on seven presidential campaigns. Advisor to eighty-eight campaigns for Governor, U.S. Senate, and Congress. Ran for Lieutenant Governor of Georgia in 2006 (first bid for elective office) but lost Republican primary. Founded the Faith & Freedom Coalition in 2009, a conservative advocacy group that Reed describes as a "21st–Century version of the Christian Coalition on steroids."[35] Emory University (Ph.D., American History, 1989).

GROVER J. REES III, *Writer; Advocate; Retired Diplomat*

State Department: Deputy Assistant Secretary, Bureau of International Organizations Affairs, 2008–2009; Special Representative for Social Issues, 2006–2008; Ambassador to East Timor, 2002–2006. Counsel to the Committee on International Relations of the U.S. House of Representatives, 2001–2002; Staff Director and Chief Counsel, Subcommittee on International Operations and Human Rights of the House of Representatives, 1995–2001. General Counsel to Immigration and Naturalization Service, 1991–1993. Chief Justice, High Court of American Samoa, 1986–1991. Assistant Professor, University of Texas Law School, 1979–1986. Special Assistant to Attorney General Edwin Meese, with respect to judicial appointments, 1986. Clerked for Albert Tate, Supreme Court of Louisiana. Louisiana State University Law School (1978).

GERALD A. REYNOLDS, *General Counsel, Eastern Division, American Water Works, Inc.*

Chairman, U.S. Commission on Civil Rights, 2004–2010. Assistant Secretary of Education, Office of Civil Rights, 2002–2003. Former President, Center for New Black Leadership. Legal Analyst, Center for Equal Opportunity. Deputy Associate Attorney General, Department of Justice. Opponent of affirmative action, stating that affirmative action is "the Big Lie."[36] Boston University School of Law (1992).

WILLIAM BRADFORD REYNOLDS, *Senior Counsel, Baker Botts*

Assistant Attorney General, Civil Rights Division, 1981–1988. Promotion to Associate Attorney General rejected by Senate because of controversial views. Opponent of affirmative action. Criticized Justice William J. Brennan Jr. for efforts to create a "radically egalitarian" society.[37] Member, Board of Visitors, Federalist Society. Vanderbilt University Law School (1967).

DAVID B. RIVKIN JR., *Partner, Baker Hostetler LLP*

Served in the Department of Justice during the Reagan and George H. W. Bush administrations, including in the White House Counsel's Office, Office of the Vice President, and the Departments of Energy and Justice. Associate Executive Director and General Counsel, President's Council on Competitiveness, 1992–1993. Associate General Counsel, Department of Energy, 1990–1991, during which time the national energy markets were deregulated. Cochairman, Center for Law and Counterterrorism, a joint initiative of the Foundation for Defense of Democracies and the National Review Institute. Visiting Fellow, Nixon Center; Contributing Editor, *National Review* magazine. Attorney, prolific author, and media commentator on issues of constitutional law, international law, and defense policy. Columbia University School of Law (1985).

JOHN G. ROBERTS JR., *Chief Justice, U.S. Supreme Court*

Judge, D.C. Circuit, 2003–2005; then appointed Chief Justice. Special Assistant to the Attorney General, Department of Justice, 1981–1982; Associate Counsel, White House Counsel's Office, 1982–1986; Principal Deputy Solicitor General, 1989–1993. Private practice, Hogan & Hartson. Clerked for Henry J. Friendly, Second Circuit Court of Appeals, and William Rehnquist, Supreme Court. Harvard Law School (1979).

MARION GORDON "PAT" ROBERTSON, *Founder and Chairman, American Center for Law and Justice*

In addition to the American Center for Law and Justice, founded the Christian Coalition, Christian Broadcasting Network (CBN), Regent University, International Family Entertainment, Operation Blessing International Relief, and Development Corporation, The Flying Hospital, and others. Former Baptist minister who led an unsuccessful campaign to become the Republican nominee in the 1988 presidential election. Yale Law School (1955); Biblical Seminary (M.Div., 1959).

MICHAEL E. ROSMAN, *General Counsel, Center for Individual Rights*

Joined Center for Individual Rights, a law firm dedicated to defend "individual liberties against the increasingly aggressive and unchecked authority of federal and state governments," in 1994.[38] Cases included: *Hopwood v. State of Texas*, 236 F.3d 256 (5th Cir. 2000), striking down affirmative action admissions policy at University of Texas School of Law; *United States v. Morrison*, 529 U.S. 598 (2000), where the Supreme Court held the Violence against Women Act was unconstitutional; and *Grutter v. Bollinger*, 539 U.S. 306 (2003), and *Gratz v. Bollinger*, 539 U.S. 244 (2003), where the Supreme Court upheld University of Michigan law school's use of diversity in admissions, but struck down use of race preferences by the college. Vice Chairman of Federalist Society's Civil Rights Practice Group. Yale Law School (1984).

WILLIAM L. SAUNDERS, *Senior Vice President of Legal Affairs, Americans United for Life*

Senior Fellow in Bioethics and Human Rights Counsel at the Family Research Council. Columnist for *National Catholic Bioethics Quarterly.* Work focuses on bioethics, abortion, human rights, and international law. Practiced in D.C. office of Covington & Burling. Taught law at the Catholic University of America. U.S. delegation to the UN Special Session on Children, 2001–2002. Chairman, Executive Committee, Federalist Society's Religious Liberties Practice Group. Harvard Law School (1980).

ANTONIN SCALIA, *Associate Justice, U.S. Supreme Court*

Appointed in 1986. Recipient of Sheldon Fellowship from Harvard University, 1960–1961. Attorney, Jones, Day, Cockley and Reavis, 1961–1967. Law Professor, University of Virginia, 1967–1974. Served as General Counsel to the Office of Telecommunications Policy, 1971–1972, and Chairman of the Administrative Conference of the United States, 1972–1974, while on leave from the University of Virginia. Assistant Attorney General for and the Office of Legal Counsel in the Nixon administration, 1974–1977. University of Chicago Law School: Professor, 1977–1982; Faculty Advisor to the first Federalist Society group. Former Chairman, Administrative Law Section, American Bar Association. Judge, D.C. Circuit, 1982–1986. Harvard Law School (1960).

JAY A. SEKULOW, *Chief Counsel, American Center for Law and Justice*

Focuses practice on First Amendment litigation, specifically religious rights and freedom of speech. Along with Federalist Society Executive Vice President Leonard A. Leo, guided President George W. Bush's judicial nominees through Senate confirmations, most notably Supreme Court Justices Roberts and Alito. Operates two talk shows discussing judiciary, First Amendment rights, and evangelism. Distinguished Professor of Law, Regent University School of Law. Mercer University School of Law (1980).

LAURENCE H. SILBERMAN, *Senior Judge, D.C. Circuit Court of Appeals*

Asserted racial job quotas were constitutional as Solicitor of Department of Labor in Nixon administration. Later, in *Wall Street Journal* article, "The Road to Racial Quotas," declared affirmative action a "fundamentally unsound policy" because "the GOP was anxious to expand employment opportunity for blacks."[39] Undersecretary of Labor, 1970–1973; Deputy Attorney General of the United States, 1974–1975; Ambassador to Yugoslavia, 1975–1977. Member, General Advisory Committee on Arms Control and Disarmament and Department of Defense Policy Board, 1981–1985. Law faculty at Georgetown University Law Center, NYU, and Harvard, 1987–1999. In 2004, appointed by President George W. Bush to cochair Iraq Intelligence Committee. Harvard Law School (1961).

ROSALIE "RICKY" SILBERMAN, *Cofounded Independent Women's Forum with Barbara Olson, wife of Ted Olson.*

Credited with exposing "the fallacies and hypocrisies of radical political interest group feminism."[40] Appointed by President Nixon to the Presidential Commission for the Education of Disadvantaged Children. In 1984, appointed by President Reagan to the Equal Employment Opportunity Commission with Clarence Thomas and became close friends. Outspoken supporter of Thomas during his Supreme Court nomination. Helped edit *The Real Anita Hill*, written by David Brock. Appointed by Defense Secretary Donald Rumsfeld to Defense Department Advisory Commission on the Status of Women. Wife of Judge Laurence H. Silberman. Died, 2007. Smith College (B.A., 1958).

ILYA SOMIN, *Associate Professor, George Mason University School of Law*

Research focuses on constitutional law, property law, and the study of popular political participation and its implications for constitutional democracy. Coeditor of the *Supreme Court Economic Review*. Quoted or interviewed by the *New York Times, Washington Post, BBC*, and the *Voice of America*, among others. Work has appeared in numerous scholarly journals, books, and reviews. Regular contributor to *Volokh Conspiracy*, a popular law and politics blog. Clerked for Jerry Smith, Fifth Circuit Court of Appeals. Yale Law School (2001).

KENNETH STARR, *President, Baylor University*

Appointed by President Reagan to D.C. Court of Appeals, serving 1983–1989. Solicitor General of the United States, 1989–1993. Independent Counsel, 1994–1999; undertook five investigations, including Whitewater, Vince Foster, and Monica Lewinsky inquiries. Partner, Kirkland & Ellis LLP, 1993–2004. Appointed Dean of Pepperdine University School of Law in 2004 and President of Baylor University in 2010. Clerked for David W. Dyer, Fifth Circuit Court of Appeals, and Warren E. Burger, Supreme Court. Duke University School of Law (1973).

CLARENCE THOMAS, *Associate Justice, U.S. Supreme Court*

Nominated by President George H. W. Bush in 1991, and later confirmed by the narrowest margin in one hundred years. Second African American appointed to the Court. Subscribes to originalist method of constitutional interpretation. Judge, D.C. Circuit Court of Appeals, 1990–1991. Assistant Attorney General of Missouri, 1974–1977; Legislative Assistant to Senator John Danforth, 1979–1981; Assistant Secretary for Civil Rights, Department of Education, 1981–1982; Chairman, Equal Employment Opportunity Commission, 1982–1990. Yale Law School (1974).

J. HARVIE WILKINSON, *Judge, Fourth Circuit Court of Appeals*

Appointed by President Reagan to the Fourth Circuit Court of Appeals in 1984 and confirmed by the Senate seven months later. Deputy Assistant Attorney General, Civil Rights Division, Department of Justice, 1982–1983; Associate Professor, University of Virginia School of Law, 1973–1978. As then-Chief Judge, wrote majority opinion in *Hamdi v. Rumsfeld*, 316 F 3d 450 (4th Cir. 2003), authorizing the indefinite detention of a U.S. citizen, which was subsequently overturned by Supreme Court, 542 U.S. 507 (2004). Paul Clement argued case for the government. Clerked for Lewis Powell, Supreme Court. University of Virginia School of Law (1972).

RALPH K. WINTER, *Senior Judge, Second Circuit Court of Appeals*

Appointed in 1981. Professor, Yale Law School, 1962–1981. Faculty Advisor, alongside Robert Bork, to original Federalist Society chapter at Yale Law School. Senior Fellow, Brookings Institute; John Simon Guggenheim Fellow and Adjutant Scholar, American Enterprise Institute. Hired Steven Calabresi as his Judicial Clerk from 1983–1984. Clerked for Caleb M. Wright, U.S. District Court for the District of Delaware, and Thurgood Marshall, Second Circuit Court of Appeals. Yale Law School (1960).

JOHN C. YOO, *Professor, University of California at Berkeley, Boalt Hall School of Law*

General Counsel, Senate Judiciary Committee, 1995–96. Deputy Assistant Attorney General in President George W. Bush's Office of Legal Counsel. Authored, with other OLC lawyers, a series of memoranda to senior Bush administration officials providing legal rationale for various torture techniques, use of military commissions, and absence of Geneva Conventions protections vis-à-vis al-Qaeda and Taliban detainees. Author of *The Powers of War and Peace: The Constitution and Foreign Affairs after 9/11* (2005), *War by Other Means: An Insider's Account of the War on Terror* (2006), and *Crisis and Command: The History of Executive Power From George Washington to George W. Bush* (2010). Recipient, Federalist Society's Paul M. Bator Award. Clerked for Laurence H. Silberman, D.C. Court of Appeals, and Clarence Thomas, Supreme Court. Yale Law School (1992).

➤ Notes ◆

INTRODUCTION

1. Steven Calabresi, Lee Liberman, & David McIntosh, Statement of Purpose, Proposal for a Symposium on the Legal Ramifications of the New Federalism (1982), *quoted in* John J. Miller, A Gift of Freedom: How the John M. Olin Foundation Changed America 89 (2006).
2. Lee Liberman & David McIntosh (1982), *quoted in* Miller, *supra* note 1, at 92.
3. George W. Hicks Jr., *The Conservative Influence of the Federalist Society on the Harvard Law School Student Body*, 29 Harv. J.L. & Pub. Pol'y 623, 628 (2006).
4. Ann Southworth, Lawyers of the Right 27 (2008).
5. Terry Carter, *The In Crowd: Conservatives Who Sought Refuge in the Federalist Society Gain Clout*, 87 A.B.A. J. 46, 47 (2001).
6. Jerry M. Landay, *The Federalist Society: The Conservative Cabal That's Transforming American Law*, Wash. Monthly, Mar. 2000, *available at* washingtonmonthly.com.
7. *Id.*
8. *Id.*
9. 2010 Federalist Soc'y Ann. Rep.
10. Justices Scalia, Thomas, and Alito are acknowledged members of the Federalist Society. During his confirmation hearings, Chief Justice Roberts claimed to have no recollection of being a member, although his name appeared in the organization's 1997–1998 leadership directory as a member of the steering committee of the Washington, D.C., chapter. Charles Lane, *Roberts Listed in Federalist Society '97–98 Directory*, Wash. Post, July 25, 2001, at A01.
11. Ann. Rep., *supra* note 9.
12. Landay, *supra* note 6.
13. Thomas B. Edsall, *Federalist Society Becomes a Force in Washington: Conservative Group's Members Take Key Roles in Bush White House and Help Shape Policy and Judicial Appointments*, Wash. Post, Apr. 18, 2001, at A04.
14. *Id.*
15. Sidney Blumenthal, *Preface to the First Edition* of The Rise of the Counter-Establishment: The Conservative Ascent to Political Power xix (2008 ed.).
16. Richard B. Cheney, *Address to 2001 National Lawyers Convention*, 3 Engage 59 (2002).
17. Abner Mikva, *ACS v. The Federalists*, Nation, Apr. 17, 2006.
18. Miller, *supra* note 1, at 88.
19. David McIntosh, *Introduction to the Federalist Society 2002 Symposium on Law and Truth: Banquet Panel on the Founding of the Federalist Society*, 26 Harv. J.L. & Pub. Pol'y ix, ix–x (2003).
20. *State AG Tracker*, Federalist Soc'y, fed-soc.org/publications (last visited Aug. 13, 2012).
21. Amanda Hollis-Brusky, Paper Prepared for the Annual Meeting of the American Political Science Association: The Federalist Society and the Unitary Executive: An Epistemic Community at Work 2, (Sept. 3, 2009) (on file with authors).
22. *Id.*
23. Federalist Soc'y Pro Bono Ctr., probonocenter.org (last visited Aug. 13, 2012).
24. Ilya Somin, *Addressing the Most Important Weakness of Conservative-Libertarian Public Interest Law*, Volokh Conspiracy (Dec. 10, 2009, 7:58 PM), volokh.com.

25. Steven M. Teles, The Rise of the Conservative Legal Movement (2008).
26. *Gideon v. Wainwright*, 372 U.S. 335 (1963) (holding Sixth Amendment right to assistance of counsel applies to states through Fourteenth Amendment). The court's landmark ruling held that an indigent defendant in a criminal case has a constitutional right to counsel appointed and paid for by the state.
27. Teles, *supra* note 25, at 42.
28. *Id.* at 44.
29. *Id.* at 56.
30. Blumenthal, *supra* note 15.
31. *Id.* at 25.
32. *Id.* at 22.
33. *Id.* at 27.
34. Charlie Savage, Takeover: The Return of the Imperial Presidency and the Subversion of American Democracy 45 (2007).
35. Southworth, *supra* note 4, at 25.
36. Charles Fried, Order and Law: Arguing the Reagan Revolution—A Firsthand Account 49–51 (1991).
37. Edwin Meese III, *The Case for "Originalism,"* Pittsburgh Trib.-Rev., June 5, 2005, *available at* pittsburghlive.com.
38. Steven G. Calabresi, *A Critical Introduction to the Originalism Debate*, 31 Harv. J.L. & Pub. Pol'y 875, 875 (2008).
39. Lynette Clemetson, *Meese's Influence Looms in Today's Judicial Wars*, N.Y. Times, Aug. 17, 2005, *available at* nytimes.com.
40. *Id.*
41. *Id.*; Calabresi, *supra* note 38.
42. Clemetson, *supra* note 39.
43. *Id.*
44. Originalism: A Quarter-Century Of Debate (Steven G. Calabresi ed., 2007).
45. Steven G. Calabresi, *Introduction* to Originalism, *supra* note 44, at 14–15.
46. Randy E. Barnett, *Interpretation and Construction*, 34 Harv. J. L. & Pub. Pol'y 65, 69 (2011).
47. *Id.* at 69–70.
48. Theodore B. Olson, *Concluding Thoughts, in* Originalism, *supra* note 44, at 335.
49. Calabresi, *supra* note 44, at 39–40.
50. David M. McIntosh, *Introduction: A View for the Legislative Branch*, 19 Harv. J.L. & Pub. Pol'y 317, 318 (1996).
51. 2009 Federalist Soc'y Ann. Rep.
52. Ann. Rep., *supra* note 9, at 27.
53. *Id.* at 28.
54. Cheney, *supra* note 16, at 59.
55. Carter, *supra* note 5, at 48.
56. Blumenthal, *supra* note 15, at xi.
57. Editorial, *The Roberts-Alito Court: Thank You, Ted Kennedy and Ralph Neas*, Wall St. J., Jan. 26, 2006, *reprinted in* 2006 Federalist Soc'y Ann. Rep. (emphasis in original).
58. Jeffrey Rosen, *Supreme Court Inc.*, N.Y. Times Mag., Mar. 16, 2008, at 38, *available at* nytimes.com (commenting on court term as friendly to business interests).
59. *Id.* (noting increase in antitrust cases heard by Roberts Court).
60. *See Leegin Creative Leather Prod., Inc. v. PSKS, Inc.*, 551 U.S. 877, 880 (2007) (rejecting per se illegality rule applied to vertical minimum-resale-price agreements); *Credit*

Suisse Sec. (USA) LLC v. Billing, 551 U.S. 264, 267–72 (2007) (affirming dismissal of antitrust claims against security underwriting firms as incompatible with securities laws); *Bell Atl. Corp. v. Twombly*, 550 U.S. 544, 571 (2007) (affirming dismissal of antitrust conspiracy action against local telephone exchange carriers due to insufficient pleading). The court's ruling in *Twombly* abrogated *Conley v. Gibson*, 355 U.S. 41 (1957) with respect to the sufficiency of pleadings in the face of a motion to dismiss. *Twombly*, 550 U.S. at 562. *See also Weyerhaeuser Co. v. Ross-Simmons Hardwood Lumber Co.*, 549 U.S. 312, 315 (2007) (applying strict test applicable to claims of predatory pricing to claims of predatory bidding). In this case, the plaintiff sawmill operator brought an action under § 2 of the Sherman Act, alleging its competitor obtained monopsony power in the Pacific Northwest market for alder sawlogs through predatory bidding; however, the court reversed the judgment in favor of the plaintiff. *Id.* at 315–19. *See also Ill. Tool Works, Inc. v. Indep. Ink, Inc.*, 547 U.S. 28, 31 (2006) (holding mere fact tying product is patented does not create presumption of market power). This decision abrogated a previous Supreme Court precedent, thereby reflecting that the court's historic disapproval of tying arrangements has substantially diminished. *Id.* at 42–43. *See also Texaco Inc. v. Dagher*, 547 U.S. 1, 3 (2006) (holding oil companies' joint venture not per se illegal horizontal price fixing agreement); *Volvo Trucks N. Am., Inc. v. Reeder-Simco GMC, Inc.*, 546 U.S. 164, 169–70 (2006) (holding truck manufacturer not liable for unfair secondary-line price discrimination under Robinson–Patman Act).

61. *See Riegel v. Medtronic, Inc.*, 552 U.S. 312, 322–25 (2008) (holding patient's negligence, strict liability, implied warranty claims preempted by FDA premarket approval process); *Safeco Ins. Co. of Am. v. Burr*, 551 U.S. 47, 66–70 (2007) (holding notice not required where rate charged equal to rate in absence of credit report). The court held that although willful failure required by the statute covers reckless action, the defendant was not liable for its mistaken belief that the statute did not apply to initial applications for insurance, because such a reading was not objectively unreasonable and thus fell short of the "unjustifiably high risk" of violating the statute necessary for recklessness. *Id.* at 70.

62. *See Philip Morris USA v. Williams*, 549 U.S. 346, 349 (2007) (holding punitive damages award violation of due process). The court held when a jury bases a punitive damage award in part on a desire to punish the defendant for harming nonparties, such award constitutes deprivation of property without due process. *Id.*

63. *See John R. Sand & Gravel Co. v. United States*, 552 U.S. 130, 132 (2008) (holding court may *sua sponte* raise special statute of limitations despite waiver by government). The decision resulted in barring a claim that the environmental protection activities of the government constituted an unconstitutional taking of plaintiff's mining leasehold rights. *See also Nat'l Ass'n of Homebuilders v. Defenders of Wildlife*, 551 U.S. 644, 671–73 (2007) (holding decision not within EPA discretion, thereby triggering no consultation requirement regarding protection of species); *Massachusetts v. Envtl. Prot. Agency*, 549 U.S. 497, 526 (2007) (holding state had standing to challenge denial of petition to make rules regarding greenhouse emissions). Further, the court held that the EPA has statutory authority to regulate such gases and can avoid promulgating regulations "only if it determines that greenhouse gases do not contribute to climate change or . . . provides some reasonable explanation as to why it cannot or will not exercise its discretion to determine whether they do." *Id.* at 533. *See also Rapanos v. United States*, 547 U.S. 715, 739 (2006) (defining term "navigable waters" under Clean Water Act narrowly). In rejecting a broader definition by the Army Corps of Engineers, the court defined "navigable waters" to include only relatively permanent, standing or continuously

flowing bodies of water, and excluded channels through which water flows inter-mittently, or channels that periodically provide drainage for rainfall. *Id.* The court reasoned that such interpretation fulfills the purpose of the act, which aims to "pro-tect the primary responsibilities and rights of the States . . . to plan the development and use of land and water resources." *Id.* at 722–23.

64. *Compare Gonzales v. Carhart*, 550 U.S. 124, 133 (2007) (holding Partial-Birth Abortion Ban Act of 2003 not unconstitutional on its face), *with Stenberg v. Carhart*, 530 U.S. 914, 929–30 (2000) (holding partial birth abortion statute unconstitutional). In *Stenberg*, the court found the statute unconstitutional where it lacked an exception for preserving the health of the mother and where it imposed an undue burden on the woman's right to choose an abortion, because it applied to the D & E procedure as well as the D & X procedure). *Id.*

65. *See Samson v. California*, 547 U.S. 843, 857 (2006) (holding suspicionless search of parolee not violation of Fourth Amendment). The court explained that parolees have a diminished expectation of privacy compared to probationers. *Id.* at 850. *See also Hudson v. Michigan*, 547 U.S. 586 (2006) (holding knock-and-announce rule violation does not require suppression of all evidence).

66. *See Parents Involved in Cmty. Sch. v. Seattle Sch. Dist. No. 1*, 551 U.S. 701 (2007) (hold-ing voluntarily adopted plans relying on race to determine student assignments to schools unconstitutional).

67. *Compare Hein v. Freedom From Religion Found.*, 551 U.S. 587, 593 (2007) (holding challenge not within exception to prohibition on taxpayer standing established in *Flast*), *with Flast v. Cohen*, 392 U.S. 83, 105–06 (1968) (setting forth narrow exception to rule against taxpayer standing).

68. *Citizens United v. Fed. Election Comm'n*, 130 S. Ct. 876 (2010).

69. *National Federation of Independent Business v. Sebelius*, 132 S. Ct. 2566 (2012).

70. Sheryl Gay Stolberg & Charlie Savage, *Vindication for Challenger of Health Care Law*, N.Y. TIMES, Mar. 26, 2012, *available at* nytimes.com; Ezra Klein, *Obamacare's Most Influential Legal Critic on Tuesday's Oral Arguments*, WONKBLOG (Mar. 27, 2012, 4:52 PM), washingtonpost.com/blogs.

71. Among others, in *Sebelius*, 132 S. Ct. 2566 (Nos. 11–393, 11–398, 11–400): Richard A. Epstein was on the Brief of Amicus Curiae Texas Public Policy Foundation Supporting Respondents on the Individual Mandate, 2012 WL 504607; Jay Sekulow was on the Amici Curiae Brief of the American Center for Law & Justice, 119 Members of the United States Congress, and More Than 144,000 Supporters of the ACLJ in Support of Respondents and Urging Affirmance on the Minimum Coverage Provision, Otherwise Known as the Individual Mandate, Issue, 2012 WL 441264; William ("Chip") H. Mellor and Dana Berliner were on the Brief of Amicus Curiae Institute for Justice in Support of Respondents (Minimum Coverage Provision), 2012 WL 484067; Ilya Somin was on the Brief of the Washington Legal Foundation and Constitutional Law Scholars as Amici Curiae in Support of Respondents (Individual Mandate Issue), 2012 WL 1680857; Carrie Severino was on the Brief of Members of the United States Senate as Amici Curiae in Support of Respondents on the Minimum Coverage Provision Issue, 2012 WL 484064; Charles J. Cooper was on the Brief of Amicus Curiae Partnership for America in Support of Respondents on the Minimum Coverage Provision Issue, 2012 WL 484065; Erik S. Jaffe was on the Brief for Docs4patientcare, Benjamin Rush Society, Pacific Research Institute, Galen Institute, and Angel Raich as Amici Curiae on the Minimum Coverage Provision Issue in Support of Respondents, 2012 WL 484068; Ilya Shapiro was on the Brief of Amici Curiae Cato Institute,

Competitive Enterprise Institute, Pacific Legal Foundation, 14 Other Organizations, and 333 State Legislators Supporting Respondents (Individual Mandate Issue), 2012 WL 504615; David B. Kopel was on the Brief of Authors of *The Necessary and Proper Clause* (Gary Lawson, Robert G. Natelson & Guy Seidman) and the Independence Institute as Amici Curiae in Support of Respondents (Minimum Coverage Provision), 2012 WL 484061. Numerous other amicus briefs were filed by conservative organizations challenging the law and by liberal organizations and others in support of the law.

72. *Health Care in the Supreme Court*, Federalist Soc'y, fed-soc.org/publications (last visited Sept. 12, 2012).
73. *Lopez v. United States*, 514 U.S. 549 (1995); *United States v. Morrison*, 529 U.S. 598 (2000).
74. For example, in *Gonzales v. Raich*, 545 U.S. 1 (2005), the court rejected the argument that the federal Controlled Substances Act was unconstitutional under the commerce clause as applied to users of medical marijuana in California.
75. *National Federation of Independent Business v. Sebelius*, 132 S. Ct. at 2589 (emphasis in original).
76. Randy Barnett, *A Weird Victory for Federalism*, SCOTUSblog (June 28, 2012, 12:56 PM), scotusblog.com.
77. The statute as written would have permitted the federal government to deny all Medicaid funds to states that refused to participate in the expansion of the program. The court's ruling struck that penalty down, and held that the government could deny new funds to states under the expanded program if they failed to comply with conditions on their use, but could not take away previously existing Medicaid funding.
78. Ann. Rep, *supra* note 9.
79. Federalism and Separation of Powers Practice Group, *2011 Separation of Powers CLE Course*, Federalist Soc'y, fed-soc.org (last visited Aug. 13, 2012).
80. James Oliphant, *Scalia and Thomas Dine with Healthcare Law Challengers as Court Takes Case*, L.A. Times, Nov. 14, 2011, *available at* latimes.com.
81. Notes of speech on file with authors.
82. For a scholarly study of several specific conservative campaigns, *see* Jean Stefancic & Richard Delgado, No Mercy: How Conservative Think Tanks and Foundations Changed America's Social Agenda (1996).
83. Miller, *supra* note 1, at 91.
84. *Id.* at 93.
85. *Id.*
86. Roger M. Williams, *Sustaining Ideas on the Right*, 47 Found. News & Comment. 1 (2006), *available at* foundationnews.org.
87. *Id.*
88. Teles, *supra* note 25, at 135.
89. *Id.* at 152, et seq.
90. Ilya Somin, *The Rise of Libertarian and Conservative Public Interest Law*, Volokh Conspiracy (Mar. 2, 2008, 12:11AM), volokh.com.
91. Southworth, *supra* note 4, at 3.
92. *Id.* at 41.
93. *Id.* at 48–49.
94. *Id.*
95. Teles, *supra* note 25, at 147 (quoting David McIntosh).
96. *Id.* at 4.
97. *Id.* at 14.

98. *Id.* at 17.
99. *Id.* Teles provides a detailed analysis of the entrepreneurs and patrons responsible for the development of conservative public interest legal institutions, the law and economics movement, the Federalist Society, and the implementation of their goals in law schools, the bar, the courts, and the government.
100. Benjamin Rush Soc'y, benjaminrushsociety.org (last visited Aug. 13, 2012).
101. Alexander Hamilton Soc'y, hamsoc.org (last visited Aug. 13, 2012).
102. Manhattan Inst., manhattan-institute.org (last visited Aug. 13, 2012). The launch of the Adam Smith Society is described in the Manhattan Institute's website as "a national organization for business schools akin to what the Federalist Society has been for law school." *See also* Philanthropy Roundtable, philanthropyroundtable.org/topic/excellence_in_philanthropy/a_federalist_solution (last visited Aug. 13, 2012); Harv. Bus. Sch., hbs.edu/mba/studentlife/clubs/ideasatwork.html (last visited Aug. 13, 2012).
103. Crystal Nix Hines, *Young Liberal Law Group Is Expanding*, N.Y. Times, June 1, 2001, *available at* nytimes.com.
104. *Id.*
105. Abner Mikva, quoted in *About ACS*, Am. Const. Soc'y, acslaw.org (last visited Aug. 13, 2012).

CHAPTER 1

1. Edwin Meese III, *Foreword* to Henry Julian Abraham et al., Judicial Selection: Merit, Ideology, and Politics, at x (1990).
2. Other Federalist Society judges who spoke at the symposium included Brett M. Kavanaugh, D.C. Circuit; William H. Pryor Jr., Eleventh Circuit; Diane Sykes, Seventh Circuit; and J. Harvie Wilkinson III, Fourth Circuit. *2011 Annual Student Symposium—"Capitalism, Markets, and the Constitution"* (Feb. 25–26, 2011), Federalist Soc'y, fed-soc.org/events.
3. In an op-ed in the *Huffington Post* the day after the fundraiser, Nan Aron of the Alliance for Justice wrote: "There are only nine federal jurists who could get away with doing what Scalia and Thomas did, and although Supreme Court spokespeople have said that the justices accept the Code's principles as 'guidance,' apparently some either don't understand the rules or simply don't care to be guided that way. This is exactly why Alliance for Justice, members of Congress, and other groups have called for immediate reform of Supreme Court ethics rules, including the formal application of the Code of Conduct to the Court, either by voluntary action by the justices themselves or by congressional action." Nan Aron, *Justices Thomas and Scalia Celebrate Their Service by Thumbing Their Noses at Ethical Rules*, Huffington Post (Nov. 11, 2011, 5:33 PM), huffingtonpost.com. Aron notes that Scalia and Thomas spoke at the dinner, were the guests of honor, and were featured on the program of a fundraising event, all prohibited by the Code of Conduct for United States Judges. *See* Canon 4C *in* Judicial Conference of the United States, Code of Conduct for United States Judges (last revised June 2, 2011), uscourts.gov. For a more detailed discussion, see Chapter 1.
4. Charles Lane, *Roberts Listed in Federalist Society '97–98 Directory*, Wash. Post, July 25, 2001, at A01.
5. John G. Roberts Jr., *7th Annual Barbara K. Olson Memorial Lecture—Event Audio/Video*, Federalist Soc'y (Nov. 16, 2007), fed-soc.org; E. Spencer Abraham et al., *25th Anniversary Tribute Video*, Federalist Soc'y (Nov. 15, 2007), fed-soc.org.

6. David D. Kirkpatrick, *In Alito, G.O.P. Reaps Harvest Planted in '82*, N.Y. Times, Jan. 30, 2006, *available at* nytimes.com.

7. Graeme Browning, *Reagan Molds the Federal Court in His Own Image*, 71 A.B.A. J. 60, 61 (1985).

8. Edward Lazarus, Closed Chambers: The Rise, Fall, and Future of the Modern Supreme Court 264 (1999).

9. Rachel Brand profile on linkedin.com (last visited Aug. 14, 2012).

10. Press Release, U.S. Chamber of Commerce, U.S. Chamber's Litigation Center Names Rachel Brand Chief Counsel for Regulatory Litigation and Kate Comerford Todd Chief Counsel for Appellate Litigation (June 1, 2011), uschamber.com/press.

11. *President Bush Discusses Judicial Accomplishments and Philosophy*, 44 Weekly Comp. Pres. Doc. 1303–06 (Oct. 6, 2008).

12. Gary L. McDowell & Edwin Meese III, *The Language of Law and the Foundations of American Constitutionalism* 3 (Heritage Lectures No. 1182, Apr. 11, 2011).

13. *Id.* at 2.

14. *Id.* at 4.

15. Gary L. McDowell, *Introduction: The Politics of Advice and Consent, in* Judicial Selection, *supra* note 1, at xvii.

16. Sheldon Goldman, Picking Federal Judges: Lower Court Selection from Roosevelt through Reagan 297, 300 (1997).

17. Ronald Reagan, Speech in North Carolina, 1986, *quoted in* Goldman, *supra* note 16, at 302.

18. Goldman, *supra* note 16, at 291.

19. Stephen J. Markman, *Judicial Selection: The Reagan Years, in* Judicial Selection, *supra* note 1, at 33.

20. Goldman, *supra* note 16, at 291.

21. George W. Hicks Jr., *The Conservative Influence of the Federalist Society on the Harvard Law School Student Body*, 29 Harv. J.L. & Pub. Pol'y. 623, 648–49 (2006).

22. Henry J. Abraham, *Beneficial Advice or Presumptuous Veto? The ABA's Committee on Federal Judiciary Revisited, in* Judicial Selection, supra note 1, at 67.

23. Browning, *supra* note 7, at 62.

24. Debra Cassens Moss, *The Policy and the Rhetoric of Ed Meese*, 73 A.B.A. J. 64, 68 (1987).

25. *Id.*

26. Douglas Martin, *Roger J. Miner, 77, Dies; Judge Valued Neutrality*, N.Y. Times, Feb. 20, 2012, *available at* nytimes.com.

27. Nina J. Easton, Gang of Five: Leaders at the Center of the Conservative Crusade 191 (2000).

28. *Id.* at 193.

29. *Id.* at 235. After the defeat of Robert Bork's nomination, commentators began to use his name as a verb, "to Bork," meaning to defeat a nomination through organized opposition.

30. *See generally* Amanda Hollis-Brusky, *The Reagan Administration and the Rehnquist Court's New Federalism: Understanding the Role of the Federalist Society*, ExpressO (2008), works.bepress.com/amanda_hollis; Charles Fried, Order and Law: Arguing the Reagan Revolution (1991); Cornell Clayton, The Politics of Justice: The Attorney General and the Making of Legal Policy (1992); David M. O'Brien, Federal Judgeships in Retrospect, in The Reagan Presidency: Pragmatic Conservatism and Its Legacies (W. Elliot Brownlee and Hugh Davis Graham eds., 2003).

31. Clayton, *supra* note 30, at 151.

32. Hollis-Brusky, *supra* note 30, at 13.

33. Off. of Legal Pol'y (OLP), Dep't of Just., Report to the Attorney General: The Constitution in the Year 2000, at v (1988).

34. OLP, Dep't of Just., Report to the Attorney General: Original Meaning Jurisprudence: A Sourcebook 1 (1987).

35. *Id.*

36. William Bradford Reynolds, *Adjudication as Politics by Other Means: The Corruption of the Senate's Advice and Consent Function in Judicial Confirmations, in* Judicial Selection, supra note 1, at 18. Stephen J. Markman, also a Federalist Society member, used almost exactly the same words as Reynolds (without attribution) in his article in the same book, Judicial Selection: The Reagan Years. Markman wrote: "The Constitution and laws passed pursuant to it, of course, have meanings; otherwise, the very idea of consent—of ratifying or amending the Constitution or voting for or against laws—would be a nullity. Consent must mean knowing consent, and knowing consent is possible only if the constitutional provisions consented to have ascertainable meanings." Markman, *in* Judicial Selection, supra note 1, at 35.

37. *Roberts: "My Job Is to Call Balls and Strikes and Not to Pitch or Bat,"* CNN (Sept. 12, 2005), articles.cnn.com .

38. Reynolds, *in* Judicial Selection, *supra* note 1, at 22.

39. Dawn E. Johnsen, *Ronald Reagan and the Rehnquist Court on Congressional Power: Presidential Influences on Constitutional Change*, 78 Ind. L.J. 363, 367 (2003).

40. *Id.* at 389–90.

41. Ed Meese articulated this distinction in his famous 1986 speech at Tulane Law School. Edwin Meese III, *The Law of the Constitution*, 61 Tul. L. Rev. 979, 981–82 (1987).

42. *Marbury v. Madison*, 5 U.S. 137 (1803); *Cooper v. Aaron*, 358 U.S. 1 (1958).

43. Johnsen, *supra* note 39, at 402–03.

44. OLP, Dep't of Just., Guidelines on Constitutional Litigation 56–59 (1988).

45. Religious Freedom Restoration Act: *City of Boerne v. Flores*, 521 U.S. 507 (1997); Age Discrimination in Employment Act: *Kimel v. Fla. Bd. of Regents*, 528 U.S. 62 (2000); Violence against Women Act: *United States v. Morrison*, 529 U.S. 598 (2000); Americans with Disabilities Act: *Bd. of Trustees of Univ. of Ala. v. Garrett*, 531 U.S. 356 (2001).

46. OLP, Dep't of Just., Report to the Attorney General: Religious Liberty under the Free Exercise Clause, at iii (1986).

47. OLP, Dep't of Just., Report to the Attorney General: Justice without Law: A Reconsideration of the "Broad Equitable Powers" of the Federal Court (1988).

48. The OLP was criticizing the decision in *Swann v. Charlotte-Mecklenburg Board of Education. Id.* at 94–95, 120–21.

49. *Id.* at 94.

50. Michael Wines, *A Counsel with Sway over Policy*, N.Y. Times, Nov. 25, 1991.

51. W. John Moore, *The White House Lawyer Nobody Knows*, 23 Nat'l J. 1357 (1991).

52. Sheldon Goldman, *The Bush Imprint on the Judiciary: Carrying On a Tradition*, 74 Judicature 294, 295–96 (1991).

53. C. Boyden Gray & Nan Aron, *Judicial Confirmations Debate Transcript*, Federalist Soc'y, Feb. 20, 2003, at 19–20, *available at* fed-soc.org.

54. Goldman, *supra* note 52, at 297.

55. Roger J. Miner, *Advice and Consent in Theory and Practice*, 41 Am. U. L. Rev. 1075 (1992).

56. *Id.* at 1080–81.

57. Sheldon Goldman, Sara Schiavoni & Elliot Slotnick, *W. Bush's Judicial Legacy, Mission Accomplished*, 92 JUDICATURE 258, 259–60 (May–June 2009).

58. Sheldon Goldman, Elliot Slotnick, Gerard Gryski, Gary Zuk & Sara Schiavoni, *W. Bush Remaking the Judiciary: Like Father Like Son?* 86 JUDICATURE 282, 284 (May–June 2003).

59. *Id.* at 309.

60. *Id.* at 261.

61. *See* Chapter 1.

62. Todd had been a judicial clerk for Justice Thomas and for Judge Michael Luttig of the Fourth Circuit Court of Appeals, also a Federalist Society member.

63. Goldman et al., *supra* note 57, at 260.

64. Goldman et al., *supra* note 58, at 285–89; Sheldon Goldman, Elliot Slotnick, Gerard Gryski, & Sara Schiavoni, *W. Bush's Judiciary: The First Term Record*, 88 JUDICATURE 244, 246–47 (May–June 2005).

65. BILL MINUTAGLIO, THE PRESIDENT'S COUNSELOR 202 (2006).

66. *Id.* at 191.

67. *Our People: Bradford A. Berenson*, SIDLEY, sidley.com (last visited Aug. 13, 2012).

68. *Id.* at 193–94.

69. Goldman et al., *supra* note 64, at 253.

70. Sheldon Goldman, Elliot Slotnick, Gerard Gryski & Sara Schiavoni, *Picking Judges in a Time of Turmoil: W. Bush's Judiciary during the 109th Congress*, 90 JUDICATURE 252, 254–55 (May–June 2007).

71. Kirkpatrick, *supra* note 6.

72. *Id.*

73. Wendy Long, *Bring It On . . .* , NAT'L REV. ONLINE (July 25, 2005, 5:37 PM), nationalreview.com.

74. Jack Newfield, *Why Estrada Went Down*, NATION, Sept. 29, 2003, at 5.

75. *Mr. Curt Levey*, FEDERALIST SOC'Y, fed-soc.org/publications (last visited Aug. 14, 2012).

76. ADMIN. OFF. OF THE U.S. COURTS, *Table B. U.S. Courts of Appeals—Appeals Commenced, Terminated, and Pending during the 12-Month Periods Ending March 31, 2010 and 2011, in* FEDERAL JUDICIAL CASELOAD STATISTICS (2011), www.uscourts.gov.

77. Goldman et al., *supra* note 70, at 255.

78. *Id.* at 257–58.

79. 149 CONG. REC. at 4,589 (2003).

80. *Hearing before the Senate Comm. on the Judiciary*, 110th Cong. 7 (Sept. 25, 2007).

81. Roger Pilon, *How Constitutional Corruption Has Led to Ideological Litmus Tests for Judicial Nominees* 4 (Cato Pol'y Analysis No. 446, Aug. 8, 2002), *available at* cato.org.

82. *Id.* at 5–12.

83. *Id.* at 12, 14.

84. PEOPLE FOR THE AM. WAY FOUND., *Appendix A: The Right Wing Dream Team at the Department of Justice: Some of the Players, in* JOHN ASHCROFT'S FIRST YEAR AS ATTORNEY GENERAL (Feb. 2002), pfaw.org.

85. 28 C.F.R. § 42.1(a) (2009); 5 U.S.C. § 2301(b) (2006).

86. OFF. OF THE INSPECTOR GEN. (OIG) & OFF. OF PROF. RESP. (OPR), DEP'T OF JUST., AN INVESTIGATION OF ALLEGATIONS OF POLITICIZED HIRING IN THE DEPARTMENT OF JUSTICE HONORS PROGRAM AND SUMMER LAW INTERN PROGRAM (2008), justice. gov [hereinafter HONORS PROGRAM INVESTIGATION].

87. OPR & OIG, DEP'T OF JUST., AN INVESTIGATION OF ALLEGATIONS OF POLITICIZED HIRING BY MONICA GOODLING AND OTHER STAFF IN THE OFFICE OF THE ATTORNEY GENERAL (2008), justice.gov [hereinafter GOODLING INVESTIGATION].

88. OIG & OPR, Dep't of Just., An Investigation of Allegations of Politicized Hiring and Other Improper Personnel Actions in the Civil Rights Division (July 2, 2008; released publicly, Jan. 13, 2009), justice.gov [hereinafter C.R. Div. Investigation].

89. OIG & OPR, Dep't of Just., An Investigation into the Removal of Nine U.S. Attorneys in 2006 (2008), justice.gov [hereinafter U.S. Att'ys Investigation].

90. Goodling Investigation, *supra* note 87, at 135.

91. *Id.* at 7.

92. *Id.* at 136.

93. *Id.* at 25, 36.

94. *Id.* at 37–38.

95. *Id.* at 95, 121, 137.

96. *Id.* at 84, 102–03.

97. *Id.* at 118–19.

98. *Id.* at 18–21.

99. *Id.* at 137–38.

100. *Id.* at 101, 138.

101. 18 U.S.C. § 1001 (2006).

102. Alan Cooper, *Ex-Bush Official Reprimanded by Bar*, Va. Law. Wkly., May 5, 2011, *available at* valawyersweekly.com.

103. Honors Program Investigation, *supra* note 86, at 98.

104. *Id.* at 22–24.

105. *Id.* at 33.

106. *Id.* at 37.

107. *Id.* at 42–45.

108. *Id.* at 55.

109. *Id.* at 75.

110. *Id.* at 92–97.

111. *Id.* at 79.

112. *Gerlich v. U.S. Dep't of Justice*, No. 08–1134, 2011 WL 6250851 (D.D.C. 2011).

113. C.R. Div. Investigation, *supra* note 88, at 14.

114. *Id.* at 17.

115. *Id.* at 25–26.

116. *Id.* at 33.

117. *Id.* at 4.

118. *Jason Torchinsky, Partner*, HoltzmanVogelJosefiak PLLC, hvjlaw.com (last visited Aug. 14, 2012).

119. *Matt M. Dummermuth*, Whitaker Hagenow GBMG, gbmglaw.com/iowa-law-firm (last visited Aug. 14, 2012).

120. *Religious Liberties* (practice group page), Federalist Soc'y, fed-soc.org (last visited Aug. 14, 2012).

121. C.R. Div. Investigation, *supra* note 88, at 2.

122. *Id.* at 30.

123. Eric Lichtblau, *Mukasey Won't Pursue Charges in Hiring Inquiry*, N.Y. Times, Aug. 12, 2008, *available at* nytimes.com.

124. C.R. Div. Investigation, *supra* note 88, at 21.

125. *Id.* at 43–44.

126. *Id.* at 53.

127. *Id.* at 1.

128. Hinkle Law Firm, hinklaw.com (last visited Aug. 14, 2012).

129. U.S. Att'ys Investigation, *supra* note 89, at 325.

130. *Id.* at 325–26.

131. Stephen Braun, *Romney Charity Has History of Donations to Conservative Groups; Will It Help His GOP Image?*, Associated Press, Dec. 23, 2011, *available at* boston.com.

132. Kirkpatrick, *supra* note 6.

133. Carrie Severino, *There He Goes Again: Obama Renominates Activist Judges*, Judicial Crisis Network (Feb. 16, 2011), judicialnetwork.com.

134. Goldman et al., *supra* note 64, at 252. *See also* Lisa Holmes & Elisha Savchak, *Judicial Appointment Politics in the 107th Congress*, 86 Judicature 232, 235 (Mar.–Apr. 2003).

135. Meese, *supra* note 1, at xi.

136. Edwin Meese III, *The Imperial Judiciary—and What Congress Can Do about It*, 81 Pol'y Rev. (Jan. 1, 1997), hoover.org.

137. Minutaglio, *supra* note 65, at 204.

138. Goldman et al., *supra* note 58, at 292.

139. *Id.* at 290.

140. Cass R. Sunstein, David Schkade, Lisa M. Ellman & Andres Sawicki, Are Judges Political? An Empirical Analysis of the Federal Judiciary 147 (2006).

141. *Id.* at 8–9. The authors also point out that their conclusions should not be overstated, and that the result of legal cases is not "foreordained by the composition of the panel." *Id.* at 12. There are many reasons why judges of different perspectives might vote the same way in a given case, including the existence of binding precedent or clear Supreme Court guidance in an area.

142. *Id.* at 116. The authors note the difficulty of reaching conclusions on comparisons over time, because of various factors, including that of the sorts of legal questions litigated changing over time.

143. *Id.* at 121.

144. *Id.* at 148.

145. *Id.* at 128.

146. Robert A. Carp, Kenneth L. Manning & Ronald Stidham, *The Voting Behavior of George W. Bush's Judges: How Sharp a Turn to the Right?*, *in* Principles and Practice of American Politics: Classic and Contemporary Readings (Samuel Kernell & Steven S. Smith eds., 3d ed., 2007); Kenneth Jost, *Courts and the Law: The Bush Bench*, Cong. Q., May 22, 2006.

147. *Id.* at 439–40.

148. *Id.* at 440–41.

149. *Id.* at 443–44.

150. Nancy Scherer & Banks Miller, *The Federalist Society's Influence on the Federal Judiciary*, 62 Pol. Res. Q. 366 (2009).

151. The Bush Sr. appointees to the Supreme Court and the Courts of Appeals whom Scherer and Miller identified as Federalist Society members were Samuel Alito, Dennis Jacobs, Michael Luttig, Sheldon Plager, and Clarence Thomas. The George W. Bush appointees were Samuel Alito, Carlos Bea, Janice Brown, Jay Bybee, Michael Chertoff, Edith Clement, Steven Collonton, Deborah Cook, Thomas Griffith, Raymond Gruender, Harris Hartz, Brett Kavanaugh, Michael McConnell, David McKeague, Priscilla Owen, William Pryor, John Roberts, John Rogers, Jeffrey Sutton, Diane Sykes, and Timothy Tymkovich.

152. Scherer & Miller, *supra* note 150, at 371–72.

153. *Id.* at 373.

154. *Id.*
155. *Id.* at 375.
156. Sunstein et al., *supra* note 140, at 147.

CHAPTER 2

1. Richard A. Epstein, Takings: Private Property and the Power of Eminent Domain 263 (1985).
2. This summary of colonial practice is based on William Michael Treanor, *The Original Understanding of the Takings Clause and the Political Process*, 95 Colum. L. Rev. 782, 786–89 (1995). The Massachusetts Body of Liberties, adopted in 1641, had a clause requiring compensation for the seizure of *personal* property. The 1669 Fundamental Constitution of Carolina required compensation when *real* property was seized. Where other charters or constitutional documents of the colonial era protected private property against government seizure, they did so by resorting to legislative mechanisms, requiring a jury or a legislature to determine any monetary award. No colonial government charter or court ruling mandated compensation when a regulation was imposed upon private property that affected its value or restricted its use. *Id.*
3. *Lucas v. S.C. Coastal Council*, 505 U.S. 1003, 1114 (1992).
4. *Pa. Coal v. Mahon*, 260 U.S. 393, 414 (1922).
5. A regulatory taking has been described as a regulation that affects a property owner's legal rights: "Indirect condemnation can be categorized as physical action, such as a county's dumping of road construction debris on a private lot, or regulatory action, such as a county's downzoning of private land from allowing apartment buildings to allowing only single-family residence construction. . . . Physical impact is illustrated by a county's dumping of debris on the owner's private lot. Regulatory impact, in contrast, affects the owner's legal rights. For example, downsizing can restrict the types of construction allowed on an owner's property. This type of action goes by many names, including 'regulatory takings,' 'indirect condemnation,' 'inverse condemnation,' and 'unintentional takings.'" John Martinez & Karen L. Martinez, *A Prudential Theory for Providing a Forum for Federal Takings Claims*, 36 Real Prop. Prob. & Tr. J. 445, 453–54 (2001).
6. The environmental laws examined include *Palazzolo v. Rhode Island*, 533 U.S. 606 (2001).
7. Erwin Chemerinsky, Constitutional Law: Principles and Policies 658 (3d ed. 2006). The court has also recognized the existence of a "temporary taking" if a governmental act that temporarily denies a landowner the use of her land is not reasonable. *Tahoe-Sierra Preservation Council v. Tahoe Regional Planning Agency*, 535 U.S. 302 (2002).
8. In some categories of land, states did not even allow for the creation or expectation of property rights, most notably in harbor and/or coastal areas.
9. For example, in *Lucas v. South Carolina Coastal Council*, the Supreme Court held that because a coastal preservation law that prevented the building of a structure on the land existed prior to the purchase of the land, the owner could have no expectation of a property right in his ability to build a structure. 505 U.S. 1003 (1992). In *Phillips v. Washington Legal Foundation*, the Supreme Court held that under Texas law, interest income generated by funds held in Interest on Lawyers Trust Account (IOLTA) accounts is private property of the owner of the principal for purposes of the Takings Clause. 524 U.S. 156 (1998).
10. In *United States v. General Motors Corp.*, the court defined property as the "group of rights inhering in the citizen's [ownership of property]." *United States v. General Motors Corp.*, 323 U.S. 373 (1945).

11. On trade secrets, see *Ruckelshaus v. Monsanto Co.*, 467 U.S. 986 (1984). On client funds, see *Brown v. Wash. Legal Fund*, 538 U.S. 216 (2003).

12. *Dames & Moore v. Regan*, 453 U.S. 654 (1981).

13. *Kelo v. City of New London*, 125 S. Ct. 2655 (2005).

14. CHEMERINSKY, *supra* note 7, at 644.

15. *Mugler v. Kansas*, 123 U.S. 623 (1887).

16. EPSTEIN, *supra* note 1, at 17.

17. *Id.* at 10.

18. Nestor M. Davidson, *Standardization and Pluralism in Property Law*, 61 VAND. L. REV. 1597, 1645 n.259 (2008).

19. Douglas T. Kendall & Charles P. Lord, *The Takings Project: A Critical Analysis and Assessment of the Progress So Far*, 25 B.C. ENVTL. AFF. L. REV. 509, 522 (1998).

20. *Id.* at 512.

21. EPSTEIN, *supra* note 1, at 299, 315, 318.

22. Charles Reich, *The New Property*, 73 YALE L.J. 733, 739–40 (1964).

23. *Goldberg v. Kelly*, 397 U.S. 262 (1970) ("It may be realistic today to regard welfare entitlements as more like 'property' than a 'gratuity.' Much of the existing wealth in this country takes the form of rights that do not fall within traditional common-law concepts of property. It has been aptly noted that '[s]ociety today is built around entitlement. The automobile dealer has his franchise, the doctor and lawyer their professional licenses, the worker his union membership, contract, and pension rights, the executive his contract and stock options; all are devices to aid security and independence. Many of the most important of these entitlements now flow from government: subsidies to farmers and businessmen, routes for airlines and channels for television stations; long term contracts for defense, space, and education; social security pensions for individuals. Such sources of security, whether private or public, are no longer regarded as luxuries or gratuities; to the recipients they are essentials, fully deserved, and in no sense a form of charity. It is only the poor whose entitlements, although recognized by public policy, have not been effectively enforced") *citing* Charles Reich, *Individual Rights and Social Welfare: The Emerging Legal Issues*, 74 YALE L.J. 1245, 1255 (1965) *and* Charles Reich, *The New Property*, 73 YALE L.J. 733 (1964).

24. *Pa. Coal v. Mahon*, 260 U.S. 393, 415 (1922).

25. William Michael Treanor, *The Original Understanding of the Takings Clause* 2 (Envtl. Law & Pol'y Inst., Geo. U. L. Ctr., Paper, 1998), *available at* law.georgetown.edu.

26. Treanor, *supra* note 2, at 787.

27. Treanor, *supra* note 2, at 711, n.95 (emphasis added).

28. EPSTEIN, *supra* note 1, at 11.

29. Kendall & Lord, *supra* note 19, at 522.

30. *Id.* at 523.

31. Joseph L. Sax, *Takings*, 53 U. CHI. L. REV. 279, 279 (1986).

32. Kendall & Lord, *supra* note 19, at 526.

33. Treanor, *supra* note 25, at 1.

34. ROBERT H. BORK, THE TEMPTING OF AMERICA: THE POLITICAL SEDUCTION OF THE LAW 230 (1990).

35. Charles Fried, *Protecting Property-Law and Politics*, 13 HARV. J.L. & PUB. POL'Y 44, 48–49 (1990).

36. NINA J. EASTON, GANG OF FIVE: LEADERS AT THE CENTER OF THE CONSERVATIVE CRUSADE 66–67 (2000).

37. Kendall & Lord, *supra* note 19, at 526. *See also* Richard A. Epstein, *Needed: Activist Judges for Economic Rights*, WALL ST. J., Nov. 14, 1985, at 32.

38. Stuart Taylor, *Newest Judicial Activists Come from the Right*, N.Y. TIMES, Feb. 8, 1987, *available at* nytimes.com.

39. Kendall & Lord, *supra* note 19, at 514.

40. CHARLES FRIED, ORDER AND LAW 183 (1991).

41. *Lochner v. New York*, 198 U.S. 45 (1905).

42. *Id.* at 53 *citing Algeyer v. Louisiana*, 165 U.S. 578, 579 (1897). The *Algeyer* Court identi-fied a right to pursue a livelihood and contract freely within the definition of liberty.

43. *Lochner*, 198 U.S. at 64.

44. *Id.* at 57–8.

45. William Consovoy, Wendy Keefer, Thomas McCarthy & Seth Wood, *Can Bush Supreme Court Appointments Lead to a Rollback of the New Deal?* 5 (Federalist Soc'y, White Paper, 2005), *available at* fed-soc.org. Notwithstanding this, the post-*Lochner* Court in fact upheld more economic regulations challenged under the due pro-cess clause than it struck down. Note, *Resurrecting Economic Rights: The Doctrine of Economic Due Process Reconsidered*, 103 HARV. L. REV. 1363, 1366 (1990).

46. Some of these institutions survive today, such as the Securities and Exchange Commission, the Federal Housing Commission, and the Social Security Administration.

47. CHEMERINSKY, *supra* note 7, at 622.

48. *Nebbia v. New York*, 291 U.S. 502, 510–11 (1934).

49. *Id.* at 523. The decision, which is still good law, contains a laundry list of governmen-tal regulations the Supreme Court had previously upheld, despite them in some way impinging on property or economic rights. Such regulations included zoning laws, construction method and materials laws, antiprostitution laws, laws that regulated consumer goods, laws prohibiting the use of child labor, laws setting maximum weekly hours for certain occupations, and laws establishing workmen's compensation. *Id.* at 527, n.25.

50. *Id.* at 526. Also in 1934, the court upheld a Minnesota law that prevented mortgage holders from foreclosing on mortgagees for a two year period, an emergency measure in response to the depression. *See Home Building & Loan Ass'n v. Blaisdell*, 290 U.S. 398 (1934). Although not argued on economic substantive due process grounds, the decision reflected the court's growing willingness to defer to governmental economic decisions. CHEMERINSKY, *supra* note 7, at 623.

51. *West Coast Hotel Co. v. Parrish*, 300 U.S. 379, 400 (1937).

52. *Adkins v. Children's Hospital*, 261 U.S. 525 (1923).

53. *West Coast Hotel Co.*, 300 U.S. at 391.

54. *Id.* at 399.

55. *United States v. Carolene Products*, 304 U.S. 144, 149 (1938).

56. *Id.* at 158.

57. *Carolene Products*, 304 U.S. at 153, n.4.

58. Consovoy et al., *supra* note 45, at 6–7.

59. Conservatives have also sought to protect property rights by breathing new life into the Privileges and Immunities Clause of the Fourteenth Amendment. We discuss these efforts later in this chapter.

60. *Pa. Coal v. Mahon*, 260 U.S. 393 (1922).

61. *Lynch v. U.S.*, 292 U.S. 571 (1934).

62. *Penn Central Transportation v. City of New York*, 438 U.S. 104 (1978).

63. *Id.* at 131.

64. *Id.* at 130.

65. *Id.* at 130–31.

66. *Penn Central*, 438 U.S. at 143 (Rehnquist, J., dissenting), citing *United States v. General Motors Corp.*, 323 U.S. 373, 377–78 (1945).

67. Brief for Pacific Legal Fund as Amici Curiae Supporting Appellants at *15, *Penn Central Transportation v. City of New York*, 438 U.S. 104 (1978), No. 77–444, 1978 WL 206886.

68. Sharon Buccino, Tim Dowling, Doug Kendall & Elaine Weiss, Hostile Environment: How Activist Judges Threaten our Air, Water and Land 11 (Natural Resources Defense Council, July 2001), *available at* nrdc.org.

69. *Nollan v. Cal. Coastal Comm'n*, 483 U.S. 825 (1987).

70. *Id.*

71. *Nollan*, 483 U.S. at 837. The court in a later takings case characterized Scalia's argument thus: "How enhancing the public's ability to "traverse to and along the shorefront" served the same governmental purpose of "visual access to the ocean" from the roadway was beyond our ability to countenance. The absence of a nexus left the Coastal Commission in the position of simply trying to obtain an easement through gimmickry, which converted a valid regulation of land use into "'an out-and-out plan of extortion." *Dolan v. City of Tigard*, 512 U.S. 374, 387 (1994).

72. *Nollan*, 483 U.S at 846 (Brennan, J., dissenting).

73. Stephen M. Teles, The Rise of the Conservative Legal Movement: The Battle for Control of the Law 86 (2008).

74. *Id.* at 87. For information on the Pacific Legal Foundation, *see* pacificlegal.org/ (last visited Aug. 9, 2012).

75. Brief of Appellant at 12–13, *Nollan v. Cal. Coastal Comm'n*, 483 U.S. 825 (1987).

76. Christopher P. Yates, *Reagan Revolution Redux in Takings Clause Jurisprudence*, 72 U. Det. Mercy L. Rev. 531, 541 (1993).

77. Richard Epstein, *Yee v. City of Escondido: The Supreme Court Strikes Out Again*, 26 Loy. L.A. L. Rev. 3, 3 (1992).

78. *Lucas v. S.C. Coastal Council*, 505 U.S. 1003 (1992).

79. Michael C. Blumm, *The End of Environmental Law? Libertarian Property, Natural Law, and the Just Compensation Clause in the Federal Circuit*, 25 Envtl. L. 171, 174 (1995).

80. Buccino et al., *supra* note 68, at 10.

81. *Id.*, citing *Lujan v. Defenders of Wildlife*, 504 U.S. 555, 564 (1992).

82. *Lucas*, 505 U.S. at 1052 (Blackmun, J., dissenting).

83. Michael C. Blumm, *Property Myths, Judicial Activism, and the Lucas Case*, 23 Envtl. L. 907, 911 (1993).

84. Blumm, *supra* note 79, at 176.

85. Blumm, *supra* note 83, at 910.

86. Epstein, *supra* note 77, at 3.

87. Blumm, *supra* note 79, at 177.

88. *Dolan v. City of Tigard*, 512 U.S. 374 (1994).

89. *Dolan*, 512 U.S. at 387–93.

90. *Id.* at 396 (Brennan, J., dissenting).

91. *Kelo v. City of New London*, 545 U.S. 469, 473–74 (2005).

92. Timothy J. Dowling, *Kelo as Trojan Horse: How the Property Rights Movement is Misusing the Kelo Decision to Advance a Radical Agenda*, 54 Fed. Law. 46 (Oct. 2007).

93. *49 WB, LLC v. Vill. of Haverstraw*, 44 A.D.3d 226 (2007).

94. Amy Brigham Boulris & Annette Lopez, *2007–2008 Update on Judicial Reactions to Kelo, in* Eminent Domain and Land Valuation Litigation 63 (American Law Institute & American Bar Association Continuing Legal Education, Coursebook SP006, 2009).

95. *Harrison Redevelopment Agency v. DeRose*, 398 N.J. Super. 361, 411 (Feb. 25, 2008).
96. Teles, *supra* note 73, at 240.
97. *Id.* at 242.
98. Dick M. Carpenter II & John K. Ross, Doomsday? No Way: Economic Trends & Post-Kelo Eminent Domain Reform 3 (Inst. for Just., Jan. 2008), *available at* ij.org.
99. Dowling, *supra* note 92, at 46.
100. *About Cato*, Cato Inst., cato.org/about.php; *Board of Directors*, Cato Inst., cato.org/people/directors.html (last visited Aug. 9, 2012).
101. *Reason Trustees and Officers*, Reason Found., reason.org/trustees_officers.shtml (last visited Aug. 9, 2012).
102. Dowling, *supra* note 92, at 46.
103. *Id.*
104. Carpenter & Ross, *supra* note 98, at 2.
105. Notes of speech on file with authors.
106. Douglas T. Kendall & Charles P. Lord, *The Origins of the Takings Project, in* The Takings Project: Using Federal Courts to Attack Community and Environmental Protections ch. 3 (Community Rights Counsel, 1998), *available at* communityrights.org/CombatsJudicialActivism/TP/chapter3.asp *citing* David Helvarg, *Legal Assault on the Environment*, Nation, Jan. 30, 1995, at 126.
107. *Id. See also* the biographies listed under *Judges*, U.S. Court of Appeals for the Federal Circuit, cafc.uscourts.gov (last visited Aug. 9, 2012).
108. Blumm, *supra* note 79, at 173.
109. Kendall & Lord, *supra* note 106. *See also* Graham, Noe & Branch, *infra* note 145.
110. *Fla. Rock Industries v. United States*, 18 F.3d 1560, 1568 (1994).
111. *Id.* at 1562.
112. *Id.* at 1564. The court remanded the case for a determination of "what economic use as measured by market value, if any, remained after the permit denial, and for consideration of whether, in light of the properly assessed value of the land, Florida Rock has a valid takings claim."
113. *Fla. Rock Industries v. United States*, 45 Fed. Cl. 21 (1999).
114. Robert L. Bunting & William W. Wade, *Average Reciprocity of Advantage: "Magic Words" or Economic Reality—Lessons from Palazzolo*, 39 Urb. Law. 319–70 (Spring 2007).
115. *Loveladies Harbor, Inc. v. United States,* 28 F.3d 1171 (Fed. Cir. 1994).
116. Blumm, *supra* note 79, at 172.
117. William W. Wade, *Sophistical and Abstruse Formulas Made Simple: Advances in Measurement of Penn Central's Economic Prongs and Estimation of Economic Damages in Federal Claims and Federal Circuit Courts*, 38 Urb. Law. 337, 342 (2006).
118. *Zoltek Corp. v. United States*, 442 F.3d 1345 (Fed. Cir. Ct. App. 2006).
119. *Zoltek*, 442 F.3d at 1352. The statute authorizing the court of claims' subject matter jurisdiction is 28 U.S.C. §1498.
120. *Id.* at 1351. The court decided three distinct issues in *Zoltek*. First, that because some of the patented manufacturing process was performed outside the United States, the government was not liable to Zoltek under the strict wording of 28 U.S.C.A. 1498 (a). *Id.* at 1350. Second, that the Supreme Court held in *Schillinger v. United States*, 155 U.S. 163 (1894), that a patentee could not sue the government for patent infringement as a Fifth Amendment Taking, and that *Schillinger* remains the law. *Id.* Third, that by enacting the Patent Act of 1910 and assigning patent infringement jurisdiction to the court of claims, Congress did not create a separate *Takings* remedy in that court. If the

right to sue under the Takings Clause already existed, the court reasoned, the creation of this statutory right would be moot. *Id.* at 1352.

121. "[T]he the trial court's remaining conjectures on Takings jurisprudence do not require consideration." *Id.* at 1352.

122. *See* Chapter 7 for a more detailed discussion of Judge Bybee's role in the George W. Bush White House; *Guggenheim v. City of Goleta*, 582 F.3d 996 (9th Cir. 2009).

123. *Guggenheim v. City of Goleta*, 638 F.3d 1111 (9th Cir. 2010).

124. FREE, free-eco.org (last visited Aug. 9, 2012).

125. *Public Policy, Risk Analysis, & the Law: A Seminar Series for Federal Judges & Law Professors*, FREE, free-eco.org/seminars/past-seminars/public-policy-risk-analysis-and -the-law.html (last visited Aug. 9, 2012). After a centenary program in September 2011, FREE stated that "Article III federal judges and law professors were a primary constituency for twenty years." *Id.*

126. *Id.*

127. *See* mediamattersaction.org/transparency/funders/ (last visited Aug. 9, 2012).

128. *Id.*

129. Christopher Lee, *Possible Nominees to the Supreme Court*, Wash. Post, July 1, 2005, *available at* washingtonpost.com.

130. Jonathan Zittrain & George Priest, *Microsoft: Did Judge Jackson Get It Right?* Slate (Dec. 2, 1999), slate.com.

131. George L. Priest, *The Abiding Influence of the Antitrust Paradox*, 31 Harv. J.L. & Pub. Pol'y 455, 455 (2008).

132. Bork's book, The Antitrust Paradox: A Policy at War with Itself (Free Press 1978) has been called the most important antitrust book ever written. Bork's argument is that the enforcement of antitrust laws has harmed consumers because they harmed efficient firms while simultaneously protecting inefficient firms. Antitrust laws, by interfering with the market, therefore increase costs to consumers because the laws supported weak companies to maintain the perception of competition. Bork updated the book in 1993 to account for changes in the antitrust legal framework.

133. Linda Greenhouse, *The Bork Hearings: Legal Establishment Divided over Bork Nomination*, N.Y. Times, Sept. 26, 1987.

134. Conservative and Libertarian Legal Scholarship: An Annotated Bibliography (originally prepared by Roger Clegg, Michael E. DeBow & John McGinnis, 1996; updated 2011), *available at* fed-soc.org.

135. Easton, *supra* note 36, at 48.

136. *Id.* at 67.

137. *David M. McIntosh*, Mayer Brown, mayerbrown.com (last visited Aug. 9, 2012).

138. Fried, *supra* note 40, at 49.

139. *Id.*

140. *Id.* at 51.

141. Malcolm D. Woolf, *Clean Air or Hot Air?: Lessons from the Quayle Competitiveness Council's Oversight of EPA*, 10 J.L. & Pol. 97, 100 (1993).

142. Alan B. Morrison, *OMB Interference with Agency Rulemaking: The Wrong Way to Write a Regulation*, 99 Harv. L. Rev. 1059, 1062 (1986).

143. *Id.*

144. *Id.* at 1065.

145. John D. Graham, Paul R. Noe & Elizabeth L. Branch, *Managing the Regulatory State: The Experience of the Bush Administration*, 33 Fordham Urb. L.J. 953, 961 (2006). In fact, centralized presidential regulatory review, instituted by the Reagan administration, stayed in place through the George H. W. Bush administration and both of

President Clinton's terms. James F. Blumstein, *Regulatory Review by the Executive Office of the President: An Overview and Policy Analysis of Current Issues*, 51 Duke L.J. 851, 853 (2001). Clinton did, however, disband the Council on Competitiveness within his first few days of office. Michael Herz, *Imposing Unified Executive Branch Statutory Interpretation*, 15 Cardozo L. Rev. 219, 223 (1993).

146. Graham et al., *supra* note 145, at 962.

147. Yates, *supra* note 76, at 551.

148. Mountain States Legal Found., mountainstateslegal.org (last visited Aug. 9, 2012).

149. *Roger J. Marzulla*, Marzulla L., marzulla.com (last visited Aug. 9, 2012).

150. Exec. Order No. 12,630 § 4(b).

151. Yates, *supra* note 76 at 551–52.

152. Jerry Elig & Jerry Brito, *Toward a More Perfect Union: Regulatory Analysis and Performance Management*, 8 Fla. St. U. Bus. Rev. 1, 27 (2009). President Clinton abolished the Council on Competitiveness and rescinded President Reagan's Executive Order 12, 291, by which Reagan had established the regulatory review process. *Id.*

153. *The Quayle Committee*, 12 Multinat'l Monitor 5 (May 1991), *available at* multinationalmonitor.org.

154. Herz, *supra* note 145, at 225.

155. Nancy Watzman & Christine Triano, *Defund Quayle's Autocratic Competitiveness Council, Regulatory Agencies: His Secretive Group Blocks Health, Safety, and Environmental Policies at the Behest of Business*, L.A. Times, June 24, 1992, *available at* latimes.com.

156. *Id.*

157. David Lauter, *Clinton Order Lifts Regulatory Review Secrecy Government: Executive Edict Requires That Contacts between White House Aides, Lobbyists Be Made Part of Public Record*, L.A. Times, Oct. 1, 1993, *available at* latimes.org.

158. Woolf, *supra* note 141 at 101–02.

159. *The ABA and Criminal Justice Issues*, Federalist Soc'y (Aug. 1, 1997), fed-soc.org.

160. *See* Off. of Legal Counsel, Dep't of Justice, *Common Legislative Encroachments on Executive Branch Authority*, 13 Op. O.L.C. 248, 249 (1989).

161. For a more detailed discussion of the unitary executive theory, *see* Chapter 7.

162. Herz, *supra* note 145, at 223.

163. *See, e.g., Past Chapter Events*, Federalist Soc'y Milwaukee Law. Chapter (last updated Oct. 21, 2006), my.execpc.com/~fedsoc/fedmk.html; Symposium, *The Presidency and Congress: Constitutionally Separated and Shared Powers*, 68 Wash. U. L.Q. 485 (1990); Symposium, *The Bill of Rights after 200 Years*, 15 Harv. J.L. & Pub. Pol'y 1 (1992); Panel, *Telecommunications: Net Neutrality: Battle of the Titans, featuring William P. Barr, Paul Misener, Christopher S. Yoo; Moderator: David M. McIntosh*, 8 Engage 2 (2007).

164. Easton, *supra* note 36, at 236.

165. Chuck Clark, *Douglas Condemns Wetland Plan Federal Proposal "A Very Bad Thing," Famed Conservationist Says*, SunSentinel.com, Jan. 22, 1992.

166. Easton, *supra* note 36, at 236.

167. *See* W. R. Walker & S. C. Richardson, The Federal Wetlands Manual: Swamped by Controversy 2 (Va. Water Resources Research Ctr., Va. Polytechnic, Special Report No. 24, Oct. 1991), *available at* vwrrc.vt.edu.

168. *Wetlands: Community and Individual Rights v. Unchecked Government Power—Hearing Before the Subcomm. on Nat'l Econ. Growth, Nat. Resources, and Reg. Aff., of the H. Comm. on Gov't Reform and Oversight*, 105th Cong., 1st Sess. (1997), *available at* gpo.gov.

169. James Warren, *Hypothetically Speaking: Congressman Finds Regulatory Potholes on a Trek from Chicago to Muncie*, Chic. Trib., Mar. 5, 1996, *available at* chicagotribune.com.

170. H.R. 3521, 106th Cong. (2000).

171. H.R. 2221, 106th Cong. (1999).

172. *Id.*

173. Nat. Resources Def. Council, *Bush's Flawed Arguments against Regulating Carbon Pollution*, NRDC (last revised Mar. 15, 2001), nrdc.org. Backing off his pledge to cut global warming pollution, President Bush cited a flawed study and got the law wrong.

174. *Id.*

175. INST. FOR JUST., ij.org (last visited Aug. 9, 2012).

176. Brief for the Inst. of Just. as Amici Curiae Supporting Defendant-Appellants at *3, *Cnty. of Wayne v. Hathcock*, 471 Mich. 445, 450 (2004), Nos. 124070–124078, 2004 WL 687795.

177. Litigation Backgrounder, *Challenging Barriers to Economic Opportunity: Uqdah v. Board of Cosmetology*, INST. FOR JUST., ij.org/washington-dc-hair-braiding-backgrounder-2 (last visited Aug. 9, 2012).

178. *Uqdah v. District of Columbia*, 785 F. Supp. 1015, 1018 (D.D.C. 1992).

179. Monica C. Bell, *The Braiding Cases, Cultural Deference, and the Inadequate Protection of Black Women Consumers*, 19 YALE J.L. & FEMINISM 125 (2007).

180. Clint Bolick, Paper Presented at Inst. for Just. Conference on *Slaughter-House: The Slaughter-House Cases: Dismantling Liberty's Slaughter-House*, Dec. 1–3, 1995, *available at* ij.org/dismantling-libertys-slaughter-house (last visited Aug. 9, 2012).

181. Litigation Backgrounder, *Uncorking Freedom: Challenging Protectionist Restraints on Direct Interstate Wine Shipments to Consumers*, INST. FOR JUST., ij.org/ny-wine-background (last visited Aug. 9, 2012).

182. Clint Bolick, *Brennan's Epiphany: The Necessity of Invoking State Constitutions to Protect Freedom*, 12 TEX. REV. L. & POL. 137, 145 (2007). See also Clint Bolick, *Arizona Erects a Federalism Shield*, ARIZ. ATT'Y, Apr. 2010.

183. Bolick, *supra* note 182, at 140–41.

184. *Id.* at 145.

185. *Cnty. of Wayne v. Hathcock*, 471 Mich. 445, 450 (2004).

186. *Poletown Neighborhood Council v. City of Detroit*, 410 Mich. 616 (1981).

187. Brief for the Inst. of Just. as Amici Curiae Supporting Defendant-Appellants, *supra* note 176, at *4-5. In *Poletown Neighborhood Council v. City of Detroit*, 410 Mich. 616, 628 (1981), the Michigan Supreme Court upheld the City of Detroit's plan to condemn a swath of residential property in order to clear space for a General Motors automobile assembly plant. *Id.*

188. *Id.* at *6.

189. *Id.* at *5. Bolick also suggested the court explicitly require that property cannot be condemned without advance assurances that it will be employed only for specified public uses. *Id.* at *29–*30.

190. *Landmark Eminent Domain Abuse Decision: Michigan Supreme Court Halts Eminent Domain For "Economic Development" Court States Poletown Was "Erroneous,"* INST. FOR JUST. (July 31, 2004), ij.org/county-of-wayne-v-hathcock-release-7-31-2004).

191. *Slaughter-House Cases*, 83 U.S. 36, 38 (1872).

192. U.S. CONST. amend. XIV, § 1.

193. Clint Bolick, *A Cheer for Judicial Activism*, WALL ST. J., Apr. 3, 2007, *reproduced at* cato.org. The EPA, under George W. Bush's administration, had interpreted the Clean Air Act to mean the agency had no authority to regulate automobile CO_2 emissions. Massachusetts and eleven other states, plus a collection of U.S. territories, districts, cities and organizations, claiming injury due to global warming caused in part by such emissions, argued the agency did have such authority. The court agreed with the states,

holding specifically that the EPA is responsible for the regulation of automobile CO_2 if it determines that the gas contributes to climate change; and that it could only avoid taking action to restrict CO_2 emissions if it determined the gas does not contribute to global warming, or if it provided some reasonable explanation as to why it cannot or will not determine whether it does. *Massachusetts v. EPA*, 549 U.S. 497 (2007). Aside from the alleged judicial activism, this decision created two more troubling results for conservatives. First, the regulatory power of the agency was effectively broadened to encompass CO_2 emissions—the "big government" problem. Second, the EPA and the Bush administration could no longer hide behind their purported statutory "powerlessness" to act with regards to global warming, and would have to face up to the political consequences of regulating—or not regulating—CO_2.

194. *Id.*
195. Letter from Ian MacKenzie, Policy Advisor, Defenders of Property Rights, to Craig L. Fuller, Senior Vice President, Corporate Affairs, Philip Morris Companies, Inc. Aug. 30, 1995 (archived in Legacy Tobacco Documents Libr., U. Cal., San Francisco), *available at* legacy.library.ucsf.edu/tid/uhs82e00. For a more in-depth analysis of the right to smoke, *see Why Smoking Bans Are a Butt to Texas: The Impact of Smoking Bans on Private Property Rights and Individual Freedom*, 39 Tex. Tech. L. Rev 345, 355 (2007) (discussing how smoking ban in Austin led to increased littering).
196. Marzulla L., Marzulla.com (last visited Aug. 10, 2012).
197. Steve France, *Dusty Doctrines*, A.B.A. J., May 2001, at 41–50. (The authors note that the article also attributes this quotation to Nancie Marzulla in a photo caption.)
198. *Id.*
199. *Philip Morris, Inc. v. Reilly*, 312 F.3d 24 (2002).
200. Steven Gieseler & Nicholas M. Gieseler, *The Supreme Court and the Judicial Takings Doctrine*, 10 Engage 3 (2009).
201. *Stop the Beach Renourishment v. Florida Department of Environmental Protection*, 130 S. Ct. 2592 (2010).
202. *Stevens v. City of Cannon Beach*, 114 S. Ct. 1332, 1344 (1994) (Scalia, J., dissenting, *citing Lucas*, 505 U.S. 1003 (1992)).
203. Teles, *supra* note 73, at 146.

CHAPTER 3

1. *Marbury v. Madison*, 5 U.S. 137, 147 (1803).
2. Adam Liptak, *Step Away from the Courthouse Doors*, N.Y. Times, May 3, 2010, *available at* nytimes.com. Justices Breyer and Ginsburg issued a statement expressing regret about the court's decision.
3. *See, e.g.*, Erwin Chemerinsky, The Conservative Assault on the Constitution (2010); Pamela S. Karlan, *Disarming the Private Attorney General*, 2003 U. Ill. L. Rev. 183 (2003).
4. Andrew M. Siegel, *The Court against the Courts: Hostility to Litigation as an Organizing Theme in the Rehnquist Court's Jurisprudence*, 84 Tex. L. Rev. 1097, 1107 (2006).
5. *Id.* at 1108.
6. Absolute immunity protects officials performing certain functions (e.g., judges, prosecutors, legislators) from suit for damages. Qualified immunity protects government officials exercising discretionary functions (e.g. police officers, municipal officials) from suit for damages unless their conduct has violated "clearly established" constitutional rights and unless a reasonable official in their position would have known that his or her conduct would violate such rights. Application of these doctrines is complicated

and beyond the scope of this book. *See* Michael Avery, David Rudovsky & Karen Blum, Police Misconduct: Law and Litigation (3rd ed. 2011), ch. 3.

7.　*Cent. Bank of Denver v. First Interstate Bank of Denver*, 511 U.S. 164 (1994); *Alexander v. Sandoval*, 532 U.S. 275 (2001).

8.　*Corr. Servs. Corp. v. Malesko*, 534 U.S. 61 (2001).

9.　*Chavez v. Martinez*, 538 U.S.760 (2003).

10.　*Stoneridge Inv. Partners v. Scientific-Atlanta, Inc.*, 552 U.S. 148 (2008).

11.　*See, e.g.*, Andrew P. Morriss, Bruce Yandle & Andrew Dorchak, *Regulation by Litigation*, 9 Engage 109 (2008).

12.　Margaret A. Little, Regulation by Litigation *by Andrew P. Morriss, Bruce Yandle & Andrew Dorchak*, 10 Engage 154 (2009).

13.　Relevant practice groups include Administrative Law and Regulation; Civil Rights; Corporations, Securities and Antitrust; Environmental Law and Regulation; Federalism and Separation of Powers; Labor and Employment Law; and Litigation.

14.　Article 6 of the Constitution provides, in part: "This Constitution, and the Laws of the United States which shall be made in Pursuance thereof; and all Treaties made, or which shall be made, under the Authority of the United States, shall be the supreme Law of the Land; and the Judges in every State shall be bound thereby, any Thing in the Constitution or Laws of any State to the Contrary notwithstanding."

15.　*Gade v. Nat'l Solid Wastes Mgmt.*, 505 U.S. 88, 98 (1992).

16.　*Id.*

17.　*Cipollone v. Liggett Grp.*, 505 U.S. 504, 524 (1992) (state tort claims for failure to warn of the dangers of smoking relied on a state law "requirement" or "prohibition" and thus were preempted by federal statutes with respect to warnings on cigarette packages); *Riegel v. Medtronic, Inc.*, 552 U.S. 312, 324–25 (2008) (confirming that common law tort actions impose "requirements" as the term is used in preemption provisions in statutes).

18.　Thomas O. McGarity, The Preemption War 30 (2008).

19.　Ronald A. Cass, Thomas W. Merrill, Catherine M. Sharkey & Daniel E. Troy, with Diarmuid F. O'Scannlain (moderator), *Agency Preemption: Speak Softly, But Carry a Big Stick?*, 8 Engage 104 (2007). Troy is a graduate of Columbia Law School who served as a clerk for D.C. Circuit Judge Robert Bork from 1983 to 1984 and later became a partner in the Washington office of Sidley Austin.

20.　Kenneth W. Starr, *Preface* to Federal Preemption, States' Powers, National Interests, at xiv–xvi (Richard A. Epstein & Michael S. Greve eds., 2007).

21.　*Id.* at 105–07.

22.　Memorandum from Lewis F. Powell Jr. to Eugene B. Sydnor Jr. (Aug. 23, 1971), re-published with analysis as *The Powell Memo*, ReclaimDemocracy.org (Apr. 3, 2004), reclaimdemocracy.org .

23.　Linda S. Mullenix, *Strange Bedfellows: The Politics of Preemption*, 59 Case W. Res. L. Rev. 837, 847 (2009).

24.　Michael L. Rustad & Thomas H. Koenig, *Taming the Tort Monster: The American Civil Justice System as a Battleground of Social Theory*, 68 Brook. L. Rev. 1, 5 (2002).

25.　See more discussion of the work of the council in Chapter 3.

26.　President's Council on Competitiveness, Agenda for Civil Justice Reform in America 1 (1991).

27.　Rustad & Koenig, *supra* note 24, at 69.

28.　Sandra F. Gavin, *Stealth Tort Reform*, 42 Val. U. L. Rev. 431, 441–42 (2008).

29.　*Id.* at 443.

30.　Rustad & Koenig, *supra* note 24, at 74.

31. Walter K. Olson, The Rule of Lawyers: How the New Litigation Elite Threatens America's Rule of Law (2004); Mark A. Behrens & Phil S. Goldberg, *Stopping Asbestos Litigation Abuse*, 6 Engage 120 (2005) (criticizing "mass screening" for asbestos-related claims).

32. Lester Brickman, Lawyer Barons: What Their Contingency Fees Really Cost America (2011); Margaret A. Little, review of Lawyer Barons, 12 Engage 1 (2011).

33. Michael S. Greve, Harm-Less Lawsuits? What's Wrong with Consumer Class Actions (2005); *Government by Litigation: Are Class Actions Subverting the Political Process?*, 3 Engage 121 (2002) (transcript of a Federalist Society panel featuring Robert Goodlatte [R-VA], Viet Dinh, Mark F. Grady [Dean of George Mason University School of Law], Richard F. Scruggs, and Brian Brooks).

34. Victor E. Schwartz, Leah Lorber & Emily Laird, *Silica Litigation: Controls Are Needed to Curb the Potential for Unwarranted Claims*, 5 Engage 103 (2004) (counseling against allowing silica litigation to create the problems that asbestos litigation created; Schwartz frequently appears at Federalist Society events and was a participant in the panel "Is Overlawyering Overtaking Democracy?" at the 2007 National Lawyers Convention [*infra* note 43]); Bert W. Rein & Kristina R. Osterhaus, *Combating Bioterrorism: The Product Liability Threat* (Federalist Soc'y, White Paper, 2003), *available at* fed-soc.org; Richard A. Epstein, *The Unintended Revolution in Product Liability Law*, 10 Cardozo L. Rev. 2193 (1989).

35. Michael I. Krauss, *Punitive Damages and the Supreme Court: A Tragedy in Five Acts*, 4 Engage 118 (2003); Theodore J. Boutrous Jr. & Thomas H. Dupree Jr., *State Farm v. Campbell: Federalism and the Constitutional Limitations on Punitive Damages*, 3 Engage 110 (2002) ("punitive damage awards have spiraled out of control and often bear little relation to the corporate conduct supposedly deserving of punishment").

36. Karen R. Harned & Jeff A. Hall, *Mississippi Supreme Court to Rule on Constitutionality of Non-Economic Damage Caps*, Class Action Watch, Apr. 2010.

37. Karen R. Harned & Zeke J. Roeser, *Resurrect Rule 11*, 9 Engage 125 (2008) (criticizing 1993 amendments to Rule 11, Federal Rules of Civil Procedure, urging that sanctions for unsupported allegations in papers filed in court should be mandatory, not discretionary with the judge); Sherman Joyce, *The Lawsuit Abuse Reduction Act: A Sound Federal Reform*, 7 Engage 135 (2006) (Joyce has been the president of the American Tort Reform Association since 1994); John Thorne, *Twombly: Naked (Alleged) Conspiracy Does Not Strip Freedom of Unilateral Action*, 7 Engage 2 (2006).

38. *See, e.g.*, Megan L. Brown, *Are Nuisance Lawsuits to Address Climate Change Justiciable in the Federal Courts: Global Warming at the Supreme Court*, 12 Engage 90, 94 (2011) (Brown is a former member of the Federalism and Separation of Powers Practice Group's executive committee; here, she recommends that the Supreme Court "close the federal courthouse doors to nuisance suits based on alleged contributions to global warming"); David B. Rivkin Jr., Carlos Ramos-Mrosovsky & Matthew S. Raymer, *"Complaints" About the Weather: Why the Fifth Circuit's Panel Decision in Comer v. Murphy Oil Represents the Wrong Approach to the Challenge of Climate Change* (Federalist Soc'y, White Paper, 2010) (Rivkin is the cochair of the International Organizations Subcommittee of the International and National Security Law Practice Group); Little, *supra* note 12; Dwight J. Davis, Ann Driscoll & Jaime Schwartz, *"Fast Food": The Next Tobacco?*, 4 Engage 121, 125 (2003) (predicting it is likely that "jurors will hold plaintiffs accountable for their dietary selections and sedentary lifestyles"); Margaret A. Little, *A Most Dangerous Indiscretion: The Legal, Economic, and Political Legacy of the Governments' Tobacco Litigation*, 33 Conn. L. Rev. 1143 (2001); Robert A. Levy, *Pistol Whipped: Baseless Lawsuits, Foolish Laws*, 10 J.L. & Pol'y 1 (2001) (criticizing attempts

to control guns through litigation; Levy is a member of the Federalist Society's board of visitors and chairman of the Cato Institute's board of directors).

39. *Attorneys*, Shook, Hardy & Bacon, shb.com (last visited Aug. 16, 2012).

40. Rustad and Koenig describe, for example, how Richard Epstein took Gregory and Kalven's *Cases and Materials on Torts*, which had generally taken a favorable view toward the expansion of tort liability, and moved it in a conservative direction. Rustad & Koenig, *supra* note 24, at 85–86.

41. *See, e.g.*, Andrew C. Cook & Emily Kelchen, *State Court Challenges to Legislatively Enacted Tort Reforms* (Federalist Soc'y, White Paper, 2011), *available at* fed-soc.org; Victor E. Schwartz & Leah Lorber, *Judicial Nullification of Civil Justice Reform Violates the Fundamental Federal Constitutional Principle of Separation of Powers: How to Restore the Right Balance*, 32 Rutgers L.J. 907 (2001), *available at* fed-soc.org.

42. Rustad & Koenig, *supra* note 24, at 72–78.

43. Theodore Eisenberg, Walter K. Olson, Victor E. Schwartz, David C. Vladeck, & David M. Schizer, *Is Overlawyering Overtaking Democracy?—Event Audio/Video*, Federalist Soc'y (Nov. 16, 2007), fed-soc.org. Olson maintains his own website on the topic at overlawyered.com (last visited Aug. 14, 2012).

44. Mullenix, *supra* note 23, at 850.

45. Common Sense Legal Reforms Act of 1995, *available at* thomas.loc.gov (last visited Aug. 16, 2012).

46. Mullenix, *supra* note 23, at 852.

47. Thomas O. McGarity, *The Perils of Preemption*, Trial, Sept. 2008, at 20, 21 (2008).

48. Codified at 28 U.S.C. § 1332 (d) (2006).

49. The act established federal jurisdiction whenever any member of the class is from a different state than any defendant (in other words, jurisdiction based on diversity of citizenship is not defeated simply because some plaintiffs and defendants are from the same state) and computed the amount in controversy requirement based on total damages sought for all plaintiffs (in other words, there is no per plaintiff amount in controversy requirement).

50. The court must decline jurisdiction if more than two-thirds of the class members are citizens of the state where the action was filed, and either the "primary defendants" are from that state, or at least one defendant from whom significant relief is sought and whose alleged conduct forms a significant basis for the claims is a citizen of that state, and the principal injuries were incurred in that state. The court has discretion, based on several factors described in the statute, to decline jurisdiction if more than one-third but less than two-thirds of the class members and the primary defendants are citizens of the state where the action was filed. The act does not apply to class actions where the primary defendants are states or state officials against whom the court may be foreclosed from ordering relief, claims relating to corporate governance based on state law, and claims for securities violations.

51. Rep. Robert Goodlatte (R-VA) was a sponsor of one version of this legislation and described it at a Federalist Society panel three years before it was enacted, *supra* note 33.

52. *Id.*

53. Margaret Jane Porter, *The Lohr Decision: FDA Perspective and Position*, 52 Food & Drug L.J. 7, 11 (1997).

54. *See, e.g.*, Brief for the United States as Amicus Curiae Supporting Petitioners, *Aetna Health, Inc. v. Davila*, 542 U.S. 200 (2004) (Nos. 02–1845, 03–83), 2003 WL 23011479 (Employee Retirement Income Security Act of 1974 [ERISA] preempts suit by patient against HMO that provided health coverage under patient's employer's ERISA plan).

55. *See* Brief for the United States as Amicus Curiae Supporting Respondent, *Bates v. Dow Agrosciences LLC*, 544 U.S. 431 (2005) (No. 03–388), 2004 WL 2681684, at 20 (Federal Insecticide, Fungicide, and Rodenticide Act preempts claim by peanut farmers that herbicide that harmed their crops was improperly labeled).

56. Am. Ass'n for Just. (AAJ), Get Out of Jail Free: How the Bush Administration Helps Corporations Escape Accountability 6, 28–33 (listing the individual rules) (AAJ, 2008), *available at* justice.org .

57. Final Rule: Standard for the Flammability (Open-Flame) of Mattress Sets, 71 Fed. Reg. 13,472, 13,496 (Mar. 15, 2006) (codified at 16 C.F.R. pt. 1633).

58. Federal Motor Vehicle Safety Standards: Head Restraints, 72 Fed. Reg. 25,512. Other examples are described in Catherine M. Sharkey, *Federalism Accountability: "Agency-Forcing" Measures*, 58 Duke L.J. 2125 (2009).

59. Federal Motor Vehicle Safety Standards: Roof Crush Resistance, 70 Fed. Reg. 49,223 (proposed Aug. 23, 2005); Catherine M. Sharkey, *Federalism Accountability: "Agency-Forcing" Measures*, Legal Workshop, Duke L.J., July 13, 2009, *available at* legalworkshop.org. (This is a later editorial that updates Professor Sharkey's article, *supra* note 58).

60. Nina A. Mendelson, *A Presumption against Agency Preemption*, 102 NW. U. L. Rev. 695 (2008); Sharkey, *supra* note 58, at 2139, n.48; AAJ, *supra* note 56.

61. Margaret H. Clune, *Stealth Tort Reform: How the Bush Administration's Aggressive Use of the Preemption Doctrine Hurts Consumers* 1–2 (Ctr. for Progressive Regulation, White Paper, 2004).

62. Tamara Loomis, *Preemptive Strike*, American Lawyer (2008), americanlawyer.com (last visited Aug. 16, 2012).

63. FDA Requirements on Content and Format of Labeling for Human Prescription Drug and Biological Products, 71 Fed. Reg. 3,922, 3,934–36 (Jan. 24, 2006).

64. Victor E. Schwartz, Cary Silberman, Michael J. Hulka & Christopher E. Appel, *Marketing Pharmaceutical Products in the Twenty-First Century: An Analysis of the Continued Viability of Traditional Principles of Law in the Age of Direct-To-Consumer Advertising*, 32 Harv. J.L. & Pub. Pol'y 333, 385 (2009); Richard A. Epstein, *Why the FDA Must Preempt Tort Litigation: A Critique of Chevron Deference and a Response to Richard Nagareda*, 1 J. of Tort L. 5 (2006). Epstein was critical of the FDA and did not think that deference to the FDA's view of preemption was a reliable solution to the issue. He was unequivocal, however, that "we should all hope that preemption will cut the tort system of an area where it cannot do any systematic good." *Id.* at 33.

65. Sharkey, *supra* note 58, at 2139–40. Sharkey described how the NHTSA followed similar tactics. *Id.* at 2141–42.

66. Daniel E. Troy, *The Case for FDA Preemption, in* Federal Preemption, *supra* note 20, at 81–105.

67. *Id.* at 103.

68. Porter, *supra* note 53, at 11.

69. McGarity, *supra* note 18, at 157–58.

70. Maurice Hinchey News (July 13, 2004), ahrp.org/infomail/04/07/13a.php.

71. Evelyn Pringle, *Daniel Troy—Bush Administration's Preemption Gang—Part I*, LawyersandSettlements.com (Feb. 25, 2008, 6:45 AM), lawyersandsettlements.com; Amicus Brief for the United States in Support of the Defendant-Appellee and Cross-Appellant, *Motus v. Pfizer, Inc.*, 358 F.3d 659 (9th Cir. 2004) (Nos. 02–55372, 02–55498), 2002 WL 32303084 (arguing that suit for damages for suicide of depression sufferer who took Zoloft, based on failure to warn of such a danger, was preempted by FDA's "repeated and contemporaneous determination that there is no scientific basis for such warning").

72. Motion for Leave to File Brief as Amicus Curiae in Support of Petitioners, *Warner-Lambert Co. v. Wakefield*, 544 U.S. 1044 (2005) (No. 04–1047), 2005 WL 1364909. The decision of the court of appeals, sub nom *Desiano v. Warner-Lambert & Co.*, 467 F.3d 85 (2d Cir. 2006) (deciding that federal law did not preempt the common law claims in Michigan), was affirmed by an equally divided Supreme Court (Chief Justice Roberts did not sit on the case).

73. Brief of Petitioners, *Warner-Lambert Co. v. Kent*, 552 U.S. 440 (2008) (No. 06–1498), 2007 WL 4205142.

74. Brief for the United States as Amicus Curiae Supporting Petitioners, *Warner-Lambert Co. v. Kent*, 552 U.S. 440 (2008) (No. 06–1498), 2007 WL 4218889 (urging preemption where Michigan law generally provided that drug manufacturer is not liable in tort when FDA had approved the drug, unless manufacturer submitted inaccurate information and FDA would have denied approval or withdrawn it based on accurate information, on ground that state determination of whether manufacturer committed fraud on FDA would affect FDA approval process and response to fraud).

75. Daniel E. Troy, *State-Level Protection for Good-Faith Pharmaceutical Manufacturers* (2006), *available at* fed-soc.org.

76. *Wyeth v. Levine*, 555 U.S. 555 (2009).

77. Brief of John E. Calfee, Ernst R. Berndt, Robert Hahn, Tomas Philipson, Paul H. Rubin, and W. Kip Viscusi as Amici Curiae Supporting Petitioner, *Wyeth v. Levine*, 555 U.S. 555 (2009) (No. 06–1249), 2008 WL 2322237.

78. Brief of the Center for State Enforcement of Antitrust and Consumer Protection Laws, Inc. as Amicus Curiae in Support of Respondent, *Wyeth v. Levine*, 555 U.S. 555 (2009) (No. 06–1249), 2008 WL 3851615, at *5. Merrill had taken a position consistent with this brief in the 2006 Federalist Society debate on preemption, suggesting that there is a danger that federal agencies might displace too much state law, and that courts should serve as a counterweight to the tendency of an agency to push the limits of federal law. Cass et al., *supra* note 19, at 112.

79. *Id*. at 2. The brief documents the existence of this movement by citing an article by Catherine M. Sharkey, *Preemption by Preamble: Federal Agencies and the Federalization of Tort Law*, 56 DePaul L. Rev. 227 (2007).

80. Preemption: Memorandum for the Heads of Executive Departments and Agencies, 74 Fed. Reg. 24,693 (May 20, 2009).

81. Exec. Order No. 13,132, 64 Fed. Reg. 43,255 (Aug. 4, 1999).

82. Catherine M. Sharkey, *Inside Agency Preemption*, 110 Mich. L. Rev. 521, 531 (2012).

83. Catherine M. Sharkey and others refer to it as a "muddle." *Id*. at 524.

84. As solicitor general, Olson argued in favor of preemption in *Engine Mfrs. Ass'n v. South Coast Air Quality Mgmt. Dist.*, 541 U.S. 246 (2004), and against preemption in *Nixon v. Missouri Mun. League*, 541 U.S. 125 (2004). Prior to his government service, he argued in favor of preemption in *Cal. Fed. Sav. & Loan Ass'n v. Guerra*, 479 U.S. 272 (1987), and *California v. ARC Am. Corp.*, 490 U.S. 93 (1989). After his service, he argued in favor of preemption in *Altria Grp. v. Good*, 555 U.S. 70 (2008); *Riegel v. Medtronic, Inc.*, 552 U.S. 312 (2008); and *Wagnon v. Prairie Band Potawatomi Nation*, 546 U.S. 95 (2005).

85. The statute is codified at 21 U.S.C. § 360c et seq.

86. *Medtronic, Inc. v. Lohr*, 518 U.S. 470 (1996).

87. *Riegel*, 552 U.S. at 322.

88. *Id*. at 334 (Ginsburg, J., dissenting).

89. Justice Ginsburg joined the dissenters, for example, in cases where the majority limited federal power under the Tenth Amendment, such as *Printz v. United States*, 521 U.S.

898 (1997) (court held Brady Bill, imposing gun purchase background check responsibilities on state officials, unconstitutional) or under the Eleventh Amendment and
the sovereign immunity of the states, such as *Bd. of Trustees of University of Alabama v.
Garrett*, 531 U.S. 356 (2001) (court held application of Americans with Disabilities Act
to state employees unconstitutional).

90. *Riegel*, 552 U.S. at 337 (Ginsburg, J., dissenting) (internal quotation marks omitted).
91. *Id.* at 326.
92. *Id.* at 330–31 (Stevens, J., concurring).
93. *Altria*, 555 U.S. at 87.
94. *Williamson v. Mazda Motor of Am.*, 131 S. Ct. 1131 (2011).
95. *Id.*; *Geier v. Am. Honda Motor Co.*, 529 U.S. 861 (2000); Brief of the Alliance of
Automobile Manufacturers, Association of International Automobile Manufacturers,
Inc., and National Automobile Dealers Association as Amici Curiae in Support of
Respondents, *Williamson*, 131 S. Ct. 1131 (No. 08–1314), 2010 WL 3820816.
96. Federalist Society members filed amicus briefs in support of preemption in *Geier*. Ted
Olson, representing the Chamber of Commerce, argued that "recent trends in state
tort law demonstrate an *enhanced* need for vigorous enforcement of implied preemption principles in order to shield our national economy from the increasing burdens
placed upon it by unconstrained, arbitrary, inconsistent, and excessive tort verdicts and
liability rules." Brief for the Chamber of Commerce of the United States of America
as Amicus Curiae in Support of Respondent, *Geier*, 529 U.S. 861 (No. 98–1811), 1999
WL 1049891, at *5–6. Brett Kavanaugh and Thomas W. Merrill, on behalf of associations of domestic and international automobile manufacturers, argued that a failure to
preempt state tort liability would lead to an "intolerable" result for the manufacturers.
Brief of the Alliance of Automobile Manufacturers and the Association of International
Automobile Manufacturers, Inc., as Amici Curiae in Support of Respondents, *Geier*,
529 U.S. 861 (No. 98–1811), 1999 WL 1049898, at *2.
97. This is the conclusion that Catherine M. Sharkey has reached. Sharkey, *supra* note 82.
98. 9 U.S.C. § 2.
99. *See, e.g.*, *Hall St. Assocs. v. Mattel, Inc.*, 552 U.S. 576 (2008) (grounds provided in FAA
for vacating, correcting, or modifying arbitration award constitute exclusive grounds
for doing so).
100. *Circuit City Stores, Inc. v. Adams*, 532 U.S. 105 (2001).
101. 9 U.S.C. § 1.
102. Brief of the States of California, Arizona, Arkansas, Colorado, Connecticut, Idaho,
Illinois, Iowa, Massachusetts, Minnesota, Mississippi, Missouri, Montana, Nevada,
New Jersey, New York, North Dakota, Pennsylvania, Vermont, Washington, and West
Virginia, as Amici Curiae in Support of Respondent, *Circuit City Stores*, 532 U.S. 105
(No. 99–1379), 2000 WL 1369472.
103. *Penn Plaza LLC v. Pyett*, 556 U.S. 247 (2009).
104. Erika Birg, *Waging War against Binding Arbitration: Will Trial Lawyers Win the Battle?*
4 ENGAGE 112 (2003). Birg is also on the executive board of the Atlanta chapter of the
Federalist Society, according to her profile on linkedin.com (last visited Aug. 15, 2012).
105. *AT&T Mobility LLC v. Concepcion*, 131 S. Ct. 1740 (2011).
106. *Discover Bank v. Superior Court*, 36 Cal. 4th 148, 162–63 (2005).
107. 9 U.S.C. § 2.
108. *AT&T Mobility*, 131 S. Ct. at 1748.
109. Brief of the Center for Class Action Fairness as Amicus Curiae in Support of Petitioner
AT&T Mobility, 131 S. Ct. 1740 (No. 09–893), 2010 WL 3167314.
110. *Id.* at *4–6.

111. Brief of Amici Curiae Marygrace Coneff et al. in Support of Respondents, *AT&T Mobility*, 131 S. Ct. 1740 (No. 09–893), 2010 WL 3973886, at *9–10, citing data from discovery in the Coneff class action against AT&T.

112. Brief of the Center for Class Action Fairness, *supra* note 109, at *28.

113. Brief of CTIA-The Wireless Association® as Amicus Curiae in Support of Petitioner, *AT&T Mobility*, 131 S. Ct. 1740 (No. 09–893), 2010 WL 709799.

114. Brief of DRI-The Voice of the Defense Bar as Amicus Curiae in Support of Petitioner *AT&T Mobility*, 131 S. Ct. 1740 (No. 09–893), 2010 WL 709798. According to the brief, DRI is an international organization of more than twenty-two thousand attorneys involved in the defense of civil litigation.

115. Brief of Distinguished Law Professors as Amici Curiae in Support of Petitioner, *AT&T Mobility*, 131 S. Ct. 1740 (No. 09–893), 2010 WL 3183856.

116. Brian T. Fitzpatrick, *Did the Supreme Court Just Kill the Class Action?*, Class Action Watch, Sept. 2011, at 1 (emphasis in original).

117. *Stoneridge Inv. Partners v. Scientific-Atlanta, Inc.*, 552 U.S. 148 (2008).

118. Joint Appendix, 94a–97a.

119. Section 10(b) of the Securities Exchange Act, 15 U.S.C. § 78j.

120. *Superintendent of Ins. of N.Y. v. Bankers Life & Casualty Co.*, 404 U.S. 6, 13, n.9 (1971).

121. *Cent. Bank of Denver*, 511 U.S. 164.

122. *Stoneridge Inv. Partners*, 552 U.S. at 160.

123. *Id.* at 161.

124. *Id.* at 163.

125. Brief of Ohio, Texas, and thirty other states and commonwealths as Amici Curiae in Support of Petitioner, *Stoneridge Inv. Partners*, 552 U.S. 148 (No. 06–43), 2007 WL 1957413 at *1.

126. Brief for Change to Win and the CtW Investment Group as Amici Curiae in Support of Petitioner, *Stoneridge Inv. Partners*, 552 U.S. 148 (No. 06–43), 2007 WL 1701933, at *2.

127. Videos of the symposium and debate are available at *Symposium: Scheme Liability, Section 10(b), and Stoneridge Investment Partners v. Scientific Atlanta*, Federalist Soc'y, fed-soc.org/publications/id.488/default.asp (last visited Aug. 15, 2012).

128. Richard A. Epstein, *Primary and Secondary Liability under Securities Law: The Stoneridge Investment Saga*, PointofLaw.com (Oct. 9, 2007), pointoflaw.com /columns/archives/004373.php.

129. Brief for the United States as Amicus Curiae Supporting Affirmance, *Stoneridge Inv. Partners*, 552 U.S. 148 (No. 06–43), 2007 WL 2329639, at *9–10.

130. Brief of the Washington Legal Foundation as Amicus Curiae in Support of Respondents, *Stoneridge Inv. Partners*, 552 U.S. 148 (No. 06–43), 2007 WL 2363255, at *3–4.

131. *Id.* at *5.

132. Larry Obhof, *Stoneridge Investment Partners: The Supreme Court Rejects "Scheme Liability,"* 9 Engage 118 (2008); Class Action Watch, Mar. 2008, at 1.

CHAPTER 4

1. *Parents Involved in Cmty. Schs v. Seattle Sch. Dist. No. 1*, 551 U.S. 701 (2007). The court consolidated the Seattle case with *Meredith v. Jefferson Co. Board of Education* for decision.

2. Lino A. Graglia, *Title VII of the Civil Rights Act of 1964: From Prohibiting to Requiring Racial Discrimination in Employment*, 14 Harv. J. L. & Pub. Pol'y 68, 71 (1991).

3. Seattle's plan allocated slots in oversubscribed high schools and Jefferson County's plan made elementary school assignments and handled transfer requests. Seattle

employed race as a "tiebreaker" between applicants at oversubscribed schools to maintain a white/nonwhite racial composition for each school that was within ten percentage points of the district's overall composition. Jefferson County assigned students to schools in part based on the racial guidelines in the district's current plan. When a school reached the "extremes of the racial guidelines," a student whose race would contribute to racial imbalance would not be assigned to that school. Jefferson County also denied transfers between schools on the basis of the racial guidelines.

4. Lee Cokorinos, The Assault on Diversity: An Organized Challenge to Racial and Gender Justice 3 (2003). Cokorinos has written a far more detailed account of the history of this campaign than it is possible to provide in this chapter. Readers interested in a full description of the individual lawyers and officials, organizations, funding sources, and the relationships between them that make up this conservative network should consult his book.

5. Edwin Meese III, *Civil Rights, Economic Progress, and Common Sense*, 14 Harv. J.L. & Pub. Pol'y, 150 (1991).

6. Nina J. Easton, Gang of Five: Leaders at the Center of the Conservative Crusade 109 (2000).

7. Clint Bolick, Unfinished Business: A Civil Rights Strategy for America's Third Century 11 (1990). Bolick's arguments in this book are also very briefly summarized in Clint Bolick, *Unfinished Business: A Civil Rights Strategy for America's Third Century*, 14 Harv. J.L. & Pub. Pol'y. 137 (1991).

8. *Id.* at 5.

9. Gerald A. Reynolds, *Gerald Reynolds reviews* Right Turn: William Bradford Reynolds, The Reagan Administration, and Black Civil Rights *by Raymond Wolters*, C.R. Prac. Grp. Newsl., May 1, 1997.

10. Robert Woodson, *Affirmative Action Is No Civil Right*, 19 Harv. J.L. & Pub. Pol'y 773, 775 (1996) (footnote omitted).

11. *Id.* at 777–78.

12. Bolick, *supra* note 7, at 7.

13. *Id.* at 25.

14. *Lochner v. New York*, 198 U.S. 45, 75 (1905) (Holmes, J., dissenting). Spencer was an influential philosopher in the nineteenth century.

15. Bolick, *supra* note 7, at 26.

16. *Id.* at 29.

17. *Parents Involved*, 551 U.S. at 747.

18. *Id.*

19. *Id.*

20. Adam Liptak, *The Same Words, but Differing Views*, N.Y. Times, June 29, 2007.

21. Robert L. Carter, *Brown's Legacy: Fulfilling the Promise of Equal Education*, 76 J. Negro Educ. 240, 249–50 (July 1, 2007).

22. *Id.* at 241.

23. *Korematsu v. United States*, 323 U.S. 214 (1944).

24. *City of Richmond v. J.A. Croson, Co.*, 488 U.S. 469 (1989); *Adarand Constructors, Inc. v. Pena*, 515 U.S. 200 (1995).

25. *Parents Involved*, 551 U.S. at 829 (Breyer, J., dissenting).

26. *Adarand Constructors*, 515 U.S. at 243 (Stevens, J., dissenting).

27. *Gratz v. Bollinger*, 539 U.S. 244, 298 (2003) (Ginsburg, J., dissenting).

28. *Id.*

29. *Id.* at 299–301 (footnotes and citations omitted).

30. *Parents Involved*, 551 U.S. at 745–46 (internal citations omitted).

31. *Adarand Constructors*, 515 U.S. at 240 (Thomas, J., concurring).

32. *Id.* 240–41.

33. *Parents Involved*, 551 U.S. at 757 (citing *Parents Involved in Cmty. Schs. v. Seattle Sch. Dist. No. 1*, 426 F.3d 1162, 1193 (9th Cir. 2005) (Kozinski, J., concurring); *Comfort v. Lynn Sch. Comm.*, 418 F.3d 1, 28–29 (1st Cir. 2005) (Boudin, J., concurring)).

34. *Parents Involved*, 551 U.S. at 758 (Thomas, J., concurring).

35. *Id.* at 746.

36. *Id.* at 867 (Breyer, J., dissenting).

37. A. Leon Higginbotham Jr., Shades of Freedom: Racial Politics and Presumptions of the American Legal Process 9 (1996).

38. As Professor Robertson has noted, Judge Higginbotham was "an ardent and outspoken defender of desegregation and affirmative action" who believed that "affirmative action promoted valuable academic diversity by ensuring that Americans of all races would have access to educational opportunities, allowing them the opportunity to fulfill their intellectual potential." Elbert L. Robertson, *Antitrust as Anti-Civil Rights? Reflections on Judge Higginbotham's Perspective on the "Strange" Case of United States v. Brown University*, 20 Yale L. & Pol'y Rev. 399, 400 (2002).

39. Pamela S. Karlan, *What Can Brown° Do for You?: Neutral Principles and the Struggle over the Equal Protection Clause*, 58 Duke L.J. 1049, 1052–53 (2009).

40. *Id.* at 1063.

41. *Id.*

42. Stephen L. Carter, *When Victims Happen To Be Black*, 97 Yale L.J. 420, 433–34 (1988).

43. *Regents of the Univ. of Cal. v. Bakke*, 438 U.S. 265 (1978).

44. *Grutter v. Bollinger*, 539 U.S. 306 (2003).

45. *Id.* at 783 (Kennedy, J., concurring).

46. *Parents Involved*, 551 U.S. at 725.

47. *Swann v. Charlotte-Mecklenburg Bd. of Educ.*, 402 U.S. 1, 16 (1971).

48. *Parents Involved*, 551 U.S. at 823 (Breyer, J., concurring).

49. *Id.* at 725–26.

50. *Id.* at 730. (internal citations and footnote omitted).

51. *Id.* at 806 (Breyer, J., dissenting).

52. *Id.* at 838–40 (Breyer, J., concurring).

53. *Id.* at 748 (Thomas, J., concurring).

54. *Id.* at 773–74.

55. Bolick, *supra* note 7, at 30.

56. Bolick, *supra* note 7, at 139.

57. *Parents Involved*, 551 U.S. at 750, n.3 (Thomas, J., concurring).

58. Lino A. Graglia, *Grutter and Gratz: Race Preference to Increase Racial Representation Held "Patently Unconstitutional" Unless Done Subtly Enough in the Name of Pursuing "Diversity,"* 78 Tul. L. Rev. 2037, 2049 (2004).

59. *Id.* 2038.

60. Graglia, *supra* note 2, at 76.

61. *Id.* 2050–51 (internal footnote omitted).

62. *Id.* 2042 (internal citation omitted).

63. *Id.* 2045.

64. Lino A. Graglia, *Fraud by the Supreme Court: Racial Discrimination by a State Institution of Higher Education Upheld on "Diversity" Grounds*, 37 Loy. U. Chi. L.J. 57, 71 (2004).

65. Graglia, *supra* note 58, at 2051.

66. Brief for the United States as Amicus Curiae Supporting Petitioners, *Wygant v. Jackson Bd. of Educ.*, 476 U.S. 267 (1986) (No. 84–1340), 1985 WL 669739 at *4.

67. Off. of Legal Pol'y, Dep't of Just., Report to the Attorney General: Justice Without Law: A Reconsideration of the "Broad Equitable Powers" of the Federal Court 132 (1988). The Reagan administration OLP reports are discussed at greater length in Chapter 2.

68. *Parents Involved*, 551 U.S. at 731. Roberts relied in part on a similar conclusion previously articulated by Justice O'Connor: "[A] governmental agency's interest in remedying 'societal' discrimination, that is, discrimination not traceable to its own actions, cannot be deemed sufficiently compelling to pass constitutional muster"). *Id.* at 731–32 (citing *Wygant*, 476 U.S. at 288 (O'Connor, J., concurring)).

69. For a good discussion of institutional racism, see Eva Paterson & Susan Serrano, *Cuyahoga Falls v. Buckeye: The Supreme Court's "Intent Doctrine"—Undermining Viable Discrimination Claims and Remedies for People of Color, in* We Dissent 54 (Michael Avery ed., 2009).

70. Graglia, *supra* note 2, at 73–74.

71. Easton, *supra* note 6, at 194.

72. Bolick, *supra* note 7, at 20 (citing *Thomas Paine, Dissertation on the First Principles of Government, in* Burke and Paine on Revolution and the Rights of Man 200 [Robert B. Dishman ed., 1971]).

73. *Adarand Constructors*, 515 U.S. at 240 (Thomas, J., concurring).

74. *Parents Involved*, 551 U.S. at 743.

75. Roger Clegg, review of America in Black and White by Stephan and Abigail Thernstrom, C.R. Prac. Grp. Newsl., May 1, 1998.

76. Dinesh D'Souza, *Improving Culture to End Racism*, 19 Harv. J.L. & Pub. Pol'y, 785, 789 (1996).

77. *Id.* at 789–90.

78. *Id.* at 794.

79. Brian W. Jones, *A Supreme Fallacy: "Diversity" and the High Court*, C.R. Prac. Grp. Newsl., May 1, 1999.

80. Laurence H. Silberman, *The D.C. Circuit Task Force on Gender, Race, and Ethnic Bias: Political Correctness Rebuffed*, 19 Harv. J.L. & Pub. Pol'y 759, 763 (1996). Judge Silberman's late wife, Ricky Gaull Silberman, was a former chair of the Independent Women's Forum board of directors and was appointed by President Reagan to the EEOC in 1984.

81. *Washington v. Davis*, 426 U.S. 229, 239 (1976). For a critique of this principle, see Paterson & Serrano, *supra* note 69, at 54.

82. Off. of Legal Pol'y, Dep't of Just., Report to the Attorney General: The Constitution in the Year 2000 (1988). The Reagan administration OLP reports are discussed at greater length in Chapter 2.

83. *Id.* at 50.

84. *Id.* at 54.

85. Paterson & Serrano, *supra* note 69, at 56–57.

86. Debera Carlton Harrell, *School District Pulls Web Site After Examples of Racism Spark Controversy*, Seattle Post-Intelligencer, June 2, 2006.

87. *Id.*

88. *Parents Involved*, 551 U.S. at 731.

89. Carter, *supra* note 21, at 240.

90. *City of Richmond*, 488 U.S. at 552–53 (Marshall, J., dissenting).

91. *Plessy v. Ferguson*, 163 U.S. 537, 559 (1896) (Harlan, J., dissenting).

92. Jamin B. Raskin, *From "Colorblind" White Supremacy to American Multiculturalism*, 19 Harv. J.L. & Pub. Pol'y 743, 744 (1996).

93. Goodwin Liu, *"History Will be Heard": An Appraisal of the Seattle/Louisville Decision*, 2 Harv. L. & Pol'y Rev. 53, 55 (2008).

94. *Id.* at 56.

95. In this connection Liu cites *Pace v. Alabama*, 106 U.S. 583 (1883), sustaining a statute that punished adultery and fornication more severely when engaged in by interracial couples, and *Cumming v. Bd. of Educ.*, 175 U.S. 528 (1899), upholding a racially separate and unequal educational system. *Id.* at 58–60.

96. *Parents Involved*, 551 U.S. at 788 (Kennedy, J., concurring).

97. Glenn C. Loury, *Individualism before Multiculturalism*, 19 Harv. J.L. & Pub. Pol'y 723, 730 (1996).

98. *Id.* at 725.

99. *Id.*

100. *Id.* at 724.

101. *Id.* at 729.

102. Raskin, *supra* note 92, at 748.

103. *Id.* at 745, 749.

104. *Id.* at 747.

105. Kimberly Schuld, *Dangerous Waters in the (Title IX) Safe Harbor*, C.R. Prac. Grp. Newsl., Aug. 1, 1999.

106. Melinda Sidak, *Brown University v. Cohen: A Pyrrhic Victory for Feminists*, C.R. Prac. Grp. Newsl., Dec. 1, 1997.

107. Ms. Sidak is a Federalist Society member; she met her husband, Greg Sidak, at a Federalist Society luncheon in Washington, D.C. Phillip Longman, *Reagan's Disappearing Bureaucrats*, N.Y. Times Mag., Feb. 14, 1988, *available at* nytimes.com.

108. Jennifer C. Braceras, *Affirmative Action & Gender Equity: New Rules Under Title IX?* C.R. Prac. Grp. Newsl., May 1, 1999.

109. Notes of speech on file with authors.

110. *See, e.g.*, Jacqueline E. King, Gender Equity in Higher Education: 2006 (Amer. Council on Educ., Ctr. for Pol'y Analysis 2006); Christianne Corbett, Catherine Hill & Andresse St. Rose, Where the Girls Are: The Facts about Gender Equity in Education (Am. Ass'n of Univ. Women 2008).

111. Corbett et al., *supra* note 110, at 2.

112. 20 U.S.C. § 1681(2009) (the statute provides for several exceptions).

113. *Cohen v. Brown Univ.*, 991 F.2d 888, 903–04 (1st Cir. 1993).

114. *Cohen v. Brown Univ.*, 809 F. Supp. 978, 991–93 (D.R.I. 1992)

115. *Cohen v. Brown Univ.*, 101 F.3d 155 (1st Cir. 1996).

116. F. Carolyn Graglia, *The Housewife as Pariah*, 18 Harv. J.L. & Pub. Pol'y 509, 515 (1995).

117. *Id.* at 516.

118. 518 U.S. 515 (1996); Anita K. Blair, *US v. Virginia: The New and Improved Equal Protection Clause*, C.R. Prac. Grp. Newsl., May 1, 1997.

119. *Civil Rights Practice Group Executive Committee Contact Information*, Federalist Soc'y, fed-soc.org (last visited Aug. 16, 2012).

120. In addition, two articles concerned the right to bear arms under the Second Amendment, one noted that the Fourth Circuit Court of Appeals had held unconstitutional the civil suit provisions of the Violence against Women Act, and one criticized the proposed Hate Crimes Prevention Act.

121. Cokorinos, *supra* note 4, at 8, 22–29.

122. Reynolds, *supra* note 9. Wolters's book provides a sympathetic account of the Reagan administration's policies with respect to civil rights. *Id.*

123. Edwin Meese III, *Dialogue, Reagan's Legal Revolutionary*, 3 Green Bag 2d 193, 199 (2000).

124. *Id.*

125. *See Nomination of William Bradford Reynolds to be Associate Attorney General of the United States: Hearings Before the S. Judiciary Comm.*, 99th Cong., 99–3374 (June 4, 5, and 18, 1985) [hereinafter Senate Hearings].

126. People for the Am. Way Found., The Federalist Society: From Obscurity to Power, (Aug. 2001), ratical.org/ratville/CAH/feddieSoc.html (citing *Senate Hearings*, *supra* note 125, at 887, 971).

127. Easton, *supra* note 6, at179.

128. *Id.* 195.

129. *Id.* 193.

130. *Id.* 196.

131. *Id.*

132. *Id.* at 197.

133. Cokorinos, *supra* note 4, at 26.

134. Brief of the United States, *supra* note 66, at 4, 8.

135. Brief for the Equal Employment Opportunity Commission, *Local 28, Sheet Metal Workers v. EEOC*, 478 U.S. 421 (1986) (No. 84–1656), 1985 WL 670084, at *10–11, *23–36.

136. *Id.* at 24.

137. Brief for the United States, *United States v. Paradise*, 480 U.S. 149 (1987) (No. 85–999), 1986 WL 727614.

138. *Id.* at *13.

139. *City of Richmond*, 488 U.S. 469.

140. For an illuminating history of the development of conservative public interest law firms, see Steven M. Teles, The Rise of the Conservative Legal Movement: The Battle for Control of the Law (2008).

141. "The Independent Women's Forum is on a mission to expand the conservative coalition, both by increasing the number of women who understand and value the benefits of limited government, personal liberty, and free markets, and by countering those who seek to ever-expand government in the name of protecting women." *About IWF*, iwf.org (last visited Aug. 16, 2012).

142. Cokorinos, *supra* note 4, at 21.

143. *Id.* at 31–117.

144. *Griggs v. Duke Power Co.*, 401 U.S. 424 (1971).

145. Edwin Meese III, *The Imperial Judiciary—And What Congress Can Do About It*, 81 Pol'y Rev. (Jan. 1, 1997), hoover.org/publications.

146. 490 U.S. 642 (1989).

147. *Id.* at 647.

148. *Id.* at 663, n.4. (Stevens, J., dissenting).

149. Brief for the United States as Amicus Curiae Supporting Petitioners, *Wards Cove Packing, Inc. v. Atonio*, 490 U.S. 642 (1989) (No. 87–1387), 1988 WL 1026056.

150. The "burden of proof" in a civil case includes two concepts—the "burden of production" and the "burden of persuasion." In most cases, the plaintiff always has the burden of persuasion. That means that at the end of a trial, the burden is on the plaintiff to persuade the judge or the jury that he has established all the elements of his claim by a preponderance of the evidence. The burden of production, however, can shift back and forth between the two sides. That means that once the plaintiff has introduced evidence on the elements of his claim, the burden may shift to the defendant

to produce evidence to establish its defense. If it has no such evidence, the plaintiff wins the case. But once the defendant offers evidence to support its defense, it has met the production burden. In that case, the plaintiff wins only if he meets the burden of persuasion—that is, if after considering all the evidence from both sides, the judge or the jury is persuaded by a preponderance of the evidence that the plaintiff has proved his case. In some cases, however, where the defendant has to establish what is known as an "affirmative defense," the burden of persuasion shifts to the defendant. One of the questions in *Wards Cove* was whether the business necessity defense was an affirmative defense that shifted the burden of persuasion to the defendant. The court held that it was not, and that the plaintiff retained the burden of persuasion. Who has the ultimate burden of persuasion is a crucially important question in close cases.

151. Brief for the Center for Civil Rights as Amicus Curiae in Support of Petitioners, *Wards Cove*, 490 U.S. 642 (No. 87–1387), 1988 WL 1026048.

152. On the evidence of race-labeling, *see* Brief of Respondents, *Wards Cove*, 490 U.S. 642 (No. 87–1387), 1988 WL 1026081, at *6. On the manipulation of labor pools, *see, e.g.*, the analysis in Brief for the American Civil Liberties Union, National Women's Law Center, Now Legal Defense and Education Fund, Women's Legal Defense Fund, Amici Curiae, on Behalf of Respondents, *Wards Cove*, 490 U.S. 642 (No. 87–1387), 1988 WL 1026070, at *13–30.

153. *Wards Cove*, 490 U.S. at 676 (Stevens, J., dissenting).

154. *Id.* at 652.

155. Brief for the Center for Civil Rights, *supra* note 151, at *16–17.

156. *Id.* at 16.

157. *Wards Cove*, 490 U.S. at 673 (Stevens, J., dissenting)

158. On "business necessity," *see Griggs*, 401 U.S. at 431. On "essential to job performance," *see Dothard v. Rawlinson*, 433 U.S. 321, 331 (1977).

159. Brief for the United States, *supra* note 149, at *25.

160. 42 U.S.C. § 2000e-2(k) (1994).

161. Amos N. Jones & D. Alexander Ewing, *The Ghost of Wards Cove: The Supreme Court, The Bush Administration, and the Ideology Undermining Title VII*, 21 Harv. BlackLetter L.J. 163 (2005).

162. *Id.* at 170–71.

163. *Wards Cove*, 490 U.S. at 662 (Blackmun, J., dissenting).

164. *Hopwood v. Texas*, 78 F.3d 932 (5th Cir. 1996).

165. *Grutter v. Bollinger*, 539 U.S. 306 (2003).

166. *Adarand Constructors, Inc. v. Pena*, 515 U.S. 200 (1995).

167. *Bakke*, 438 U.S. 265.

168. *Sweatt v. Painter*, 339 U.S. 629 (1950).

169. *Hopwood*, 78 F.3d at 952.

170. *Id.* at 953 (citing *Md. Troopers Ass'n v. Evans*, 993 F.2d 1072, 1079 (4th Cir. 1993)).

171. *Hopwood v. Texas*, 236 F.3d 256, 272 (5th Cir. 2000).

172. *Gratz*, 539 U.S. 244.

173. *Id.* at 326–27.

174. *Id.* at 328.

175. *Id.* at 330.

176. *Id.* at 335–36.

177. *Id.* at 323–24.

178. *Id.* at 341–42.

179. *Id.* at 343.

180. *Grutter*, 539 U.S. at 346–47 (Scalia, J., concurring & dissenting).

181. *Id.* at 350 (Thomas, J., dissenting); *id.* at 355, n.3; (Thomas, J., dissenting).

182. *Id.* at 371–74 (Thomas, J., dissenting).

183. Conservatives would also win a significant victory in *Ricci v. DeStefano*, 557 U.S. 557 (2009), the New Haven firefighters case. There the court held that concern about a potential disparate impact claim by African American firefighters in connection with a promotion examination did not justify disregarding the examination to the detriment of white and Hispanic firefighters who had done well on it. The court said that concern about disparate impact litigation could only justify using race to make employment decisions where there is a "strong basis in evidence" to believe the employer would be held liable for a disparate impact. Several Federalist Society members and allies wrote amicus briefs in the case arguing that New Haven's rejection of the test results was illegal. Amicus Brief of the Center for Individual Rights, the Center for Equal Opportunity, and the American Civil Rights Institute in Support of Petitioners, *Ricci*, 557 U.S. 557 (Nos. 07–1428, 08–328), 2009 WL 564458; Brief of the Cato Institute, Reason Foundation, and the Individual Rights Foundation as Amici Curiae in Support of Petitioners, *Ricci*, 557 U.S. 557 (Nos. 07–1428, 08–328), 2009 WL 507012; Brief Amicus Curiae of Law Professors and other Academics in Support of Petitioners, *Ricci*, 557 U.S. 557 (Nos. 07–1428, 08–328), 2009 WL 564457.

184. Cokorinos, *supra* note 4, at 20.

185. Shaw was lead counsel for the coalition of African American and Latino students in *Gratz v. Bollinger*, the University of Michigan undergraduate admissions affirmative action case. The description of this panel is based on notes on file with the authors. Videos of the panel are available through fed-soc.org.

186. Chavez's views were echoed by conservative pundit David Horowitz on his "Newsreal" blog, in *Fire General Casey*, David's Blog (Nov. 9, 2009, 7:24 AM), newsrealblog.com.

187. The lawsuit in question was ultimately settled when the Massachusetts Department of Correction agreed to stop using the challenged physical abilities test, to consider women who failed it for future employment with retroactive seniority, and to pay $736,000 in damages to women who failed the test. The DOJ's announcement of the settement terms is available at justice.gov (last visited Aug. 15, 2012).

188. Roger Clegg, *Unfinished Business: The Bush Administration and Racial Preferences*, 32 Harv. J.L. & Pub. Pol'y 971, 972 (2009).

189. Cokorinos, *supra* note 4, at 35 (citing data from the California Secretary of State's Office).

190. *Id.* at 35–36.

191. Tom Wood, *How Honest Is the Debate over the California Civil Rights Initiative?* C.R. Prac. Group Newsl., Dec. 1, 1996.

192. Easton, *supra* note 6, at 333.

193. *Id.* at 330.

194. German is an acknowledged Federalist Society member. *G. Michael "Mike" German: Candidate for United States Representative, District 8*, League of Women Voters (Nov. 4, 2002, 8:24 PM), smartvoter.org/2002/11/05/ca/state/vote/german_g/.

195. In July 2009, Gary G. Kreep called for a mass campaign of fax communications to the attorney generals of every state to investigate the alleged fraud surrounding the location of President Barack Obama's birth and announced the USJF campaign on this issue. *From the Desk of Gary G. Kreep*, The Steady Drip (July 26, 2009, 12:45 AM), the steadydrip.blogspot.com. In 2009, Kevin T. Snider was chief counsel for the Pacific Justice Institute, which specializes in the defense of religious freedom, parental rights, and other civil liberties.

196. The appellate briefs were signed by Michael E. Rosman, Hans Bader, Manuel S. Klausner, Michael A. Carvin, Charles J. Cooper, Michael W. Kirk, and David H. Thompson.

197. *Coal. for Econ. Equity v. Wilson*, 122 F.3d 692 (9th Cir. 1997).

198. Hans Bader, *The California Civil Rights Initiative Goes to Court*, C.R. Prac. Group Newsl., May 1, 1997.

199. Ward Connerly, *The American Civil Rights Institute: Taking CCRI to the National Stage*, C.R. Prac. Group Newsl., May 1, 1997.

200. The Bradley Foundation, the John M. Olin Foundation, the Sarah Scaife Foundation, and the Donner Foundation made several significant six-figure contributions to the funding of ACRI. Cokorinos, *supra* note 4, at 32.

201. Charlie Savage, *Affirmative-Action Foe Is Facing Allegations of Financial Misdeeds*, N.Y. Times, Jan. 17, 2012. The article describes allegations of financial misconduct made, ironically, by Jennifer Gratz, who went to work for ACRI after winning her case against the University of Michigan.

202. Charles T. Canady, *The Civil Rights Act of 1997*, C.R. Prac. Group Newsl., Dec. 1, 1997.

203. Ward Connerly, *Achieving Equal Treatment through the Ballot Box*, 32 Harv. J.L. & Pub. Pol'y 105, 111–12 (2009).

204. *Id.* at 53.

205. *Id.* at 234.

206. *Parents Involved*, 551 U.S. at 782, n.30 (Thomas, J., concurring).

207. *Id.*

208. *Id.* at 263.

209. Cokorinos, *supra* note 4, at 45; Easton, *supra* note 6, at 399.

210. U.S. Comm'n on Civil Rights (USCCR), usccr.gov (last visited Aug. 15, 2012).

211. *Gerald A. Reynolds*, USCCR, usccr.gov (last visited Aug. 15, 2012).

212. Brief of the Center for New Black Leadership as *Amicus Curiae* in Support of Petitioners, *Grutter v. Bollinger*, 539 U.S. 306 (Nos. 02-241, 02-516), *available at* supreme.lp.findlaw.com (last visited Aug. 15, 2012).

213. Biographies of the commissioners can be found at usccr.gov.

214. In 2003, the commission stated, "Today's Supreme Court decisions in the University of Michigan affirmative action cases are consistent with the United States Commission on Civil Rights' longstanding support of diversity and equal education opportunity." Press release, USCCR (June 23, 2003), usccr.gov/pubs/pubsndx.htm.

215. USCCR, Affirmative Action in American Law Schools (June 16, 2006), usccr.gov/pubs/AALSreport.pdf.

216. *Id.* at 5–7,141–44.

217. ABA Council of the Section of Legal Education and Admissions, Standard 212, *Id.* at 1–2.

218. Letter from Gerald A. Reynolds, Chair, and Jennifer C. Braceras, Peter N. Kirsanow & Ashley L. Taylor Jr., Commissioners, USCCR, to Sally Stroup, Assistant Secretary for Postsecondary Education, USCCR (Mar. 20, 2006), usccr.gov/correspd/060606Letter Chairetal.pdf, and letter from Abigail Thernstrom, Vice Chair, USCCR, to Stroup, USCCR (Mar. 8, 2006), usccr.gov/correspd/060606LetterVCThernstrom.pdf.

219. Briefing Report, *supra* note 215, at 186, 199–209 (joint dissent of Commissioners Arlan D. Melendez and Michael J. Yaki). The majority defended their methodology in a response to the dissent. *Id.* at 216–20.

220. *Id.* at 186. In their dissent, Melendez and Yaki provide a review of the academic literature critical of the materials on which the majority of the commissioners relied.

221. *Id.* at 187 (joint dissent).

222. *Id.* at 212 (dissent of Commissioner Michael J. Yaki).

223. *Id.* at 189.

224. *Id.* at 198.

225. *Id.*

226. The letters cited below (notes 227–30) were signed by the conservative majority members of the commission. Commissioners Melendez and Yaki either dissented from the letters or simply did not sign them.

227. Letter to President George W. Bush (Aug. 4, 2008), usccr.gov/correspd /080108DoTDBEprogram.pdf.

228. Letter to Senator Ray Miller, at 3 (July 21, 2009), usccr.gov/correspd /RacialPreferenceSB146.pdf.

229. *Id.* at 4.

230. Letter to President Obama and Members of Congress (Oct. 9, 2009), usccr.gov/correspd /CommissionHealthCareBill100909.pdf, and Letter to President Obama and Senators (Dec. 11, 2009), usccr.gov/correspd/LetterPresidentSenatorsHealthCare12-11-09.pdf.

231. Theodore M. Shaw, *Introduction* to Cokorinos, *supra* note 4, at x.

232. *Fisher v. University of Texas at Austin*, 2012 WL 538328 (cert. granted Feb. 21, 2012).

233. Among others, one by the conservative members of the U.S. Civil Rights Commission discussed above. Brief Amicus Curiae of Gail Heriot, Peter Kirsanow & Todd Gaziano, Members of the United States Commission on Civil Rights, in Support of Petitioner, 2011 WL 5007903.

234. Clegg, *supra* note 188.

CHAPTER 5

1. *Lawrence v. Texas*, 539 U.S. 558, 602 (2003) (Scalia, J., dissenting).

2. Janet Hadley, Abortion: Between Freedom and Necessity 3 (1997)

3. *Roe v. Wade*, 410 U.S. 113 (1973).

4. *See generally*, John P. Heinz, Ann Southworth & Anthony Paik, *Lawyers for Conservative Causes: Clients, Ideology, and Social Distance*, 37 L. & Soc'y Rev. 1, 5–55 (March 2003).

5. *About Focus on the Family*, Focus on the Fam., focusonthefamily.com (last visited Aug. 10, 2012).

6. For example, in *About AUL* (aul.org; last visited Aug. 10, 2012), Americans United for Life states that its legislative goals are to:
   - Mandate standards for abortion clinics to protect the health and safety of women and correct often substandard conditions.
   - Protect the rights of conscience of all healthcare professionals.
   - Protect parental rights, ensuring parents and guardians are involved in medical decisions of children.
   - Protect unborn victims from criminal violence, including homicide.
   - Ban all forms of human cloning.
   - Promote adult stem cell, cord blood and other forms of life-affirming stem cell research.
   - Prevent euthanasia and assisted suicide.
   - Inform women of the health risks of abortion including the link between abortion and breast cancer.

7. Joan Crawford Greenburg, Supreme Conflict 251 (2008).

8. Laurie Goodstein, *For Bishops, A Battle over Whose Rights Prevail*, N.Y. Times, Dec. 28, 2011, at A16.

9. Focus on the Fam., *Focus on Social Issues: Position Statement on Federal Judicial Appointments*, Mar. 7, 2005, *quoted in* Robert C. Post & Reva B. Siegel, *Originalism as a Political Practice: The Right's Living Constitution*, 75 Fordham L. Rev. 545, 560, 556–57 at n.54 (2006–2007).

10. David G. Kirkpatrick, *The Conservative-Christian Big Thinker*, N.Y. Times, Dec. 16, 2009, at MM24. Kirkpatrick describes the timing of the meeting with the bishops, discussed here, as "last spring." *Id.*

11. *Id.*

12. U.S. Comm'n on Religious Freedom, uscirf.gov (last visited Aug. 10, 2012).

13. *NRLC Expresses Confidence Supreme Court Nominee "Will Abide by the Text and History of the Constitution,"* Nat'l Right to Life Committee (Oct. 4, 2005), nrlc.org.

14. Kirkpatrick, *supra* note 10.

15. Kirkpatrick, *supra* note 10.

16. Monica Hesse, *Profile of Brian Brown, Executive Director of the National Organization for Marriage*, Wash. Post, Aug. 28, 2009, washingtonpost.com.

17. *About the American Principles Project*, Am. Principles Project, americanprinciplesproject.org/?p=398 (last visited Aug. 10, 2012).

18. Kirkpatrick, *supra* note 10.

19. *Id.*

20. Hadley Arkes, *Gonzales v. Carhart: What Hath Kennedy Wrought?* 8 Engage 3, at 24 (June 3, 2007).

21. *Id.* at 22.

22. *About AUL*, Americans United For Life, aul.org (last visited Aug. 10, 2012).

23. *Id.*

24. *William Saunders*, Americans United for Life, aul.org/william-saunders (last visited Aug. 10, 2012). *See also* Berkley Center for Religion, Peace & World Affairs, Georgetown University, *William L. Saunders, Jr.*, Resources on Faith, Ethics, and Public Life, berkleycenter.georgetown.edu (last visited Aug. 10, 2012).

25. Charles Tiefer, Veering Right: How the Bush Administration Subverts the Law for Conservative Causes 54 (U. Cal. Press 2006).

26. *Kevin J. "Seamus" Hasson*, Becket Fund for Religious Liberty, becketfund.org/author/KevinHasson (last visited Aug. 10, 2012).

27. *NRLC General Counsel James Bopp Named Republican Lawyer of the Year*, 36 NRL News, Issue 9 (Sept. 2009), *available at* nrlc.org/news/2009/NRL09/Bopp.html.

28. *Legislation*, Americans United for Life, aul.org (last visited Aug. 10, 2012). States with directors are: Alabama, Florida, Georgia, Illinois, Mississippi, Missouri, Oklahoma, and Utah. *Id. See also Issues*, Americans United for Life, aul.org (last visited Aug. 10, 2012).

29. *Planned Parenthood of Southeastern Pa. v. Casey*, 505 U.S. 833 (1992).

30. Americans United for Life, *supra* note 28.

31. Linda Greenhouse, *U.S. Supports Bid to Uphold Ohio Limits on Abortions*, N.Y. Times, Feb. 8, 2002, at A18.

32. James Madison Ctr. for Free Speech, jamesmadisoncenter.org (last visited Aug. 10, 2012).

33. David D. Kirkpatrick, *A Quest to End Spending Rules for Campaigns*, N.Y. Times, Jan. 24, 2010, at A11.

34. James Bopp, *Electioneering Communication Versus Abortion*, 3 Elect. L.J. 205 (2004); Matthew Mosk, *Citizens United v. the FEC: The Return of Corporate Influence Peddling?* ABC News, Jan. 13, 2010, *available at* abcnews.go.com.

35. *Fed. Election Comm'n v. Wis. Right to Life, Inc.*, 551 U.S. 449 (2007). *Citizens United v. Fed. Election Comm'n*, 130 S. Ct. 876 (2010). *Citizens United* concerned *Hillary*, a critical documentary of then-senator Hillary Clinton, at the time a candidate for the Democratic Party's presidential nomination. Citizens United, a nonprofit corporation, sought to make *Hillary* available through on-demand cable TV within thirty days of the Democratic primary elections, in violation of the Bipartisan Campaign Reform Act of 2002. *Id.*

36. Kirkpatrick, *supra* note 33.

37. James Bopp Jr., Resume, *available at* bopplaw.com/attorneys/James_Bopp_Jr /Boppresume0208.pdf (last visited Aug. 10 2012).

38. NRL News, *supra* note 27.

39. Stephanie Simon, *Evangelical Group Seeks Broader Tent*, WALL St. J. (Aug. 10, 2010), online.wsj.com.

40. Focus on the Fam. 2010 IRS Form 990, *available at* media.focusonthefamily.com/fotf /pdf/about-us/financial-reports/2010-990.pdf (last visited Aug. 10, 2012).

41. *Id.* at 53.

42. *Id.* at 39–44.

43. Press Release, Focus On The Fam., Focus' Option Ultrasound Program Saves Lives in U.S. and Abroad (Feb. 6, 2012), *available at* focusonthefamily.com. In its February 2012 news release, Focus noted its first Option Ultrasound (formerly known as "Operation Ultrasound") "international placement" in Bucharest, Romania. *See also* Rachel Benson Gold, *All That's Old Is New Again: The Long Campaign to Persuade Women To Forego Abortion*, 12 GUTTMACHER INST. POL'Y REV. (Spring 2009), *available at* guttmacher.org.

44. *Requirements for Ultrasound*, GUTTMACHER INST., STATE POLICIES IN BRIEF, *available at* guttmacher.org/statecenter/spibs/spib_RFU.pdf (data to Aug. 1, 2012).

45. For a more detailed discussion of their work on judicial selection, *see* Chapter 2.

46. *About Jay Sekulow*, AM. CTR. FOR LAW & JUST., aclj.org/jay-sekulow (last visited Aug. 10, 2012).

47. See *Fed. Election Comm'n v. Christian Coal.*, 52 F. Supp. 2d 45, 49 (D. D.C., 1999).

48. *Fed. Election Comm'n v. Christian Coal.*, 52 F. Supp. 2d 45 (D. D.C., 1999).

49. *Meyer v. Nebraska*, 262 U.S. 390 (1923).

50. *Pierce v. Soc'y of Sisters*, 268 U.S. 510, 534–35 (1925).

51. *Stanley v. Illinois*, 405 U.S. 645, 651 (1972).

52. *Moore v. City of East Cleveland*, 431 U.S. 494, 503 (1977).

53. *Santosky v. Kramer*, 455 U.S. 745, 753 (1982).

54. *Skinner v. Oklahoma*, 316 U.S. 535 (1942).

55. *Loving v. Virginia*, 388 U.S. 1, 12 (1967).

56. Justice Louis Brandeis had argued for the recognition of a right of privacy under the Fourth Amendment in his dissent in *Olmstead v. United States*, 227 U.S. 438 (1928), in which the court upheld a criminal conviction that was based upon wiretap evidence. Olmstead challenged the use of this evidence, arguing that the wiretap was an illegal search under the Fourth Amendment's guarantee against "unreasonable searches and seizures." The Supreme Court rejected the argument, holding that because there was no physical invasion or search of material things such as the defendant's person, house, papers, or effects, there was no "search" or "seizure." In dissent, Justice Brandeis, joined by three other members of the court, argued for protection of an expansive right of privacy: "The makers of our Constitution undertook to secure conditions favorable to the pursuit of happiness. They recognized the significance of man's spiritual nature, of his feelings and of his intellect. They knew that only a part of the pain, pleasure

and satisfactions of life are to be found in material things. They sought to protect Americans in their beliefs, their thoughts, their emotions and their sensations. They conferred, as against the government, the right to be let alone—the most comprehensive of rights and the right most valued by civilized men. To protect, that right, every unjustifiable intrusion by the government upon the privacy of the individual, whatever the means employed, must be deemed a violation of the Fourth Amendment." *Olmstead*, 227 U.S. at 478 (Brandeis, J., dissenting). As a question of Fourth Amendment jurisprudence, *Olmstead* was subsequently overruled. In *Katz v. United States*, 389 U.S. 347, 353 (1967), the court recognized that a physical invasion of a person's space was not required for a violation of the Fourth Amendment, because it "protects people—and not simply 'areas'—against unreasonable searches and seizures."

57. *Griswold v. Connecticut*, 381 U.S. 479 (1965).

58. For a more detailed discussion of substantive due process during the *Lochner* era, *see* Chapter 3.

59. *Griswold*, 381 U.S. at 488 (Goldberg, J., concurring). The Ninth Amendment provides that "[t]he enumeration in the Constitution, of certain rights, shall not be construed to deny or disparage others retained by the people."

60. *Id.* at 485–86.

61. *Eisenstadt v. Baird*, 405 U.S. 438, 453 (1972).

62. *Roe v. Wade*, 410 U.S. 113, 152–53 (1973).

63. *Id.* at 154.

64. *Bowers v. Hardwick*, 478 U.S. 186 (1986).

65. John A. Jenkins, *Mr. Power: Attorney General Edwin Meese*, N.Y. Times, Oct. 12, 1986, at 19. The Supreme Court of Georgia later held the state's sodomy statute unconstitutional as violating the right of privacy guaranteed by the due process clause of the Georgia Constitution. *Powell v. State*, 270 Ga. 327 (1998).

66. Laurence H. Tribe, *On Reading the Constitution*, Tanner Lectures on Human Values, 58–59 (Nov. 17 and 18, 1986), tannerlectures.utah.edu (Lecture Library).

67. Off. of Legal Pol'y, Dep't of Just., Report to the Attorney General: The Constitution in the Year 2000, at 11–43 (1988).

68. *Id.* at 16.

69. *Id.* at 16–17.

70. *Id.* at 17.

71. *Id.* at 18.

72. *Id.* at 29.

73. *Id.* at 25, n.31.

74. *Id.* at 32.

75. *Id.* at 25.

76. *Planned Parenthood of Southeastern Pa. v. Casey*, 505 U.S. 833, 851 (1992).

77. *Lawrence v. Texas*, 539 U.S. 558, 562 (2003).

78. *See, e.g.*, William Saunders, *Health Care Reform and Respect for Human Life: How the Process Failed*, 25 Notre Dame J.L. Ethics & Pub. Pol'y 593 (2011); William Saunders & Thomas F. Farr, *The Bush Administration and America's International Religious Freedom Policy*, 32 Harv. J.L. & Pub. Pol'y 949 (2009); William Saunders, *Lethal Experimentation on Human Beings: Roe's Effect on Bioethics*, 31 Fordham Urb. L.J. 817 (2004).

79. James Bopp Jr. and Curtis R. Cook, *Partial-Birth Abortion: The Final Frontier of Abortion Jurisprudence*, 14 Issues L. & Med. 3 (1998).

80. *See, e.g.*, Hadley Arkes, *The Constitution and Its Moral Warnings*, 33 Harv. J. L. & Pub. Pol'y 495 (2010); Hadley Arkes, *Great Expectations and Sobering Truths: Partial-Birth*

Abortion and the Commerce Clause, 1 U. St. Thomas J.L. & Pub. Pol'y 5 (2007); Hadley Arkes, *News for the Libertarians: The Moral Tradition Already Contains the Libertarian Premises*, 29 Harv. J.L. & Pub. Pol'y 61 (Fall 2005).

81. Hadley Arkes, *A Response to David Forte*, 1 U. St. Thomas J.L. & Pub. Pol'y 42, 47 (2007). Delahunty was one of the "early recruits" to the Federalist Society at Harvard in the early 1980s. George W. Hicks Jr., *The Conservative Influence of the Federalist Society on the Harvard Law School Student Body*, 29 Harv. J.L. & Pub. Pol'y 624, 656 (2006).

82. Patrick Lee & Robert P. George, *The Wrong of Abortion, in* Contemporary Debates in Applied Ethics 3–15 (Andrew I. Cohen and Christopher Wellman eds., 2005).

83. Manhattan Declaration, *available at* manhattandeclaration.org/the-declaration/read.aspx (last visited Aug. 10, 2012). Alongside the sanctity of human life, the remaining principles are the "dignity of marriage as the conjugal union of husband and wife, and religious liberty and freedom of conscience." Interview by Kathryn Jean Lopez with Robert George, Nat'l Rev. Online, Dec. 1, 2001, *available at* nationalreview.com.

84. Manhattan Declaration, *supra* note 83.

85. Steven Calabresi, *How to Reverse Government Imposition of Immorality: A Strategy for Eroding Roe v. Wade*, 31 Harv. J.L. & Pub. Pol'y 85 (2008).

86. Linda Greenhouse & Reva B. Siegal, *Before (and After) Roe v. Wade: New Questions about Backlash*, 120 Yale L.J. 2028, 2048 (2011).

87. John R. Vile, Encyclopedia of Constitutional Amendments, Proposed Amendments, and Amending Issues, 1789–2001, 387 (ABC-CLIO, 2003).

88. Charles E. Rice, *Overruling Roe v. Wade: An Analysis of the Proposed Constitutional Amendments*, 15 B.C. L. Rev. 307, 314 (1973).

89. *Id.* at 388.

90. *Roe v. Wade*, 410 U.S. 113, 159 (1973).

91. S. J. Res. 137, 97th Cong. (1981).

92. James Bopp Jr. & Richard E. Coleson, Memorandum re: Pro-life Strategy Issues, Aug. 7, 2007 (on file with authors).

93. S. J. Res. 137, 97th Cong. (1981). *See also* Nat'l Committee for a Human Life Amendment, *Human Life Amendments:1973–2003*, *available at* nchla.org/issues.asp?ID=46 (last visited Aug. 10, 2012).

94. S. J. Res. 110, 97th Cong. (1981).

95. Nat'l Committee for a Human Life Amendment, *Human Life Amendments: United States Congress (1973–2003)*, nchla.org/datasource/idocuments/HLAhghlts.pdf (last visited Aug. 10, 2012).

96. Vile, *supra* note 87, at 388.

97. Bopp & Coleson, *supra* note 92.

98. Vile, *supra* note 87, at 387. *See also* Edward Keynes with Randall K. Miller, The Court v. Congress: Prayer, Busing, and Abortion 245 (1989) and *Monthly State Update: Major Developments in 2012*, Guttmacher Inst., *available at* guttmacher.org/statecenter (data to Aug. 1, 2012). As of December 2011, six states are considering personhood or human life constitutional amendments.

99. *Harris v. McRae*, 448 U.S. 297 (1980).

100. *Id.*

101. *H. L. v. Matheson*, 450 U.S. 398 (1981).

102. *Id.* at 413.

103. The challenged portions of the ordinance were as follows: (1) the requirement that all abortions performed after the first trimester of pregnancy be performed in a hospital (§ 1870.03); (2) the prohibition of a physician from performing an abortion on an

unmarried minor under the age of fifteen unless he obtains the consent of one of her parents or unless the minor obtains an order from a court having jurisdiction over her that the abortion be performed (§ 1870.05(B)); (3) the requirement that the attending physician inform his patient of the status of her pregnancy, the development of her fetus, the date of possible viability, the physical and emotional complications that may result from an abortion, and the availability of agencies to provide her with assistance and information with respect to birth control, adoption, and childbirth (§ 1870.06(B)), and also inform her of the particular risks associated with her pregnancy and the abortion technique to be employed (§ 1870.06(C)); (4) the prohibition of a physician from performing an abortion until twenty-four hours after the pregnant woman signs a consent form (§ 1870.07); and (5) the requirement that physicians performing abortions ensure that fetal remains are disposed of in a "humane and sanitary manner" (§ 1870.16). A violation of the ordinance is punishable as a misdemeanor. *City of Akron v. Akron Center for Reproductive Health, Inc.*, 462 U.S. 416, 416, (1983) (syllabus).

104. President Nixon, although privately believing that abortion was a matter best left to the states, seized upon the abortion issue in his reelection campaign as a means to attract, from traditionally democratic affiliations, the votes of Catholics and social conservatives. After *Roe* was handed down, however, the Nixon administration stayed out of the case. *See* Greenhouse & Siegal, *supra* note 86 at 2054, 2058.

105. Solicitor General Rex E. Lee, Oral Argument, *City of Akron v. Akron Center for Reproductive Health, Inc.*, 462 U.S. 416 (1983) (Nov. 30, 1982).

106. David Binder, *Rex Lee, Former Solicitor General, Dies at 61*, N.Y. Times, Mar. 13, 1996, *available at* nytimes.com.

107. *Thornburgh v. Am. Coll. of Obstetricians & Gynecologists*, 476 U.S. 747, 760–761 (1986).

108. *Thornburgh*, 476 U.S. at 761.

109. *Id.* at 765.

110. Memorandum from Samuel A. Alito to Solicitor General Charles Fried, *Thornburgh v. Am. Coll. of Obstetricians & Gynecologists*, No. 84–495; *Diamond v. Charles*, No. 84–1379 (June 3, 1985).

111. *Id.* at 10.

112. *Id.* at 11.

113. *Id.* at 14–15.

114. *Id.* at 15.

115. *Id.* at 16.

116. *Id.* at 17.

117. *Id.*

118. Ari Shapiro, *Alito Documents: "We Disagree with Roe v. Wade,"* NPR (Nov. 30, 2005), npr.org.

119. Brief for the National Right to Life Committee, Inc. as Amicae Curiae Supporting Appellants, *Thornburgh v. Am. Coll.of Obstetricians & Gynecologists*, 476 U.S. 747 (1986) (No. 84–495), 1985 WL 669702.

120. *Doe v. Bolton*, 410 U.S. 179, 192 (1973).

121. Brief for Olivia Gans, Terryl Carlson, and Suze Dewing as Amicae Curiae Supporting Appellants, *Thornburgh v. Am. Coll. of Obstetricians & Gynecologists*, 476 U.S. 747 (1986) (No. 84–495), 1985 WL 669701.

122. *Thornburgh v. Am. Coll. of Obstetricians & Gynecologists*, 476 U.S. 747, 759 (1986).

123. *Thornburgh*, 476 U.S. at 766.

124. Tinsley E. Yarbrough, The Reagan Administration and Human Rights 226 (1985).

125. *Webster v. Reproductive Health Services*, 492 U.S. 490 (1989).

126. The statute's provision forbidding the use of public funds or employees to "encourage or counsel" a woman to have an abortion was moot because the challengers stated they were no longer adversely affected by the State's interpretation of that provision. *Webster*, 492 U.S. at 512.

127. *Id.* at 509–10.

128. Brief for the National Right to Life Committee as Amici Curiae Supporting Appellants at *2, *Webster v. Reproductive Health Services*, 492 U.S. 490 (1989) (No. 88–605), 1989 WL 1127669.

129. *Id.* at *11.

130. *Id.* at *18–*20.

131. Brief for the American Academy of Medical Ethics as Amici Curiae in Support of Appellants, *Webster v. Reproductive Health Services*, 492 U.S. 490 (1989) (No. 88–605), 1989 WL 1127668.

132. *Harris v. McRae*, 448 U.S. 297 (1980).

133. *Id.* at 22.

134. *Planned Parenthood of Southeastern Pa. v. Casey*, 505 U.S. 833 (1992).

135. Brief for National Right to Life, Inc. as Amici Curiae Supporting Respondents/Cross-Petitioners, *Planned Parenthood of Southeastern Pa. v. Casey*, 505 U.S. 833 (1992) (Nos. 91–744, 91–902), 1992 WL 12006425.

136. *Planned Parenthood of Southeastern Pa. v. Casey*, 947 F.2d 682, 720 (Alito, J., dissenting).

137. Brief for Life Issues Institute as Amici Curiae Supporting Respondents/Cross-Petitioners, *Planned Parenthood of Southeastern Pa. v. Casey*, 505 U.S. 833 (1992) (Nos. 91–744, 91–902), 1992 WL 12006426.

138. Brief for the United States as Amicus Curiae Supporting Respondents/Cross-Petitioners, *Planned Parenthood of Southeastern Pa. v. Casey*, 505 U.S. 833 (1992) (Nos. 91–744, 91–902), 1992 WL 12006421.

139. *Casey*, 505 U.S. at 878.

140. James Bopp Jr. & Curtis R. Cook, *Partial-Birth Abortion: The Final Frontier of Abortion Jurisprudence*, 14 ISSUES L. & MED. 3 (1998).

141. *Id.*

142. *Id.*

143. Bopp & Coleson, *supra* note 92.

144. *Stenberg v. Carhart*, 530 U.S. 914 (2000).

145. Brief for U.S. Rep. Charles T. Canady and Other Members of Congress as Amici Curiae in Support of Petitioners, *Stenberg v. Carhart*, 530 U.S. 914 (2000) (No. 99–830), 2000 WL 228464.

146. Brief for Virginia, Alabama, Idaho, Illinois, Iowa, Michigan, North Dakota, Ohio, Pennsylvania, South Carolina, South Dakota, Utah, the Governor of Rhode Island, the Governor of West Virginia, and the State Legislature of New Jersey as Amici Curiae in Support of Petitioners, *Stenberg v. Carhart*, 530 U.S. 914 (2000) (No. 99–830), 2000 WL 228466.

147. Brief for National Right to Life Committee, Christian Legal Society, Concerned Women for America, The Southern Center for Law and Ethics, and Focus on the Family as Amici Curiae in Support of Petitioners, *Stenberg v. Carhart*, 530 U.S. 914 (2000) (No. 99–830), 2000 WL 228496.

148. *Stenberg*, 530 U.S. 914 (2000).

149. *Ayotte v. Planned Parenthood of Northern New England*, 546 U.S. 320 (2006). The challenge was a facial challenge. *Id.*

150. Cruz previously served as associate deputy attorney general at the U.S. Department of Justice and as Department of Justice coordinator for the Bush transition team. From June 1999 until December 2000, he served as domestic policy advisor to President George W. Bush on the Bush-Cheney 2000 campaign, where he had primary responsibility for all legal policy. *See Hon. R. Ted Cruz*, Federalist Soc'y, fed-soc.org /publications (last visited Aug. 10, 2012).

151. Brief for the Horatio R. Storer Foundation, Inc. as Amici Curiae in Support of Petitioners, *Ayotte v. Planned Parenthood of Northern New England*, 546 U.S. 320 (2006) (No. 04–1144), 2005 WL 2012348.

152. Brief for the United States as Amici Curiae in Support of Petitioners, *Ayotte v. Planned Parenthood of Northern New England*, 546 U.S. 320 (2006) (No. 04–1144), 2005 WL 1900328, citing *United States v. Salerno*, 481 U.S. 739, 745 (1987).

153. Brief for Texas, Alabama, Arkansas, Colorado, Delaware, Florida, Idaho, Kansas, Michigan, Mississippi, North Dakota, Ohio, Pennsylvania, South Dakota, Tennessee, Utah, Virginia, and Wyoming as Amici Curiae in Support of Petitioners, *Ayotte v. Planned Parenthood of Northern New England*, 546 U.S. 320 (2006) (No. 04–1144), 2005 WL 1941279.

154. *Planned Parenthood of Southeastern Pa. v. Casey*, 505 U.S. 833, 895 (1992).

155. The court in *Casey* applied the *Salerno* standard to the twenty-four-hour waiting period, but used a different test when considering the constitutionality of the spousal notification requirement. *Casey*, 505 U.S. 833 (1992). The "controlling class," according to the court, was not all women seeking an abortion, but "married women seeking abortions who do not wish to notify their husbands of their intentions and who do not qualify for one of the statutory exceptions in the notice requirement." *Id.* at 2829–30.

156. Kevin C. Walsh, *Frames of Reference and the "Turn to Remedy" in Facial Challenge Doctrine*, 36 Hastings Const. L.Q. 667, 681–82 (2009).

157. *Gonzales v. Carhart*, 550 U.S. 124 (2007). The challenge was a facial challenge. *Id.*

158. Hadley Arkes, *Great Expectations and Sobering Truths: Partial-Birth Abortion and the Commerce Clause*, 1 U. St. Thomas J.L. & Pub. Pol'y 5, 9 (2007).

159. Federal Born-Alive Infants Protection Act of 2002, 1 U.S.C. § 9 (2002).

160. Brief for the United States as Petitioner at *3, *Gonzales v. Planned Parenthood Federation of America*, 550 U.S. 124 (20007) (No. 05–1382), 2006 WL 2282123.

161. *Id.* at 140.

162. Brief for the American Center for Law and Justice as Amicus Curiae in Support of Petitioner, *Gonzales v. Carhart*, 550 U.S. 124 (2007) (Nos. 05–380, 05–1382), 2006 WL 2317063.

163. *Id.* at *3.

164. Brief for the American Center for Law and Justice, 78 Members of Congress, and the Committee to Protect the Ban on Partial Birth Abortion as Amici Curiae in Support of Petitioner, *Gonzales v. Carhart*, 550 U.S. 124 (2007) (No. 05–380), 2006 WL 1436694.

165. Brief for Professor Hadley Arkes and the Claremont Institute Center for Constitutional Jurisprudence as Amici Curiae in Support of Petitioner, *Gonzales v. Carhart*, 550 U.S. 127 (2007) (No. 05–380), 2006 WL 2252506.

166. *Id.* at *8.

167. *Id.* at *30.

168. Brief for the Family Research Council and Focus on the Family as Amici Curiae in Support of Petitioner, *Gonzales v. Carhart*, 550 U.S. 127 (2007) (No. 05–380), 2006 WL 1436686.

169. *Id.* at *14.

170. Brief for the Horatio R. Storer Foundation, Inc., as Amicus Curiae in Support of Petitioner, *Gonzales v. Carhart*, 550 U.S. 127 (2007) (No. 05–380), 2006 WL 1436695.

171. *Id.* at *2.

172. *Id.* at *3.

173. Brief for Petitioners at *9, *Gonzales v. Planned Parenthood Federation of America, Gonzales v. Carhart*, 550 U.S. 127 (2007) (No. 05–1382), 2006 WL 2282123.

174. *Gonzales v. Carhart*, 550 U.S. 124, 167 (2007).

175. *Carhart*, 550 U.S. at 169 (Thomas, J., concurring).

176. Bopp & Coleson, *supra* note 92.

177. Sarah Kliff, *2011: The Year of the Abortion Restrictions*, WASH. POST (Dec. 29, 2011), washingtonpost.com. *See also* Chuck Raasch, *Abortion Restrictions Gain Steam in the States*, USA TODAY (Apr. 6, 2012), usatoday.com.

178. *Counseling and Waiting Periods for Abortion*, GUTTMACHER INST., STATE POLICIES IN BRIEF, guttmacher.org/statecenter (data to Aug. 1, 2012).

179. *Requirements for Ultrasound*, GUTTMACHER INST., STATE POLICIES IN BRIEF, guttmacher.org/statecenter (data to Aug. 1, 2012).

180. *Requirements for Ultrasound*, GUTTMACHER INST., STATE POLICIES IN BRIEF, guttmacher.org/statecenter (data to Dec. 1, 2011).

181. *An Overview of Abortion Laws*, GUTTMACHER INST., STATE POLICIES IN BRIEF, guttmacher.org/statecenter (data to Aug. 1, 2012). Thirty-six of those states have a judicial bypass procedure whereby the minor may, in the alternative, seek approval from a state court. *Id.*

182. Kate Sheppard, *Personhood Amendments: Coming to a Ballot Near You?* MOTHER JONES (Nov. 8, 2011, 4:00 AM), motherjones.com.

183. Naral Pro-Choice America Found., *"Personhood" Measures: Extreme and Dangerous Attempts to Ban Abortion* 1, *available at* prochoiceamerica.org/media/fact-sheets /abortion-personhood.pdf (data current as of Aug. 1, 2012).

184. *Bans on "Partial-Birth" Abortion*, GUTTMACHER INST., STATE POLICIES IN BRIEF, guttmacher.org/statecenter (data to Aug. 1, 2012). Of the thirty-one, thirteen have been specifically blocked by a court or are not in effect. *Id.*

185. *An Overview of Abortion Laws*, GUTTMACHER INST., STATE POLICIES IN BRIEF, guttmacher.org/statecenter (data to Aug 10, 201). Thirty-two states and the District of Columbia follow the federal standard and provide abortions in cases of life endangerment, rape, and incest. *Id.*

186. *Id.*

CHAPTER 6

1.   George Washington, Farewell Address, Sept. 17, 1796 (reprinted for 106th Congress, 2d. Session, S. Doc. No. 106–21 (2000), at 25).

2.   Peter J. Sprio, *The New Sovereigntists*, FOREIGN AFF., Nov.–Dec. 2000.

3.   2 ALEXIS DE TOCQUEVILLE, DEMOCRACY IN AMERICA pt. 1, ch. 9, at 517–18 (Arthur Goldhammer trans., Libr. of America 2004).

4.   *Id.* See also *id.* at 273.

5.   Damon Linker, *Calvin and American Exceptionalism*, NEW REPUBLIC, July 9, 2009, *available at* tnr.com.

6.   Theodore Roosevelt, *quoted in* NATSU TAYLOR SAITO, MEETING THE ENEMY: AMERICAN EXCEPTIONALISM AND INTERNATIONAL LAW 159 (2010).

7. FREDERICK JACKSON TURNER, THE FRONTIER IN AMERICAN HISTORY (1921). Turner presented his thesis, *The Significance of the Frontier in American History*, to a gathering of American historians in Chicago on July 12, 1893. *Id.* at 1. He wrote that the heart of American Exceptionalism was a compact between nature's God (in the Jeffersonian sense—that is, the god from whom came reason and morality, rather than religious doctrine) and the immigrants who ventured west to the frontier and beyond. According to Turner, it was not the Atlantic Coast, but rather the frontier, which constituted the "line of most rapid and effective Americanization. *Id.* at 3–4.

8. SAITO, *supra* note 6, at 11.

9. *Id.* at 78.

10. John Bolton, Address to 2003 Federalist Society National Lawyers Convention (Nov. 3, 2003), fed-soc.org/doclib/20070324_bolton.pdf. "Thank you very much, Ron. It's a real pleasure to be here today. I consider it not just an honor to appear before the Federalist Society, but a real opportunity to see a lot of old friends and to be in a generally friendly audience, which is not always my pleasure." *Id.*

11. Robert Costa, *Bolton: "A Post-American Speech By Our First Post-American President,"* NAT'L REV. ONLINE (Sept. 23, 2009, 2:09 PM), nationalreview.com.

12. Al Gaspari, *Bolton Calls Obama's Foreign Policy Post-American*, CHIC. MAROON (Oct. 16, 2009, 9:27 AM), chicagomaroon.com.

13. Steven Calabresi, *"A Shining City on a Hill": American Exceptionalism and the Supreme Court's Practice of Relying on Foreign Law*, 86 B.U. L. REV. 1335, 1338 (2006).

14. *Id.* at 1355, citing works by Daniel Bell and Jon Meacham.

15. Michael Stokes Paulsen, *The Original Meaning of the Commerce, Spending, and Necessary and Proper Clauses*, 31 HARV. J.L. & PUB. POL'Y 991 (2008).

16. Michael Stokes Paulsen, *The Constitutional Power to Interpret International Law*, 118 YALE L.J. 1762, 1765–66 (2009). Paulsen continues, "The power to interpret and apply international law for the United States is a power vested in officers of the U.S. government, not in any foreign or international body . . . As a matter of U.S. constitutional law, no international body authoritatively determines the content of international law for the United States." *Id.* at 1766–67.

17. AMERICAN EXCEPTIONALISM AND HUMAN RIGHTS 11–20 (Michael Ignatieff ed., 2005).

18. Harold Hongju Koh, *On American Exceptionalism*, Foreword, 55 STAN. L. REV. 1479 (2003).

19. On America's human rights vernacular: For example, Koh refers to one of his appearances before the Committee Against Torture in Geneva to defend U.S. compliance with the Torture Convention. When asked why the United States does not "maintain a single, comprehensive collation of statistics regarding incidents of torture and cruel, inhuman or degrading treatment or punishment," he answered that "the myriad bureaucracies of the federal government, the fifty states, and the territories did gather statistics regarding torture and cruel, inhuman, or degrading treatment, but we called that practice by different labels, including 'cruel and unusual punishment,' 'police brutality,' 'section 1983 actions,' applications of the exclusionary rule, violations of civil rights under color of state law, and the like." *Id.* at 1484.

20. The International Criminal Court came into force in 2002 and is a permanent court, independent of the United Nations, set up to prosecute individuals for genocide, crimes against humanity, and war crimes. *See generally About the Court*, INT'L CRIM. CT., icc-cpi.int (last visited Aug. 10, 2012). Article 98(2) of the Rome Statute, which created the International Criminal Court, states, "The Court may not proceed with a request for surrender which would require the requested State to act inconsistently

with its obligations under international agreements pursuant to which the consent of a sending State is required to surrender a person of that State to the Court, unless the Court can first obtain the cooperation of the sending State for the giving of consent for the surrender." *Id.*

21. *Printz v. United States*, 521 U.S. 898, 921, n.11 (1997).
22. Antonin Scalia, Speech at Federalist Society meeting, Faneuil Hall, Boston (Oct. 1, 2008) (notes of speech on file with authors).
23. Koh, *supra* note 18, at 1494
24. *Id.* at 1487.
25. Jonathan Riehl, The Federalist Society and Movement Conservatism: How a Fractious Coalition on the Right Is Changing Constitutional Law and the Way We Talk and Think about It 283 (2007) (Ph.D. dissertation, U.N.C. at Chapel Hill) (on file with authors).
26. John Bolton, Surrender Is Not an Option: Defending America at the United Nations and Abroad 12 (2007).
27. Riehl, *supra* note 25, at 283.
28. Bolton, *supra* note 26, at 442.
29. "[A]gainst the insidious wiles of foreign influence . . . the jealousy of a free people ought to be constantly awake, since history and experience prove that foreign influence is one of the most baneful foes of republican government." Washington, *supra* note 1, at 25.
30. *Id.* at 27–28
31. Bolton, *supra* note 26, at 88–89.
32. Kyoto Protocol to the United Nations Framework Convention on Climate Change art. 20, Dec. 10, 1997, 37 I.L.M. 22 (1998) [hereinafter Kyoto Protocol], *available at* unfccc.int/resource/docs/convkp/kpeng.html.
33. Michael C. Dorf, *Dynamic Incorporation of Foreign Law*, 157 U. Pa. L. Rev. 103, 115 (2008).
34. Bolton, *supra* note 26, at 88.
35. *About Global Governance Watch*, Global Governance Watch, globalgovernancewatch.org (last visited Aug. 10, 2012).
36. *Id.*
37. UN Universal Declaration of Human Rights, *available at* un.org/en/documents/udhr (last visited Aug. 10, 2012).
38. Chanler believed that the Kellogg-Briand pact deprived the Nazis of the "shield of lawful belligerence." Bradley F. Smith, The Road To Nuremberg 106 (1981).
39. David F. Schmitz, Henry L. Stimson, the First Wise Man 204 (2001).
40. Robert H. Jackson, *International Military Tribunal: Opening Address for the United States of America*, 13 Dep't St. Bull. 850–60 (1945).
41. *Id.*
42. *Prosecutor v. Tadic* (Judgment), Case No. IT-94-1-A, Judgment, 38 I.L.M. 1518 (1999) (Int'l Crim. Trib. for the Former Yugoslavia, Appeals Chamber, July 15, 1999).
43. *Prosecutor v. Taylor* (Sentencing Judgment), Case No. SCSL-03-01-T (2012) (Special Court for Sierra Leone, Trial Chamber II, May 30, 2012). *See also* The Special Court for Sierra Leone, www.sc-sl.org/HOME (last visited Aug. 8, 2012).
44. *Filartiga v. Pena*, 630 F.2d 876 (2d Cir. 1980).
45. *Sosa v. Alvarez-Machain*, 542 U.S. 692, 729–730 (2004).
46. *Hearing on the United Nations International Criminal Court*, 105th Cong. (July 23, 1998) (statement of Sen. Jesse Helms). Helms continued, "[I]f Madison and our other Founding Fathers were here today, I believe they would support my assertion that any

treaty which undermines those Constitutional protections—as this one clearly does—will be dead-on-arrival at the Senate Foreign Relations Committee. Let's close the casket right now, Mr. Chairman." *Id.*

47. Bolton, *supra* note 26, at 85.
48. As of May 3, 2005, the United States had conducted one hundred legally binding bilateral agreements that would prohibit the surrender of U.S. persons to the court. Jennifer K. Elsea, U.S. Policy regarding the International Criminal Court, CRS Report for Congress 16 (Aug. 29, 2006).
49. Antonia Chayes, *How American Treaty Behavior Threatens National Security*, 33 Int'l Security 1, 74, *quoting* Moravcsik, *Why Is U.S. Human Rights Policy So Unilateralist?* at 185.
50. Saito, *supra* note 6, at 182.
51. *Id.* at 210.
52. *Id.* at 213.
53. As Edwin Meese explained, "[I]t was out of step with the concepts of economic liberty and free enterprise that Ronald Reagan was to inspire throughout the world." David Ridenour, *Ratification of the Law of the Sea Treaty: A Not-So-Innocent Passage* (Nat'l Ctr. for Public Pol'y Res., Paper, 2006), *available at* nationalcenter.org.
54. Andrew Moravcsik, *Why is U.S. Human Rights Policy so Unilateralist?* in The Cost of Acting Alone: Multilateralism and US Foreign Policy 360 (Shepard Forman & Patrick Stewart eds., 2001).
55. Bolton, *supra* note 26, at 441–42.
56. *Id.* at 90. *See also* Interview by Ginny Simone with John Bolton, in *Bolder Bolton*, NRA-ILA (May 7, 2009), nraila.org.
57. Bolton, *supra* note 26, at 90.
58. *Convention on the Rights of the Child*, UNICEF (last updated Nov. 29, 2005), unicef.org/CRC/.
59. Alison Dundes Renteln, *Who's Afraid of the CRC: Objections to the Convention on the Rights of the Child*, 3 ILSA J. Int'l & Comp. L. 629, 631 (1997).
60. UNICEF, *supra* note 58. The seven major UN human rights treaties are the Convention against Torture and Other Cruel, Inhuman or Degrading Treatment or Punishment (Convention against Torture), the International Convention on the Elimination of All Forms of Racial Discrimination, the Convention on the Elimination of All Forms of Discrimination against Women (CEDAW), the International Covenant on Civil and Political Rights, the Genocide Convention, the International Covenant on Economic, Social and Cultural Rights, and the Convention on the Rights of the Child (CRC). Lainie Rutkow & Joshua T. Lozman, *Suffer the Children? A Call for United States Ratification of the United Nations Convention on the Rights of the Child*, 19 Harv. Human Rights J. 161, 166 (2006).
61. David D. Kirkpatrick, *Alito Memos Supported Expanding Police Powers*, N.Y. Times, Nov. 29, 2005, *available at* nytimes.com.
62. For a more detailed discussion of the shared membership and leadership between family values organizations and the Federalist Society, *see* Chapter 6.
63. Donald Hodel was appointed by President Reagan to be secretary of energy; he went on to be president of the Christian Coalition and then Focus on the Family, a conservative evangelical Christian organization dedicated to nurturing and defending the "God-ordained institution of the family." *See* focusonthefamily.com. For further information on Hodel and Focus on the Family, *see* Chapter 6. Press Release, Catholic Family & Human Rights Institute, Focus on the Family Calls on Governments to De-Ratify Child Convention (June 8, 2001), *available at* c-fam.org.

64. Renteln, *supra* note 59, at 633.

65. *Id.* Focus on the Family, alongside many other conservative groups, subscribes to the theory that the CRC portrays parents as threats to children's interests, rather than as their protectors, nurturers, and educators. *Id.*

66. *Whitney v. Robertson*, 124 U.S. 190, 194 (1888), held: "By the constitution, a treaty is placed on the same footing, and made of like obligation, with an act of legislation. Both are declared by that instrument to be the supreme law of the land, and no superior efficacy is given to either over the other. When the two relate to the same subject, the courts will always endeavor to construe them so as to give effect to both, if that can be done without violating the language of either; but, if the two are inconsistent, the one last in date will control the other: provided, always, the stipulation of the treaty on the subject is self-executing." *Id.*

67. Rutkow & Lozman, *supra* note 60, at 177. Critics (including Focus) argue that legal determinations regarding family separation and reunification, child custody, foster care placement, and child protection should remain the exclusive ambit of the states and ought not to be the subject of an international treaty. *Id.* at 58.

68. Jackie Ammons, *Children's Rights Fundamentally Flawed under U.N. Convention on the Rights of the Child*, GLOBAL GOVERNANCE WATCH, globalgovernancewatch.org (last visited Aug. 10, 2012).

69. *See* UN TREATIES COLLECTION, treaties.un.org (last visited Aug. 10, 2012).

70. Melana Zyer Vickers, *The Convention on the Elimination of All Forms of Discrimination against Women: A Leading Example of What's Wrong with International Law* 3 (Federalist Soc'y, White Paper, 2003), *available at* fed-soc.org.

71. Jim Kelly, *Ratification of CEDAW Would Give UN Experts Control Over U.S. Domestic Policies*, GLOBAL GOVERNANCE WATCH (July 22, 2009), globalgovernancewatch.org.

72. Thomas J. Lipping & Wendy Wright, *CEDAW Treaty Would Undermine American Sovereignty* 1 (Federalist Soc'y, White Paper, n.d.) (on file with authors).

73. *Id.*

74. *Id.* Hyperbole noted in Laura Roskos, *International Law, National Sovereignty, and Local Norms: What's to Become of CEDAW in the United States?* 24 (Boston Consortium on Gender, Security, and Human Rights Working Paper Series, Paper No. 103, 2003), *available at* genderandsecurity.umb.edu.

75. Vickers, supra note 70, at 3.

76. CONG. RES. SERVICE, TREATIES AND OTHER INTERNATIONAL AGREEMENTS: THE ROLE OF THE UNITED STATES SENATE: A STUDY PREPARED FOR THE SENATE COMMITTEE ON FOREIGN RELATIONS 40 (106th Cong. S. Prt. 106–71, Jan. 2001). Up to and including the year 1989, the United States had conducted 890 treaties and 5,117 executive agreements. *Id.*

77. Warren Mass, *Obama's Canada Visit Spotlights NAFTA*, NEW AM. (Feb. 20, 2009), thenewamerican.com.

78. Douglas Seay, *Why Conservatives Should Support The NAFTA* (Heritage Foundation, Executive Memorandum No. 366, Sept. 27, 1993), *available at* heritage.org.

79. Christopher Magee, Paper Prepared for Columbia University Conference in Honor of Jagdish Bhagwati: Robert Peel, Bill Clinton, and the George Bushes 3 (Aug. 5, 2005), *available at* columbia.edu .

80. These benefits are still being extolled by the current administration. *See, e.g.*, ECON. REP. OF THE PRESIDENT 137 (Jan. 2009), gpoaccess.gov.

81. Dan Druck, *Not a Free Trade Agreement*, COUNCIL ON DOMESTIC RELATIONS NEWSL. (Council on Domestic Relations, Millerton, PA), Nov. 1993. These fears may not have been entirely unfounded. In 2000, seven years after NAFTA came into force,

Mexico's Vicente Fox unveiled his country's agenda for North America during the Summit of the Americas in Ottawa. Luis Rubio & Susan Kaufman Purcell, Mexico under Fox149 (Lynne Rienner Publishers 2004). President Fox advocated for common external tariffs, monetary policy, policy coordination, mobile pools of labor and investment aid to Mexico—ideas that were loosely modeled on policies of the European Union. *Id.*

82. Barnali Choudury, *Recapturing Public Power: Is Investment Arbitration's Engagement of the Public Interest Contributing to the Democratic Deficit?* 41 Vand. J. Transnat'l L. 775, 782 (2008).

83. Charles N. Brower & Stephan W. Schill, *Is Arbitration a Threat or Boon to the Legitimacy of International Investment Law?* 9 Chi. J. Int'l L. 471, 474 (2009).

84. John Bolton, *Should We Take Global Governance Seriously?* 1 Chi. J. Int'l L. 205, 220 (2000).

85. Jeremy Rabkin, The Case for Sovereignty 139 (2004).

86. *Id.* at 131.

87. *Id.* at 151.

88. Bolton, *supra* note 84, at 220.

89. The idea of derailing a scheduled fourth UN Atomic Energy Conference in favor of a conference on the problems surrounding the human environment was initiated by Swedish diplomat Inga Thorsson and convened at the urging of the Swedish delegation to the United Nations. *Moving Forward by Looking Back: Learning from UNEP's History, in* Global Environmental Governance: Perspectives on the Current Debate 28 (Lydia Swart & Estelle Perry eds., 2007).

90. Steven Hayward, 2008 Federalist Society National Lawyers Convention, Panel, Environmental Law: The Policy Implications of the Reaction to Climate Change, Nov. 20, 2008 (notes of speech on file with authors).

91. Bolton, *supra* note 84, at 219.

92. Saito, *supra* note 6, at 212.

93. *Missouri v. Holland*, 252 U.S. 416 (1920).

94. The full text of the Tenth Amendment is: "The powers not delegated to the United States by the Constitution, nor prohibited by it to the States, are reserved to the States respectively, or to the people."

95. *McCulloch v. Maryland*, 17 U.S. 316, 415 (1816). In *Holland*, Justice Holmes suggested that the founders had created an "organism" in the Constitution, the development of which they could not have completely foreseen. He said the court must consider "what this country ha[d] become" in deciding what rights the Tenth Amendment reserved to the states. *Id.* at 434.

96. Saito, *supra* note 6, at 212.

97. H. R. 568, 108th Congress (2004).

98. *Bowers v. Hardwick*, 478 U.S. 186 (1986); *Lawrence v. Texas*, 539 U.S. 554, 576 (2003).

99. The American Justice for American Citizens Act, H.R. 4118, 108th Cong. § 2(7) (2004).

100. Bolton, *supra* note 26, at 446.

101. Michael Stokes Paulsen, *The Constitutional Power to Interpret International Law*, 118 Yale L. J. 1762, 1766 (2009).

102. *Id.* at 1769.

103. *The Paquete Habana*, 175 U.S. 677, 700 (1900). Justice Gray delivered the opinion of the court, stating: "International law is part of our law, and must be ascertained and administered by the courts of justice of appropriate jurisdiction as often as questions of right depending upon it are duly presented for their determination. For this purpose,

where there is no treaty and no controlling executive or legislative act or judicial decision, resort must be had to the customs and usages of civilized nations, and, as evidence of these, to the works of jurists and commentators who by years of labor, research, and experience have made themselves peculiarly well acquainted with the subjects of which they treat. Such works are resorted to by judicial tribunals, not for the speculations of their authors concerning what the law ought to be, but for trustworthy evidence of what the law really is." *Id.* (citation omitted).

104. *Murray v. Schooner Charming Betsy*, 6 U.S. 64 (1804). "It has also been observed that an act of Congress ought never to be construed to violate the law of nations if any other possible construction remains, and consequently can never be construed to violate neutral rights, or to affect neutral commerce, further than is warranted by the law of nations as understood in this country." *Id.* at 118.

105. John Bolton, Address at the Federalist Society 2003 National Lawyers Convention (Nov. 30, 2003), *available at* fed-soc.org.

106. Paulsen, *supra* note 101, at 1776.

107. *Id.* at 1770.

108. For example, unlike in civilian courts, evidence may not be excluded on the basis that it was obtained without a search warrant. Dep't of Defense, *Fact Sheet, Military Commissions, 8/30/2007, available at* defense.gov. Also, the military judge may admit any evidence that would have "probative value to a reasonable person." *Id.*

109. David B. Rivkin, *The Use of Military Commissions in the War on Terror*, 24 B.U. Int'l L.J. 123 (2006).

110. *Id.* at 142.

111. David B. Rivkin, *The Virtues of Preemptive Deterrence*, 29 Harv. J.L. & Pub. Pol'y 85, 99 (2005)

112. *Id.*

113. *Id.*

114. Jeremy Rabkin, Introduction and Book Presentation at the American Enterprise Institute Conference: War, International Law, and Sovereignty: Reevaluating the Rules of the Game in a New Century (June 24, 2004), *available at* aei.org.

115. Po-Jen Yap, *Transnational Constitutionalism in the United States: Toward a Worldwide Use of Interpretive Modes of Comparative Reasoning*, 39 U.S.F. L. Rev. 999, 1007, citing Federalist No. 63 (James Madison).

116. *Id.*

117. Federalist No. 63 (James Madison).

118. Yap, *supra* note 115, at 1007, citing Gary Wills, Inventing America: Jefferson's Declaration of Independence 317 (1979).

119. Article II's articulation of presidential powers, combined with the Federalist Papers, which extol the separation of powers and an executive who has "energy" and "accountability," gives rise to the theory of the Unitary Executive. For an exposition of the theory of the Unitary Executive and its foundations in the Federalist Papers, *see* Steven G. Calabresi, *Some Normative Arguments for the Unitary Executive*, 48 Ark. L. Rev. 23, 37–47 (1995).

120. Amanda Hollis-Brusky, Paper Prepared for the Annual Meeting of the American Political Science Association: The Federalist Society and the Unitary Executive: An Epistemic Community at Work 17 (Sept. 3. 2009) (on file with authors). As in many other issue areas, Federalist Society members are not always in agreement. One high-profile member who disagrees with the unitary executive theory is libertarian Richard Epstein. While participating in a panel at the 2006 Federalist Society National Lawyers Convention entitled "Federalism and Separation of Powers: Executive Power

in Wartime," Epstein stated that "looking to the constitutional text, it seems clear to me that the President's claim of extensive powers under Article II of the Constitution is woefully overstated and generally insupportable." 8 ENGAGE 2 (2007), at 51.

121. Calabresi, *supra* note 119, at 28.

122. Hollis-Brusky, *supra* note 120, at 22.

123. *Presidential Signing Statements under the Bush Administration: A Threat to Checks and Balances and the Rule of Law? Hearing Before the H. Comm. on the Judiciary*, 110th Cong. 106 (Jan. 31, 2007).

124. *Marbury v. Madison*, 5 U.S. (1 Cranch) 137 (1803).

125. *Cooper v. Aaron*, 358 U.S. 1 (1958); *United States v. Nixon*, 418 U.S. 683 (1974).

126. This is a vision that the founding fathers explicitly rejected. In FEDERALIST NO. 69, Alexander Hamilton assured the people of New York that the president's commander-in-chief powers were inferior to that of the English king: "The President is to be commander-in-chief of the army and navy of the United States. In this respect his authority would be nominally the same with that of the king of Great Britain, but in substance much inferior to it. It would amount to nothing more than the supreme command and direction of the military and naval forces, as first General and admiral of the Confederacy; while that of the British king extends to the declaring of war and to the raising and regulating of fleets and armies—all which, by the Constitution under consideration, would appertain to the legislature."

127. The account of the memos produced by the OLC that follows is not exhaustive. It primarily relies upon the list of memos outlined in the order denying Yoo's motion to dismiss in *Padilla v. Yoo*, 633 F. Supp.2d 1005 (N.D. Cal. 2009).

128. JACK GOLDSMITH, THE TERROR PRESIDENCY 22 (2009).

129. Memorandum from John Yoo, Deputy Assistant Attorney General, and Robert Delahunty, Special Counsel, to Alberto R. Gonzales, Counsel to the President, and William J. Haynes, General Counsel, Department of Defense, Authority for Use of Military Force to Combat Terrorist Activities within the United States 25 (Oct. 23, 2001) [hereinafter Oct. 23, 2001 Memo] *available at* gwu.edu/~nsarchiv/torturingdemocracy/documents/theme.html (last visited Aug. 16, 2012). The authors determined that the amendment's prohibitions would not apply, regardless of whether the terrorists were foreign or not. *Id.* at 27. *See also* Hollis-Brusky, *supra* note 120 at 26.

130. Oct. 23, 2001 Memo at 34–37.

131. *Id.* at 4–14.

132. *Id.* at 24. *See also* Hollis-Brusky, *supra* note 120, at 26.

133. Oct. 23, 2001 Memo, at 34.

134. *See* Memorandum from John Yoo, Deputy Assistant Attorney General, and Robert Delahunty, Special Counsel, to William J. Haynes, General Counsel, Department of Defense, Re: Application of Treaties and Laws to Al Qaeda and Taliban Detainees (Jan. 9, 2002) [hereinafter Jan. 9, 2002 Memo] *available at* gwu.edu/~nsarchiv/torturing-democracy/documents/theme.html, *and* Memorandum from Jay S. Bybee, Assistant Attorney General, to Alberto R. Gonzales, Counsel to the President, and William J. Haynes, General Counsel, Department of Defense, Re: Application of Treaties and Laws to Al Qaeda and Taliban Detainees (Jan. 22, 2002) [hereinafter Jan. 22, 2002 Memo] *available at* gwu.edu/~nsarchiv/torturingdemocracy/documents/theme.html (last visited Aug. 16, 2012).

135. The authors analyzed the language of the Geneva Conventions in reference to the state of international law at the time the conventions were signed, noting that they structured "legal relationships between nation-States, not between nation-States and private, transnational or subnational groups or organizations." Jan. 22, 2002 Memo,

at 4, 7. They noted the modern understanding that individuals were the subjects of international law (citing *Prosecutor v. Tadic*), and that this understanding proposes that Article 3 is a "catch all," enabling the conventions to apply to armed conflicts of any description. *Id.* at 8. The authors rejected this interpretation. *Id.*

136. Jan. 22, 2002 Memo at 1.

137. The authors argued that because the Taliban were not a high contracting party to the conventions, the conflict did not fall under common article 2 of the conventions, which addressed conflict between high contracting parties. Jan. 22, 2002 Memo at 3–4. They argued that it was also not "armed conflict not of an international character," under common article 3, which according to the authors was most likely to refer to civil war or conflict between a state and an armed movement within its territory. *Id.* at 6.

138. *Id.* at 32–33.

139. Memorandum from Alberto R. Gonzales, Counsel to the President, to President George W. Bush, Decision Re: Application of the Geneva Conventions on Prisoners Of War to the Conflict with Al Qaeda and the Taliban (Jan. 25, 2002), *available at* gwu.edu/~nsarchiv/torturingdemocracy/documents/theme.html (last visited Aug. 16, 2012).

140. *Id.* at 2. See also Neil A. Lewis, *Justice Memos Explained How to Skip Prisoner Rights*, N.Y. Times, May 21, 2004, *available at* nytimes.com, and 18 U.S.C. § 2441.

141. Memorandum from Jay Bybee, Assistant Attorney General, to Alberto R. Gonzales, Counsel to the President, Standards of Conduct for Interrogation under 18 U.S.C. §§ 2340–2340A (Aug. 1, 2002) [hereinafter Aug. 1, 2002 Memo], *available at* gwu.edu/~nsarchiv/torturingdemocracy/documents/theme.html (last visited Aug. 16, 2012).

142. *See* Letter from John Yoo to Alberto R. Gonzales, Aug. 1, 2002 [hereinafter Aug. 1, 2002 Letter], summarizing the Aug. 1, 2002 Memo *available at* gwu.edu/~nsarchiv/torturingdemocracy/documents/theme.html (last visited Aug. 16, 2012).

143. For a discussion of the ratification history, *see* Aug. 1, 2002 Memo, at 16–21.

144. The full definition continues: "[A]nd that mental pain or suffering refers to prolonged mental pain caused by or resulting from (1) the intentional infliction or threatened infliction of severe physical pain or suffering; (2) administration or application, or threatened administration or application, of mind altering substances or other procedures calculated to disrupt profoundly the senses or the personality; (3) the threat of imminent death; or (4) the threat that another person will imminently be subjected to death, severe physical pain or suffering, or the administration or application of mind-altering substances or other procedures calculated to disrupt profoundly the senses or personality." *See* Aug. 1, 2002 Letter, at 3.

145. Aug. 1, 2002 Memo, at 1.

146. *Id.* at 22–30.

147. *See, e.g., id.* at 8.

148. *Id.* at 12.

149. *Id.* at 31–39.

150. Memorandum from Patrick F. Philbin, Deputy Assistant Attorney General, to Counsel to the President, Legality of the Use of Military Commissions to Try Terrorists 1, 6–10 (Nov. 6, 2001), *available at* gwu.edu/~nsarchiv/torturingdemocracy/documents/theme.html (last visited Aug. 16, 2012).

151. *Id.*

152. *Hamdan v. Rumsfeld*, 548 U.S. 557, 613 (2006).

153. *Id.* at 678–83.

154. *Id.* at 725.

155. *Id.* at 733.

156. Military Commissions Act of 2006, Pub. L. No. 109–366, 120 Stat. 2600 (2006).

157. Military Commissions Act of 2006, § 948b-(g).

158. Edwin Meese, *The Double Standard in Judicial Selection*, 41 U. Rich. L. Rev. 369, 376 (2007).

159. *Id.*

160. Daniel A. Farber, *The Supreme Court, The Law of Nations, and Citations of Foreign Law: The Lessons of History*, 95 Cal. L. Rev. 1335, 1336 (2007). Farber argues that foreign law has influenced American Law—constitutional and private—since the founding of the Republic. Farber surmises that Chief Justice John Marshall would not necessarily have found Justice Kennedy's reference to a European Court of Human Rights decision in *Lawrence v. Texas* surprising or invalid. *Id.*

161. Steven G. Calabresi & Stephanie Dotson Zimdahl, *The Supreme Court and Foreign Sources of Law: Two Hundred Years of Practice and the Juvenile Death Penalty Decision*, 47 Wm. & Mary L. Rev. 743, 755 (2005). The authors surveyed Supreme Court decisions from 1789 to 2005 to uncover the extent to which foreign law was cited. The early Supreme Court considered the laws of European nations, the views of foreign scholars, and the decisions of English judges in interpreting what constitutes the law of nations.

162. *Id.* at 760, 883. Justice Breyer has stated that the "willingness to consider foreign judicial views in comparable cases is not surprising in a Nation that from birth has given a 'decent respect to the opinions of mankind.'" *Id.* at 884.

163. *Chisholm v. Georgia*, 2 U.S. 419, 474 (1793).

164. *Schooner Exchange v. McFaddon*, 11 U.S. 116 137, 146–47 (1812).

165. *Murray v. Schooner Charming Betsy*, 6 U.S. 64 (1804).

166. *Charming Betsy*, 6 U.S. at 118, holding that "an act of Congress ought never to be construed to violate the law of nations if any other possible construction remains."

167. *The Paquete Habana*, 175 U.S. 677, 700 (1900).

168. *Thirty Hogsheads of Sugar v. Boyle*, 13 U.S. 191, 198 (1815).

169. *Dred Scott v. Sandford*, 60 U.S. 393 (1856).

170. Calabresi & Zimdahl, *supra* note 161, at 884. In *Roe v. Wade*, 410 U.S. 113 (1973), and *Lawrence v. Texas*, 539 U.S. 558 (2003), the court found state exercises of police power to be unreasonable and in its determination turned to foreign law. *Id.* at 886. In *Lochner v. New York*, 198 U.S. 45, 71 (1905), Justice Harlan compared the average daily working hours restriction of the New York law at issue to the average daily working hours of "working men" in other countries. The countries compared were almost exclusively "similarly situated"—developing countries: Australia, Great Britain, Denmark, Norway, Sweden, France, Switzerland, Germany, Belgium, Italy, Austria, and Russia. *Id.*

171. *Trop v. Dulles*, 356 U.S. 86 (1958).

172. *Trop*, 356 U.S. at 102–103.

173. Adam Liptak, *U.S. Court Is Now Guiding Fewer Nations*, N.Y. Times, Sept. 17, 2008, at A1. "Justice Michael Kirby of the High Court of Australia said that his court no longer confined itself to considering English, Canadian and American law. 'Now we will take information from the Supreme Court of India, or the Court of Appeal of New Zealand, or the Constitutional Court of South Africa. . . . America . . . is in danger of becoming something of a legal backwater.'" *Id.*

174. Adam Liptak, *"We the People" Loses Appeal with People around the World*, N.Y. Times, Feb. 6, 2012, at A1.

175. *Atkins v. Virginia*, 536 U.S. 304, 347–48 (2002) (Scalia, J., dissenting).

176. *Roper v. Simmons*, 543 U.S. 551, 624 (2005) (Scalia, J., dissenting).

177. *Id.*

178. Denial of Certiorari, *Foster v. Florida*, 537 U.S. 990, n.1 (2002).

179. *Atkins*, 536 U.S. at 322, 324–25 (Rehnquist, C.J., dissenting).

180. Federalist No. 20, *quoted in Printz v. United States*, 521 U.S. 898, 921, n.11 (1997).

181. *The Relevance of Foreign Legal Materials in U.S. Constitutional Cases: A Conversation between Justice Antonin Scalia and Justice Stephen Breyer*, 3 Int'l J. Const. L. 519, 521 (2005) [hereinafter *Scalia-Breyer Conversation*].

182. *Id.*

183. *Washington v. Glucksberg*, 521 U.S. 702, 710–11 (1997).

184. Jeffrey Toobin, *Swing Shift: How Anthony Kennedy's Passion for Foreign Law Could Change the Supreme Court*, New Yorker, Sept. 12, 2005, at 50.

185. *Roper v. Simmons*, 543 U.S. 551, 575 (2005).

186. *Graham v. Florida*, 130 S. Ct. 2011, 2033 (2010).

187. The companion case, *Sullivan v. Florida*, 130 S. Ct. 2059 (2010) (No. 08–7621), raised similar issues, but the writ of certiorari was ultimately dismissed as improvidently granted.

188. Brief for Amnesty International et al. as Amici Curiae in Support of Petitioners at *3, *Graham v. Florida*, 130 S. Ct. 2011 (2010) (Nos. 08–7412, 08–7621), 2009 WL 2219304.

189. Brief for Center for Constitutional Jurisprudence as Amicus Curiae Support of Respondents at *1–2, 130 S. Ct. 2011 (2010) (Nos. 08–7412, 08–7621), 2009 WL 3022910.

190. *Id.* at 24.

191. *See* Claremont Institute Center for Constitutional Jurisprudence as Amicus Curiae in Support of Petitioners at *1, *Boy Scouts of America v. Dale*, 530 U.S. 640 (2000) (No. 99–699), 2000 WL 228580. In *Hamdi v. Rumsfeld*, Meese argued that Yaser Esam Hamdi, held as an enemy combatant in the war on terror, did not have a constitutional right to citizenship of the United States, despite the fact that he was born in Louisiana, because he did not also have allegiance to the United States. Claremont Institute Center for Constitutional Jurisprudence as Amicus Curiae in Support of Respondent, *Hamdi v. Rumsfeld*, 542 U.S. 507 (2004) (No. 03–6696), 2004 WL 871165. In *Elk Grove Unified School District v. Newdow*, Meese argued that an atheist father's objections to his daughter's compulsory saying of the pledge of allegiance featuring the words "under God" did not violate the constitutional clause prohibiting the state-sanctioned establishment of religion, because the founders who wrote it never intended it to prohibit "a profound respect for the Creator who is the source of all our rights." Claremont Institute Center for Constitutional Jurisprudence as Amicus Curiae in Support of Petitioners at *6, *Elk Grove Unified Sch. Dist. v. Newdow*, 542 U.S. 1 (2004) (No. 02–1624), 2003 WL 23011471. In *Boy Scouts of America v. Dale*, 530 U.S. 640 (2000), Meese claimed that a New Jersey Supreme Court decision to allow an openly gay man to be a part of the Boy Scouts, against the organization's wishes, would have "astounded our nation's Founders." Meese's fundamental argument was that the Boy Scouts should not be compelled to admit to its ranks an "activist homosexual," because his sexuality was anathema to its moral canons, and moral virtue in the eyes of the founders is a necessary prerequisite for republican government. Claremont Institute Center for Constitutional Jurisprudence as Amicus Curiae in Support of Petitioners at *4, *Boy Scouts of Am. v. Dale*, 530 U.S. 640 (2000) (No. 99–699), 2000 WL 228580.

192. *Graham v. Florida*, 130 S. Ct. 2011, 2034 (2010).
193. *Id.*
194. Calabresi, *supra* note 13, at 1355.
195. *Scalia-Breyer Conversation, supra* note 181, at 540–41.

APPENDIX B

1. Jane Mayer, *The Hidden Power: The Legal Mind behind the White House's War on Terror*, New Yorker, July 3, 2006, *available at* newyorker.com.
2. Chitra Ragavan, *Cheney's Guy*, U.S. News & World Rep., May 29, 2006, *available at* usnews.com.
3. David Kirkpatrick, *In Alito, G.O.P. Reaps Harvest Planted In '82*, N.Y. Times, Jan. 30, 2006, *available at* nytimes.com.
4. *Dossier: John D. Ashcroft*, Forbes.com (Jan. 16, 2001, 3:00 PM).
5. Jennifer C. Braceras, *Affirmative Action and Gender Equity: New Rules under Title IX?* 3 C.R. Prac. Group Newsl. 1 (Spring 1999), *available at* fed-soc.org.
6. Janice Rogers Brown, Associate Justice, California Supreme Court, Speech at the University of Chicago Law School Federalist Society Chapter: A Whiter Shade of Pale: Sense and Nonsense—The Pursuit of Perfection in Law and Politics (Apr. 20, 2000).
7. *Id.*
8. *Id.*
9. Randy James, *Jay Bybee: The Man behind Waterboarding*, Time, Apr. 28, 2009, *available at* time.com.
10. Roger Clegg, *No Reason for "Preferences" in Contracting*, Philly.com (Jan. 22, 2011); Roger Clegg, *Racial Discrimination, in Black and White*, N.Y. Times, Nov. 27, 2010, *available at* nytimes.com.
11. Charlie Savage, *Affirmative-Action Foe Is Facing Allegations of Financial Misdeeds*, N.Y. Times, Jan. 17, 2012, at A10.
12. Jason DeParle, *Debating the Subtle Sway of the Federalist Society*, N.Y. Times, Aug. 1, 2005, *available at* nytimes.com.
13. *Focus on the Family's Foundational Values*, Focus on the Fam., focusonthefamily.com (last visited Aug. 10, 2012).
14. John Schwartz, *Conservatives Split Deeply over Attacks on Justice Dept. Lawyers*, N.Y. Times, Mar. 10, 2010, *available at* nytimes.com.
15. Naftali Bedavid, *Hate Crime Bill Stalls*, Chi. Trib., Oct. 19, 1998, *available at* chicagotribune.com.
16. David D. Kirkpatrick, *The Conservative-Christian Big Thinker*, N.Y. Times, Dec. 16, 2009, *available at* nytimes.com.
17. Steven Lee Myers & Philip Shenon, *Embattled Attorney General Resigns*, N.Y. Times, Aug. 27, 2007, *available at* nytimes.com.
18. Sam Howe Verhovek, *Texas Law Professor Prompts a Furor over Race Comments*, N.Y. Times, Sept. 16, 1997, *available at* nytimes.com.
19. Lino Graglia, *The "Affirmative Action" Fraud*, 54 J. Urb. & Cont. L. 31, 31 (1998).
20. Jesse McKinley, *In a Filmdown Premiere, A Foe For Gore*, N.Y. Times, Apr. 4, 2007, *available at* nytimes.com.
21. Focus on the Fam., focusonthefamily.com/about_us.aspx (last visited Aug. 10, 2012).
22. Peter Kirsanow, *Blacks, Democrats, and Republicans*, Nat'l Rev. Online (Mar. 15, 2011, 3:08 PM), nationalreview.com.
23. Amy Bach, *Movin' On Up with The Federalist Society*, Nation, Sept. 13, 2001 (print edition, Oct. 1, 2001), *available at* thenation.com.

24. Opinion, *Another Unworthy Judicial Nominee*, N.Y. TIMES, Apr. 24, 2003, *available at* nytimes.com.

25. *About Us*, COMM. FOR JUST., committeeforjustice.org (last visited Aug. 10, 2012).

26. Stephen J. Markham, *The Coming Constitutional Debate*, IMPRIMIS, Apr. 2010, at 1, *available at* hillsdale.edu.

27. *How EPA Has Taken the Environment out of Environmental Enforcement: An Exclusive Interview with Roger Marzulla*, HEARTLANDER (Sept. 1, 1998), news.heartland.org.

28. MARZULLA L., marzulla.com (last visited Aug. 10, 2012).

29. Keith Schneider, *Washington at Work: Administration's Regulation Slayer Has Achieved a Perilous Prominence*, N.Y. TIMES, June 30, 1992, *available at* nytimes.com.

30. Editorial, *The House Strikes, and Wins, Again*, N.Y. TIMES, Apr. 24, 2011, at A24.

31. Times Topics, *Theodore B. Olson*, nytimes.com (updated Aug. 19, 2009).

32. Colleen Rowley, *Calling Out the Torture Enablers at St. Thomas Law School*, HUFFINGTON POST (Aug. 26, 2009, 9:46 AM), huffingtonpost.com.

33. Michael Stokes Paulsen, *A Government of Adequate Powers*, 31 HARV. J.L. & PUB. POL'Y 991, 991 (2008).

34. Sheryl Gay Stolberg, *A Different Timpanist*, N.Y. TIMES, June 10, 2005, *available at* nytimes.com.

35. Erik Eckholm, *A Political Revival*, N.Y. TIMES, June 1, 2011, *available at* nytimes.com. *See also* Adele M. Stan, *Religious Right's Ralph Reed Field-Tests Plan for Beating Obama*, alternet.org (last visited Aug. 10, 2012).

36. Randal C. Archibold, *Shift toward Skepticism for Civil Rights Panel*, N.Y. TIMES, Dec. 10, 2004, *available at* nytimes.com.

37. Robert Pear, *Aide in Justice Dept. Holds That Brennan Has "Radical" Views*, N.Y. TIMES, Sept. 13, 1995, *available at* nytimes.com.

38. *CIR's Mission*, CTR. FOR INDIVIDUAL RIGHTS, cir-usa.org (last visited Aug. 10, 2012).

39. Seymour Martin Lipset, *Equality and the America Creed: Understanding the Affirmative Action Debate*, 5–6, DEMOCRATIC LEADERSHIP COUNCIL, dlc.org/documents/equality_lipset.pdf (last visited Aug. 10, 2012).

40. Joe Holley, *Rosalie Silberman: Created Independent Women's Forum*, WASH. POST, Feb. 21, 2007, *available at* washingtonpost.com.

→ Index ←